T0317774

Trading the Fixed Income, Inflation and Credit Markets

Trading the Fixed Income, Inflation and Credit Markets

A Relative Value Guide

Neil C. Schofield
Troy Bowler

A John Wiley & Sons, Ltd., Publication

Registered office
John Wiley & Sons Ltd, The Atrium, Southern Gate, Chichester, West Sussex, PO19 8SQ, United Kingdom

For details of our global editorial offices, for customer services and for information about how to apply for permission to reuse the copyright material in this book please see our website at www.wiley.com.

Library of Congress Cataloging-in-Publication Data

Schofield, Neil C.
  Trading the fixed income, inflation and credit markets : a relative value guide / Neil C. Schofield, Troy Bowler.—1
        p. cm.—(The wiley finance series)
    Includes bibliographical references and index.
    ISBN 978-0-470-74229-7 (hardback)
  1. Investments. 2. Finance, Personal. I. Bowler, Troy. II. Title.
  HG4521.S35623 2011
    332.63′2—dc23

                                                                      2011028230

A catalogue record for this book is available from the British Library.

ISBN 978-0-470-74229-7 (hardback)   ISBN 978-1-119-95297-8 (ebk)
ISBN 978-1-119-96077-5 (ebk)   ISBN 978-1-119-96078-2 (ebk)

Set in 10/12pt Times by Laserwords Private Limited, Chennai, India
Printed and bound by CPI Group (UK) Ltd, Croydon, CR0 4YY

Dedicated to RBS
To Bren, Robert and Gillian
To Nicki

NCS

To my family and my friends;
who always support me

TB

Contents

Preface

If you have ever tried to read a finance textbook and bemoaned the fact that your brain starts to wander (or even wonder) after the first paragraph, then we think this book is for you. If you have ever been suckered into paying the best part of £100 for a finance textbook that you have opened only once, then again, we think this book is for you – clearly though for the right reason! If you have ever opened a finance textbook to be told "obviously" when it is patently far from it, then we also think this book is for you.

On the other hand, if you are looking for a heavy-duty academic text, then this book is definitely not for you. There are plenty of those available. Try, for example, *An Introduction to the Mathematics of Financial Derivatives* by Salih N. Neftci or the classic *Options, Futures and Other Derivatives* by John C. Hull. A slightly less academic but highly worthwhile read is *The Mathematics of Financial Derivatives: A Student Introduction* by Jeff Dewynne. Likewise, if you are looking for a cheaper version of one of the popular product handbooks that proliferate the market, put our book back on the shelf right now. It is not for you. We are not planning on discussing mortgage-backed bonds, Munis, REITs or 401Ks.

That is not to say that our book is not rigorous in its descriptions and its workings. It most certainly is. It is just that we want readers to come away from this book with a clear understanding of the intuition behind the theory, some practical examples to aid the understanding of that theory, some shortcuts that can be used to cut to the chase and some jargon-lite explanations of concepts such as PCA and Monte Carlo. As such, this book will be useful for students about to embark on a university course in finance and who want a book that is not dedicated to "squiggly d's" and stochastic calculus. It will also be useful for those people about to embark on a career in finance, whether on a well-structured graduate training course or not.

We have adopted a relative value approach to analysing the fixed income, credit and inflation market. The phrase "relative value" is perhaps most commonly interpreted in a literal sense; the value of one asset relative to another. From this notion the argument extends towards the definition of "value", which is often expressed as some notion that an asset can be considered cheap or expensive ("rich" in the market jargon). As any regular shopper will no doubt frequently report when they consider something to be a bargain, this notion is expressed with respect to some given benchmark or accepted norm.

This definition of relative value is a valid one, although we will argue that it is also somewhat limiting. Our definition of relative value is therefore "*what is the optimal way in which a particular view of the market can be expressed*". To grasp the significance of this definition, consider the following simple example. Let us assume that we are an investor who is looking to earn a return in euros with a minimum degree of credit risk (i.e., the risk that the issuer of a security will be unable to repay its debts). If the investor chose to invest in AAA-rated EUR-denominated sovereign bonds, they would be able to pick between a variety of different countries. In theory, since the currency and the credit risk are identical, all of these bonds should return the same amount for a given yield. The investor may be able to identify one bond that they consider cheap relative to the universe of other assets and so purchase that asset. This type of transaction would conform to the traditional definition of relative value. Using the wider definition of relative value the investor would look at alternative structures that may afford the same exposure but offer a greater degree of return. So, for example, an investor may choose to purchase a bond future or enter into an interest rate swap transaction where they receive fixed or execute an option transaction that will show a profit if market rates move as expected. We will use this framework of spot–forward–swap–optionality as the basis of our trade design as we progress through the different asset classes.

Chapter 1 presents an overview of the different products that will be analysed in later chapters. It is not imperative to go through this chapter slavishly if you are confident of your product knowledge, but we include the chapter for the sake of completeness. *Chapter 2* introduces our relative value framework and considers the pricing relationships that exist between the spot, forward, swap and volatility markets. *Chapter 3* is essentially an extension of the pricing relationships developed in the previous chapter as it considers the market risk of the different instruments. *Chapter 4* considers how the relative value framework can be applied to express trading opinions within a fixed income context. *Chapter 5* takes a traditional "cheap/rich" approach to relative value within a sovereign bond context. *Chapter 6* looks at different ways to express views on expected yield curve movements. *Chapters 7 and 8* apply the relative value framework within a credit and inflation context, respectively. *Chapter 9* concludes the text on a slightly light-hearted note by considering some of our favourite trading axioms.

Finally, by the time that you have finished reading this book you will understand why, amongst other things, forward prices are not expected prices (Troy's pet hate!) and why most financial commentators need a little more humility. This book is the result of more than 50 years' combined working in various roles at the coal face of the capital markets rather than in the comfort of academia. We hope that it is worth the journey.

Acknowledgements

It's scary to think that Troy and I first met at Loughborough University many years ago; more than we care to remember. We went our separate ways and it wasn't until about 2002 that we bumped into each other at Barclays Capital. It was at Troy's instigation that we decided to embark on the project and I am personally grateful to him for his intellectual input into the text over the two to three years it took us to compile the material. His insight into all of these markets is remarkable and I am lucky to have been the scribe who documented his thoughts.

Troy has always been a big supporter of graduate education within Barclays Capital and the text was written with this audience in mind. The book is designed to both complement and supplement the existing classroom training that such a "bootcamp" course would deliver. However, we have tried to make the text accessible to any reader wishing to deepen their understanding of these complex financial markets.

I must also take the opportunity to extend a very big "thank you" to Stuart Urquhart of Barclays Capital. I first met Stuart at Barclays in about 2002, and ever since day one he has proved to be one of life's true gentlemen. Not only did he arrange for access to Barclays Capital Live for all of the data in the text, but he added value to some of the chapters with insightful suggestions and constructive observations. His professionalism and kindness are truly an example to us all. Thanks also to Dr Andy Bevan for help in shaping my thoughts on certain aspects of the yield curve.

I would also like to thank the late Paul Roth, who shaped my understanding on many aspects of derivatives. Sadly my late father, Professor Reg Schofield, passed away during the writing of the book and all his family and friends still miss him. He perhaps didn't realize it at the time, but his explanation in 2007 of yield curve modelling was a useful addition to the text – not bad for a Civil Engineer! As ever, Nicki never complained about me writing, even during (at least) two holidays.

Many thanks go to the team at John Wiley (Caitlin, Aimee and Pete in particular), who came to know me as Neil *"can I have another extension for delivery of the manuscript"* Schofield.

Although many people helped to shape the book, any mistakes are entirely our responsibility. I would always be interested to hear any comments about the text and so please feel free to contact me at neil@fmtuk.com or via my website (www.fmtuk.com).

P.S. Alan and Roger – two slices of white toast and a cuppa for me!

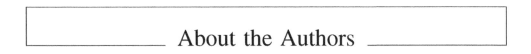

About the Authors

TROY BOWLER

Troy Bowler joined Barclays Capital in London in 2002 and is currently a Managing Director within Distribution, based in Singapore. Before joining Barclays Capital, he held positions at Deutsche Bank in London, where he was part of their highly-regarded global fixed income and relative-value research team, at PaineWebber and Bank of Tokyo Capital Markets (UK), where he was Chief Economist, and Charterhouse Investment Management Limited, where he managed money-market funds, including the #1 ranked GBP unit trust according to Micropal (acquired by McGraw-Hill Companies in 1997).

Although Troy's membership of the Institute of Investment Management and Research (IIMR), now known as CFA UK, has lapsed, he was a member of the Examination Committee in the mid-1990s, helping to revamp the IIMR's examinations. Previously, the examinations had focused almost exclusively on equity markets and the IIMR looked to widen the remit to encompass fixed income professionals. Those of you who went through the IIMR examinations prior to 2002, especially the "Economics & Applied Statistical Analysis" paper, may wish to thank or curse Troy in equal measure. He happily admits that he passed his examinations well before this.

Troy holds a BSc in Economics from Loughborough University and an MSc in Economics from London University.

NEIL C. SCHOFIELD

Neil Schofield is the principal of FMT Ltd, a UK-based company offering training services in the areas of treasury, derivatives, capital markets and risk management to financial institutions, Central Banks and corporations worldwide.

Neil was global head of Financial Markets training at Barclays Capital from 2001 to 2008. He teaches primarily on the rates business, covering all of the major asset classes and their respective derivative products from foreign exchange through to commodities.

Before joining Barclays Capital, he was a director at Chisholm-Roth Training for 4 years, where he was responsible for provision of training services for a number of blue-chip global investment banks. Clients included Citigroup, Deutsche Bank, Goldman Sachs and JP Morgan Chase.

He started his training career at Chase Manhattan Bank, where he was originally employed as an internal auditor. Over a period of 9 years, he conducted numerous internal and external training seminars including the Bank of England and the Federal Reserve System in the USA. He has also held positions with Security Pacific Hoare Govett (now trading as Bank of America) and Lloyds TSB.

Neil holds a BSc in Economics from Loughborough University and an MBA from Manchester Business School. He was elected as a Fellow of the IFS School of Finance (formerly the Chartered Institute of Bankers) in 1999.

Neil was appointed as a Visiting Fellow at the University of Reading ICMA centre in April 2007.

He is author of the book *Commodity Derivatives: Markets and Applications* published by John Wiley in October 2007.

1

Product Fundamentals

1.1 CHAPTER OVERVIEW

In this chapter we consider the features of a number of instruments that will be the focus of subsequent sections. The coverage is not intended to be comprehensive; the aim is to make sure that the reader is armed with sufficient terminology to be able to understand the more detailed concepts that will follow. Pricing and risk management will be the subject of Chapters 2 and 3, respectively.

This chapter starts with a discussion of the main "cash" (i.e., non-derivative) markets of fixed income, inflation and credit. The coverage then widens to incorporate the derivative building blocks, namely futures, forwards, swaps and options. Within this section the material occasionally leans towards the detail of specific products in certain asset classes that are considered key. However, the discussion relating to options is asset class neutral to keep the chapter size manageable.

Readers with a good knowledge of these subjects can skip this chapter but we would suggest a quick skim of the pages just in case a review is needed!

1.2 BOND FUNDAMENTALS

A key building block for the first part of the text will be bonds. A bond is an IOU that evidences the indebtedness of a borrower. Borrowers comprise mainly sovereign and corporate entities, although there have been issues made by individuals such as the pop star David Bowie.

1.2.1 Fixed income structures

Although bonds have many different forms we will initially focus on standard ("vanilla") structures. In return for borrowing a given sum of money, the issuer of the bond will pay a series of contractual interest payments to the owner of the instrument. When bonds were issued in physical form, the owner would detach a small coupon and present this to a bank appointed on behalf of the borrower as their eligibility to receive interest. As a result of this practice, interest payments on bonds have become termed coupons. At the maturity of the instrument the investor will be repaid the value stated on the face of the bond, but this may not be the sum that was originally paid to acquire the asset. This is because bonds are traded on a price basis, which is quoted as a percentage of the face value. Bonds are priced by present valuing all of the future cash flows, but this concept will be considered in Chapter 2. Suffice to say that with a limited amount of any bond in issue, the relative attractiveness of the fixed coupon will be the key determinant of how much an investor will pay to acquire the bond. If a bond has a fixed coupon of 5% but investors could earn a greater return on an equivalent investment (equivalent in terms of maturity and the risk of default), the bond will have to be priced at less than its face value in order to make the investment attractive. If it were priced at say 95.00 and the investor held the instrument to maturity, they would be repaid 100% of the face value and would enjoy a capital gain of just over 5% over the period. The opposite would be true for a bond that has a relatively attractive coupon. Through the interaction of demand and supply, investors will seek to possess the bond, which will drive up its price. If held to maturity the investor will incur a capital loss but will have earned an above-market interest rate. The market uses the concept of a yield, which captures any capital gain or loss in addition to the receipt of a particular coupon.

1.2.2 Floating-rate notes

Floating-rate notes (FRNs) are interest-bearing securities that pay a variable coupon on a regular basis (usually quarterly). The coupon is usually a spread to a given margin relative to an interest rate index such as LIBOR (London Interbank Offered Rate) or Euribor. For example, the instrument may pay 3-month USD LIBOR + 0.15% (15 basis points). The instrument is economically equivalent to a series of consecutive fixed-term bank deposits, where the interest rate is reset on a periodic basis. The fixed percentage margin over the specified interest rate index is referred to as the quoted margin. The quoted margin is a function of the issuer's default risk relative to the interbank rate to which the interest payments are referenced. The better the credit rating the lower the quoted margin and vice versa.

FRN issuance is driven by the desire of the issuer to match their assets and liabilities. For example, banks will tend to be big issuers of FRNs (which will represent a liability) as the assets that the bond proceeds are used to purchase will tend to pay a variable rate of interest (e.g., mortgages). This ensures that if interest rates change, interest costs and income will move in tandem. The concept of banks being able to borrow on a LIBOR basis will become key to much of the analysis that follows. This is because investment opportunities are often analysed based on the return they generate relative to LIBOR. FRN investors will include many different entities:

- Bank treasuries with excess cash who are looking to match floating-rate liabilities.
- Central Banks, retail investors and credit-conscious fund managers will buy sovereign-issued FRNs.
- Money market funds and corporates can earn an enhanced yield compared to alternatives such as cash and commercial paper.

1.2.3 Inflation

Definitions

Although most people would argue that they understand the concept of inflation, both authors have found that in reality a number of market participants often struggle when trying to verbalize a definition. Inflation represents rising prices, deflation falling prices and disinflation is where price increases slow down.

Within the inflation world a nominal frame of reference looks at investments in terms of cash paid without taking into account the loss of purchasing power. So if an item costs €1 today, with 2% inflation it will cost €1.02 by the end of the year. Alternatively we could say that at the end of the year, €1 will only buy 0.98 of the item. How would this relate to bonds? Consider a 1-year bond that pays a principal of €100 plus one interest payment of €5 at its maturity. The real value of this final cash flow will depend on what happens to prices over the period. If an investor expected inflation to be 3% then it will cost €103 in 1 year to buy something that costs €100 presently. However, the bond will pay a cash flow of €105 and so you expect to have €2 of extra purchasing power – a 1.94% increase in purchasing power.

The Fisher equation is used extensively by the market to express the relationship between the yields on nominal bonds and expected inflation. The equation expresses the relationships as:

$$(1 + n) = (1 + r)(1 + f)(1 + p)$$

where:

n = yield on nominal bond

r = real yield on inflation-linked bond

f = inflationary expectations

p = risk premium

However, the market has shortened the expression:

$$n = r + f + p$$
$$n = r + \text{bei}$$

where:

bei = breakeven inflation

In essence, the formula states that the yield on a nominal bond is made up of three components:

- A required real yield that investors demand over and above expectations of inflation.
- Inflationary expectations over a particular period of time ("breakeven inflation").
- A factor that captures the combination of a risk premium and a liquidity discount.
    - The risk premium is the compensation an investor earns for accepting undesirable inflation risk when holding nominal bonds. One interpretation is that it represents the risk premium demanded by nominal bond investors for unexpected inflation.
    - The liquidity discount represents the yield premium that investors demand to hold a less liquid inflation-linked bond.

However, the third component is generally considered to be difficult to disaggregate and so is generally ignored by the market.

The breakeven rate can be thought of as the average rate of inflation that will equate the returns on an inflation-linked bond and a comparator nominal bond issue of the same return. To illustrate how it should be interpreted, consider the following example. Suppose there are a nominal 5-year sovereign bond that is yielding 4.5% and an inflation-linked sovereign bond of the same maturity whose yield on a real basis is 1.5%. Using the principles of the Fisher equation this implies a breakeven inflation rate of 3.0%. An investor could use the value of breakeven inflation to assess which bond should be purchased:

- If the investor expects inflation to average less than 3.0% over the period, they should hold the nominal bond.

- If the investor expects inflation to average more than 3.0% over the period, they should hold the inflation-linked bond.
- If the investor expects inflation to average 3.0% over the period, they will be indifferent between the two assets.

Arguably the difficulty experienced by practitioners in trying to grasp the concept of inflation lies in defining the concept of a real yield. If one looked at the Fisher equation, a simple but somewhat unsatisfactory definition of real yields is simply the difference between nominal yields and inflation expectations. We present three other definitions:

- A real rate of interest reflects the amount earned or paid after taking into account the impact of inflation.
- It is the market clearing rate of return in excess of expected future inflation that ensures supply meets demand for a particular investment opportunity.
- The return for forgoing consumption today to consume more goods and services tomorrow.

Real yields should also:

- Reflect the growth in an economy's productivity.
- Represent the rate at which investments are rewarded. Investments compete for capital on the basis of the real yield they offer given their associated risk.

What can be even more confusing is when real rates of interest become negative, an example of which occurred in the US Treasury market in 2008. This happened when inflation expectations were higher than nominal interest rates. These negative real yields were attributable to:

- Slower economic growth prospects, which lowered rates of expected returns across investments.
- The US Federal Reserve was expected to cut interest rates such that inflation would be greater than nominal rates.
- A "flight to quality" by investors, which drove up the price of government securities, reducing their nominal returns.

So in general terms, negative real yields could occur if:

- An asset is not considered a productive use of capital.
- The asset is attractive but faces excess demand relative to its supply. As a result, its price rises and the nominal return falls.
- The existence of negative real yield can create an incentive to drive capital to other more potentially attractive investments.

Inflation-linked bonds

An inflation-linked bond is one whose value is linked to movements in a specific price index in order to maintain its purchasing power. An inflation index measures the way in which prices change. This is achieved by analysing and recording thousands of prices for a selection of goods and services on a monthly basis. Inflation figures for a particular month are then typically issued two to three weeks later. Some of the goods and services will carry a higher weighting, reflecting the fact that consumers will spend more money on some items than others. The basket and the constituent weightings are revised on an annual basis. The most common inflation index used is the consumer price index (CPI) for the respective country of issue, although each country will typically calculate and quote a number of indices. In the USA the "Treasury Inflation Protected Securities" (TIPS; also sometimes referred to as the Treasury Inflation Indexed Securities – TIIS) reference their return to the consumer price all urban non-seasonally adjusted inflation index. In Europe a common index is the Harmonised Index of Consumer Prices (HICP) for all items excluding tobacco, while the UK mainly uses the Retail Price Index (RPI).

1.3   REPURCHASE AGREEMENTS

One important aspect of the fixed income world relates to how the purchase of a bond will be financed. It would be fair to say that most banks will not have large piles of cash lying around idle and so will look to manage their cash efficiently. The implication is that the cash required to purchase an asset will need to be borrowed and the proceeds from any sale will be reinvested. The most popular technique used in the financing of fixed income transactions is the repurchase agreement or "repo". A repo involves the simultaneous sale and future repurchase of an asset. The seller of the asset buys it back at the same price at which it was sold. On the second leg of the transaction the seller pays the buyer interest on the implicit loan that has been created. This interest is termed the repo rate.

The main cash flows associated with a typical repurchase agreement are illustrated in Figure 1.1.

A reverse repo is the opposite of a repo. From this perspective the transaction is viewed as the purchase of an asset for cash, with an agreement to resell at some future date. The market distinguishes between two different types of repo in relation to the asset that is transferred. A specific repo involves a bond that is specified by the two counterparties, whereas a general collateral ("GC") transaction involves a bond that meets some pre-agreed criteria.

Economically, the repo can be viewed as a collateralized loan rather than a pair of securities trades. Legally, however, the transaction is a sale and repurchase, which will

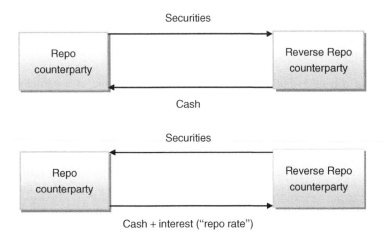

Figure 1.1   Repurchase agreements.

have important implications in the event of the default of one of the counterparties. If the securities had merely been pledged, then the default of the repo counterparty would result in the reverse repo counterparty becoming an unsecured creditor. However, the sale and repurchase structure means the reverse repo counterparty has the right of close out and set off – they get to keep the securities in lieu of the money lent. Similar principles would apply if the reverse repo counterparty were to fail.

Repos are quoted on a bid and offer basis. From a quoting institution's perspective a quote may be expressed as:

Bid	Offer
3.98%	3.92%
Buy securities	Sell securities
Earn interest	Pay interest

Although the convention of a high bid/low offer price may appear counter-intuitive, it allows for the market maker (i.e., the quoting institution) to make a profit through earning more interest than they would pay if they were able to execute offsetting trades simultaneously.

Appreciating that the transaction economically resembles a collateralized loan gives an insight into the popularity of the transaction. The interest that is payable on the second leg of the transaction will be lower than that of an unsecured borrowing and as a rule of thumb the rate that is agreed by the two counterparties is about 1/8th less than the LIBOR rate of the equivalent maturity.

It is important to appreciate that the legal title of the bonds is transferred to the reverse repo counterparty as part of the first leg of the transaction. This will allow them to sell on the bonds as part of an unrelated transaction if necessary. However, any economic benefit or risk is retained by the repo counterparty. This has a number of implications:

- If the bond issuer defaults over the period of the repo they will receive the security back but will still be forced to repay the price agreed in the first leg of the transaction.
- If the issuer of the bond being repo'd defaults, the repo counterparty will receive back the asset but will still be obliged to pay the original price agreed on the first leg of the transaction.
- If the bond pays a coupon during the period, this will have to be remitted back to the repo counterparty immediately.

Suppose that a bank is bullish on the prospects of the value of a particular bond and decides to use the repo mechanism to finance its purchase. The steps in the transaction are:

- Buy the bond for an agreed value and an agreed cash amount (an outright purchase).
- Sell the bond under repo and receive the market value with an agreement to repurchase the bond at a future date.
- The cash proceeds received from the first leg of the repo are used to settle the outright purchase.
- When the repo matures the bank retakes delivery of the bond and then sells it in the open market to any counterparty.
- The proceeds received from this sale are used to settle the outstanding principal and interest amount due under the repo.

It can be confusing as to why an investor would buy a bond outright and then sell it under repo to pay for it. However, the key to grasping the logic of this trade is to recall that all of the economic benefit of the transaction is retained by the repo seller (i.e., the outright buyer of the bond). So as long as the final sale generates sufficient cash to cover the initial purchase and the interest on the repo, the transaction will show a profit.

A similar procedure could be used if the market participant thought that a particular bond was going to fall in value:

- The target bond is purchased under a repo transaction.
- The bond is sold to a market participant in an outright sale.
- At the maturity of the repo the trader buys back the bond in the market to satisfy his commitment to redeliver the bond under the second leg of the repo.
- The proceeds of the repo (initial price plus interest received on the cash leg) are used to pay for the purchase of the bond.

As in the bullish scenario, as long as the cash received from selling the bond is greater than the cash paid to buy it, the transaction will be profitable.

Although this section is designed to give the reader an awareness of the key issues associated with a repurchase agreement, there is one particular aspect of the market that is worth highlighting. On occasion certain bonds will be in very high demand in the market and as a result the asset will "go on special" in the repo market. The excess demand for the bond may occur as a result of traders being very bearish in relation to a particular issue and there is significant demand to obtain the bond using the repo mechanism. Another example, which will be considered later, is that the bond futures contract may require a particular government bond to be delivered if it is held to its final maturity.

The impact of specialness in the repo market will result in repo rates going down. Intuitively, it would seem that the relative scarcity of an asset would cause rates to rise, but this is not the case. The participant who needs to take delivery of the asset will buy it under repo and deliver cash in return. Given the scarcity of the asset the cash that he has now lent out will only earn a very low rate of interest; this is the "cost" he must pay. Looked at from the repo seller's perspective, if they own the asset, they are able to profit from its scarcity by borrowing money at very low rates of interest. Depending on the level of demand for the asset, it is possible for the repo rate to turn negative; that is, the buyer of the bond in the repo transaction gets back less cash than they initially forwarded. This would occur if the penalty costs for failing to deliver are greater than the reduction in their repo proceeds.

1.4 CREDIT FUNDAMENTALS

One fundamental distinction made in the fixed income world is the importance of credit risk. This is defined as the risk that an entity will be unable to repay interest or principal due on monies that have been borrowed. The probability that an issuer will repay a particular debt is assessed by independent rating agencies, of which Standard and Poor's, Moody's and Fitch are examples. For example, Standard and Poor's defines a credit rating as an "independent opinion of the general creditworthiness of an obligor or an obligor's financial obligation based on relevant risk factors".[1] Each of the rating agencies applies different methods to assess this creditworthiness and express it using a mixture of letters and numbers. For example, Standard and Poor's express credit ratings for both short and long-term instruments. For long-term credit ratings, the AAA designation reflects the strongest credit quality while D reflects the lowest. It is also possible to add a degree of granularity to the credit ratings by adding a plus or minus sign to show the relative standing with the major rating categories from AA to CCC.[2] Obligations rated as BBB– or better are termed by the market as "investment grade", while ratings lower than this threshold are termed "high yield". This is an important distinction, as some investors may have restrictions on the nature of the assets in which they can invest.

From a market perspective an investor who buys a bond with a certain element of credit risk is rewarded in the form of an enhanced return. That is, they will earn a certain percentage amount over and above the so-called default-free return. This enhanced return is referred to as a credit spread. A generalized approach to estimating this spread can be stated in the following relationship:

Credit spread = Probability of entity defaulting × loss incurred in the event of default

However, there are a number of different ways in which this credit spread is measured, and this will be addressed in Chapter 3.

1.5   DERIVATIVE FUNDAMENTALS

A derivative is defined as an instrument that derives its value from the price of an underlying asset. The three main building block instruments that comprise the derivative world are forwards/futures, swaps and options. So, taking crude oil as an example, the market trades crude oil futures and forwards, crude oil swaps and crude oil options. Derivatives can be traded on an organized exchange or directly between counterparties on an over-the-counter (OTC) basis.

1.5.1   Futures

A future is an exchange-traded contract that fixes a price on the trade date for delivery of an asset at some future time period. An interest rate future fixes an interbank rate for some future time period – say the 3-month rate in 3 months' time. A bond future fixes the price of a bond for delivery at some future time period. An example of a bond future referenced to German sovereign Bunds is given in Table 1.1.

Table 1.1   Contract specifications for Euro Bund future

Trading unit	€100,000 nominal value, notional Bund, 6% coupon
Delivery months	March, June, Sept, Dec
Delivery day	The 10th calendar day of the respective delivery month (at seller's choice)
Quotation	Per €100 nominal (in decimals to 2 places)
Minimum price movement	0.01 (1 tick = €10)
Last trading day	11.00 a.m., two trading days prior to delivery date

Source: Eurex.

Although the detail of the Bund future will be considered later, there are a number of general features that are worth highlighting:

- Futures are generally traded in fixed amounts (€100,000 in this case), although there are exceptions to this such as futures on equity indices. The monetary value of this type of future changes in line with the value of the index.
- The contract is linked to a specific underlying asset so that both counterparties know exactly what will be delivered.
- Upon expiry of the contract the underlying can be delivered according to an agreed schedule of dates (in the case of the Bund it expires on the 10th calendar day of March, June, September and December).
- The underlying asset may be physically delivered (e.g., Bund futures) or cash settled, where the nature of the underlying asset makes it operationally impractical (e.g., FTSE 100 equity index).
- The smallest price movement is predefined by the exchange and is referred to as a "tick". This tick movement will have an associated monetary value. In the case of the Bund, since the contract size is €100,000 and the tick is defined as 0.01%, the tick value is €10.

Another feature of exchanges is the requirement of both counterparties to post collateral. Termed "margin", this is generally seen in two forms. Initial margin is posted at the outset of the trade, while variation margin is the mechanism whereby profits and losses are transferred between entities on a daily basis. To facilitate the settlement of exchange-traded contracts, a central clearing house will act as the counterparty to both sides of the transaction. So once a transaction is executed between two entities, the clearing house will become the buyer to every seller and the seller to every buyer. This feature removes the counterparty credit risk that would result if a transaction were executed on an OTC basis. However, it is clear that this argument is somewhat flawed in that each original party to the trade has merely transferred its credit exposure to the clearing house. However, the clearing house is often very heavily capitalized in order to mitigate this potential default risk.

1.5.2 Forwards

A forward contract is economically equivalent to a futures contract in that it will involve the fixing of a price at the point of execution for delivery at some future date. An entity trading an OTC forward will not be faced with the constraints of contract standardization that are a feature of exchange-traded contracts. Forwards allow the user greater flexibility in specifying deal parameters such as transaction size and maturity dates. Although something of a generalization, the majority of forward contracts will be cash settled. So, a cash-settled bond forward would fix the price of the bond for future delivery but the final settlement would not require the exchange of the asset for cash. Instead, the seller of the contract will pay a cash sum equal to the current market value of the bond and the buyer will pay the fixed price originally agreed upon. A forward deal is a contractual commitment which cannot be terminated unless both parties to the deal agree mutually to end the transaction.

Forward rate agreements

A forward rate agreement (FRA) is an OTC transaction that fixes a single interest rate for a single period at an agreed date in the future. The start of the period the rate will be fixed for and its length are negotiated between the contract buyer and seller. So an FRA transaction that locks in the 3-month rate in 3 months' time is referred to as a 3/6 or 3s6s transaction. The first number indicates the effective date of the transaction, the final number the maturity and the difference between the two indicates the tenor of the interest rate that is being fixed. Interest rate tenors will typically reflect those most commonly traded in the cash markets and so will have a maximum maturity of 12 months. The effective and maturity dates for FRAs could extend as far as 5 years depending on the currency.

These instruments have never been adopted by the corporate community to hedge exposures and are arguably most often used by traders as a way of expressing a view on expected short-term interest rate movements. Schofield recalls a conversation with an FRA trader where the dealer pointed out that he created his quote based on where he thought the Central Bank rate would be at some future date (plus a few basis points to reflect the difference in credit risk).

These instruments are quoted on a bid and offer basis and so a hypothetical quotation could be:

3/6	3.11%–3.12%
6/9	3.15%–3.16%
9/12	3.25%–3.26%

The interpretation of the quotation from a market maker's perspective is:

Bid	Offer
Buy FRA	Sell FRA
Pay fixed rate	Receive fixed rate
Receive LIBOR	Pay LIBOR

From this quoting convention we can start to see that an FRA is a contract for difference, which involves an exchange of cash flows. On the trade date the parties to the deal agree a fixed contract rate for an agreed future period and then will make or receive compensation depending on the actual level at which LIBOR settles. As we will show in the next section, an FRA can be thought of as a single-period interest rate swap.

To illustrate the concept, consider the following example. Suppose that 3-month interbank rates are 3.00% and the market believes that Central Bank rates will increase over the next year. The trader sees the market quoting a 9/12 rate as 3.25%–3.26%. He believes that actual 3-month rates in 9 months' time will be lower than this and so decides to sell the FRA at the bid price of 3.25% (he is a market user not a market maker) on a notional of USD 10m. This will contract him to receive 3.25% and pay the prevailing LIBOR rate in 9 months' time. If market rates evolve as per his view (i.e., 3-month LIBOR is lower than 3.25%) he will end up being a net receiver of cash.

Let us say that 9 months later, the 3-month LIBOR rate fixes at 3.20%. The parties to the FRA agreement can calculate the settlement amount due. The market user who sold the contract expects to be a net receiver of 5 basis points per annum on a USD 10 million notional amount. However, there is something of a quirk in the settlement convention.

Normally, interest rate contracts will settle in arrears but in the FRA market the settlement takes place as soon as LIBOR fixes. This means that the recipient of the cash flow has use of the funds in advance of normal market practice and as a result the settlement amount is present valued. The discount rate is the same LIBOR rate used in the numerator of the equation. The contract settles according to the following formula:

$$\frac{\dfrac{(+/-\ \text{Settlement rate}\ -/+\ \text{FRA Contract rate})}{100} \times \text{Notional amount} \times \dfrac{\text{No. of days}}{\text{Day basis}}}{1 + \left(\dfrac{\text{Settlement rate}}{100} \times \dfrac{\text{No. of days}}{\text{Day basis}}\right)}$$

The +/− signs are used to indicate if the participant is a receiver (+) or payer (−) of a particular rate. This will quickly allow the participants to decide who will be the receiver or payer of the cash settlement. Since interest rates are quoted as a percentage per annum it is necessary to pro rate the settlement according to the tenor of the interest rate. The day basis will either be 360 or 365 depending on the currency of the transaction.

So in our example the settlement amount would be:

$$\frac{(-3.20\% + 3.25\%) \times 10,000,000 \times \dfrac{90}{360}}{1 + \left(3.20\% \times \dfrac{90}{360}\right)} = \frac{1250}{1.008} = 1240.08$$

The calculation assumes an exact 90-day quarter.

1.5.3 Swaps

Interest rate swaps

In its most basic form an interest rate swap consists of a periodic exchange of cash flows with one referenced to a fixed rate while the other is referenced to a floating rate of interest, such as a particular maturity of LIBOR (Figure 1.2). Swaps are traded on a notional amount basis, which is usually fixed. The notional amount of a swap is merely a reference value and does not represent an actual cash flow. It will simply determine the magnitude of any cash flow that is subsequently exchanged. Swaps are typically long term, with maturities that may extend out to 30 or 50 years. Although the deals have a long-term maturity, the exchange of cash flows will take place on a more frequent basis. The cash flows are calculated on a simple interest basis and are paid in arrears. Each market has adopted its own conventions as to the frequency of these payments. For example, in the USD market the convention is a semi-annual payment of fixed for a quarterly payment of LIBOR. Where the payment dates coincide, it is market convention for the cash flows to be netted. However, since the transaction is OTC, all of the terms and conditions are negotiable and so there are many different variations of the simple vanilla "fixed/float" structure.

Figure 1.2   Illustration of fixed vs. floating interest rate swap.

To illustrate the principles involved, let us assume that both fixed and floating are paid semi-annually, with the rates for the period being 5.00% and 4.50%, respectively. We will assume that the cash flows are denominated in GBP, the notional amount is £10 million and that in the 6-month period there are 182 days.

The fixed cash flows will therefore be:

$$£10,000,000 \times 5.00\% \times 182/365 = £249,315.07$$

The floating cash flows will be:

$$£10,000,000 \times 4.50\% \times 182/365 = £224,383.56$$

Since the two payments coincide, there will be a net payment of £24,931.51 in favour of the receiver of fixed.

Swaps are quoted on a bid–offer basis. So if we were to analyse a typical quote from the perspective of a market maker (i.e., the institution giving the quote), it may look as follows:

Bid	Offer
4.5050%	4.5450%
Pay fixed	Receive fixed
Receive LIBOR	Pay LIBOR

A market user (i.e., the institution requesting the quote) would interpret the same values in the opposite manner. The key learning point from this is that the quotation is given in terms of the fixed rate. Since many investment banks will be running "matched positions" (i.e., they will try and structure their portfolio such that they will have a mix of pay and receive positions that are profitable overall), the LIBOR cash flows are assumed to cancel out.

Some practitioners will also say that they are "long" or "short" the swap. This is not our favoured quoting convention but for the sake of completeness, we include a short explanation. At the bid price the market maker is said to be "long" the swap – it is a "buying" position. However, the convention assumes that the market maker is buying a stream of LIBOR cash flows, for which they will pay a single fixed rate. By the same logic the offer price represents a short or "selling" swap position in that the market maker is delivering a stream of LIBOR cash flows for which their compensation is a single fixed price.

Schofield recalls one swaps class where an experienced swaps dealer disagreed vehemently with these definitions, stating that the entire swap market-making community defined "long" and "short" in the opposite way. After a flurry of phone calls, which yielded no consensus, he realized that he had been arguing at cross purposes with the participant. It would seem that some market makers reasonably viewed the offer side of the market as similar to buying a bond. The buyer receives a fixed coupon and finances the purchase at a LIBOR cash flow. Hence at the offer side of the quote perhaps it would be more helpful to describe a market maker as being long the market (as opposed to the swap) and being short the market at the bid price. It is no shame to use the terms "pay and receive fixed" to describe one's intention, and will ensure no costly mistakes are made!

It is also worth mentioning one other aspect of swap quotes. The customer may well end up paying more or receiving less than the quoted interbank rates as many banks will apply a dealing margin. There are two main factors that will impact the margin, which comprise the liquidity and credit charge. The liquidity charge is the "cost" of hedging the interest rate risk of entering into a single swap. It may not be possible for the bank to immediately offset the risk of a new swap by entering into an equal and opposite position. Alternatively, if the swap transaction is executed on a large notional amount, it may be difficult to hedge the entire position with one transaction. The credit charge has become more important in recent years and has recently become termed the "credit value adjustment". In simple terms, if there is a greater risk of a client defaulting this will have to be reflected in the price that they pay. Most interbank and hedge fund clients will have cash collateral agreements and so the credit charge may be fairly small. But if the collateral they provide is of lower quality or less liquid there will still be a credit charge, although this will be less than that applied to unsecured accounts.

In the next chapter we will show that there is a linkage between swaps and financially settled forwards in that a swap can be thought of as a multi-period, cash-settled forward contract, executed at a uniform fixed rate.

Asset swaps

An asset swap is a combination investment package where an investor buys a fixed-rate bond and simultaneously enters into a "pay fixed" interest rate swap. Asset swaps can be structured in a number of ways, the details of which will be covered in Chapter 5. Here we will consider one variation, which is the "par in, par out" (or just "par–par") structure. Here the investor pays 100% of the face value of the bond (i.e., its par value) at the start of the transaction, holds the bond to maturity and then receives par from the issuer at maturity. If the market value of the asset is anything other than par at the point of purchase this will create an advantage to either the buyer or seller. If the bond is trading below par this means the investor will be disadvantaged as he will "overpay" for the bond. For bonds that are trading at a price greater than their face value this bestows a cash flow advantage on the investor (i.e., if the bond is trading at 120 the investor only pays 100). The second element of the asset swap structure is that the fixed rate on the swap is set equal to the coupon on the bond. Again, since it is unlikely that these two parameters will be exactly equal it will create an advantage for one of the parties.

Figure 1.3 shows the cash flows associated with an asset swap and gives a visual depiction of the rationale for entering into this type of transaction. Since the fixed coupon on the bond and the fixed rate on the swap are equal and opposite to each other (and have the same maturity), the cash flows have no net economic impact on the investor. As a result, the investor owns a structure that pays them LIBOR plus or minus a spread, which makes the structure economically equal to a floating-rate note.

In the previous section we had shown that the majority of interest rate swaps involved a LIBOR cash flow without any associated spread. However, in the asset swap package the spread to LIBOR acts as a balancing mechanism to ensure that any advantage or disadvantage incurred as a result of the investor paying par and entering into an off-market swap is returned over the life of the deal. In this way the entire package will then become an equitable exchange of cash flows.

An asset swap structure has more credit than interest rate exposure. Suppose that interest rates were to rise. The bond element of the structure would lose money but since the investor

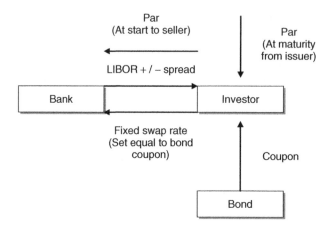

Figure 1.3   Asset swap package.

is paying fixed on a swap, this deal now becomes a more attractive transaction and will therefore increase in value. As a result, the two elements more or less cancel each other out. The same effect in the opposite direction would happen for a fall in interest rates. However, if interest rates remain unchanged but there is a perception that the issuer is more likely to default then the bond element will lose value with no offsetting profit on the swap. Overall there will be a net loss.

There are a number of reasons why an investor may wish to enter into an asset swap package:

- They may wish to reduce the market risk of holding a fixed-rate bond (bond market risk will be covered in Chapter 3).
- Since floating-rate notes offer an investor credit exposure rather than interest rate exposure, the investor may wish to take a view on how this component will evolve.
- The corporate entity to which the asset swap is linked does not have any floating-rate debt in issue and so the investor may have to create this synthetically using the asset swap.
- If the fixed-rate bond is trading cheap to its fair value then asset swapping the asset will create an attractively priced FRN.
- It is possible to buy a fixed-rate bond in, say, USD and asset swap it using a currency swap where the fixed rate is also USD but the LIBOR cash flows are denominated in, say, EUR.

Overnight index swap

An overnight index swap (OIS) is an interest rate swap where the floating leg of the swap is equal to the average of an agreed overnight index such as SONIA or EONIA (see Appendix 2.1 for more detail on these indices). As we will show in Chapter 2, the fixed leg of the swap is set at such a level that the transaction will be considered an equitable exchange of cash flows.

Figure 1.4 shows one simple application of the swap. A bank has agreed to take money on deposit on a fixed rate but can use the swap to transform the nature of their interest rate risk. They enter into an OIS where they receive a fixed rate and pay an overnight index rate. If we assume that the two fixed rates cancel out then the bank accepting the

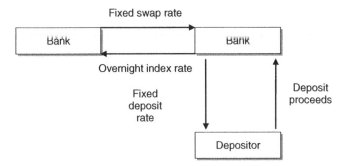

Figure 1.4 Overnight index swap.

deposit has acquired the funds and on a net basis is paying the overnight index rate. For deals with a maturity of less than one year, the fixed versus compounded floating payments are exchanged at maturity. For OIS transactions of greater than one year the payments are exchanged annually.

Credit default swaps

A credit default swap (CDS) is a bilateral contract that allows one entity to buy protection against the possibility that a particular reference entity (or basket of reference entities) will suffer a specific credit event. The buyer of this credit protection pays a fixed premium that is typically paid quarterly (although some markets pay semi-annually) to a protection seller. The protection seller will agree to "make whole" the protection buyer by agreeing to pay an amount of compensation if the agreed credit event occurs. The fee that the protection buyer agrees to pay is referred to as a premium or a spread. Upon the occurrence of the credit event the premium payments stop and the contract will terminate. The buyer of protection is considered to be short the credit risk as economically their position is equivalent to selling the credit risky asset. The protection seller is long the credit risk; similar to the buyer of a bond they are accepting the risk that a particular entity will suffer a credit event and are being paid a regular cash flow as compensation. By convention the protection seller is sometimes termed an investor as this position can be viewed as being economically equivalent to buying a bond.

Diagrammatically the CDS can be represented as in Figure 1.5.

In the credit fundamentals section of this chapter (Section 1.4) we derived an intuitive approach to pricing credit that suggested the magnitude of the spread was a function of the expected loss and the probability of default. In the USA and Europe, CDS trade with fixed coupons: 100 and 500 basis points for the USA; 25, 100, 500 and 1000 basis points for Europe. Higher-yielding names will trade with higher coupons, while investment grade names will trade with lower coupons. These coupons will not necessarily reflect the current market value of the spread and so an upfront cash adjustment will be necessary. Suppose an investment grade name is trading with a fixed coupon of 100 basis points but the market believes that the current value of the spread is 90 basis points. The buyer of protection will be required to pay the spread on a quarterly basis but is locking into a value that is 10 basis points higher than the market spread at the time the deal is executed. As a result he will receive an upfront cash adjustment of 10 basis points per annum, discounted to reflect the

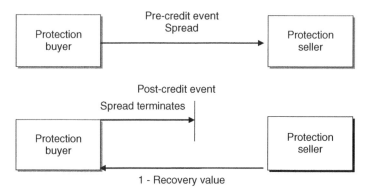

Figure 1.5   Credit default swaps.

time value of money and the probability that the company may default. This is covered in more detail in Chapter 3.

Two quoting methods have evolved for single-name CDS transactions. For investment grade names, the quote is given in terms of a "par spread". In effect this spread is a reflection of the market's current perception of the creditworthiness of the reference entity. Once the trade is executed, an upfront adjustment is paid or received and all subsequent cash flows are based on the agreed fixed coupon. For high-yield names the quotation is given in terms of "points upfront" but again all subsequent cash flows are executed on a fixed coupon basis. There is a standard market methodology to convert between par spreads and points upfront.

Originally, physical settlement was the norm upon the advent of a credit event and it required the protection seller to deliver the agreed notional amount of the transaction to the protection buyer. In return, the protection buyer delivered an asset issued by the agreed reference entity that conformed to the terms of the agreed contract. This could have been a defaulted asset or a non-defaulted asset that was considered pari passu. Physical settlement was preferred because banks typically ran a "matched position", i.e., they held an offsetting position with identical terms and conditions. As a result, if a credit event were to occur, physical settlement would allow the bank to pay and receive the notional amounts on the offsetting contracts and receive and deliver the agreed obligation. In this situation there is no price risk on the delivered obligation as long as the notional amounts on the transactions were equal. The market value of the delivered obligation was irrelevant as the notional amounts that are associated with the trades are for a fixed monetary value and the transfer of the obligation involves nothing other than a change of title of an asset.

Cash settlement was less popular as a bank holding a matched position would be subject to price risk. In the early days of the market, if a credit event were to occur, unless the institution were able to ensure that the settlement of both legs coincided there was no guarantee that the value of the delivered obligation on one side of the transaction would match that of the obligation received.

As the CDS market grew, inevitably the total notional amount of outstanding transactions outstripped the supply of outstanding obligations. This meant that if a credit event occurred, the protection buyers (who are not obligated to actually own obligations issued by the reference entity) often encountered difficulties in sourcing the required obligations. To avoid the introduction of price risk in the settlement of the CDS contract the market has now moved to an auction process where a panel of traders agree on a post-default value of the deliverable obligations. This single value is then used by all market participants, removing the potential price mismatch.

The CDS contract has a number of key characteristics.

Reference entity: It is very important for the two counterparties to agree the exact legal entity on which protection is being bought or sold.

Reference obligation: Stated in the deal confirmation is a debt obligation issued by the reference entity that identifies the exact nature of the credit risk being transferred. This is because different obligations within a capital structure will have different degrees of credit risk depending on the amount that would be recovered by the lender in the event of a default. Typically the reference obligation represents the senior unsecured portion of the reference entity's capital structure, but some transactions may be based on a different component (i.e., subordinated debt) in order to express a different view. Knowing the reference obligation will allow the contracts to be fairly priced (as the price must reflect the potential loss to the protection seller) and will also determine the nature of the asset that will be delivered if a credit event is activated.

Credit events: The market participants will agree a number of market standard events that will cause the contingent compensation to be paid by the protection seller. These are:

- bankruptcy
- failure to pay
- restructuring (of which there are different variations)
- obligation acceleration/default
- repudiation/moratorium (for sovereign reference obligations).

Not all contracts will include all of the default terms. Over time, each market has developed particular conventions as to which terms should be included. For example, in the USA the convention is to trade bankruptcy and failure to pay.

Obligations: Once the credit events have been specified the entities must agree the population of the issuer's obligations that could lead to a credit event being triggered. The market standard is typically "borrowed money" (although there are differences between markets). This is defined to include such things as bonds, loans and certificates of deposit.

Deliverable obligations: If a credit event is triggered and the deal is physically settled then the protection seller will deliver a cash sum equal to the agreed notional amount. In return the buyer will be required to deliver an acceptable asset issued by the reference entity. This need not be the reference obligation as the supply of this component may be limited. As a result, the market allows for some leeway in terms of the actual asset. Although a number of criteria apply, the most significant is that it should not be subordinated to the reference obligation as those assets possess a different degree of credit risk.

In recent times the credit derivatives market and principally the CDS component have experienced considerable growth. The spread of the CDS is viewed by market participants as representative of the "pure" credit risk of a particular reference entity. As such it is now used as a benchmark to assess and price credit risk in the bond markets. CDS instruments will trade with many different maturities even where there is no debt of an equivalent maturity. This has given rise to the concept of the credit curve, which is a representation of CDS spreads of different maturities.

1.5.4   Vanilla options

An option is a contract that gives the holder the right but not the obligation to buy or sell an asset at a pre-agreed price in the future. Essentially, it is a forward contract that allows the buyer to walk away if at maturity the market rates that prevail make execution of the deal unattractive. An option that gives the holder the right to buy an underlying asset is referred to as a call option, while the right to sell the asset is referred to as a put option. The price at which the counterparty agrees to deal is referred to as either the strike rate or the exercise price. When the buyer ("holder") of the option can use the option is a function of whether the contract is European, American or Bermudan ("semi-American") in style. A European-style option allows the holder to exercise the option only at expiry. An American-style option allows the holder to exercise the option at any time prior to its stated maturity. A Bermudan option allows the holder to exercise the option according to a pre-agreed schedule of dates.

The decision to exercise the option will depend on whether the option is in-, out-of- or at-the-money. An in-the-money (ITM) option is an option where the strike rate is more favourable than the underlying price. If this were the case it would be logical to exercise the option. An out-of-the-money (OTM) option is one where the strike rate is less favourable than the underlying price and so the option would not be exercised. An at-the-money (ATM) option is one where the underlying market price is equal to the strike price. In this case the holder would be indifferent as to whether they would exercise the option.

Assume an investor buys a 3-month European-style call option on an asset which is trading at a price of 100. Suppose that the strike rate for the option is also 100 and that the agreed premium is 5 units. If at maturity the underlying asset is trading at 90, the holder would not exercise the option to buy at the strike. The option would lapse as it is OTM and their losses would be equal to the premium paid. If the underlying asset was 110 at expiry, the holder would exercise the option. They would deliver a cash amount equal to the strike (100) and take delivery of the asset, which has a current value of 110. As a result they would have a profit of 5 units. This is calculated as the difference between the strike price of the option (100) and the expiry value of the underlying asset (110), less the premium paid (5). Note that if the underlying asset is between 100 and 105 at maturity the option would still be ITM as a result of our definition; however, the holder will not have broken even. The holder would still exercise the option as in this range of prices they will be seeking to minimize their losses and recoup some of the premium paid. An option seller is faced with a profit and loss profile opposite to that of the buyer. If the option is not exercised they will retain the premium but their losses will increase as the underlying price rises. However, the use of the terms ITM, OTM and ATM would remain the same and they are defined by convention from the buyer's perspective. So, if the underlying price is 90 at the expiry of the option, the option is OTM but is the preferred outcome from the seller's perspective.

The outcome for the buyer of a put with the same characteristics as the call would follow similar principles. However, a put option will be ITM if the strike price is greater than the underlying price, and OTM if the strike price is less than the underlying price.

From the profiles illustrated in Figure 1.6, it can be seen that for buyers of options, the maximum loss can never exceed the premium paid. The buyer's maximum loss represents the maximum profit that could be made by the seller of the option. The maximum profit for the option buyer appears to be unlimited, which is true for the call profile but not for

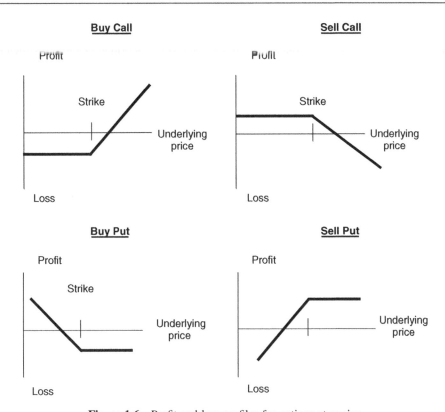

Figure 1.6   Profit and loss profiles for options at expiry.

the put. The maximum payoff on a put option is the difference between the strike rate and zero as the price of the underlying asset cannot go negative. Selling options can lead to unlimited losses for sellers of calls and significant losses for put writers, with the latter's losses "benefiting" from the restraint of a zero price boundary.

The payoff of calls and puts at expiry is often represented using the following expressions:

$$\text{Expiry payoff of call option} = \text{Max}(\text{underlying price} - \text{strike}, 0)$$

$$\text{Expiry payoff of put option} = \text{Max}(\text{strike} - \text{underlying price}, 0)$$

So for the holder of the call option the payoff will be the greater of either the underlying price less the agreed upon strike, or zero. For the holder of the put option they will exercise the option if the strike rate less the underlying price is greater than zero. These expressions do not measure the profit or loss of the position as they do not take into account the premium paid.

The premium is normally paid at the outset of the option and will be expressed in the same units as the underlying asset. So, if the option is referenced to an interest rate the premium will be paid in percentage points; crude oil options will be expressed in USD per barrel while options on equity indices will be quoted in index points.

Interest rate options

The two most common types of option within the interest rate world are cap/floor structures and swaptions. A cap structure is a strip of OTC interest rate call options on a series of forward rates, all traded with a single strike. The cap gives the buyer protection against an agreed index or reference rate such as LIBOR of a stated maturity rising above a pre-agreed strike rate. The term "cap" is the collective name for the component options, which are individually referred to as caplets. The premium payable on a cap structure is simply the sum of the individual caplet premia. It can be paid as a lump sum upfront or amortized over the life of the transaction.

Suppose that a company has taken in USD 100m for a period of 2 years on which 3-month USD LIBOR is payable. The Treasurer decides to insure himself against the possibility of an unfavourable rise in rates and so buys a 2-year cap referenced to 3-month LIBOR. Although the underlying transaction covers eight 3-month periods, there are by convention $n - 1$ options, i.e., seven caplets. This is because LIBOR interest rates are always set at the start of the period to which they apply but any associated payment is made at the end. As a result it would be impossible to buy protection against a known interest rate for the first period of the cap structure. The payoff on a cap for any single period is:

$$\text{Max}((\text{Reference rate} - \text{strike rate}) \times \text{notional} \times \text{days/day basis}, 0)$$

If we were to assume that the previously mentioned borrower agreed a strike rate of 5.00% and that in the second period, 3-month LIBOR fixed at 5.25%, then assuming a 92-day period and a 360-day year they would receive a sum equal to:

$$\text{USD } 100\text{m} \times 0.25\% \times 92/360 = \text{USD } 63,888.89$$

This could be used to offset the cost of the underlying borrowing which would now incur an interest charge of 5.25%. Similar to the underlying loan the payout on the cap would be known at the start of the quarter but payable in arrears. The net cash flows received under the cap combined with the payment on the underlying loan would result in a net interest cost of 5.00% – equal to the strike on the option. If the value of LIBOR had been equal to or less than the 5.00% strike rate then there would be no receipt under the terms of the option. The borrower would let the option lapse and enjoy the benefits of borrowing at a lower rate.

A floor gives the holder the protection again an agreed reference rate of interest falling below a pre-agreed strike. Again, a floor is a collective name for the component options which individually are referred to as floorlets. The mechanics of the floor are the same as the cap, but the payoff to a holder would only occur if the reference interest rate was less than the strike rate:

$$\text{Max}((\text{Strike rate} - \text{reference rate}) \times \text{notional} \times \text{days/day basis}, 0)$$

Swaptions

A swaption is an option that gives the holder the right but not the obligation to enter into an interest rate swap. A payer swaption allows the holder to pay fixed in a swap of a predefined maturity and so the buyer of a payer swaption would benefit if rates were to rise. A receiver

Table 1.2   The positions that result from the exercise of swaptions

	Receivers	Payers
Buy	Right to receive fixed on an interest rate swap	Right to pay fixed on an interest rate swap
Sell	Obligation to pay fixed on an interest rate swap	Obligation to receive fixed on an interest rate swap

swaption allows the holder to receive fixed in an interest rate swap and would benefit if rates were to fall. The different permutations are shown in Table 1.2.

If one were to draw the "hockey stick" at maturity payoffs for these options similar to those documented in Figure 1.6, the purchase of a payer swaption would resemble a long call, while the purchase of a receiver swaption would resemble a long put option. There is a slight difference in that the non-horizontal part of the profile will display some curvature as the instrument into which the option is exercised exhibits a non-linear profit and loss profile (the pricing of swaps is explained in greater detail in Chapter 2).

Although there are exceptions, the majority of swaptions are cash settled at expiry. So, rather than enter into an actual interest rate swap the buyer will receive the current market value of an interest rate swap with a fixed rate equal to the strike of the swaption. Swaptions are quoted in terms of the option maturity followed by the tenor of the swap. For example, an option to enter into a 5-year swap, 1 year in the future, would be written as 1y × 5y or "1 into 5".

1.5.5   Exotic options

The description of options has so far concentrated on those that are classified as being "vanilla", which means that their expiry profit and loss profiles at maturity conform to those shown in Figure 1.6. However, there is a larger family of options that are designated as being exotic. Somewhat unhelpfully, the only definition of an exotic option is one whose profit and loss expiry profile does not conform to the four vanilla building-block positions. The two most common exotic options are barriers and binaries.

Barrier options

A barrier option is an option that has an additional price performance feature, sometimes referred to as a trigger, which if hit by a movement in the spot price will result in an option position being either activated ("knocked in") or deactivated ("knocked out"). Although not universally adopted language, it is useful to classify barrier options in terms of the position of the barrier in relation to the spot price. A standard barrier option is one where the barrier is placed in the OTM region. A reverse barrier option represents an instance where the barrier is placed in the ITM region. Within either of these two categories it is possible to categorize the structure according to whether it is knocked in or knocked out, and then according to whether it is a call or a put. This results in 16 different permutations, which are shown in Table 1.3. It is possible to extend the number to 32 by distinguishing between buyers and sellers, but we will restrict our analysis to the 16 key positions. It is market convention to refer to these barrier options using terms such as "down and out". Take, for example, a standard knock out call option. Suppose an option has a strike rate of 100 and a

Table 1.3   Taxonomy of barrier option positions

	Standard knock ins	Standard knock outs	Reverse knock ins	Reverse knock outs
Calls	Down and in Barrier below spot	Down and out Barrier below spot	Up and in Barrier above spot	Up and out Barrier above spot
Puts	Up and in Barrier above spot	Up and out Barrier above spot	Down and in Barrier below spot	Down and out Barrier below spot

barrier at 90. Unless the spot rate trades at 90 prior to maturity, the option is for all intents and purposes a European-style call option. As soon as 90 trades, the option position is terminated and no further rights or obligations accrue. Hence the name; if the spot rate goes down, the option position gets knocked out.

Arguably the main motivation for executing a barrier option is one of cost. Although an extensive treatise on barrier pricing is beyond the scope of this book, since there is a possibility that the option will either survive or be terminated the price of a barrier option will always be cheaper than that of an equivalent European-style contract.

Binary options

A binary option is also sometimes referred to as a "digital", "all or nothing" or "bet" option. If exercised, the structure will pay out a fixed sum irrespective of how deeply the option is in-the-money. There are some variations on this basic description. An "at expiry" binary option is a European-style option that pays out a fixed amount only if the option is ITM at expiry. Since the payout at maturity is limited to a fixed amount, they will be cheaper than an equivalent non-binary option. A "one touch" option is an American-style digital option, which pays out a fixed amount at the point that the strike is hit, which could be any time prior to expiry. A "no touch" option is a digital option that pays out a fixed sum at expiry if the underlying price does not touch the strike.

Depending on their style, digital options may or may not be path dependent. Path dependent means that the magnitude of the option's payout is affected by the movement of the underlying price prior to expiry. One touch and no touch options are path dependent and will cost more than the European digital. As a rule of thumb, American-style digitals will cost twice as much as European digitals due to the increased probability of exercise.

Since the option has a fixed payout and a fixed premium cost there is no need to have a principal amount. The premium is often quoted as a percentage of a 100% payout. So if the trader wished to have a payout of USD 1m, the premium might be quoted as 10% (USD 100,000). Somewhat confusingly, the strike rate on a binary option may be referred to as a "barrier" and the words call and put may be replaced by "up" and "down". Reference is also made to "knock ins" and "knock outs" for touch and no touch structures, respectively.

2

Pricing Relationships

2.1 RELATIVE VALUE

The phrase "relative value" (RV) is most commonly interpreted by practitioners in a literal sense; the value of one asset with respect to another. In isolation, the term "value" is typically used when describing an asset that is believed to be either cheap or expensive ("rich" in the market jargon). As any regular shopper will no doubt testify, when considering if something is a bargain it is usually measured relative to some benchmark or accepted norm.

This definition of relative value is a valid one, although we will argue that it is also somewhat limiting. Our definition of relative value is therefore *"what is the optimal way in which a particular view of the market can be expressed"*. To grasp the significance of this definition, consider the following simple example. Let us assume that we are an investor who is looking to earn a return in euros with a minimum degree of credit risk. If the investor chose to invest in AAA-rated EUR-denominated sovereign bonds, they would be able to pick between a variety of different issuers. In theory, since the currency and the credit risk are identical, all of these bonds should return the same amount for a given yield. Using the traditional definition of relative value, if the investor were able to identify one bond that they considered cheap relative to the universe of other equivalent assets (i.e., it has a higher yield), it could represent a potential purchase. Using the wider definition of relative value the investor would look at alternative structures that may afford the same exposure but offer a greater return. In addition to buying the underlying instrument, an investor should also consider if their return could be further enhanced by:

- Purchasing a bond future.
- Receiving fixed in an interest rate swap.
- Executing an option transaction that will show a profit if market rates move as expected.

We will use this framework of spot–forward–swap–option as the basis of our trade design as we progress through the different asset classes. Another interpretation of RV relates to the notion of arbitrage. This term has been subject to misuse over time and so it is worth defining it to ensure consistency. True arbitrage is said to occur when an asset is trading at two different prices in the same market. This allows the asset to be bought and sold at a risk-free profit. Although there is clearly nothing wrong with arbitrage, it is not our intention to include this concept within our definition of RV.

2.2 THE RELATIVE VALUE TRIANGLE

At the core of the analysis is our relative value triangle (Figure 2.1), which gives a visual description of the relationships that exist between the four core components of any market.

The triangle can be interpreted either as a way of representing pricing relationships or to identify trading opportunities. Without wishing to get ahead of ourselves, the following is a

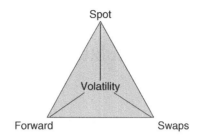

Figure 2.1   The relative value triangle.

brief overview of the direction the chapter will take and considers the nature of fixed income relationships within this framework. We will show there is a mathematical link between the spot price of a bond in the cash market and a bond for future delivery through the concept of "net carry". Equally, we will show that one way of valuing a swap is to think of the position as being equivalent to a pair of cash bonds, one with a fixed coupon and the other with a floating coupon. In short-term money markets a forward rate of interest could also be derived if we know the value of two spot-starting instruments with different maturities. It is possible to derive the value of a forward-starting instrument with a maturity equal to the difference between the maturities of the two spot instruments. For example, if the value of a 3-month and a 6-month instrument can be observed in the market, it is possible to derive the value of a 3-month instrument in 3 months' time. Using similar principles it is possible to calculate the value of a swap as the weighted average of a series of forward rates. The triangle will also help identify the relationships between the option world and the three corners of the triangle. The term "volatility" is used as this is the unknown pricing variable within an option pricing model. Although somewhat more involved, it is possible to create mathematical relationships between the underlying price of the asset (be it a spot or a forward price) and the value of an option. For example, we will show the relationship between options and their underlying market through the very useful (but underrated) concept of put–call parity.

2.3 SPOT PRICING

Kay (2009) points out that there are broadly two approaches to valuing any asset:

- The value of an asset is what someone will pay for it.
- The value of an asset is a function of the cash flows it will generate over its life.

   To illustrate the main concepts of valuation, we will initially consider the second aspect with a bias towards fixed income.

2.3.1 Pricing fixed income securities

To illustrate the concept of pricing an asset in the spot market, let us consider the example of a bond that has no default risk. By convention, the price to be paid for a bond is expressed as a percentage of its face value. So if the bond is trading at a full settlement price of 98.00

and the investor wishes to buy £10,000,000 nominal of the issue, they will be required to pay £9,800,000. However, we are more interested in determining how the price of the bond is derived. Suppose the bond has a maturity of 4 years and pays the investor an annual coupon of 5%. When pricing this particular bond the first step is to identify the associated cash flows. The cash flows on our 4-year bond per £100 nominal are therefore:

Year 1	£5
Year 2	£5
Year 3	£5
Year 4	£105

To value these cash flows they must be placed on an equal footing, which means that we must take account of their timing. For example, if I had the choice of receiving £5 today rather than in 12 months' time, I would prefer to take possession of the cash today. This has nothing to do with the fact that the £5 may not be there in 1 year's time (i.e., credit risk), but is simply a reflection of the fact that if I took receipt of £5 today I would be able to invest this sum for 12 months and earn interest at the prevailing rate. This "time value of money" concept is the foundation of all financial computations. Suppose that 12-month rates are currently 4.5%; investing my £5 now, this would mean in 12 months' time I would have £5.23 (rounded). This value is calculated using the following generalized relationship:

$$\text{Future value} = \text{Present value} \times (1 + \text{interest rate})^n \tag{2.1}$$

where:

n = whole number of years

So, substituting our values gives:

$$£5.23 = £5.00 \times 1.045$$

For periods of less than 1 year, the formula is:

$$\text{Future value} = \text{Present value} \times \left(1 + \text{interest rate} \times \frac{\text{days in period}}{\text{day basis}}\right) \tag{2.2}$$

Since interest rates are expressed as a percentage per annum, the final part of the equation prorates the interest rate by the maturity of the transaction. The equation's denominator ("day basis") will be 365 for GBP and 360 for EUR and USD.

With some simple rearrangement we can use this to value the bond cash flows presented earlier. In order to derive the present value of a sum of money, the formulas are as follows. For cash flows with a maturity of 12 months or longer:

$$\text{Present value} = \frac{\text{Future value}}{(1 + \text{interest rate})^n} \tag{2.3}$$

For cash flows with a maturity of less than 12 months:

$$\text{Present value} = \frac{\text{Future value}}{\left(1 + \text{interest rate} \times \dfrac{\text{days in period}}{\text{day basis}}\right)} \tag{2.4}$$

So far we have been non-specific about the choice of interest rates which will be applied to our cash flows. Traditional bond theory relies on the use of a single interest rate to present value all of the cash flows, irrespective of their maturity. The use of a single rate is, on the one hand, intuitively attractive as it should represent the rate of returns on assets with the same degree of credit risk and maturity. So if I were trying to price a 4-year bond, I would seek to ensure that the price offered to the market is in line with alternative equivalent investments. However, it is also intuitively incorrect – interest rates for different maturities are different and so it would make sense to use a different rate to present value each of the cash flows. We will return to this issue shortly.

When using a single interest rate to present value a stream of cash flows, this rate is referred to as the "yield to maturity" (YTM). A yield is a measure of expected return that tries to capture, in a single number, the income received by virtue of the coupon and any capital gain or loss that will be incurred by the investor. As the name suggests, the YTM measures the rate of return that an investor will earn if they buy the bond at the prevailing price and hold it to maturity.

However, there is one major caveat associated with a bond's YTM. It will only be an accurate measure of return if the investor is able to reinvest the interim cash flows at a rate equal to the original YTM. An example will help clarify these issues.

Suppose that yields on alternative equivalent assets are 4.5%, which we decide to use as the discount rate in order to present value the bond's cash flows. Present valuing our example bond's cash flows using equation (2.3) gives the following values:

Year 1	£4.7847
Year 2	£4.5787
Year 3	£4.3815
Year 4	£88.0489

The price of the bond is simply the sum of these cash flows, namely £101.7938. This figure represents how much an investor would need to pay to acquire the asset and is referred to as the "dirty price" of the bond. Typically bonds are issued with their coupons close to current market yields, which means that they will initially trade at a price close to 100 or "par". For every day that the bond is held, the investor earns the right to receive one day's worth of coupon, referred to as accrued interest. However, bonds are quoted on a "clean basis", which means that the quoted price is the dirty price less any accrued interest. If bonds were quoted on a dirty basis their value would rise every day because of the increasing accrued interest and so to strip out this upward price bias they are quoted on a "clean" basis.

So far we have calculated the "fair value", "theoretical value" or "fundamental value" of the bond. The market price of the bond is what someone is prepared to pay for it. If the market value of the bond is lower than the fair value, the bond is said to be trading "cheap" to fair value. If the market value is greater than the fair value, then the bond is trading "rich".

We highlighted earlier that the yield to maturity of a bond is only accurate as a measure of return if all of the subsequent cash flows received by the investor are reinvested at the yield to maturity that prevailed at the time the bond was purchased. To illustrate that principle consider the following example, again based on the previous bond example. If an investor were to earn the yield to maturity over the life of the bond they would need to invest the initial dirty value at this rate until the note's maturity. This would return the following amount:

$$£101.7938 \times 1.045^4 = £121.3910$$

This amount can be replicated by investing the interim coupons that are received at the end of each year at the original yield until the final maturity of the bond. The values at the maturity of the bond would be:

- £5 invested for 3 years at 4.5% returns £5.7058.
- £5 invested for 2 years at 4.5% returns £5.4601.
- £5 invested for 1 year at 4.5% returns £5.2250.
- Principal of £100 plus final coupon of 5% gives £105.00.

Total cash flows are £121.3909 (small rounding difference).

From this example, it is possible to see that the actual return earned by the bond investor will be a function of the interest rate at which the coupons can be reinvested. If the reinvestment rate is higher than the original yield, the total proceeds will be increased; equally, the opposite will apply. This concept is referred to as "reinvestment risk" and the assumption is considered to be the main weakness of YTM as an accurate measure of return. To estimate the true return on an investment to be held for a specific period one would need to have a yield that is not subject to any concepts of reinvestment risk. This rate does exist; it is referred to as a zero-coupon yield and will be considered in Section 2.3.3.

2.3.2   Par yield curves

A yield curve is a graphical representation of the yields on bonds with the same credit risk but with different maturities. The introduction of credit risk means that it is impossible to talk about a single overarching yield curve. However, the situation is somewhat confused by the existence of different types of yield curve. In its simplest form it is possible to derive the curve that comprises the YTMs of different bonds with the same credit risk. This is sometimes referred to as the "par" curve as it is often constructed from the most recently issued bonds whose yields are close to their coupons and as such their prices are trading close to par (i.e., close to a price of 100).

2.3.3   Zero-coupon yield curves

Zero-coupon yields represent the rates of return on zero-coupon structures. Traditionally the phrase "zero coupon" is used to describe bonds where there is no interest paid during the life of the deal but it is instead "rolled up" and paid at maturity. It is useful to redefine the phrase to describe any structure that has just two cash flows – one at the start and one at maturity. This means that there is no reinvestment risk. Consequently, one could invest a sum of money today and know exactly how much would be returned at maturity. For example, suppose we were to deposit £100 for 12 months at 4.5%. At the maturity of the deposit we know exactly how much would be returned (£104.50) as there are no interim coupons between the first and final cash flow. This means the final proceeds are unaffected by reinvestment considerations and so simple deposits that pay interest at maturity are zero coupon in style – the rate you see is the rate you get. This simple investment example shows the appeal of using a zero-coupon rate to calculate the future value of a cash flow. It would seem reasonable to suggest that when trying to calculate the present value of any cash flow, the most appropriate type of interest rate to use is a zero-coupon rate of the same maturity.

Using the concept of zero-coupon structures it is possible to decompose a coupon-paying bond into a series of zero-coupon cash flows, each of which can be valued separately. The value of each of these cash flows could then be summed to return the overall price of the bond. However, it should be stressed that this zero-coupon approach is not "better" than using the YTM and should not return a different value. As such it is perhaps useful to think of the YTM as a form of average of each of the zero-coupon discount rates used to value the constituent cash flows. To calculate the present value of a cash flow discounted by a zero-coupon interest rate, equations (2.3) and (2.4) are redefined slightly such that the denominator is now specified as a zero-coupon interest rate of a given maturity.

It is more common for the markets to express a zero-coupon rate as a discount factor rather than a percentage value. To move from zero-coupon rates to discount factors we could take equation (2.3) and move the numerator from the top to the right-hand side of the expression to give:

$$\text{Present value} = \text{Future value} \times \frac{1}{(1 + \text{interest rate})^n} \qquad (2.5)$$

The discount factor is the final part of equation (2.5). It is a number that has a maximum value of one (for cash flows that will be paid today) and a minimum (theoretical) value of zero. So, if a 1-year discount factor was calculated as 0.958313 it would mean that 1,000,000 currency units receivable in 12 months' time would be worth 958,313 units today.

One issue faced by practitioners is the sourcing of market-determined zero-coupon rates for longer-dated maturities. There are broadly two different approaches to this problem: the values can either be observed directly or calculated from alterative types of rates. Traditionally, zero-coupon rates are difficult to observe directly from quoted market prices as the population of zero instruments is relatively small. As a result, it is more common to derive them mathematically from their YTM equivalent. To illustrate the concept let us assume that the following par yields have been observed in the market for different maturities:

	Par rates
Year 1	4.35%
Year 2	4.40%
Year 3	4.45%
Year 4	4.50%

Since a 12-month rate with only one payment has no interim cash flows and therefore no reinvestment risk, the YTM and zero-coupon yields for this maturity will be identical. This information can then be used to derive a 2-year zero-coupon equivalent. We will assume that a bond exists with 2 years to maturity with a coupon of 4.40% and is therefore trading at par given its YTM of 4.40%. The cash flows associated with buying the bond today and holding it to maturity are:

Purchase:	(100)
Year 1	4.40%
Year 2	104.40%

To derive a 2-year zero-coupon rate we must effectively convert this coupon-paying bond into a zero-coupon structure. This could be achieved by selling for the right to receive the first year's coupon for spot value. The fair spot price to be paid for this coupon would be the present value of the cash flow. Since we know the 1-year zero rate is 4.35%, then the present value of the year one cash flow is 4.2166. So for spot settlement the cash flows comprise the 100 units needed to buy the bond less the 4.2166 received from selling the first coupon, which gives a net outgoing cash flow of 95.7834. This now gives us a zero-coupon structure – the investor pays 95.7834 today to receive back 104.40 in 2 years' time. Since the present and future values of the bond are known, it is possible to rearrange equation (2.3) to solve for the zero-coupon interest rate:

$$\text{Zero-coupon rate} = \sqrt{\frac{\text{Future value}}{\text{Present value}}} - 1$$

$$= \sqrt{\frac{104.40}{95.7834}} - 1$$

$$= 4.4011\%$$

Using these principles the zero-coupon rates for all the maturities can be calculated. For example, the 3-year zero rate is calculated by first assuming there is a 3-year bond trading at par. The first and second-year coupons could be sold off for spot settlement using the zero-coupon rates that have been calculated for these maturities to determine their present value. Having converted the bond into a zero-coupon structure, equation (2.3) could be applied to solve for the zero-coupon rate. The full set of par rates, zero rates and associated discount factors is given in Table 2.1.

Note that it is only possible to derive zero-coupon rates sequentially. To calculate the 2-year zero rate we need the 1-year zero rate; to calculate the 3-year rate we need the values for both the first and second years. This process has become known as "bootstrapping", which suggests that when lacing shoes you should start at the bottom and work towards the top. A feature of this process is when the par curve is upward sloping, zero rates are

Table 2.1   Par rates, zero-coupon rates and discount factors

	Par rates	Zero rates	Discount factors
Year 1	4.3500%	4.3500%	0.958313
Year 2	4.4000%	4.4011%	0.917466
Year 3	4.4500%	4.4530%	0.877480
Year 4	4.5000%	4.5058%	0.838375

numerically greater than their par curve equivalent. If we were to repeat the exercise in a downward-sloping par curve environment the zero rates would be below the par curve.

Let us return to our original example of a 4-year bond paying a 5% annual coupon. We can use the zero-coupon rates shown in Table 2.1 to present value the individual cash flows in order to derive the instrument's fair value:

Year 1	£5 × 0.958313 = £4.791565
Year 2	£5 × 0.917466 = £4.58733
Year 3	£5 × 0.877480 = £4.387400
Year 4	£105 × 0.838375 = £88.029396

The sum of the present values of the cash flows is £101.795691, which (allowing for rounding errors) is close to the value calculated using a single yield to maturity rate (i.e., £101.7938).

2.3.4 Forward yield curves

Forward rates are the final part of the yield curve jigsaw puzzle. A forward rate of interest is a rate of interest whose value is known today but which applies to some future time period. Arguably this rate is central to all fixed income analysis, as we will try to demonstrate. However, in our experience it is still the most widely misunderstood of the three generic yield curves.

Suppose that a company is looking to borrow USD 10m for a period of 3 months starting in 3 months' time and asks a bank for a quotation. If the bank is committing today to lend to a client in the future, it will need to borrow money for the same future maturity in order to finance the obligation. If the bank merely guessed a rate at which they would lend to the client in the future they run the risk of rising interest rates, i.e., the cost of financing the client's loan would be in excess of the amount earned. As a result, the rate quoted to the client will be based on the cost to the trader of putting on an offsetting hedge to mitigate any possible losses. This highlights an important principle of derivative theory: the price of any derivative is driven by the cost of hedging the resultant exposure – if you can hedge it, you can price it!

Let us assume that current 3-month interest rates are quoted as 5.50%–5.51% and that 6-month rates are 5.58%–5.59%. The bank could lock in a lending rate for the 3- to 6-month period by entering into two spot-starting transactions. The hedge could be achieved by borrowing for 6 months at 5.59% and lending for 3 months at 5.50%.

On the spot date there should be no net cash flow effect as the amount borrowed and lent will be the same. At the end of the 3-month period, the bank receives back the proceeds of the deposit, which could be used to finance the loan to the client. The repayment of the original 6-month borrowing is financed by the repayment of the monies due from the client. The following example will illustrate this.

At time period 0, the bank will lend a sum of money that will generate the required USD 10m for the client in 3 months' time (91 days). This is calculated as:

$$\text{USD } 10,000,000 \times \frac{1}{1 + \left(0.055 \times \dfrac{91}{360}\right)} = \text{USD } 9,862,878$$

To finance this loan, the bank will borrow this amount for 6 months, which (assuming a 182-day period) will require them to repay

$$\text{USD } 9{,}862{,}878 \times 1 + \left(0.0559 \times \frac{182}{360}\right) = \text{USD } 10{,}141{,}608$$

So at time period 0, there is no net cash flow as the amount borrowed and lent (USD 9,862,878) will net out. At the 3-month period the interest and principal received on the initial deposit is received back and exactly finances the USD 10m loan to the client. When the client finally repays the loan the interest payable should be sufficient to cover the interest payable by the bank on their original 6-month borrowing (i.e., USD 141,608). The cash flows are shown in Figure 2.2.

Therefore the percentage per annum quoted to the client for the 91-day forward-starting loan should be:

$$\frac{141{,}608}{10{,}000{,}000} \times \frac{360}{91} = 5.60\%$$

In this example we used short-term deposit rates to derive the forward rate. In the last section we argued that short-term deposits are zero coupon in style and so it follows that single-period forward rates are derived from zero-coupon rates. The formula that links them together is:

$$(1 + {}_aR_c)^{c-a} = (1 + {}_aR_b)^{b-a} \times (1 + {}_bR_c)^{c-b} \tag{2.6}$$

where:

$R =$ zero-coupon rate

a, b, c are periods of varying maturity

To illustrate the application of equation (2.6), consider the derivation of a 1-year rate in 1 year's time (also referred to as "1 × 2" rate or the "12/24" rate). To derive this value we need a 1-year and a 2-year zero-coupon rate, which we derived in Section 2.3.3 (4.35% and 4.4011%, respectively):

$$(1 + {}_aR_c)^{c-a} = (1 + {}_aR_b)^{b-a} \times (1 + {}_bR_c)^{c-b}$$

$$(1 + {}_0R_2)^2 = (1 + {}_0R_1) \times (1 + {}_1R_2)$$

$$_1R_2 = \frac{(1 + {}_0R_2)^2}{(1 + {}_0R_1)} - 1$$

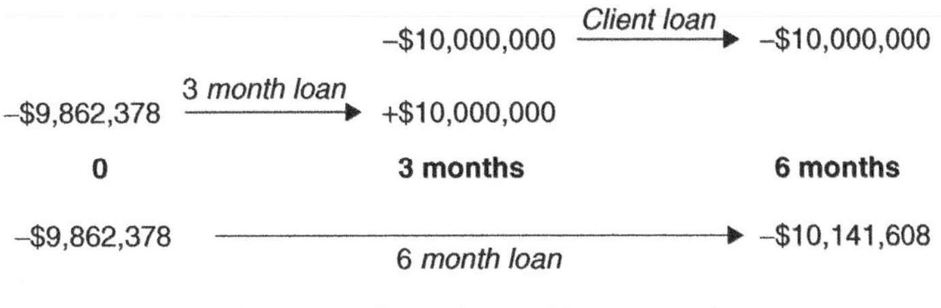

Figure 2.2   Hedging a forward loan commitment.

Table 2.2   Par, forward and zero rates

	Par rates	Zero rates	Forward rates
Year 1	4.3500%	4.3500%	4.3500%
Year 2	4.4000%	4.4011%	4.4522%
Year 3	4.4500%	4.4530%	4.5569%
Year 4	4.5000%	4.5058%	4.6642%

$$_1R_2 = \frac{(1.044011)^2}{(1.0435)} - 1$$

$$_1R_2 = 4.4522\%$$

Using this formula we can now derive the remaining forward rates from the zero-coupon values derived in Section 2.3.3 (see Table 2.2).

The par and zero rates in the table are of different tenors (1 to 4 years), whereas the forward rates all have a maturity of 12 months. The first value in the forward column (4.3500%) is not really a forward rate; it is the current 12-month rate. The second value of 4.4522% is the 1-year forward rate (the 12-month rate in 1 year's time); the third figure of 4.5569% is the 12-month rate in 2 years' time.

The table also shows that in an upward-sloping yield curve environment, forward rates will lie above both the par and zero equivalents. In a downward-sloping yield curve environment the order would be reversed, i.e., par, zero and forward.

Discount factors can also be used to calculate the forward rates. The discount factors calculated in Section 2.3.3 were:

	Discount factors
Year 1	0.958313
Year 2	0.917466
Year 3	0.877480
Year 4	0.838375

The forward rate for any period can also be calculated as the ratio of successive discount factors. For example:

Current 1-year rate

$$(1/0.958313) - 1 \times 100 = 4.3500\%$$

1-Year rate in 1 year's time

$$(0.958313/0.917466) - 1 \times 100 = 4.4522\%$$

1-Year rate in 2 years' time

$$(0.917466/0.877480) - 1 \times 100 = 4.5569\%$$

Note that the original par values were set up with "steps" of five basis points (0.05%) between each observation. This resulted in a set of forward rates that was consistently

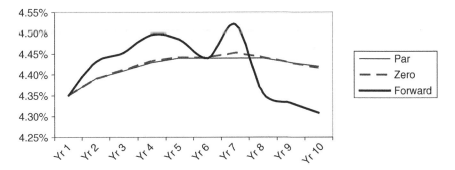

Figure 2.3   Par and forward curves; the effects of a flat par curve.

upward sloping. If the par curve was to flatten out at longer maturities then the mathematics of forward rate derivation would show a different result. Consider the values in Figure 2.3.

In this figure, the par and zero curves are flat but as a result the derived forward observations are somewhat jagged in nature. Consequently, an investor may consider there is no fundamental justification for this shape. Perhaps they do not believe that interest rates will evolve in such a discontinuous manner, and a smoother evolution would be a more reasonable outcome. As a result, this anomaly could be exploited using a number of strategies, which we consider in later chapters.

Forwards as breakevens

Suppose a market participant with a 1-year time horizon is considering two competing investment opportunities. Zero-coupon bond A has a 1-year maturity and yields 5%, while zero-coupon bond B has a 2-year maturity and yields 6%. Both bonds have the same probability of defaulting. When deciding which bond to purchase, the temptation is to make a judgement based on whether yields are expected to rise or fall. However, the correct approach for the investor is to base the decision relative to current forward rates. Using the principles introduced earlier in this section, the 1-year rate in 1 year's time is 7.01%. It would seem logical for the investor to buy the bond that would generate the greatest investment returns at the point of sale in 1 year's time. The first step is to calculate the current price of bond B, which has a 2-year maturity:

$$100/1.06^2 = 88.9996$$

If spot rates were to evolve in line with the current forward curve, the price of this 2-year zero bond in 1 year's time would be:

$$100/1.0701 = 93.4492$$

Having calculated these two prices it is possible to calculate the return on the 2-year instrument over the 1-year holding period:

$$(93.4492/88.9996) - 1 = 5.00\%$$

Table 2.3   12-month holding period returns from two zero-coupon bonds under different yield scenarios

	Return if yields evolve slower than the forward rate (e.g., 6.50%)	Return if yields evolve as per forward rate (7.01%)	Return if yields evolve faster than the forward rate (e.g., 7.50%)
Bond A (1-year maturity, initial yield 5%)	5.00%	5.00%	5.00%
Bond B (2-year maturity, initial yield 6%)	5.5024%	5.00%	4.5210%

This yield is the same as the current 1-year zero-coupon rate and indicates that if yields evolve in line with forward rates, bonds of the same credit quality will earn the same holding period return irrespective of their maturity.[1]

Suppose the investor had a different view of how rates would evolve and they believed that the actual 12-month rate in 1 year's time was more likely to be closer to 6.50%. In this case the price of bond B at that future time period would be 93.8967, and the holding period return would be 5.5024%. If the investor believed that the 12-month rate in 1 year's time was 7.50%, then the price of the bond B would be 93.0233, giving a holding period return of 4.5210%.

Table 2.3 shows the different scenarios. Based on these different scenarios we can derive some simple principles regarding the selection of fixed income investments.

The investor would choose bond B (the 2-year bond) over bond A if they believed that actual yields would be below those implied by the forward curve. If they expected actual rates to evolve in line with the forward curve, then they would be indifferent between holding the two bonds. If they believed that actual rates would be higher than the forward rate then they would select bond A. Note that in each of the scenarios the actual 1-year rate in 1 year's time had increased from the initial level of 5.00%, so the choice of investment was not based on whether rates would rise or fall. The choice of bond was different in each instance depending on the investor's view as to how the rate would evolve relative to the forward rate.

Central Bank activity

Let us develop the ideas presented in the previous section in order to understand the importance of short-term Central Bank rates in the investment process. Suppose a bank has lent money out for 3 months to earn 4% and decides to finance this by borrowing for 3 months at 3.95%. Structuring the transaction in this manner means that the bank is immune to any changes in interest rates. Suppose, however, the trader had thought that he may be able to make more money by taking a view on the evolution of shorter-dated interest rates and so decided to finance the loan with a shorter-dated transaction that is renewed ("rolled over") at the end of its maturity. For example, the trader might have decided to use three consecutive 1-month borrowings. Equally, the trader may have chosen an even shorter-term maturity such as the overnight rate, which is often used by Central Banks as a monetary policy target (see Appendix 2.1). This type of view implies that the trader believes the actual short-term rates for the future periods will be below that currently implied by the forward curve. From this we can perhaps conclude that a trader's view on interest rates will be driven by the expected path of short-term interest rates, which in turn will be driven by Central Bank activity.

Forwards as a forecast of future spot rates

One of the most widely held beliefs in relation to forward rates is that they represent some form of forecast of future spot rates. So with 1-year zero rates at 5.00% and the 1-year forward at 7.01%, the notion that a forward rate is a forecast of future spot rates would imply that 7.01% is the market's "best guess" of where the 12-month zero rate will be in 1 year's time. This practice is still perpetuated by the press, who use market values of short-term interest rate futures as a way of trying to second guess possible future changes in Central Bank rates. These exchange-traded contracts can be used to fix 3-month LIBOR rates for set future time periods, so if the rates implied from their prices are increasing with respect to maturity then this is taken as a sign that the Central Bank is likely to increase their rates. However, this is something of a flawed argument as forward rates are derived using the principle of "no arbitrage" and are therefore not the same as the expected future rate. Anecdotally, there is some suggestion that "humps" at the short end of the curve may be driven by the beliefs and actions of those participants who do believe that forward rates are forecasts.

In our view there is no justification for this view of forwards as forecasts in either theory or practice. A forecast is a value that we expect a variable to take at the end of some future time period. The forward rate calculation has no element of expectation or subjective belief built in – it is an objective calculation. There is a world of difference between a forward price and an expected future price.

Empirically there is also little evidence that forward rates are accurate predictors. Consider Figure 2.4, which shows the evolution of 3-month USD LIBOR over a 15-year period.

Each "hair" represents the forward curve out to 2 years on a single date. By looking at the difference between the "hair" at any point and the actual level of LIBOR that sits immediately below that observation, we can determine the accuracy of the forwards in predicting LIBOR.

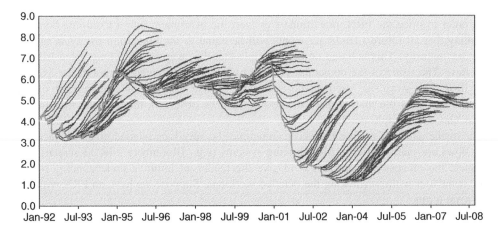

Figure 2.4   Forwards as predictors of future spot rates: 3-month LIBOR from 1992 to 2007.

This vertical distance is the extent to which the forward rate over- or under-predicted the actual value of LIBOR. As the figure shows, the ability of the forward rate to accurately predict the value of LIBOR is very poor. In the majority of cases, the forward rates over-predicted actual LIBOR and by a considerable amount. Interestingly, when forward rates under-predicted LIBOR they did so by a smaller margin.

2.3.5   Pricing floating-rate notes

In Chapter 1 we defined a floating-rate note (FRN) as an interest-bearing security whose coupon is paid on a regular basis (usually quarterly) at a given margin to an interest rate index such as LIBOR. This fixed spread over or under the index is often referred to as the "quoted margin" or the "given margin" (e.g., 3-month LIBOR + 10 basis points).

It is impossible to calculate an absolute yield for an FRN as the exact levels of future coupons are unknown. As a result, FRNs are quoted on what is termed a "discount margin basis". Recall that in conventional fixed income theory a bond price is derived by present valuing each cash flow using the following relationship, which is a variation of equation (2.3):

$$\text{Present value of cash flow} = \frac{\text{Future value of cash flow}}{(1 + \text{yield to maturity})^n} \tag{2.7}$$

It is possible to price an FRN by modifying the formula as follows:

$$\text{Present value of cash flow} = \frac{\text{Future value of LIBOR cash flow} + \text{quoted margin}}{(1 + \text{swap rate} + \text{discount margin})^n} \tag{2.8}$$

This approach to valuing the cash flows has a number of implications:

- Since the equation uses an observable par interest rate swap value in the denominator, the discount margin becomes the yield on the note.
- The discount margin becomes the mechanism by which changes in the issuer's creditworthiness are reflected in the value of the FRN.
- The discount margin is a function of the quoted price, maturity, the quoted margin, the magnitude of the LIBOR cash flow and the prevailing swap rate.

In order to price the FRN, practitioners convert the instrument into a fixed-rate bond by assuming that all future LIBOR payments will be equal to the prevailing par swap rate of the same maturity. This is based on the principle that the swap rate is a long-dated LIBOR cash flow. The value of the numerator is fixed by adding the quoted margin to the LIBOR cash flow. The swap rate used in the numerator is also used in the denominator of the equation and so if the market price of the FRN can be observed, the discount margin can be calculated by simple iteration.

The mathematics of pricing FRNs can sometimes be very long winded given the fact that cash flows are paid quarterly. Most pricing systems (e.g., Bloomberg's BC13 screen) will automate the process and our aim is to give the reader an intuitive understanding of the price behaviour without showing the detailed workings. Suppose we have an FRN with the following terms:

- 5-year maturity
- Quarterly payments
- Coupon set at 3-month LIBOR + 25 basis points

- Price 99.75 (no accrued interest)
- Discount margin of 30.511 basis points
- 5-year par swap rates are 4.00%

The discount margin – the FRN's yield to maturity – is slightly higher than the quoted margin due to the fact that if the investor were to hold the bond to maturity they would enjoy a 25 basis point capital gain. Spread over 5 years this would equate to about 5 basis points per annum (ignoring the time value of money), which accounts for the difference between the two values.

Change in the discount margin

Suppose that the market's perception of the issuer's creditworthiness declined, resulting in a higher discount margin. If the discount margin increased to 50 basis points, the price of the bond would fall, in this case to 98.87146.

Change in short-term interest rates

If current 3-month LIBOR were to fall instantaneously by 50 basis points to 3.50%, the discount margin would increase by 2.795 basis points to 33.295. This suggests that the instrument is relatively immune to changes in short-term interest rates. Once LIBOR resets to the current market level in 3 months' time, the discount margin will be equal to the quoted margin.

Change in long-term interest rates with bond trading close to par

If swap rates move from 4.00% to 5.00% the discount margin falls by a very small amount (to 30.638), leaving the price virtually unchanged. This reinforces the argument that the instrument is largely unaffected by interest rate changes.

Change in long-term interest rates with bond trading away from par

Suppose that the bond is trading significantly away from par at a price of 90 due perhaps to a deterioration in the creditworthiness of the issuer. Assuming all other market rates remain unchanged, this would correspond to a discount margin of 258.43 basis points. If swap rates were to increase from 4.00% to 5.00% the discount margin would increase to 263.993 basis points – again a relatively small move of about 5 basis points. However, the effect would be more pronounced the longer dated the bond.

From this analysis we can conclude that an FRN is relatively immune to changes in long-term and short-term interest rates. Additionally, its price is more sensitive to changes in the perception of the issuer's credit risk. This conclusion will become relevant when we consider asset swap structures, which are in effect synthetic FRNs. This will be covered in Chapter 4.

2.3.6 Inflation pricing

When calculating the price of an index-linked bond there are two different approaches, the so-called Canadian model or the UK model. We will focus on the Canadian model, which is the more popular technique and paradoxically is also the pricing approach for all UK bonds issued after 2005. Central to the pricing of inflation-linked bonds using this approach is the concept of the index ratio. This ratio uplifts the cash flows on the bond by the amount of inflation to ensure that the instrument's purchasing power is maintained.

The index ratio is calculated by dividing the CPI figure applicable to a given settlement date by the CPI that prevailed at the bond's issue date. As a result, the numerator will be common to all linkers for a given settlement date, while the denominator will be specific to a given linker. Since the index ratio is a function of a particular settlement date it will adjust on a daily basis. If settlement is going to take place on the first day of the month, the CPI value used in the numerator is the CPI figure that occurred exactly 3 months earlier. For other days in the month the CPI value used is calculated by linear interpolation. A similar approach is used to calculate the "base" CPI used in the denominator.

Consider the following example for settlement on 1 December 2009:

- 5/8th% Index-linked Treasury Gilt
- Issued: 24 July 2009
- Maturity: 22 November 2042
- Payment frequency: semi-annual (22 May and November)
- Inflation lag: 3 months

The first step is to work out the interpolated index value for the date of issue. The formula for this is:

$$\text{Index} = \text{CPI}_{m-3} + \frac{t-1}{D} \times (\text{CPI}_{m-2} - \text{CPI}_{m-3})$$

where:

$\text{CPI}_{m-2} = $ price index for month $m - 2$

$\text{CPI}_{m-3} = $ price index for month $m - 3$

$D_m = $ number of days in month m

$m = $ month in which settlement takes place

$t = $ day of the month on which settlement takes place

The first step is to obtain the values for the Retail Price Index (RPI) for 3 and 2 months prior to the issue date (i.e., April 2009 and May 2009), which were 211.5 and 212.8, respectively. Substituting these values into the equation gives us the following value:

$$211.5 + \frac{23}{31} \times (212.8 - 211.5) = 212.46452$$

The index ratio is rounded to five decimal places by convention. Since we are trying to derive the index ratio for settlement on 1 December 2009, the value of the numerator is simply the RPI value that prevailed 3 months before that date (September 2009), which was 215.3. Having derived both constituents, the index ratio for settlement on 1 December 2009 is 1.013346 (215.3/212.4645). An investor buying the bond for settlement on this date would pay the full dirty price (which is quoted in real terms) uplifted by the index ratio to ensure that the bond retains its real purchasing power. If the agreed dirty real price was 108.507320 then the nominal cash flow paid by the investor would be 108.507320 × 1.013346 = 109.955422.

On a side note, some readers may query what would happen if the inflation index were to fall. Although the coupon payments would be reduced, the majority of countries impose a deflation floor on the principal amount to be repaid at maturity (the exceptions being the UK, Canada and Japan).

The pricing of inflation-linked bonds in the Canadian model follows conventional discounted cash flow techniques considered earlier in the chapter. However, the input parameters are very different.

$$\text{Price} = \text{Index ratio}_{\text{SETT}} \times \left[\sum_{j=1}^{n} \frac{C_r}{(1+r)^j} + \frac{R_r}{(1+r)^n} \right]$$

where:

C_r = real coupon

R_r = real redemption payment

r = real yield

As with conventional bonds, the dirty price of the bond is simply the present value of the future cash flows. However, the equation highlights some key learning points:

- The bond's cash flows comprise a real coupon and principal (i.e., 5/8th% of the 2042 is the real coupon; an investor receives this plus an uplift for inflation according to the magnitude of the index ratio).
- The discount factor is a real as opposed to a nominal yield.
- The equation solves for the nominal settlement price. However, similar to other bonds they would be quoted on a clean basis, which would not include either the inflation adjustment (which is the role of the index ratio) or the accrued interest.
- By convention, inflation-linked bonds priced under the Canadian model are quoted on a real price and real yield basis. A change in inflation (all other things being equal) will have no effect on the value of inflation-linked bonds; the instrument is only impacted by a change in real yields.

2.3.7   Credit pricing

So far the analysis has been conducted in the absence of any potential for default. An investor buying a specific corporate bond where there was the possibility of default would earn an enhanced yield over the sovereign rate, which was termed the credit spread. This credit spread can be estimated intuitively using the following relationship:

$$\text{Credit spread} = \text{Probability of default} \times \text{loss in the event of default} \qquad (2.9)$$

Loss in the event of default relates to how much the investor would recover if the entity were to be liquidated. As such, the relationship could be restated as:

$$\text{Credit spread} = \text{Probability of default} \times (100\% - \text{recovery rate}) \qquad (2.10)$$

where the 100% relates to the initial amount invested. So, if the probability of an entity defaulting is 1% and the recovery rate is 40%, the fair value of the credit spread is 0.60%.

Although this technique may appear somewhat simplistic, it does allow a market participant to derive a "ball park" figure for the spread.

One of the problems of this approach is the estimation of the various parameters. Firstly, the actual recovery rate will only be known after a particular entity has defaulted, so when pricing a new transaction some form of estimate will be required. The market has adopted the convention of applying a value of 40%, which is believed to be indicative of the recovery rate of investment grade, senior unsubordinated debt. The choice of this recovery rate relates to the fact that the reference obligation of a CDS contract is typically based on this same degree of subordination within the company's capital structure. For contracts that are referenced to subordinated debt, the recovery rate used by the market is 20%. The second issue relates to the estimation of the default probability. Although it may be possible to use publically quoted information provided by the rating agencies, it will be historic in nature and not necessarily an accurate reflection of possible future default rates. Although some readers may feel it is a circular argument, observed CDS premia are used to derive forward-looking default probabilities. By taking an observed traded spread and rearranging the formula for estimating the credit spread, it is possible to back out an implied probability of default (assuming a given recovery rate). Market participants could use this value as a benchmark to assess their own views of the probability of the asset defaulting. If they believe that the implied probability of an entity defaulting is too high, this would suggest the contract is overpriced and therefore should be sold. The opposite would also apply.

2.4   THE SPOT–FORWARD RELATIONSHIP

In this section we will illustrate the pricing relationship that exists between spot and forward instruments based again on fixed income principles. However, the different approaches for other asset classes will be considered towards the end of the section.

2.4.1   Fixed income

Suppose a customer wants delivery of EUR 10m of the January 2018 Sovereign Bund in 20 days' time. For spot settlement on 26 March 2008, the bond was trading at a clean price of 100.92, a yield to maturity of 3.88% and a coupon of 4.00%. Short-term borrowing costs in the repo market for 20-day maturities were 4.25%.

The quoting bank derives a forward price based on how they would hedge themselves. The most popular hedging technique is sometimes referred to as a "cash and carry" strategy. That is, the price given by the quoting bank will be based on the net cost or income that will result from buying the bond now and holding the asset until the point of delivery. The net income or expense that results from this strategy is referred to as the "net carry" and is a function of:

- The purchase price.
- The cost of financing the purchase.[2]
- The coupon accrued during the holding period.

To calculate the purchase price, the first step is to calculate the interest accrued since the last payment date. Bunds pay interest annually on the anniversary of their maturity, which in this case is taken to be 4 January. For settlement on 26 March 2008, 82 days have elapsed since the last payment date and so the accrued interest per EUR 100 nominal is therefore:

$$100 \times 4.00\% \times 82/365 = 0.89863$$

This means that the purchase price to the bank (i.e., the dirty price) is:

$$100.92 + 0.89863 = 101.81863$$

The bank must borrow this amount until they receive the proceeds from the customer upon the eventual sale of the bond in 20 days' time. Since the bank will most likely use the repo market to finance this purchase, then assuming short-term borrowing costs of 4.25% this would incur a cost of:

$$101.81863 \times 4.25\% \times 20/360 = 0.240405$$

However, during the holding period the bank will earn 20 days' worth of accrued interest:

$$100 \times 4.00\% \times 20/365 = 0.219178$$

As a result of carrying this asset the bank will incur more expense (0.240405) than they earn in income (0.219178). It is reasonable to say that this expense should be passed on to the institution who wishes to take eventual delivery of the bond. As a result, the net cost to the client is:

$$101.81863 + 0.240405 - 0.219178 = 101.839857$$

If the bank were to quote a price of 101.839857 to their client, this would represent a breakeven price resulting in zero profit or loss at the point of delivery irrespective of how bond prices and repo rates subsequently evolve.

The example illustrates that the difference between the spot price and the forward price can be attributed to the net carry – the expense incurred less the income earned by holding the asset. This means that the spot–forward pricing relationship could be expressed as follows:

$$\text{Forward dirty price} = \text{Spot dirty price} + \text{borrowing cost}$$

Since bond prices are expressed on a clean basis, this could be rewritten as:

$$\text{Forward clean price} = \text{Spot clean price} + \text{borrowing cost}$$
$$- (\text{forward accrued} - \text{spot accrued})$$

which could be further refined to:

$$\text{Forward clean price} = \text{Spot clean price} + \text{borrowing cost} - \text{coupon income earned}$$

One final step is to replace the final parts of the expression with one phrase:

$$\text{Forward clean price} = \text{Spot clean price} + \text{net carry}$$

From this relationship we can see that if the coupon on the bond is greater than the repo rate, the bond is said to have positive carry. That is, for every day that the bond is held, more income is generated than will be paid in interest. Note that positive carry means that the net carry element is subtracted from the spot clean price, with the result that the forward clean price will be lower. This should not be interpreted to mean that the bond is cheap or that bond prices are expected to fall. If the coupon on the bond is less than the repo rate, the bond is said to have negative carry with the result that the forward clean price will be above the spot clean price.

From this analysis it can be seen that the movement in forward bond prices is influenced primarily by two factors: spot bond prices and repo rates. An increase in a bond's price will cause its forward price to rise and vice versa (all other things being equal). An increase in repo rates will cause the forward price to rise and vice versa (again, all other things being equal). It may appear to be something of a contradiction to say that a rise in both bond prices and repo rates will cause the forward price to increase given the inverse relationship between prices and yields. However, we are describing two different points on the yield as bond prices are driven by long-term yields while repo rates will be short term in nature. So a rise in prices (i.e., a fall in long-term yields) and a rise in short-term interest rates will cause the yield curve to flatten, driving up forward prices.

If the net carry for delivery on one specific future date were to be recalculated on a daily basis, its value would gradually fall towards zero. However, this overall decline will not necessarily happen on a linear basis as spot prices and repo rates may fluctuate. However, a forward and cash price for delivery on one particular date will converge by the final maturity as the time component of the net carry will tend towards zero.

2.4.2 Credit markets

At the time of writing, forward pricing of credit instruments is less well defined than in other markets. In theory, the forward price of a credit-risky bond could be derived using the same principles outlined in Section 2.4.1. In this section we will consider the forward pricing of credit default swap contracts. Using principles introduced in Section 2.3.4, it is possible to derive a forward CDS spread using time value of money principles. This would involve creating a synthetic forward position by buying and selling protection with different maturities. Forward positions could be created as follows:

Buying forward protection = Buy long-dated protection + sell short-dated protection

Sell forward protection = Sell long-dated protection + buy short-dated protection

By way of illustration,[3] suppose an investment grade name has a 5-year CDS premium of 24 basis points and a 10-year premium of 45 basis points (for ease of illustration we will ignore the use of standardized coupons). A buyer of protection for a 10-year horizon is considering the most effective way of implementing the trade. Broadly speaking, he could either:

- Buy protection for 10 years at 45 basis points p.a. (costing a total of 450 bps).
- Or, buy protection for 5 years at 24 basis points p.a. (costing 120 bps for the period) and in 5 years' time enter another 5-year transaction at the prevailing spot rate.

The first step is to calculate his breakeven rate, which is the difference between the 10-year and 5-year costs divided by the time in the second period – 66 bps (i.e., (450 – 120)/5). If the trader believes that the 5-year CDS spread in 5 years' time will be less than 66 bps, he should buy the 5-year contract and roll into a new 5-year contract at its maturity.

2.5 THE SPOT–SWAP RELATIONSHIP

The easiest way to illustrate the spot–swap relationship is to consider how interest rate swaps are valued. A similar approach is adopted by Galitz (1996).[4] This approach decomposes the swap into instruments that have a similar economic value. Suppose we are considering entering into a 5-year interest rate swap, where we receive fixed and pay floating LIBOR. For ease of illustration let us assume that both payments will occur on an annual basis. This position could be compared to a position in a pair of bonds with the same degree of credit risk. So the receipt of fixed under a swap would be equivalent to buying a fixed-coupon bond, while the payment of LIBOR could be replicated by issuing a floating-rate note.[5] If we make the assumption that both bonds are trading at par, then the initial and final principal amounts will net out. This leaves a structure that comprises the receipt of a stream of fixed cash flows in exchange for a stream of LIBOR cash flows. Since the cash flows coincide they can be netted out, resulting in a single payment or receipt in each individual period. This means that since a swap is economically equivalent to a pair of bonds, we can use bond pricing concepts to price and value interest rate swaps.

So, valuing a swap now becomes a case of valuing the constituent cash flows, which can be achieved by using discount factors derived from zero-coupon swap rates. The timing of the cash flows is sketched out in Table 2.4.

Algebraically, the value of the swap can be represented as follows:

$$V_{float} = D_1 F_1 + D_2 F_2 + D_3 F_3 + D_4 F_4 + D_5 F_5$$

and

$$V_{fixed} = D_1 C + D_2 C + D_3 C + D_4 C + D_5 C$$
$$= (D_1 + D_2 + D_3 + D_4 + D_5)C$$

where:

C = fixed cash flow

F = floating cash flow of a particular maturity

D = discount factor of a particular maturity

Table 2.4 Mapping swap cash flows

Date	Floating cash flow	Fixed cash flow	Discount factor
1	F_1	C	D_1
2	F_2	C	D_2
3	F_3	C	D_3
4	F_4	C	D_4
5	F_5	C	D_5

The value of any swap is simply the difference between the value of the fixed and floating legs expressed in present value terms. So,

$$V_{swap} = V_{fixed} - V_{float}$$
$$= [(D_1 + D_2 + D_3 + D_4 + D_5)C] - [D_1F_1 + D_2F_2 + D_3F_3 + D_4F_4 + D_5F_5]$$

It is possible to use this relationship to price swaps by rearranging the formula to solve for C, the fixed cash flow. Arguably, the key concept in pricing swaps is that on the trade date the swap has to be considered an equitable exchange of cash flows by both participants. Logically, no market participant would knowingly enter into a transaction where they were going to lose money.[6]

So, using the previous notation to illustrate the principle of pricing swaps:

$$V_{swap} = V_{fixed} - V_{float} = 0$$

Therefore:

$$V_{fixed} = V_{float}$$

and so:

$$[(D_1 + D_2 + D_3 + D_4 + D_5)C] = [D_1F_1 + D_2F_2 + D_3F_3 + D_4F_4 + D_5F_5]$$

From this, the fixed cash flow could be calculated by dividing the present value of the floating cash flows by the sum of the discount factors. To illustrate the principles, suppose the swap rates shown in Table 2.5 are observed in the market.

Table 2.5   Market rates

Years	Swap rate	Zero-coupon rate	Discount factor	Forward yield
1	6.00%	6.0000%	0.94340	6.0000%
2	6.70%	6.7236%	0.87797	7.4522%
3	6.85%	6.8767%	0.81913	7.1835%
4	6.90%	6.9256%	0.76502	7.0726%
5	6.92%	6.9436%	0.71487	7.0153%

Note: Bid–offer spreads have been removed for ease of illustration. The forward rates in the final column are all 12-month LIBOR rates that become effective at different times in the future, i.e., 1-year rate in 1 year's time, 1-year rate in 2 years' time.

In this example we will consider whether a 5-year swap executed at the prevailing rate of 6.92% is fairly valued. We will assume that the notional amount is 10 million, both sides of the swap will pay annually and the day basis is identical for both legs of the trade (i.e., an actual/actual day basis).

The cash flows on the swap are calculated on a simple interest basis:

Notional amount × applicable interest rate × days in period/days in year

The resultant cash flows are shown in Table 2.6.

Table 2.6   Pricing an interest rate swap

Year	Fixed cash flows	Discounted fixed cash flows	Floating cash flows	Discounted floating cash flows
1	692,000	652,830	600,000	566,038
2	692,000	607,554	745,217	654,277
3	692,000	566,835	718,353	588,422
4	692,000	529,394	707,258	541,066
5	692,000	494,690	701,528	501,501
	Totals	2,851,303		2,851,303
		Swap value	0	

To illustrate how the numbers are derived, let us consider the cash flows that occur in the fifth year. The fixed cash flow is calculated as:

$$10,000,000 \times 6.92\% = 692,000$$

The present value of this cash flow is calculated as:

$$692,000 \times 0.71487 = 494,690$$

The floating cash flow is calculated as:

$$10,000,000 \times 7.0153\% = 701,530$$

The present value of this floating cash flow is:

$$701,528 \times 0.71487 = 501,501$$

Since the sum of the present values of both fixed and floating net to zero, we can say that the swap is fairly valued. A commonly asked question is why a market participant would enter into an interest rate swap that has no initial profit. The answer is again based on the concept of using forward rates as a breakeven benchmark. If the participant believed that LIBOR was going to evolve faster than the values implied by the forward curve used to derive the fixed rate, they should receive LIBOR and pay fixed. Conversely, if they believed that LIBOR was going to evolve more slowly than the values implied by the forward curve they should pay LIBOR and receive fixed.

However, there is an element of circularity in this pricing process. Our end objective is to identify a single fixed swap rate that will be payable or receivable on a particular transaction. This can only be derived if there is a set of forward rates and discount factors. However, to obtain these inputs we require a set of zero-coupon swap rates which were derived from a set of observed par swap rates! However, this circularity can be resolved by recognizing that for the majority of main currencies there is a deep and liquid market for "plain vanilla" swaps where quotes are readily observable. These vanilla swaps are priced as the yield on a domestic sovereign bond of the same maturity plus a market-determined spread, referred to as the swap spread. The factors that determine the magnitude of this spread and how it will move are considered in Chapter 4.

So, for a vanilla swap there would be no need to price the instrument using discounted cash flow (DCF) techniques. Arguably, the DCF technique becomes relevant when the

Table 2.7 Pricing a forward-starting swap

Year	Fixed cash flows	Discounted fixed cash flows	Floating cash flows	Discounted floating cash flows
1	0	0	0	0
2	692,000	607,554	745,217	654,277
3	692,000	566,835	718,353	588,422
4	692,000	529,394	707,258	541,066
5	692,000	494,690	701,528	501,501
	Totals	2,198,473		−2,285,266
		Swap value	−86,792	

Table 2.8 Pricing a forward-starting swap; 1-year into 4-year structure

Year	Fixed cash flows	Discounted fixed cash flows	Floating cash flows	Discounted floating cash flows
1	0	0	0	0
2	719,319	631,540	745,217	654,277
3	719,319	589,213	718,353	588,422
4	719,319	550,293	707,258	541,066
5	719,319	514,219	701,528	501,501
	Totals	2,285,260		−2,285,266
		Swap value	0	

market participant needs to price a swap that is not vanilla in style. The quoting bank would then use the prevailing market prices to derive the specific rate for this bespoke transaction.

At this stage it is convenient to consider how to price a forward-starting interest rate swap, which we define as a swap that becomes effective at some period in the future. An example of this would be a 5-year swap starting 3 months in the future. We will use the same market values as those used to price the previous 5-year swap, but with the intention of pricing a 4-year swap, starting in 1 year's time.

The pricing of a forward-starting swap follows the same general principles used in pricing spot-starting structures. To price our example, all that is required is to remove the cash flows from spot value up until the swap's effective date. For our example this means leaving out the first year's cash flows. Using the spot-starting 5-year fixed rate of 6.92% initially, the cash flows are shown in Table 2.7.

With the first year's cash flows removed and using the original 5-year rate, the swap no longer has an NPV of zero and is therefore not an equitable exchange of cash flows. The fixed swap rate that will yield a net present value of zero can be found iteratively and can be shown to be 7.19319% (see Table 2.8).

2.5.1 Pricing swaps – counterparty credit risk

It's difficult to stand in front of regulators and say the over-the-counter derivatives market is functioning well when we can't even agree how to price a plain vanilla interest rate swap.[7]

From early 2010 the approach used to price interest rate swaps underwent a significant change as institutions became more conscious of the importance of counterparty credit risk. Prior to the financial crisis, swap traders would subjectively adjust swap prices to reflect their perception of a counterparty's default risk. As a result of the crisis, the market introduced more formalized techniques to manage this risk. One popular method used by the market is the "credit value adjustment". This approach requires the traders to adjust their quoted prices to reflect the default risk embedded within their counterparty's observed credit default swap spread.[8]

The other significant change was the choice of discount rate to present value swap cash flows. As we have seen, swap cash flows were traditionally discounted using LIBOR as the market always assumed that their interbank counterparties would not default. The procedures that banks had in place prior to the financial crisis would require counterparties to deposit acceptable collateral to support any transaction that was "in-the-money" from the bank's perspective. These procedures would vary between different institutions and interested readers are referred to Gregory (2010) for more detail.

Under the documentation that governs the procedures for managing collateral (the ISDA credit support annex), any cash collateral held by an institution would require them to pay interest at the overnight interbank rate. Overnight interbank rates are discussed in detail in Appendix 2.1, but they are introduced briefly at this point. In many countries the overnight unsecured interbank rate is often targeted by the Central Bank to influence monetary policy and as such is seen as being the closest the market has to a "true" risk-free rate. The overnight rate is the shortest tenor available, carries negligible counterparty credit and liquidity risk, and is taken by the market to be the best available proxy for a risk-free rate. Examples of this rate are:

- Fed Funds effective rate (USD)
- Sterling Overnight Index Average (SONIA)
- Euro Overnight Index Average (EONIA)

Prior to the financial crisis there was often a small mismatch between the value of the collateral (valued using the OIS rate) and the value of the swap (valued using LIBOR), but since this was a relatively small difference it was ignored by most participants. However, as the crisis developed the difference between the two rates became more pronounced, highlighting the mismatch in value between the two components of the transaction (see Figure 2.5).

As a result of this dislocation, banks now vary the discount rate applied to a particular swap transaction depending on whether it is collateralized or not. For deals that are subject to collateralization, cash flows are discounted using a zero-coupon overnight index swap (OIS) curve. An OIS is an interest rate swap where the floating rate is referenced to the average of an overnight interest rate index calculated each day over the agreed payment period. Similar to our previous explanation of swap pricing, the fixed rate on an OIS is the weighted average of all the future floating payments.

To illustrate the concept, consider a hedge fund that has an off-market/loss-making USD swap exposure to a bank and has posted USD collateral against it. The hedge fund will earn the Fed Funds rate, which will be paid by the bank on this collateral. If the hedge fund were to decide to cancel the swap, then it would have to pay cash to the bank rather than post the collateral. The issue faced by the bank is whether it should calculate the termination value of the swap using either a LIBOR rate or an OIS rate. It should calculate the present value of the swap using the OIS curve, since this more accurately highlights the "value" of the collateral it is currently holding.

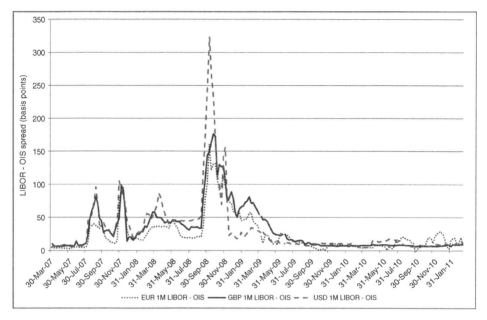

Figure 2.5   LIBOR–OIS spread for EUR, GBP and USD 2006–2011.
Source: Data sourced from Barclays Capital Live. Reproduced with permission.

Suppose the swap is out-of-the-money from the hedge fund's perspective by 0.5%. If we assume that the notional is $100, the transaction has exactly one year to expiry and that current 12-month LIBOR rates are 3%, then the mark to market is $(0.5\% \times \$100)/(1.03) =$ $0.4854. However, the counterparty bank would demand collateral in excess of this amount as they will only earn interest at an OIS rate, which is lower than LIBOR. The higher sum demanded by the bank will ensure that the collateral and the interest earned will cover the cash payments due under the swap. So if we assume that the 12-month OIS rate is 2% then the discounted value of the collateral is $(0.5\% \times \$100)/(1.02) = \$0.4902$. It follows that this higher sum of money invested at the current OIS rate will return $0.5 at the end of the swap.

The issue of swap valuation using different discount rates raises a number of problems:[7]

- The Credit Support Annex (CSA) states that the collateral should be valued using the currency of the collateral not the currency of the swap. This raises the issue of how to discount, say, a EUR swap supported by USD cash collateral.
- Some CSAs allow for collateral in different forms and different currencies. As a result, the counterparty that is required to post collateral will most likely post whatever is the "cheapest to deliver". This delivery option would need to be valued.
- Whatever asset is currently the cheapest to deliver will not necessarily remain so over the life of the transaction, which poses a challenge for valuing and hedging future swap cash flows.
- The CSA may also allow for substitution of collateral, creating a "collateral switch option" which would be very difficult to price as several assumptions on volatility and correlation would be required.
- Transactions that are not subject to collateral agreements are valued using the bank's own cost of borrowing, i.e., typically a LIBOR value. Since banks borrow at different levels there is no common benchmark for pricing uncollateralized trades. In general terms we can conclude that the rate used to discount a swap should be consistent with how the swap is collateralised or financed.

2.6   THE FORWARD–SWAP RELATIONSHIP

The relationship between swap rates and forward rates was originally outlined in equation (2.6). The equation highlights that the product of the two short-term rates should be equal to a long-term rate of the equivalent maturity. So, if this logic was extended, with a known deposit rate and sequence of futures prices, it would be possible to derive a swap rate of the same maturity.

The simplest way to conceptualize the issue is to consider the relationship between FRAs and swaps. In Chapter 1, we argued that an FRA was simply a single-period interest rate swap, so if we were to extend the argument we could say that an interest rate swap could be decomposed into a strip of FRAs all with the same single fixed rate.

The actual mathematics of deriving a swap rate from a strip of futures is slightly different in that the swap rate is calculated as a weighted average with the weights being a series of discount factors derived from the futures rates. Readers interested in this technique are referred to either Dubil (2004) or Chisholm (2009).

2.7   PRICING OPTIONS–RELATIONSHIP WITH THE UNDERLYING MARKET

Option pricing is probably one of the most well documented subjects in finance. In order to avoid reinventing the wheel but to ensure completeness of coverage, we have chosen to take an approach which will be consistent with our theme of identifying the pricing linkages between markets. Readers interested in a more formal approach are referred to texts such as Hull (2008) or Natenberg (1994).

In the 1970s, Fisher Black, Myron Scholes and Robert Merton developed a method that allowed market participants to calculate the "fair value" of an option by means of a closed-form equation. However, it is important to stress that the model will not determine the actual price of the option, which is simply a function of what someone is prepared to pay for it in an open market transaction. As a result, it is better to view the role of the option model as a tool that allows a market participant to judge how the option is expected to change in value as a result of a change in the inputs to the model.

In their original work, which focused on the fair value of a European-style non-dividend-paying stock, they argued that the fair value of the contract could be calculated as a function of five parameters:

- The spot price of the share.
- The option's exercise price.
- The option's time to expiry.
- Risk-free interest rates.
- The volatility of the share's return.

Intuitively, the premium charged by the seller of an option has to be slightly more than the amount they expect to pay out if the option were to be exercised against them. Since the payout on the option will take place in the future, the premium payable at the start of the deal can be thought of as the present value of the expected payoff at maturity.

The premium of an option can be broken down into two components:

- Intrinsic value – what is the option worth if it were to expire right now?
- Time value – how much do I see myself making from this option from now until maturity?

The intrinsic value of the option is the advantage to the option holder of the strike over the underlying price. So if the strike rate is less favourable than the underlying price, the option confers no advantage to the holder and so has no intrinsic value. The implication of this is that an option cannot have negative intrinsic value; it will either be positive or zero. The second component of the premium is time value, which is the extra amount charged by the seller to reflect the uncertainty of whether the option will be exercised. Time value could be viewed as the potential future intrinsic value of the option. Time value is greatest when an option is at-the-money as this is where there is the greatest degree of uncertainty of exercise. Therefore, time value is a function of the degree of "moneyness" of the option, time to maturity and implied volatility.

2.7.1 Black–Scholes–Merton: an intuitive approach

Suppose a gambler says he will pay you USD 10 a point for any rollover 7 based on the single throw of two dice. How much would you be willing to pay to play this game? To determine the fair price of this game you would need to know the range of possible outcomes and the probability of any particular outcome occurring. To work out the probabilities suppose you were to throw a pair of dice 1,000 times and record the results. The incidents of extreme values occurring (i.e., 2 and 12) would be relatively low as there are a limited number of ways in which the outcome could occur ($1 + 1$ and $6 + 6$, respectively). However, there are six different ways in which the outcome could total $7(1 + 6, 2 + 5, 3 + 4, 4 + 3, 5 + 2$ and $6 + 1$) and so it is reasonable to assume that this is the most likely outcome. If, as a result of throwing the dice 1,000 times, the value of 2 was observed on 30 occasions we could say there is a 3% probability of occurrence.

Table 2.9 shows how the fair value of the dice game could be assessed.

Table 2.9 Calculating the "fair value" of the dice game

Result	2	3	4	5	6	7	8	9	10	11	12
Payoff	0	0	0	0	0	0	10	20	30	40	50
Probability	3%	5.5%	8%	11%	14%	17%	14%	11%	8%	5.5%	3%
Expected value	0	0	0	0	0	0	1.40	2.20	2.40	2.20	1.50

The top line of the table shows the payoff offered by the gambler (i.e., USD 10 for a roll of 8, USD 20 for a roll of 9). The middle line shows the probability of a number being thrown based on the sample of 1,000 throws. The expected value shown on the lower line is derived by taking each payoff and multiplying it by the probability of its occurrence. So if the number 8 is rolled the gambler will pay you USD 10; since the probability of this value being thrown is 14%, the expected value is USD 1.40. The fair value of the game is simply the sum of the expected values, which in this case is USD 9.70. In effect, the gambler is selling a call option with a strike of USD 7 on a principal amount of USD 10. The payoff is:

$$\text{USD } 10 \times \text{Max}(0, \text{ result} - \text{strike})$$

Let us extend these principles to price an at-the-money call option on crude oil (Table 2.10), assuming the current price of the underlying asset is USD 50/barrel. So the reader can see the continuity of the argument, we will use the same distribution from the dice game example.

Table 2.10   Pricing a call option on crude oil

Result	45	46	47	48	49	50	51	52	53	54	55
Payoff	0	0	0	0	0	0	1	2	3	4	5
Probability	3%	5.5%	8%	11%	14%	17%	14%	11%	8%	5.5%	3%
Expected value	0	0	0	0	0	0	0.14	0.22	0.24	0.22	0.15

Table 2.11   The impact on the value of a call option when the underlying price rises

Result	46	47	48	49	50	51	52	53	54	55	56
Payoff	0	0	0	0	0	1	2	3	4	5	6
Probability	3%	5.5%	8%	11%	14%	17%	14%	11%	8%	5.5%	3%
Expected value	0	0	0	0	0	0.17	0.28	0.33	0.32	0.28	0.18

The sum of the expected values is USD 0.97, which is the "fair value" for the premium on a per barrel basis.

Suppose that a few minutes later the price of crude oil moves up to USD 51. Table 2.11 shows how this changes the value of the option (which is now in-the-money) assuming the distribution is unchanged.

Note that the probability distribution is centred on the current price of USD 51 and the sum of the expected values has increased to USD 1.56. The impact of a fall in the price of the asset to USD 49 is shown in Table 2.12.

In the case of a fall in price the sum of the expected values has decreased to USD 0.56; having the right to buy at USD 50 is now less valuable if the market has moved down to USD 49.

The next stage is to analyse what would happen to the value of the option if the underlying market is expected to be relatively stable. Table 2.13 illustrates an example of where the probability of extreme price movements is now less likely.

The ATM call option struck at USD 50 a barrel now costs USD 0.56 compared to the original value of USD 0.97. It follows that if the market is expected to be very volatile the probability of extreme events occurring increases, leading to an increase in the expected values as well as the overall premium.

Table 2.12   The impact on the value of a call option when the underlying price falls

Result	44	45	46	47	48	49	50	51	52	53	54
Payoff	0	0	0	0	0	0	0	1	2	3	4
Probability	3%	5.5%	8%	11%	14%	17%	14%	11%	8%	5.5%	3%
Expected value	0	0	0	0	0	0	0	0.11	0.16	0.17	0.12

Table 2.13   Pricing a call option in conditions of low volatility

Result	45	46	47	48	49	50	51	52	53	54	55
Payoff	0	0	0	0	0	0	1	2	3	4	5
Probability	0	0	5%	11%	19%	30%	19%	11%	5%	0	0
Expected value	0	0	0	0	0	0	0.19	0.22	0.15	0	0

In all of our examples, the probability distribution was symmetrical and so is referred to as a normal distribution. The normal distribution possesses a number of statistical properties that are useful when analysing options. The two key properties of a normal distribution are its mean and its standard deviation. The mean of the distribution is the peak of the curve and is statistically the most probable outcome. The standard deviation is a measure of spread from the mean; it describes the "fatness" of the distribution. The standard deviation tells us the likelihood that a particular value or a range of values will occur. If we try to link the statistical properties of the normal distribution to the analysis of options, the first step is to decide which market parameter represents the mean of the distribution. If we consider the pricing of European-style options, then the mean is the forward price. Since a European-style option cannot be exercised until maturity, it is reasonable to assume that the degree of "in-the-moneyness" of the option should be assessed relative to an underlying price of the same maturity, i.e., the forward price. Another argument for using the forward price is based on the notion that it represents a breakeven price for a cash trade that has a holding period equal to the maturity of the option. If I were to buy a barrel of crude oil today at a price of USD 45 with the intention of selling it in 12 months, I must finance the purchase, ship it, store and insure it. If these costs amount to USD 5, I need to make at least USD 50 to break even. Therefore, USD 50 is the fair value of the forward price as at the trade date.

The standard deviation of the distribution is referred to under another name in financial markets – volatility. In financial markets the volatility of an underlying asset is expressed as one standard deviation in per cent per annum. Statistically, one standard deviation will cover 68.3% of all possible outcomes. In our original example in Figure 2.13, one standard deviation is equal to USD 3.32 per barrel. So intuitively we would expect the asset to trade within the range of USD 46.68 to USD 53.32 on 68.3% of all occasions over the next 12 months. Equally, the seller of the option should realize there is a 31.7% chance it will be outside these boundaries.

A shortcut for pricing options

A very common "back-of-the-envelope" technique used as a shortcut for pricing options is given by the following formula:

$$\text{Premium} = 0.4 \times \sigma \sqrt{T} \times \text{DF}$$

where:

σ = implied volatility

T = time to maturity (years)

DF = discount factor

Pricing a 1-year at-the-money call option using a Black–Scholes–Merton model at a strike rate of USD 50.00, an implied volatility of 10% and interest rate of 5% generates a fair value of USD 1.8966, which expressed as a percentage of the strike price gives a value of 3.79%. The shortcut formula returns a value of 3.81% ($0.4 \times 0.10 \times 1 \times 0.952381$).

2.7.2   From closed-form to binomial pricing techniques

It would be fair to say that no trader should enter into a transaction without hedging their exposure to any potential payout. One of the key insights that resulted from the initial research into option pricing was that the payout on the option could be replicated in the underlying market. As a result, the cost of the option can be linked to the cost of the underlying hedge – "If you can hedge it, you can price it".

Suppose there is an unspecified asset that does not generate any income and is currently trading at price of $100. Our aim is price an at-the-money European call option with a 12-month maturity where interest rates are 5%. Initially, we will impose some unrealistic conditions about how the price will evolve over the life of the transaction, which we will subsequently relax. We will assume that the underlying asset will have one of two values at expiry, namely $105 or $95. Given a strike rate of $100, the payoff of the option at maturity will either be $5 or $0, respectively. To hedge this exposure, the trick is to create a portfolio whose value matches the payoff of the option; this can be achieved by buying or selling the underlying asset in certain proportions. This ratio can be calculated by considering how the price of the option will move over the life of the transaction relative to the movement in the price of the underlying asset. This is given by the following formula:

$$\frac{\text{Option value}_{up} - \text{Option value}_{down}}{\text{Asset price}_{up} - \text{Asset price}_{down}} \quad \frac{\$5 - \$0}{\$105 - \$95} = \frac{\$5}{\$10} = 0.50$$

where:

Option value$_{up}$ = the value of the option when the underlying price has risen

Option value$_{down}$ = the value of the option when the underlying price has fallen

Asset price$_{up}$ = the price of the asset assuming its value has increased

Asset price$_{down}$ = the price of the asset assuming its value has decreased

The formula indicates that the value of the option has only moved by 50% of the movement in the underlying price. This suggests that to replicate the payoff on the option position the appropriate hedge is to purchase half of the underlying asset. This hedge ratio means that for every two options sold we would only need to buy and hold one of the underlying assets. Figure 2.6 shows the value of the replicating portfolio assuming we sell two call options and hedge the exposure by purchasing one underlying asset.

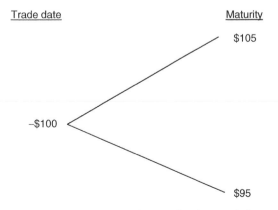

Figure 2.6   The value of the replicating portfolio.

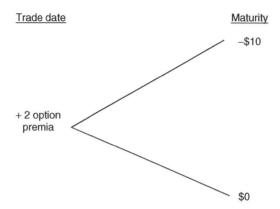

Figure 2.7   The option exposure.

Figure 2.7 shows the value of the option portfolio over the same period. The figure indicates that having sold two options and received a premium inflow, the trader could be faced with a possible payout at the option's maturity. The −$10 in the upper right-hand side of the tree represents the total payout if both options were exercised. This is derived assuming an expiry value of $105 and a strike price of $100.

Figure 2.8 combines Figures 2.6 and 2.7 to show that at maturity, having sold two options and bought one asset, we have created a portfolio that has a value of $95.

Since the portfolio is worth $95 in 12 months' time, the present value of the portfolio with interest rates at 5% (and assuming an actual/actual day basis for ease of illustration) is $90.48 (i.e., $95/1.05). Since we purchased one asset for spot settlement at the current price of $100, the premium receivable from both options would need to be $9.52 ($4.76 per share) to ensure that the current value of the portfolio is $90.48.

Note, however, that on the trade date there is a net outflow of funds. The trader must buy one asset at $100 to hedge the portfolio and will receive $9.52 from the sale of the two options. The difference between the two cash flows ($90.48) will have to be borrowed and will be financed at current rates of interest (5%), with $95 being repaid at maturity. The repayment on this loan is equal to the value of the portfolio at maturity, irrespective of whether the price rises or falls.

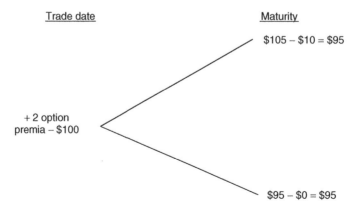

Figure 2.8   The option exposure combined with the underlying hedge.

Consider the cash flows at maturity. In the "price up" scenario:

- The option holder exercises the option.
- The trader receives $200 from the holder of the option (i.e., twice the option's strike).
- The trader delivers the share they are holding as a hedge but must buy one more share at the prevailing market price of $105.
- The trader repays the $95 principal and interest due on the loan.
- The net cash flow is zero.

In the "price down" scenario the option is not exercised and the trader sells the hedge position at the prevailing price of $95 and uses these proceeds to repay the underlying loan. Again the net cash flow is zero, illustrating that in both scenarios the trader is fully hedged.

The value of a put option with the same maturity and strike with the same market conditions could be calculated using the same principles.

This approach has sometimes been described as risk-neutral valuation. This means that whether a market participant believes the underlying price will rise or fall, there can only be one solution for the fair value of the option. If this were not the case then it would be possible to exploit a potential mispricing. If a trader saw the call option trading at higher than its fair value, the option should be sold and the duplicating portfolio purchased. If the option was trading below its fair value the option should be purchased and the duplicating portfolio sold.

A reasonable observation at this stage would be to note that the model as presented is not realistic:

- It is only a one-period model.
- Prices are assumed to move only once.
- The underlying price movement was assumed to be a fixed amount.
- No account has been taken of any possible income receivable by the asset.

However, when building a more realistic model, all of these restrictions can easily be relaxed while still applying the principles of the one-period model. For example, if one were trying to price a 12-month option, the modeller could simply decide to split the periods into smaller amounts – one day, one hour, one second. Since it is not our intention to write a full treatise on option pricing, interested readers requiring a more detailed explanation should refer to other texts such as Galitz (1996) or Hull (2008).

2.7.3 Monte Carlo simulation

Monte Carlo simulation is a technique that is used to price options when a closed-form solution such as Black–Scholes–Merton does not exist. Intuitively it is similar to the binomial process and involves generating a large number of randomly generated price scenarios. This means that the model has to make some assumptions about how the asset price will evolve over a particular period. In simple terms the Monte Carlo process makes two assumptions about how the asset price will move:

- The price will grow exponentially over time in line with the cost of carrying the underlying asset. So if holding the asset incurs expense (i.e., negative carry), the asset price will trend upwards and will trend downwards if the asset carries positively.
- The price will deviate unpredictably from its trend based on a random disturbance.

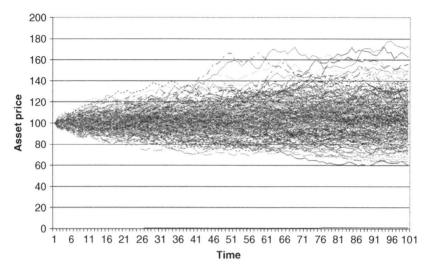

Figure 2.9   Monte Carlo simulation.

So to calculate the price of the option using the Monte Carlo process the steps are:

- Simulate the path of the asset using today's price and a period equal to the option's maturity.
- Use the final values of each simulation to calculate the payoff on the option.
- Perform this scenario analysis thousands of times over the same horizon.
- Calculate the average of all the option payoffs.
- The present value of this average is the value of the option.

Figure 2.9 shows how the process might work with an asset whose price is initially 100. Many thousands of paths are simulated over a given time horizon of 100 days, resulting in a series of expiry prices that range from about 60 to 170. Knowing the strike of the option it would then be possible to calculate the at-maturity payoffs under each of these different scenarios. These payoffs are averaged and the present value of the result is considered to be the fair value of the option premium.

2.7.4   Put–call parity

Put–call parity is a very useful and under-rated concept that attempts to link the value of an option to its underlying market. The conditions of put–call parity will hold as long as the strike, maturity and amount are the same. If the conditions do not hold then it is possible for a trader to exploit a possible arbitrage. Put–call parity will vary according to the nature of the underlying asset and Tompkins (1994) details the concept in its different forms. In its simplest form it can be represented by the following expression:

$$C - P = F - E$$

where:

C = price of a call option

P = price of a put option

F = the forward price of the underlying asset

E = the strike rate for the option

However, the significance of this relationship is perhaps not intuitive and so we could simplify the relationship to:

$$C - P = F$$

where F is redefined as a long forward position in the underlying asset. Each of the symbols will be expressed either with a "+" or a "−" to indicate either a buying or selling position, respectively. So by way of the previous expression one could link the underlying market and the option by rewriting the equation as:

$$+C - P = +F$$

That is, buying a call and selling a put is equivalent to a long position in the underlying. By rearranging this simple formula a number of different permutations could be derived. For example:

$$-C + P = -F$$

That is, a short forward position can be replicated by selling a call and buying a put option.

Although at this stage the concept may appear somewhat dry, it is commonly used in the construction of a variety of different structures and as such we will return to it in subsequent chapters.

APPENDIX 2.1 MONETARY POLICY AND OVERNIGHT INTEREST RATES

Bank of England

The main focus of the Bank of England's monetary policy is the Bank Rate, most commonly referred to as the Base Rate. One of the Bank's stated monetary policy objectives is to maintain overnight interbank interest rates in line with the Bank Rate. To achieve this they operate a reserves averaging mechanism supplemented by "Operational Standing Facilities" (OSFs).

Within the UK a certain number of institutions are authorized as clearing banks. These institutions hold accounts at the Bank of England and as a result all transactions with other clearing banks will be settled by debiting or crediting these accounts. Non-clearing institutions (for example overseas institutions) will need to hold a GBP bank account with a clearing bank in order to settle GBP transactions. As a result all interbank transactions will end up being directly or indirectly settled at the Bank of England. The level of these balances at the Bank of England is referred to as reserves.

The Bank of England operates a monthly reserve averaging scheme for the clearing banks, which runs between the dates on which the Monetary Policy Committee (MPC) meets to make decisions on the level of the Bank Rate. The clearing banks will set a target in advance for the average amount of reserves they will hold during this period based on their expectations of how business is expected to evolve. The banks are only required to meet this target for the month that they have forecast; they are free to change the target level of reserves for future months. On a day-to-day basis a commercial bank can vary the amount of reserves it holds as long as the average level of reserves over the period is no less than their stated target. All reserves held at the Bank of England earn interest at the Bank Rate. If a bank has sufficient reserves to meet its target it could lend the excess in the interbank market but is unlikely to do so at a rate less than the Bank Rate. Conversely, if a bank is short of reserves it will have to borrow in the interbank market at a rate that will most likely be higher than the Bank Rate.

If a bank is unable to maintain its average balance it will attract a charge from the Bank of England. To help avoid a situation where a bank with a reserve shortfall may be faced with the prospect of having to pay a punitive interest rate in the interbank market, the Bank of England offers OSFs. These allow banks to borrow on an overnight basis above the Bank Rate or to deposit excess reserves below the Bank Rate. As a result, a commercial bank with a reserve shortfall would not borrow at interbank rates that were less favourable than those offered by this mechanism. As a result, the interbank overnight rates should trade within this corridor of rates set by the Central Bank, i.e., the Bank Rate $+/-$ the spread of rates offered under the OSF.

The Bank of England will manage the overall supply of reserves using "Open Market Operations". The Central Bank will supply reserves by either lending against high-quality collateral (i.e., a reverse repo) or by the outright purchase of securities. It can reduce the level of reserves in the system and therefore reduce liquidity by borrowing against high-quality collateral (i.e., a repo) or by the issue of short-term government debt ("Bills").

European Central Bank

The European Central Bank (ECB) is able to shape short-term rates by managing the liquidity of the money market using a number of different instruments. The principal aim of ECB monetary policy is to maintain price stability, i.e., to manage inflation. The main tools are the use of a reserve requirement, weekly refinancing operations and communications that indicate its stance on monetary policy.

One of the key elements of the ECB's monetary policy is the concept of the reserve requirement. The reserve requirement sets out the minimum amount of cash that commercial banks are required to hold with their respective National Central Bank over a specified period of time based on the structure of their short-term liabilities. This specified period is known as the "maintenance period" and lasts for approximately one month. It follows the meeting of the ECB's Governing Council at which an assessment of the current monetary policy stance is made.

In order to ensure that the banks can finance their overall borrowing and lending operations in light of the reserve requirement, the ECB will lend money for a limited time. One of these tools is the "Main Refinancing Operation" (MRO), where banks will bid for money on a weekly basis. The commercial banks will pay interest on these borrowings and lodge acceptable collateral. At the maturity of the transaction the banks repay the loan and their collateral is returned.

During the MRO the ECB sets a minimum bid rate below which it will not provide liquidity to banks at a lower rate. This minimum bid rate is set once a month by the ECB's

Governing Council during their assessment of the current monetary policy stance. Banks submit their bids on a Monday evening and early Tuesday morning. These are then analysed by the Liquidity Committee, who submit a recommendation to the Advisory Board, who determine the total amount of funds to be allocated. Banks offering the highest interest rates will be served first until the full amount is allocated. The banks that fail to borrow using this mechanism would be forced to borrow in money markets; however, these rates are typically close to the minimum ECB bid rate. It is also possible for banks to lend or borrow at any time outside the scheduled weekly operations. The marginal lending facility allows commercial banks to borrow (albeit at a higher rate than the minimum bid rate) while the deposit facility allows them to lend any excess balances. However, this rate is lower than the minimum bid rate.

Overnight Index Markets

The Sterling Overnight Index Average (SONIA) was introduced in 1997 and represents a benchmark for rates traded in the overnight GBP money market. According to the British Bankers Association,[9] it is calculated as the weighted average of all unsecured sterling overnight cash transactions brokered in London by Wholesale Markets Brokers' Associations' members. Eligible trades are conducted between midnight and 4:15pm and must have a minimum deal size of £25 million.

The Euro Overnight Index Average (EONIA) is the weighted average of all overnight unsecured lending transactions of the contributing panel banks that happen in the euro market on a given day. The ECB determines the rate every business day and publishes it at 19:00 Central European Time. The biggest driver of EONIA rates is ECB monetary policy.

The minimum rate at which one can borrow cash from the ECB (the MRO rate) essentially sets the minimum rate at which a bank can refinance itself through the weekly tenders. Clearly, this marginal rate will affect EONIA fixings in the market. This is because the EONIA fixings are based on all the unsecured overnight lending transactions that happen in a given day. If the secured weekly lending rate increases (perhaps due to a Central Bank rate increase), then banks will want to lend cash to the market at a higher rate than that at which they borrow it from the ECB.

APPENDIX 2.2 OIS DISCOUNTING

In this appendix we consider a number of aspects relating to the discounting of interest rate swaps using an OIS curve. The approach taken is similar to that first outlined in 'Understanding OIS discounting' by Amrut Nashikkar (2011).

OIS curves

The first issue relates to the sourcing of OIS rates. One of the simplest ways to build an OIS curve is to use observed market values. The rates quoted for maturities of less than one year are zero coupon in style but those of longer maturities are par rates. Where the market does not quote an OIS rate it would be possible to derive a value using LIBOR rates and then adjusting them by the LIBOR−OIS basis which is quoted out to 30 years (see Figure 2.10).

	0m	3m	6m	12m	2y	3y	4y	5y	7y	10y	15y	20y	25y	30y
3m	12.6	19.5	21.6	25.9	27.9	27.9	24.4	22.1	18.1	12.3	6.2	6.3	6.3	6.3
6m	16.1	20.6	22.8	27.3	28.1	27.6	24.2	22.0	18.1	12.2	6.3	6.4	6.4	6.4
1y	19.4	22.8	25.1	28.2	28.1	26.7	23.7	21.6	17.6	11.8	6.3	6.4	6.4	6.4
2y	23.7	25.7	26.8	28.1	27.3	25.1	22.6	20.6	16.6	10.8	6.4	6.4	6.4	6.4
3y	25.0	26.4	27.0	27.5	26.0	23.9	21.6	19.6	15.7	10.0	6.4	6.4	6.4	6.4
4y	25.2	26.0	26.3	26.4	24.9	22.8	20.6	18.6	14.8	9.4	6.4	6.4	6.4	6.4
5y	24.7	25.3	25.4	25.3	23.8	21.8	19.7	17.7	13.9	8.8	6.4	6.4	6.4	6.4
6y	24.0	24.4	24.4	24.3	22.7	20.8	18.8	16.8	13.0	8.5	6.4	6.4	6.4	6.4
7y	23.2	23.5	23.5	23.3	21.8	19.9	17.9	15.9	12.3	8.2	6.4	6.4	6.4	6.4
8y	22.4	22.6	22.6	22.3	20.8	19.0	17.0	15.1	11.7	8.0	6.4	6.4	6.4	6.4
9y	21.6	21.8	21.7	21.4	19.9	18.1	16.2	14.4	11.2	7.9	6.4	6.4	6.4	6.4
10y	20.8	20.9	20.9	20.5	19.0	17.3	15.5	13.8	10.9	7.8	6.4	6.4	6.4	6.4
15y	17.2	17.3	17.2	16.9	15.8	14.5	13.1	11.9	9.7	7.5	6.4	6.4	6.4	6.5
20y	15.2	15.3	15.2	15.0	14.2	13.1	12.0	11.0	9.2	7.3	6.4	6.4	6.5	6.5
25y	14.0	14.1	14.1	13.9	13.2	12.3	11.4	10.5	8.9	7.2	6.5	6.5	6.6	6.5
30y	13.3	13.4	13.4	13.3	12.6	11.8	11.0	10.2	8.7	7.2	6.5	6.6	6.6	6.6

Figure 2.10   LIBOR–OIS basis report. Report shows the difference between LIBOR and OIS rates of a given maturity in basis points. Effective dates are read vertically, maturities horizontally. Example: the spot starting 12-month LIBOR–OIS basis is 16.7 basis points.
Source: Barclays Capital Live. Reproduced with permission.

Value of swap at inception

When pricing a new swap under an OIS discounting framework, the floating cash flows will still be referenced to LIBOR but valued using OIS discount factors. The basic premise of swap pricing – that the transaction should be an equitable exchange of cash flows at inception – still remains true under the OIS discounting regime.

Suppose the following swap rates are observed in the market for annual payments against 12-month LIBOR.

	Swap rates	OIS rates
1 year	3%	1%
2 year	4%	2%

The 1-year swap discount factor is:

$$1/1.03 = 0.970874$$

The formula for calculating the second year discount factor is

$$DF_t = \frac{1 - R_t \sum_{i=1}^{t-1} \alpha_i DF_i}{1 + R_t \alpha_t} \tag{A1}$$

where:

R_t = Fixed swap rate

DF_i = Discount factor for reset date i

α_t = Accrual factor from $t - 1$ to t

Using equation A1, we derive the 2-year swap discount factor:

$$1 - 4\% \times 0.970874/1 + 4\% = 0.924197$$

The 1-year LIBOR rate 1 year forward is then the ratio of the two discount factors (see section 2.3.4):

$$0.970874/0.924197 - 1 = 5.05\%$$

Applying the same approach to the OIS rates, the 1-year and 2-year discount factors are:

$$1/1.01 = 0.990099$$

$$1 - 2\% \times 0.990099/1 + 2\% = 0.960978$$

The formula for deriving forward LIBOR rates from OIS discount factors differs from the approach used under the LIBOR discounting regime:

$$\text{LIBOR}_{t-1,\,t} = \frac{R_t \sum_{i=1}^{t} \alpha_i DF_i - \sum_{i=1}^{t-1} \alpha_i DF_i L_{i-1,\,i}}{DF_i \alpha_i} \qquad (A2)$$

where:

$L_{t-1,\,t}$ = Forward LIBOR rate from $t - 1$ to t

Applying formula A2 we derive the 1-year forward rate:

$$(4\% \times (0.990099 + 0.960978) - 3\% \times 0.990099)/0.960978 = 5.03\%$$

The result is 2 basis points lower than the forward rate derived from LIBOR discount factors.

If we used OIS discount factors to price a new swap, the first step would be to derive a series of forward LIBOR rates from the OIS curve and then solve for the swap rate that returns a zero net present value. However, since the forward rates derived using OIS discount factors are different than those derived using LIBOR discount factors the resulting fixed swap rate will be different. We can calculate the par swap rate from forward yields and discount factors using the following formula:

$$\text{Par swap rate} = \frac{\sum F_{i,i+1}/t * DF_{0,i}}{\sum DF_{0,i}} * t \qquad (A3)$$

where:

F = Forward rate

DF = Discount factors

t = payment frequency

Applying formula A3 returns a par swap rate of 3.99%

$$3\% \times 0.990099 + 5.03\% \times 0.960978/(0.990099 + 0.960978) = 3.99\%$$

Changing swap valuations from LIBOR to OIS

The impact of moving from a LIBOR to OIS discounting regime for a swap that pays a fixed rate of 'R' when the par rate is 'r' can be approximated by estimating the DV01 of a stream of cash flows that pays the difference between R and r ($DV01_{R-r}$):

$$\text{Change in value} = (\text{LIBOR} - \text{OIS}) \times DV01_{R-r} \times \text{notional amount}$$

The formula also highlights that:

- ITM swaps will gain under OIS discounting as long as the LIBOR–OIS basis remains positive. This means that OTM swaps will lose value.
- The change in value of deeply OTM swaps will be significant if the LIBOR–OIS basis is volatile.
- Any swap valued under an OIS regime will be impacted by a change in the LIBOR–OIS basis even if the swap rate does not change.

3

Market Risk Management

3.1 WHAT DO WE MEAN BY RISK?

Look on any newswire service on any day and you will probably see market analysts commenting on "high-risk" or "low-risk" trades. But what does this mean and does it matter? The implication much of the time is that a high-risk trade is somehow "bad", while a low-risk trade is "good". But, should we be concerned if a trade is high risk as long as the potential return is substantial? The acquisition of Lehman Brothers by Barclays was certainly a high-risk trade, but it may well turn out to have been the "deal of the decade" within the banking sector. Likewise, if the returns from a low-risk trade are inconsequential, one should question whether the money should be invested elsewhere. In fact, a better way to look at risk is "high quality" versus "low quality". So, a high-risk trade could be viewed as low quality if the potential return is limited, while it could be seen as high quality if the potential return is significant. Many hedge funds investors, for example, are more than happy to buy out-of-the-money options where the payoffs are, say, 10 times the premium paid, despite the fact that, in all probability, they will lose all of their upfront investment if they hold the position to maturity. In these cases, the investor realizes that he will in all likelihood lose money on such trades but if the unexpected happens, he will make substantial returns relative to his premium paid.

A further consideration when discussing the implied risk of a particular trade is the impact that it will have on the investor's existing portfolio. For example, let us assume that an investor is long UK equities and decides to hedge this by buying puts. Suppose he is going on a business trip for a few days and does not want to leave his portfolio at risk as there is a significant economic release about to be published which might impact the equity market adversely. Regardless of his reason for wanting to hedge, he still likes the equity exposure but wants to protect some of the previous gains. Again, his expectation is that he will lose his entire upfront premium on the put. So, looked at in isolation, buying puts is not a particularly attractive trade, from an expected risk–return perspective. From a portfolio point of view, however, buying puts may be a very smart move indeed.

This brings us to the following piece of advice. The implied value of trade cannot be quantified in isolation. The payoff profile from a bullish trade may look great but, if you already have a portfolio of great bullish trades, then does it really have any value? The value of a trade is dependent heavily on its marginal contribution to the overall risk–reward profile of the portfolio. In fact, a well-diversified portfolio may have a combination of both essentially bullish and essentially bearish trades, even if the portfolio manager is bullish. So, the next time you recommend a trade to a client, perhaps try to think of one that fits well into his existing portfolio and not just one that offers a sizeable risk–reward payoff.

3.2 DEFINING MARKET RISK

Throughout this book we will mainly consider two types of financial risk. Our analysis of credit risk will focus on the inability (or unwillingness) of a borrower to repay monies they have borrowed. However, in this chapter we will focus on market risk, which we will define as the risk that something that is owned (an asset) or something that is owed (a liability) changes in value as a result of a change in some market price. Some writers may break this down further into things like FX risk or equity risk, but in essence this is simply a variation on the "big picture" definition of market risk.

3.3   SPOT MARKET RISK

In the following sections we will focus on the main measures of fixed income market risk. However, we will subsequently show that a number of the principles will have applicability in other markets.

3.3.1   Macaulay duration

The oldest measure still used in the fixed income markets is that of Macaulay duration. This is a measure of a bond's or a portfolio's exposure to interest rate risk. We define interest rate risk as the change in the price of a bond for a given change in yields. However, Macaulay duration is arguably the least intuitive measure of interest rate risk given its unit of measurement, which is years. Its technical definition is "the present value-weighted time to receipt of cash flows".[1] Choudhry (2005) points out that a bond's maturity tells us little about when an investor would receive their return. A high-coupon bond will pay more of the return during the life of the bond, but the return from a zero-coupon bond is all paid at maturity. So at first glance it would be tempting to use some form of average time to receipt. Since coupons and their respective payment dates will vary between bonds, it would seem reasonable to use a form of weighted average based on the present value of the coupons. He argues: "The average maturity of a bond's cash flow stream calculated in this manner provides a measure of the speed at which a bond pays out its return, and hence of its price risk relative to other bonds having the same maturity."

However, knowing that the interest rate exposure of a bond is 5.34 years does not really help one's understanding of the concept or the inherent risk. However, it would be fair to say that the larger a bond's duration, the greater the investor's price exposure to changes in yields. In addition, it is useful to appreciate that the measure can be used for comparative purposes so when comparing two bonds with different durations, the bond with the higher value has a greater degree of market risk. The formula to calculate the value of the Macaulay duration is:

$$\frac{\sum_{t=1}^{n} \frac{t \times \mathrm{CF}_t}{(1+r)^t}}{\sum_{t=1}^{n} \frac{\mathrm{CF}_t}{(1+r)^t}}$$

where:

t = timing of the cash flow

CF_t = cash flow paid at period t

r = the bond's yield to maturity

Table 3.1 Calculation of Macaulay duration

Cash flow	Time to receipt (years)	Present value of cash flow (denominator)	Present value-weighted time to receipt (years) (numerator)
6	1	5.7692	5.7692
6	2	5.5473	11.0947
6	3	5.3340	16.0020
6	4	5.1288	20.5152
106	5	87.1243	435.6215
	Totals	**108.9036**	**489.0026**

To bring the concept to life, the calculation for a hypothetical bond is shown in Table 3.1. We will assume that the bond has the following characteristics:

- 5-year maturity.
- 6% coupon paid annually.
- 4% yield to maturity.

From the values returned at the bottom of the table, we can calculate the Macaulay duration as 4.49 years (489.0026/108.9036). The calculation shows that the duration is influenced by three factors:

- The bond's maturity.
- The coupon.
- The yield to maturity.

The relationship between the duration and these three factors can be summarized as follows:

- Longer-dated bonds have a higher duration than shorter-dated bonds, but the duration increases at a lower rate than the increase in maturity.
- Lower-coupon bonds have a higher duration than higher-coupon bonds. Zero-coupon bonds have a duration equal to their maturity.
- The greater the frequency of the coupons the lower the duration.
- Lower-yielding bonds have a higher duration than higher-yielding bonds.

Readers interested in a more detailed description of duration are referred to Kopprasch (1985). He presents the subject in a visually appealing manner, which saves the reader from becoming mired in the mathematics.

3.3.2 Modified duration

Given the lack of intuition surrounding Macaulay duration, it was perhaps inevitable that a more user-friendly version would be developed. The formula for modified duration is:

$$\text{Modified duration} = \frac{\text{Macaulay duration}}{1 + \dfrac{\text{yield to maturity}}{\text{Frequency of coupon payment}}}$$

One of the initially confusing aspects of the formula is trying to guess the units of measurement, since one is dividing a value expressed in years by the periodic yield, which is a percentage. Like Macaulay duration, the unit of measurement is years. Irrespective of any debate over the units of output, modified duration has a standard definition and application. It is defined as the percentage change in the dirty price of the bond for a one percentage change in its yield. It is also important to realize that some market participants somewhat confusingly will often refer to modified duration as just "duration".

If we were to take the bond introduced in Table 3.1 with Macaulay duration of 4.49 years, the modified duration for this annual coupon-paying bond with a 4% yield to maturity is 4.32 years. However, the interpretation of this measure is very different – for a 1% change in the bond's yield, modified duration predicts that the present value of the bond (its dirty price) will change by 4.32%. Kopprasch (2004) presents a formula that estimates the change in the dirty price of the bond:

$$\Delta \text{Price} = -\text{Modified duration} \times \Delta \text{yield} \times \text{price}/100$$

The price of the bond is the dirty value, and yield is expressed in absolute percentage terms (i.e., 1% is expressed as 1). The modified duration has a negative sign in front of it to preserve the inverse relationship between price and yield. So if the yield change is negative, the change in the price of the bond will be positive. So using our previous bond example, where the dirty value was 108.9036, a 1% fall in its yield to maturity with a modified duration of 4.32 will cause the price to increase by 4.7046 points:

$$4.7046 = -4.32 \times -1 \times 108.9036/100$$

As a result of the 1% fall in yields, the dirty price will increase to 113.6082.

3.3.3 Convexity

One of the drawbacks of using modified duration as a measure of market risk is that it works on the basis of linear estimation. However, the mathematics used in pricing bonds results in a price–yield relationship that is convex in nature. In the previous worked example of modified duration, we had shown that a 1% change in modified duration would lead to a 4.32% change in the dirty price. So if yields were to increase by 1%, then the price would be predicted to fall to 104.1990; a fall in yields by 1% would predict the price to increase to 113.6082.

However, if we were to calculate the prices of these bonds at the new level of yields using either a spreadsheet or bond calculator, then we would see very different results. Re-pricing the 5-year bond with a 6% coupon at a 5% yield to maturity returns a clean price of 104.3295. The same bond priced at a 3% yield returns a price of 113.7391. From this we can conclude that modified duration as an accurate predictor of market risk has its limitations. Figure 3.1 shows the convex price–yield relationship along with the linear predictions made by modified duration. Modified duration will tend to overestimate the fall in bond prices when yields rise and underestimate the rise in price for a fall in yields. The figure also illustrates an advantageous property for an investor who has bought the bond. Note that when yields fall, prices rise at an accelerating rate; when yields rise, prices fall at a decelerating rate. This effect is referred to as "positive convexity" and is a desirable property in a bond.

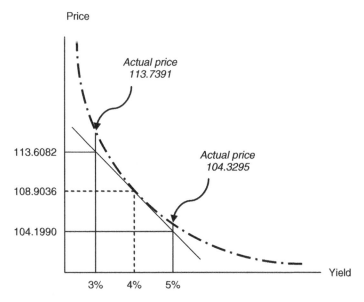

Figure 3.1   Price–yield relationship for fixed income securities.

It is possible to calculate the predicted price of the asset for a given change in yields that will take into account the degree of curvature that the instrument displays and hence account for the degree of "error" when using modified duration. Mathematically, convexity is a second-order function and so is defined as the change in the modified duration of the bond for a 1% change in yield. It is unlikely that the majority of readers will be required to perform this calculation, and so the interested reader is referred to Watsham and Parramore (1997) who provide a complete mathematical derivation.

Blake (1990) suggests a useful shortcut method of calculating convexity:

$$\text{Convexity} = 10^8 \left(\frac{\Delta P'_{\mathrm{d}}}{P_{\mathrm{d}}} + \frac{\Delta P''_{\mathrm{d}}}{P_{\mathrm{d}}} \right)$$

where:

$\Delta P'_{\mathrm{d}}$ = change in the dirty price of the bond for a one basis point increase in yield

$\Delta P''_{\mathrm{d}}$ = change in the dirty price of the bond for a one basis point decrease in yield

So using our previous example but expanding the number of decimal places in the answer, this would return the following value:

$$\text{Convexity} = 10^8 \left(\frac{-0.0470064}{108.9036447} + \frac{0.0470325}{108.9036447} \right) = 23.96$$

Similar to Macaulay duration, the units of measurement of convexity are not intuitive but are periods squared. There is one final step in the calculation, and that is to divide the result by the square of the number of cash flows per year. Since there is only one cash flow per year in this example, this step is unnecessary.

However, in this instance the exact interpretation of the figure is somewhat secondary to how it should be applied. Using the following expression we can now make a prediction as to how the dirty price of the bond will change for a 1% change in yields, allowing for the effects of convexity.

$$= -\text{Modified duration} \times \text{yield change} \times \text{dirty price} + \frac{\text{convexity}}{2} \times \text{yield change}^2$$

$$\times \text{dirty price}$$

$$= -4.32 \times 0.01 \times 108.9036 + \frac{23.96}{2} \times 0.01^2 \times 108.9036$$

$$= -4.7046 + 0.130467$$

$$= -4.5741$$

Looking at the above formula, everything to the left of the "+" sign is the original formula used to apply modified duration. All the elements to the right of the sign allow for the effect of convexity.

Also note that the worked example is based on a positive yield change of 1%. If the change were negative, the left-hand side of the formula would return a value of +4.7046, to which the convexity adjustment of 0.130467 would be added to give a total value of 4.8351.

As a result, these "modified" duration measures can be applied directly to the dirty price to calculate the impact of a 1% change in yields:

- If yields increase by 1%, the dirty price is predicted to fall to 104.3295 (108.9036 − 4.5741).
- If yields fall by 1%, the dirty price of the bond is predicted to increase to 113.7387 (108.9036 + 4.8351).

Note that in both instances the new predicted prices are virtually identical to the actual calculated prices shown in Figure 3.1.

Although a full proof of the following statements would be somewhat tedious, we ask the reader to take it on trust that the following properties hold for convexity:

- The lower the coupon, the higher the convexity.
- The longer the maturity, the higher the convexity.
- The lower the yield, the higher the convexity.
- The greater the coupon frequency, the higher the convexity.

3.3.4 Dollar value of an 01

Modified duration is usually defined with respect to a 1% move in the yield curve. However, in "normal" markets, movements of this magnitude are rare. As a result, traders have developed measures that are considered to be a more accurate reflection of actual market movements. Arguably, the most popular metric is the "dollar value of an 01" (DV01), which is defined as how much the clean price of the bond will change for a one basis point move in its yield to maturity. Essentially, this involves calculating the change in the (clean) price of the bond for a one basis point change in its yield to maturity. Somewhat annoyingly, the market has developed several alternative terms to describe this concept – basis point value, present value of a basis point, "risk", price risk and delta to name but a few.

There are two ways in which this number can be calculated. The first way is to derive the value from the bond's modified duration using the following formula:

$$DV01 = \frac{\text{Modified duration}}{100} \times \frac{\text{dirty price}}{100}$$

To illustrate the concept, let us take the bond that we have been analysing in this chapter:

$$DV01 = \frac{4.32}{100} \times \frac{108.9036}{100} = 0.047046$$

This means that if the yield to maturity of the bond changes by one basis point, the bond will lose 0.047 per 100. Although our example bond is currency neutral, if it were denominated in euros or dollars this would represent 4.7 cents per €100 or 4.7 cents per $100. Note that the calculation is linear and so, like modified duration, will suffer from the same predictive inaccuracy when analysing larger movements in the yield curve. However, as a rule of thumb some practitioners suggest that DV01 will be reasonably accurate in predicting price changes for yield movements of up to 10 basis points. So for a five basis point change in yield, the price change would simply be five times the DV01.

The other way of calculating the DV01 would be to use a spreadsheet or specialist bond calculator and price the bond with a yield which is one basis point different from its original value. To have a high degree of accuracy, a DV01 figure should be calculated for both a one basis point increase and decrease in yield with the final figure being an average of the two derived values.

Very often there is some confusion as to why the DV01 is applied to the clean rather than the dirty price. All of the market risk measures considered so far measure the instantaneous change in price of a bond. When trading bonds, dealers will be more interested in changes in the clean, rather than the dirty price. Recall that bonds are quoted on a clean rather than a dirty basis to ensure that any change in price does not include the natural increase in value that arises from the daily accrual of interest. So if a trader is considering an instantaneous change in the price of the bond, the accrued interest will be of little concern as this will not change on an intraday basis.

A related concept is the "dollar value of an 01" (also sometimes called the "dollar duration"), which produces a monetary estimate of how much a position will be affected by a change in yields. Suppose we were trying to calculate the profit or loss in cash terms on a $10m position in a bond with a DV01 of 0.047046 per $100. The dollar value of an 01 for the entire position is $+/-\$4,704.60$ for a one basis point change in yield.

3.3.5 Market risk of a floating-rate note

In Chapter 2, Section 2.3.5, we considered the price characteristics of an FRN. FRNs are credit rather than interest rate-sensitive instruments. We argued that the price of an FRN would not move by a large amount as a result of a move of either long or short-term interest rates. In duration terms the instrument will have a maximum duration equal to the frequency with which the interest rate resets – typically 3 months. The duration will decline as the next LIBOR reset period approaches, to reach its maximum level at the reset date. Recall that duration is a measure of interest rate risk and on the reset date the investor is receiving the current market rate and so is not disadvantaged; as a result, the FRN trades at par. This is an important concept, to which we will return in Section 3.5 when we consider the market risk of spot and forward interest rate swaps.

3.3.6 Market risk of credit instruments

With the move to fixed coupons on credit default swaps, the market now quotes two measures of market risk in relation to the instrument. The risky PV01 (also sometimes referred to as the credit duration) is defined as the amount by which the CDS contract will change for a one basis point change in its credit spread. This measure could be thought of as the value today of receiving one basis point per year for the life of the contract, which is either maturity or default, whichever occurs sooner. The credit DV01 (sometimes referred to as the delta) measures the change in value of a CDS contract for a one basis point parallel shift in the credit curve.

Suppose we have a 5-year CDS which pays an annual spread. The risky PV01 will tell us how an increase in this spread by one basis point across all maturities will impact the value of the contract.

The first step is to discount this one basis point change using a credit risk-free interest rate to take account of the time value of money. It may initially seem strange, but the market convention is to use zero-coupon interest rate swap rates. However, since the majority of bank counterparties who dominate the market will have a similar credit rating, it would seem reasonable to apply this particular rate.

The second step is to take account of the probability that the cash flow may not actually be received. This is done by introducing two related concepts. The survival probability measures the probability that an entity will survive without defaulting to a particular period, while the hazard rate is the probability that an entity will default between any two periods. So at a simple level, the difference between two survival probabilities for different maturities will be equal to the hazard rate. To illustrate the concepts let us work through a simple example.

Suppose that the spread on a 1-year CDS is observed as 50 basis points. Assuming a recovery rate of 40%, the implied probability of default can be calculated using the shorthand formula introduced in Chapter 2:

$$\text{CDS spread} = \text{Probability of default} \times (1 - \text{recovery rate})$$

$$0.50\%/60\% = 0.8333\%$$

If there is a 0.8333% chance that the underlying asset will default by the end of the year, we can suggest that the probability that the asset will survive to the end of the year is 99.17% (100% − 0.8333%).

Suppose that market rates are quoted for 2-year, annual-paying CDS structures such that the probability of the asset surviving to the end of the second year is 98.90%. Having derived two different survival probabilities it is possible to derive the hazard rate – i.e., the probability that the asset will default between year one and year two. The survival probability is:

$$99.17\% - 98.90\% = 0.27\%$$

Table 3.2 Calculation of the risky PV01

(1)	Undiscounted one basis point CDS cash flow	Discounted using interest rate swap rate	Discounted using interest rate swap rate and allowing for the probability of default
	(2)	(3)	(4)
Year 1	1.0000	0.9524	0.9430
Year 2	1.0000	0.9070	0.8891
Year 3	1.0000	0.8638	0.8384
Year 4	1.0000	0.8227	0.7906
Year 5	1.0000	0.7835	0.7455
Totals	**5.0000**	**4.3294**	**4.2066**

In Table 3.2 we calculate the risky PV01 of a 5-year CDS assuming a flat interest rate swap curve of 5% and a constant hazard rate for each period of 1%.

To calculate the value in column 3, the CDS spread value in column 2 is divided by $(1 + \text{interest rate swap rate})^n$, where n corresponds to the maturity of a particular cash flow.

To calculate the value of the cash flow that takes into account the probability that the entity will survive to a given period (i.e., column 4), the value in column 3 is divided by $(1 + \text{hazard rate})^n$. The sum of column 4 is the risky PV01. So we can say that the value today of receiving one basis point over the life of the CDS deal is 4.2066 basis points per 100 nominal. The risky PV01 can be solved for using the following formula:

$$PV01 = \frac{1}{N} \sum DF_k \times P_k$$

where:

N = coupon frequency

DF_k = discount factor to the kth time period

P_k = survival probability to the kth period

This formula is the same as that for a "risk-free" duration calculation but with an extra discounting factor given by the survival probability.

With the movement to fixed-coupon CDS structures, the market evolved to develop the "delta" (or risky DV01) which gives the expected change in profit and loss for a one basis point parallel shift in the underlying credit curve. It can be calculated as:

$$DV01 = \frac{\partial PV}{\partial S}$$

$$= PV01 + (S - C)\frac{\partial PV01}{\partial S}$$

where:

PV = present value

S = current CDS spread

C = fixed CDS coupon

Thus for a contract trading at par (i.e., where the current spread is equal to the fixed coupon), the risky DV01 and PV01 measures are identical.

To illustrate how the PV01 could be applied, consider the following examples. Suppose that a market participant decides to buy protection on this 5-year CDS on a notional amount of USD 10m and that the reference entity trades in the market with a fixed coupon of 100 basis points per annum. If the current market spread was observed at 90 basis points the buyer would be locked into paying a spread that was 10 basis points per annum higher than the current market rate. As a result, the protection buyer will receive an upfront cash adjustment to make the transaction equitable. If we use the risky PV01 calculated previously, the calculation is:

$$\$10 \text{ m} \times (90 - 100 \text{ bps}) \times 4.2066 = \$42,066$$

The PV01 could also be used to calculate the mark to market of a CDS contract using the same principles:

$$= (\text{Current spread} - \text{fixed coupon}) \times \text{present value of 1 basis point}$$

Suppose that immediately after executing the trade the observed spread increases by 20 basis points. Using the previous values, the buyer of protection would enjoy a market to market profit of $84,132.

CDS contracts represent contractual commitments that cannot be unilaterally terminated prior to their maturity. However, mutual termination is possible and the existence of fixed coupons facilitates this. Consider the previous example where the participant had bought protection on an entity that was trading at a fixed coupon of 100 basis points. Suppose that the participant has disposed of the underlying asset and has no further need for the CDS. One possibility is that the exposure could be unwound with the mutual agreement of the original counterparty. The counterparties would calculate the current mark to market using the process described earlier and would then pay the contract's value in cash. The settlement amount will be paid to the party for whom the contract is in-the-money. If the original counterparty refused to terminate the deal then the alternative would be to find another participant who is willing to take an equal and opposite position. As long as the notional amount, residual maturity and fixed coupon match that of the original trade, the resulting transaction should be a mirror image of the original deal. Since the second transaction is traded with another entity, there would be some form of upfront cash flow to be paid or received if the spread of the reference entity is trading away from the fixed coupon. If the spread has moved considerably since the original deal with the result that the reference entity is trading at a different fixed coupon, then on the overall matched position there will be a risky annuity that will need to be serviced until the earlier of default or contract maturity.

3.4   FORWARD RISK

In Chapter 2 we considered the forward pricing within the context of fixed income and credit. The market risk of a forward position arises from the nature of the forward pricing relationship, which in general terms is expressed as:

$$\text{Forward price} = \text{Spot price} + \text{net carry}$$

So in general terms, the forward price could move as a result of the spot price or the net carry components. To illustrate the principles, let us consider the risk of a long forward position in some of the asset classes we have already introduced.

3.4.1 Fixed income

Within this asset class the net carry for a forward position comprises the repo borrowing cost less any coupon income earned. A decrease in repo rates will force the forward price down and would result in a mark to market loss for a long position. The coupon element is of course fixed and so this component cannot vary. A decrease in the spot price of the bond will also lower the forward price of the position while an increase will cause the forward price to rise. As a result, we can say that the forward risk of a fixed income position represents an exposure to a change in the shape of the yield curve; repo rates representing the short end, while bond prices (via their inverse relationship to yields) represent the long end of the curve. Specifically, a long forward position will lose money on a mark to market basis if the curve were to steepen.

3.4.2 Credit

At the time of writing, the forward market for credit products (namely forward-starting CDSs) is less well defined than other markets. We pointed out in Chapter 2 that a forward position could be replicated by taking offsetting positions in credit default swaps of different maturities. Namely:

Buying forward protection = Buy long-dated protection + sell short-dated protection

Sell forward protection = Sell long-dated protection + buy short-dated protection

So a forward position is impacted by the shape of the credit curve. Buying protection forward will result in a loss if the credit curve were to flatten.

3.5 SWAP MARKET RISK

3.5.1 Spot swap risk

In Chapter 2 we derived a process to price and value virtually any type of swap structure. From a risk management point of view it may be useful to derive an intuitive understanding of the risk properties of an interest rate swap by decomposing the instrument into a number of equivalent positions. For example, receiving fixed and paying LIBOR on an interest rate swap can be considered economically similar to buying a fixed-rate bond and shorting (or issuing) a floating-rate note of the same nominal amount which pays LIBOR. So at a very simplistic level one perhaps could consider the market risk of a swap position as simply the duration of the fixed-rate bond less the duration of the FRN. Although perhaps illuminating on an intuitive basis, this way of measuring swap risk is not used in the markets. However, the market risk of a swap will follow the same fixed income principles outlined in Section 3.3. As a result, it is common to talk about the DV01 of a swap transaction (sometimes referred to as its "delta" exposure) and the convexity of the position (the swap's "gamma").

Table 3.3   Pricing a 5-year par swap with a fixed rate of 6.92% and a 10m notional

Year	Fixed cash flows	Discounted fixed cash flows	Floating cash flows	Discounted floating cash flows
1	692,000	652,830	600,000	566,038
2	692,000	607,554	745,217	654,277
3	692,000	566,835	718,353	588,422
4	692,000	529,394	707,258	541,066
5	692,000	494,690	701,528	501,501
	Net	2,851,303		2,851,303
		Swap value	0	

Table 3.4   Calculating the DV01 of an interest rate swap position

Year	(1) Fixed cash flows	(2) (1) × discount factor	(3) Floating cash flow	(4) (3) × discount factor
1	692,000	652,769	−600,000	−565,984
2	692,000	607,440	−746,224	−655,038
3	692,000	566,676	−719,358	−589,079
4	692,000	529,195	−708,261	−541,630
5	692,000	494,458	−702,530	−501,982
	TOTALS	2,850,537		−2,853,713
	Swap net present value = (2) + (4)		−3,176	

For consistency we will analyse the 5-year swap that was introduced in Chapter 2. The initial valuation of the swap is reproduced in Table 3.3.

To calculate the DV01 of the position, the yield curve is moved by one basis point across all maturities. Table 3.4 shows the worked example of the impact of a one basis point parallel increase in the swap curve.

A one basis point decrease will increase the value of the swap position by 3,178 and so the DV01 of the position would be calculated as the average of these two values, namely 3,177.

The impact of a non-parallel movement in the yield is not as obvious. Suppose, in the above example, the 3-year swap rate were to increase by one basis point but all other rates remain the same. The market factors for years one and two will remain unchanged but the values from years three to five will move. The higher swap rate will translate into lower discount factors but a higher forward curve. The result will be that although the present values of the fixed and floating sides of the swap will change, there will be no overall change in the position's net present value. Only a movement in the swap rate of the same maturity will have an impact on the overall NPV.

When considering a parallel movement in the curve we showed that the impact of a one basis point change was to move the value of the swap by 3,177. However, what may hold for a one basis point change does not hold for a 100 basis point movement. Using the above data, a 100 basis point parallel movement upwards in the curve would cause the swap to decrease in value by 307,737; a 100 basis point parallel fall in the curve causes the position to increase in value by 328,117. So since a swap position can be decomposed into a fixed income equivalent exposure, it is logical that it will display convexity. Since the swap position we are analysing is equivalent to buying a bond, the instrument is displaying positive convexity; losses decelerate as yields rise, while profits accelerate as yields fall.

3.5.2   Carry and roll down

Roll down is the change in value of the swap as it approaches maturity assuming no movement in the yield curve. The concept of roll down is also used in non-derivative fixed income structures, but is arguably somewhat easier to illustrate using interest rate swaps. Using the original set of par swap rates introduced earlier, suppose an investor were to receive fixed on a 5-year swap at 6.92%. One year later this position would be a 4-year structure, which if the yield curve remains unchanged will be valued at the 4-year rate of 6.90%. Since the process of revaluing a transaction estimates the profit or loss from the hypothetical closing out of the position, the trader could terminate the transaction by paying fixed at this lower rate and realize a profit.

In terms of explicit cash flows the roll down on the swap can be viewed simply as a 5-year swap without the final year's cash flows. Table 3.5 illustrates this principle.

Table 3.5   Illustration of roll down for an interest rate swap

Year	Fixed cash flows	Discounted fixed cash flows	Floating cash flows	Discounted floating cash flows
1	692,000	652,830	600,000	566,038
2	692,000	607,554	745,217	654,277
3	692,000	566,835	718,353	588,422
4	692,000	529,394	707,258	541,066
5	0	0	0	0
	Net	2,356,614		2,349,803
		Swap value	6,811	

Since the trader was originally receiving fixed at 6.92% and the position is now revalued at 6.90%, the roll down effect has been positive. From this example we can see that the steeper the curve, the greater the roll down effect. Hence we could conclude from this that a trader may consider the shape of the curve in order to determine where roll down will have the most optimum impact on their position.

The second significant concept is that of carry. With respect to a bond position, carry is defined as the coupon earned by holding a bond less the (repo) interest cost paid to finance the position. Since a swap can be considered analogous to a fixed income position, carry is defined in a similar way – the income received from the fixed leg less the LIBOR paid on the floating leg.

We can see from this analysis that carry is calculated using observed market prices, whereas roll down makes an assumption about the shape of the curve at the horizon.

3.5.3   Application of DV01

We are now in a position to combine the concepts of DV01, carry and roll down within a simple trading example. Let us assume that a trader believes that the swap curve will steepen between the 2 and 5-year point. The 2-year swap rate is 6.70% (with a DV01 on a 10m position of 2,764) and the 5-year swap rate is 6.92% (with a DV01 on a 10m position of 3,177). In order to immunize the position against a parallel movement in the curve, the trade must be made duration (or "delta") neutral. The first step is to calculate the ratio of the two DV01s, which is 1.1494 (3,177/2,764). This tells us that the longer-dated position is 1.1494 times more sensitive to a given change in swap rates than the shorter-dated exposure.

In order to profit from this expected move in the curve, the trader decides to pay fixed on a 5-year swap with a notional of 10m and receive fixed on a 2-year swap with a notional that is 1.1494 times greater. Since it may be difficult to execute positions that have odd notional amounts, we will assume that the 2-year trade is executed on a notional of 11,500,000.

To profit from an anticipated steepening of the curve, the trader decides to receive fixed on the 2-year maturity and pay fixed on the 5-year transaction. If the curve does steepen, the 5-year rate should increase by more than the 2-year rate and so the trader could then close out the exposure by entering into an offsetting position with the same residual maturity.

The carry on the trade can be calculated by breaking the transaction down into its component parts (using the rounded transaction size rather than the original hedge ratio).

2-year position

$$+1.150 \times 6.70 - 1.150 \times \text{LIBOR (i.e., the trader receives fixed at 6.70\% and}$$

$$\text{pays LIBOR on a notional of 11.5m)}$$

5-year position

$$-1 \times 6.92 + 1 \times \text{LIBOR}$$

This reduces to:

$$+0.785 - 0.150 \times \text{LIBOR}$$

So if LIBOR is less than 5.23, this delta-neutral trade will carry positively.

3.5.4   Forward-starting swap risk

Forward-starting swaps are often used by traders in preference to spot-starting transactions when expressing views on expected rate movements.

To illustrate the concept we will use the figures in Table 3.6, which illustrates the present value of a stream of one basis point cash flows from the fixed leg of a 4-year swap. We will assume that in the following swap transactions the participant is receiving fixed against 12-month LIBOR and that all cash flows are calculated on an actual/actual day basis for ease of illustration.

Table 3.6   Deriving the DV01 of a swap position

Date of payment	Undiscounted one basis point stream from fixed leg	Zero-coupon swap rate	Present value of one basis point on fixed leg
Year 1	1 bp	4.8500%	0.953743
Year 2	1 bp	4.9012%	0.908738
Year 3	1 bp	4.9533%	0.864990
Year 4	1 bp	5.0064%	0.822501

One useful formula for pricing swaps from their discount factors is:

$$\text{Swap rate}_{m,n} = \frac{\text{Discount factor}_m - \text{Discount factor}_n}{\displaystyle\sum_{i=n+1}^{n} (\text{Discount factor}_i \times \alpha_i)}$$

where:

α = fraction of a year

From this we can derive the 3-year swap rate and the 3-year swap rate, 1 year forward:

$$\text{3-year swap rate} = \frac{1 - 0.864990}{(0.953743 + 0.908738 + 0.864990)} = 4.95\%$$

$$\text{1 year into 3-year swap rate} = \frac{0.953743 - 0.822501}{(0.908738 + 0.864990 + 0.822501)} = 5.06\%$$

The DV01 of a 3-year spot-starting swap is 2.727471 (0.953743 + 0.908738 + 0.864990), whereas the DV01 of a 3-year swap, 1 year forward is 2.596229 (0.908738 + 0.864990 + 0.822501).

To understand the market risk of a forward-starting swap we must consider how LIBOR contributes to the market risk of a swap. Until LIBOR is actually fixed, the LIBOR leg has no interest rate risk. To grasp the significance of this idea, suppose a bank which normally borrows and lends at LIBOR is looking to issue a bond in the near future which will pay a single interest rate equal to the prevailing 12-month LIBOR rate. Suppose that at the point of issuance LIBOR fixes at 5% with the result that at the end of the year the bond will repay 105. The present value of the bond at issuance will be par (i.e., 100) as the coupon payment will be discounted by a zero-coupon rate of the same maturity and credit risk – in this case 5%. So there is no exposure to LIBOR as the bond will be issued at the prevailing rate and will trade at par on the day of issue. The interest rate exposure occurs after fixing, when the LIBOR cash flow will have a duration exposure equal to its residual maturity. Additionally, the bank will receive 100 from the bond buyers, which it can then lend in the market for a year to earn 12-month LIBOR. When the deposit matures, the principal and interest is used by the bank to finance the redemption payment. From this second example we can see that the bank is immune to LIBOR movements, so it follows that a bank which finances at LIBOR has no interest rate exposure to LIBOR cash flows that have not been set. We can apply this logic to a series of LIBOR cash flows on an interest rate swap; until LIBOR is fixed, there is no market risk.

For a 3-year swap where the participant receives fixed, the interest rate risk should be equal to the risk of buying a 3-year par fixed bond less the risk of issuing a 3-year floating-rate note. However, the interest rate risk on a 3-year swap effective in 1 year's time will only be a function of forward rates of the same maturity as there is no interest rate risk on a floating cash flow where the interest rate has not been set. When the forward-starting period has elapsed, the transaction will have the same market risk as a spot-starting 3-year swap.

Another way of looking at the problem is to consider the 3-year spot-starting swap shortly before the first LIBOR setting. The calculation of the DV01 of this position was shown in Table 3.6. As soon as LIBOR fixes, the first floating cash flow will have some market risk and Table 3.7 illustrates the impact using the same set of zero-coupon rates.

Table 3.7 Impact of LIBOR setting on 3-year spot-starting receiver swap

Date of payment	Undiscounted one basis point stream from fixed leg	Present value of one basis point on fixed leg	LIBOR cash flows	Present value of one basis point on floating leg
Year 1	1 bp	0.953743	−1 bp	−0.953743
Year 2	1 bp	0.908738	−LIBOR	0
Year 3	1 bp	0.864990	−LIBOR	0
Year 4	1 bp	0.822501	−LIBOR	0
	Total	2.727471		−0.953743
	DV01 of swap		1.773728	

When the initial value of LIBOR is fixed it will acquire some degree of market risk and the present value of paying one basis point is shown in column four (Table 3.7). Since the payment dates of the fixed and floating cash flows coincide, the present value of these cash flows partly nets out, reducing the overall DV01 of the 3-year swap to 1.773728. However, the DV01 of a "one into three" forward-starting swap is unchanged (all other things being equal) as this initial LIBOR fixing contributes nothing to the position's market risk.

At the start of this section we argued that traders will often prefer to use forward-starting swaps to express a view on potential market movements. Suppose that the trader is looking to express a view on the spread between 2 and 5-year swap rates and creates a spot-starting DV01-weighted trade. As soon as LIBOR fixes, the DV01 values of each trade will change by different amounts with the result that the position becomes a mis-weighted trade: 6-month into 18-month against a 6-month into 54-month position. It may prove advantageous to express the view using forward-starting swaps using, say, a "2s5s" position effective in 3 months' time. This means that the position will only be exposed to movements in forward rates and any LIBOR settings between the trade date and the effective date will have no impact on the transaction's DV01.

For those readers whose heads are now spinning, we reframe the issue in a less formal way. Assume two coupon swaps, paying 12m LIBOR. One is a 2-year swap paying 4% fixed and one is a 3-year swap paying 5%. Suppose you were to receive fixed on a notional of 100m on the 3-year and pay fixed on a notional of 100m on the 2-year. The resultant exposure would be a 1-year receive fixed position, 2 years forward. What is your effective instantaneous market risk, i.e., your DV01 exposure? The way to see the intuition behind this is to break the equal nominal trade into two components. The first component is a 2-year to 3-year duration-weighted spread trade. For ease of illustration, let us suppose that a duration-weighted trade in the two swaps would require a nominal position of 100m in the 2-year and 70 million in the 3-year. Therefore the second component is a 30m residual receive fixed outright position in the 3-year. If the swap market bear steepens (i.e., long-term rates rise by more than short-term rates; see Figure 5.5), the 2-year to 3-year spread component of the trade will lose money as will the outright residual 3-year exposure. If the market bull flattens (i.e., long-term rates fall by more than short-term rates), both the spread and the outright market components will gain. Equally, if the market bear flattens (short-term rates rise relative to long-term rates) or bull steepens (short-term rates fall relative to long-term rates), then the net profit and loss impact will again be a combination of the effects of the spread curve and outright risk exposures. Empirically, yield curves have tended to bull steepen and bear flatten (see Figure 5.8), so one could legitimately argue that the *ex-post* DV01 risk of a forward-starting swap is less than one would assume from the *ex-ante* formulaic calculation. That said, bid–offer spreads tend to be wider on forward-starting swap trades than on spread trades since there is a residual DV01 exposure borne by the trader.

What if we hold the exposure for 2 years, the tenor of the forward start? Since the nominal size of each trade is the same, the cash flows from the LIBOR fixings offset each other. The profit and loss from the trade at the end of the first 2 years would be the net present value (NPV) of the difference in the 2-year and 3-year swap rates earned for the first 2 years. In this example it would be 1% per annum for 2 years in addition to the NPV of the fixed rate on the 3-year leg (in this case 5%) versus the prevailing 1-year swap rate in 2 years' time. This, of course, is unknown. At that time, the risk of the trade will likely be that of an off-market swap.

Why use forward-starting swaps?

There are a number of reasons why a trader might prefer to use forward-starting swaps:

- There is a wider set of trading opportunities due to the fact that the swap can become effective at any time in the future for any desired maturity.
- This wider set of opportunities allows the trader to pinpoint forward dates where the roll down is highest or maybe the spread between two rates is most advantageous.
- It may be easier to increase or decrease an existing position if the exposure is taken in the forward market rather than the spot market. The maturities of the different legs will remain "round" numbers (e.g., 3 years) until they remain effective. The maturity of a swap transaction will gradually decline, making it difficult to obtain a quote for an odd residual value (e.g., 2 years 11 months and 3 weeks).
- The unwind price for a 5-year swap 3 months after it has become effective may not be particularly favourable. A 5-year swap effective in 3 months' time could be unwound into a straight 5-year exposure after the same period has elapsed.

3.6 OPTION RISK MANAGEMENT

In Chapter 2, we considered an intuitive approach to pricing options and determined that a number of market factors were needed to determine the theoretical value of the option:

- The underlying price.
- The implied volatility of the underlying asset.
- The time to expiry.
- The net cost of carrying the asset.

In reality, very few market participants will use a model to price an option. The price is simply what someone is prepared to pay in an open market transaction. This should not imply, however, that models have no role. Arguably, the key role of models is to help understand how the value of the option will change as the various market factors vary. To facilitate this risk management process the market uses the concept of option "Greeks". The main Greeks and their associated market factors are:

- Delta – the underlying price.
- Vega – implied volatility.
- Theta – the passage of time.
- Gamma – the rate of change of delta.

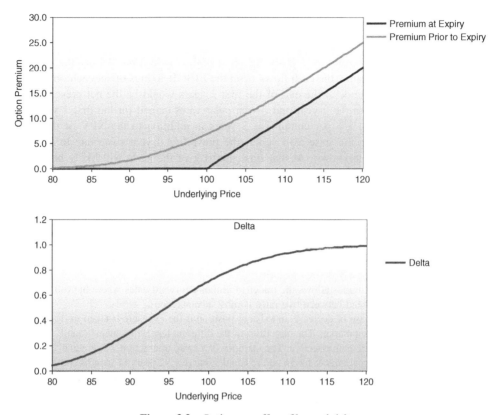

Figure 3.2   Option payoff profiles and delta.

3.6.1   Delta

Delta measures the sensitivity of the option premium to a change in price (see Figure 3.2).

The upper part of the figure shows the relationship between the premium on a call option prior to expiry and at expiry. The lower part of the figure shows the value of delta, which is measured as the slope of the price line in the upper panel prior to expiry.

Prior to expiry an option's premium with respect to its underlying price will possess some degree of curvature. The at-expiry payoff is linear in nature and conforms to the payoff shown in Figure 1.6. However, in Figure 3.2 the y-axis in the upper part of the diagram is defined as the option premium rather than the overall profit or loss shown in Figure 1.6.

Delta is defined as the slope of the price line at any single point. When the call option is out-of-the-money the slope is shallow and the delta tends towards zero. When the option is in-the-money the slope is steeper and tends towards one. An at-the-money option will have a delta of approximately 0.5; it is something of an urban myth to say that all ATM options will have a delta of exactly 0.5.

Figure 3.2 only illustrates the concepts for a long call option but a number of principles will apply to all types of vanilla option positions:

- The delta of an option will have a value between zero and one depending on the "moneyness" of the position.
- As the underlying price moves the delta will change since it is not a constant number.

- It is more common to describe the delta of an option not as 0.25 but as "25 delta".
- The Greeks will also by convention take a positive or negative sign. The sign taken by delta is dependent on whether the option position is equivalent to being long or short the underlying asset. So, being long a call or short a put will result in a long position in the underlying asset if the option is exercised. As a result, deltas for these option positions will be positive. Selling a call or buying a put will result in a short position in the underlying asset if the option is exercised and as a result delta will take a negative value.

One simple but powerful property of delta is that the metric is additive across positions. So, combining an option with a delta of +30 with an option that has a delta of −30 will result in a position that is delta neutral. That is, the position has no exposure to small movements in the price of the underlying asset.

There are also a number of other interpretations of delta:

A trader's directional exposure – If a trader has a position that is overall delta positive, he will benefit from a rise in price and lose when prices fall. Equally, if the trader's position is delta negative he will benefit from a fall in price and suffer when they rise. However, one school of thought suggests that an option trader should remain delta neutral as their job is to trade the one property that is unique to options, namely implied volatility.

The sensitivity of the option premium to a change in the underlying price – The classic definition of delta is given as:

$$\text{Delta} = \frac{\text{Change in option price}}{\text{Change in underlying price}}$$

The formula can also be rearranged to predict how the premium will change for a small change in the underlying price. So if the underlying price change was $0.01 and the delta of the option was, say, 30, we would expect the premium to change by 30% of this amount, i.e., $0.003.

The hedge ratio – In this context delta expresses the market risk of an option relative to an equivalent position in the underlying market. As we have argued, it is possible to combine various options so that the net delta of the overall position is the market risk that the participant wishes to achieve. Suppose a trader has sold a call on 10,000 shares with a delta of −30 and does not wish to have any exposure to price movements in the underlying asset. The delta value suggests that the option position will behave as if the trader had actually sold 3,000 of the underlying asset. To neutralize the position against small movements in the underlying price – a process known as delta hedging – the trader has two alternatives in order to achieve delta neutrality:

1. The position must be combined with other options which have a delta of +0.3.
2. The trader should purchase 3,000 shares in the underlying market.

The probability of exercise – Although not true in a statistical sense, delta can be viewed intuitively as the probability of exercise. Since values of delta can range from 0 (out-of-the-money) to +/−1 (in-the-money), it is appealing to suggest that an option with a delta of 60 has a 60% probability of exercise.

Delta possesses two other important properties. Firstly, delta changes as a function of time even if there is no movement in the underlying asset price. In Figure 3.3 the evolution of delta is shown through time. The upper figure shows the value of delta for a 12-month option, while the lower figure shows the value of delta for the same position much closer to expiry. This follows from the upper part of Figure 3.2, which illustrates how the price line of the option evolved through time, losing its curvature and becoming more linear. This

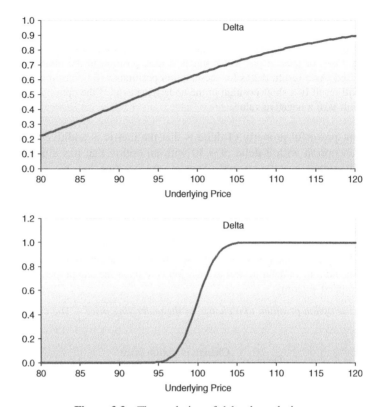

Figure 3.3   The evolution of delta through time.

evolution of delta is sometimes referred to as "delta bleed", and would be of concern to a trader looking to hedge his directional exposure.

The second important property of delta is the sensitivity of its value to the magnitude of the implied volatility input used to price the option. As the implied volatility of the underlying asset increases, the delta of both calls and puts will tend towards zero, all other things being equal. This is because the range of expected prices at maturity widens and so intuitively the probability of exercise tends towards 50:50.

3.6.2   Gamma

Arguably, gamma is the least intuitive of the option Greeks, probably due to the fact that it is a second-order function. The textbook definition of gamma is normally given as:

$$\text{Gamma} = \frac{\text{Change in delta}}{\text{Change in underlying price}}$$

Possibly the most confusing aspect of gamma is that it does not relate directly to the option's premium but rather delta. Since our aim in writing this book is to equip the reader with an intuitive understanding of financial concepts, we will endeavour to interpret gamma in a variety of ways. Perhaps one useful reference is Sections 3.3.1–3.3.3, which make reference to the DV01 of the bond and its related second-order function, convexity. These are the fixed income cash equivalents of delta and gamma, respectively.

Gamma tells us by how much delta will change for a given move in the underlying price. Consequently, one subtle but vital aspect of gamma relates to the fact that a range of underlying price movements needs to be associated with every gamma measurement. So a statement such as "the option had a gamma of 0.03" is meaningless; it would be far more accurate to say "the gamma for a 1% change in the underlying price is 0.03".

An option trader who is attempting to neutralize a position against moves in the underlying price has a keen interest in knowing the value of gamma as it will tell them how rapidly a delta-hedged position becomes unhedged, due to changes in the option's delta. So the greater the gamma, the greater the change in delta for a given change in the underlying price. This change in delta could force the trader to re-hedge their directional exposure in order to maintain delta neutrality.

Figure 3.4 shows the value of delta (the two left-hand panels) at different maturities for a given option. Gamma (the two right-hand panels) is simply the slope of the opposite delta profile with respect to the underlying price. Gamma is highest when the slope of the delta profile is steepest (note that the values of the y-axis on the Gamma charts are different). This is when the option is at-the-money and has little time left to maturity. It is possible to represent gamma using a three-dimensional graph (Figure 3.5), which illustrates the concepts in an alternative fashion. Figure 3.5 also shows that gamma will decline as longer-dated OTM and ITM options approach maturity.

Unlike delta, gamma's sign is somewhat easier to remember. Buyers of options are gamma positive, while sellers of options are gamma negative. This can be inferred from the profile in Figure 3.4, which is the delta profile for a long call option. In this example the slope of delta is positive with respect to the underlying price; since gamma is the slope of the delta function it will therefore have a positive value. Although not shown, we could consider a long put position where the delta is negative. A rise in the underlying price will make the option's delta tend towards zero as the position moves out-of-the-money. Since delta is increasing (i.e., becoming less negative) with respect to rising prices, its slope will also be positive, hence gamma will also take a positive value. The logic for short option positions is identical but will result in negative gamma values for both calls and puts.

To illustrate the application of gamma, consider the following examples. The change in delta for a 1% move in the underlying price could be expressed as:

$$\text{Change in delta} = \text{Gamma} \times \frac{\text{underlying price}}{100}$$

Suppose an asset is trading with a price of €50 and the delta value for a long call option is +0.50. We will assume that the option pricing model returns a gamma value of 0.757 for a 1% move in the underlying asset. This means that if the price moves to €50.50, the delta on the option should increase by 0.3785 (0.0757 × €50/100) to 0.53785.

The second example of gamma relates to its impact on the delta hedging activities of an option trader. Suppose an option trader has sold a very short-dated call on 10,000 shares, which are trading at a price of 700p. The trader has decided to implement a trade that is delta neutral as he wishes to express a view on the volatility of the underlying asset. We will assume the delta of the option is −0.50, meaning the market risk on the option position is equivalent to being short 5,000 of the underlying shares. To delta hedge this exposure

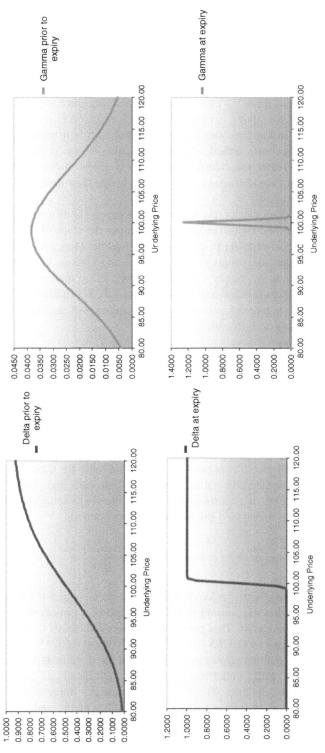

Figure 3.4 The relationship between delta and gamma.

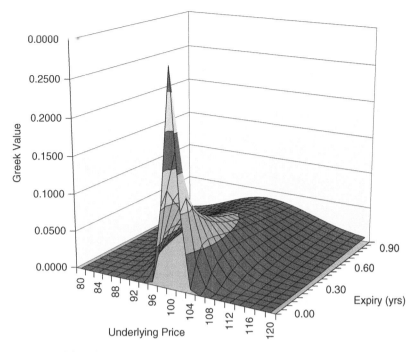

Figure 3.5 The value of gamma in three dimensions (option strike = 100).

the trader buys 5,000 shares at the prevailing price of 700p. However, shortly after the trade has been hedged the underlying share price rallies to 720p, which according to the trader's option model corresponds to a delta of -0.92. As a result, the option position now has the same market exposure as a short position of 9,200 shares. However, his existing delta hedge comprises a long position of 5,000 shares. If the price of the underlying asset continues to rise, the option position will show a mark-to-market loss greater than the profit on the offsetting hedge. This is because the loss on his option is nonlinear and so will increase at a faster rate than the increase in the linear profit on the underlying hedge. As a result, he decides to re-hedge at the higher price and new delta value, which means he must buy 4,200 shares at 720p to maintain his delta neutrality. However, shortly after putting on the hedge the share price slips back to its original starting value of 700p, which means that the option's delta falls back to -0.50. If the price of the underlying asset continues to fall, the mark-to-market profits on the trader's option position (as measured from the higher price of 720p) will be greater than the losses on the delta hedge. This time the option profits are decelerating while the losses on his hedge increase at a faster rate. As a result, the trader decides to rebalance again by selling 4,200 shares at the prevailing price of 700p. If the market were to close at this point the trader would be facing a loss after their trading activities. Since the underlying price started and finished the session at the same price and the analysis has been performed intraday, the value of the option position will be unchanged. The source of loss was the trader's hedging activities. He started and finished the session with a long position of 5,000 shares but bought an additional 4,200 at a price of 720p before selling them at 700p. This results in a net loss of £840.

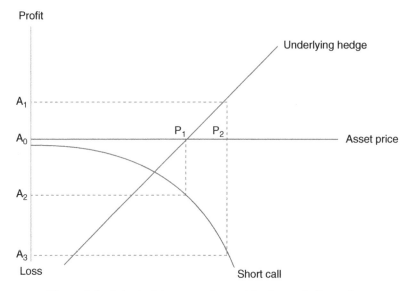

Figure 3.6   Delta hedging an option position in a volatile market.

Figure 3.6 illustrates the intuition of delta hedging a short option position when the market moves. If we assume that the initial price of the underlying asset is P_1, then a rise in price to P_2 will lead to a loss on the short option position equal to $A_2 - A_3$. This loss is greater than the profit made on the underlying delta hedge, which is equal to $A_0 - A_1$. Although not shown on the diagram, the reader is invited to consider the impact of a falling price from point P_1. Here the profits on the option position will decelerate, while the losses on the hedge increase at a faster rate.

In this case the trader would initially be forced to sell some of the initial hedge at a lower price as the delta on the option will have tended towards zero. If the price were subsequently to rise back to its starting point, the trader would then have to buy back the position at a delta value close to the original value of -0.50.

This example illustrates the concept of negative gamma exposure as the trader believed that when establishing the position the underlying asset price would display actual price volatility less than the implied volatility that was used to price the option. With the benefit of hindsight, the trader would have been better off establishing a long gamma position. This would have entailed buying an option (either a call or a put) and then delta hedging the directional exposure. In that scenario the option trader would make money from rebalancing their portfolio in a volatile market.

Table 3.8 summarizes the trading implications of a positive and negative gamma position.

The example of negative gamma allows us to derive some alternative and intuitive definitions for this risk management measure. Some traders define gamma as the rate of change of their profit and loss with respect to movements in the underlying price. The logic for this definition arises from the fact that if gamma is numerically large, then for a given movement in the underlying price, delta will change by a large amount. This will require the trader to rebalance their portfolio, which will mean they will incur profits or losses depending on the sign of their gamma exposure.

Table 3.8   Summary of delta-hedging activities of an option position

Initial position	Delta exposure	Gamma exposure	Initial delta hedge	Asset price up	Asset price down
Buy call	+	+	Sell asset	Sell more of the asset	Buy asset
Buy put	−	+	Buy asset	Sell asset	Buy more of the asset
Sell call	−	−	Buy asset	Buy more of the asset	Sell asset
Sell put	+	−	Sell asset	Buy asset	Sell more asset

Another definition is that gamma is a trader's exposure to actual volatility. This is not the same as implied volatility, which is measured by vega (see Section 3.6.4). Consider a scenario where a trader has sold a short-dated ATM option. If the underlying price moves by a significant amount and results in a large movement in delta, then a trader will need to rebalance a delta-neutral exposure. Since the trader is short the option this price volatility will result in delta hedge losses; if they had been long the price volatility would have generated profits. Implied volatility describes the range of values that the underlying asset is expected to take at the expiry of the option. It says very little about current price movements, which we define as actual volatility.

3.6.3   Theta

Theta measures how the value of an option will change with respect to the passage of time. Theta describes how time value amortizes as the option approaches maturity and is normally expressed in terms of one day.

In Section 2.7 we pointed out that the option premium can be decomposed into two components: intrinsic and time value. The intrinsic value element is influenced only by movements in the underlying price relative to the strike price. Although beyond the scope of this book to prove, the time value element is essentially driven by changes in volatility and the passage of time.[2]

One of the features of the impact of time is the nonlinear way in which prices decay. At first the change in the value of the option with respect to time will be fairly limited, but the sensitivity will increase as the option approaches maturity.

Theta for option buyers is negative, which implies that time will work against the buyer of an option. However, it is positive for sellers, which means the impact of time will be favourable for option sellers.

Table 3.9 shows how the values of three different types of option decay with respect to time. This table follows the principles outlined in Vine (2005).

Table 3.9   The time decay for a long call option position with initially 1 year to maturity but at different degrees of "moneyness"

Option type	1 year	0.75 year	0.5 year	0.25 year	Expiry
ITM	10.4197	10.2313	10.0501	9.9321	10.0000
ATM	3.7933	3.3267	2.7507	1.9697	0.0000
OTM	0.6776	0.4288	0.1961	0.0297	0.0000

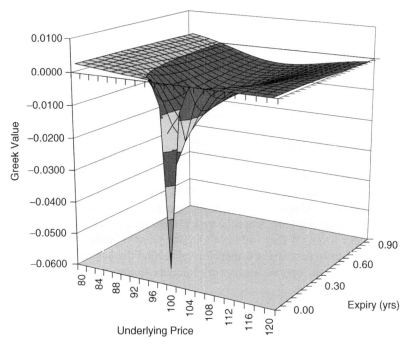

Figure 3.7   Evolution of theta in three dimensions (option strike = 100).

A number of features can be identified from this table:

- The ITM option displays both negative and positive theta, with the value of the option being comprised entirely of intrinsic value.
- The ATM option loses most value in absolute terms.
- The OTM option loses the greatest value in percentage terms.

The evolution of theta with respect to maturity and the underlying price is shown in Figure 3.7.

Theta is sometimes referred to as "gamma rent". This can be shown by reconsidering the trading example introduced in Section 3.6.2, which illustrated the concept of the delta–gamma relationship. In the example, selling short-dated options close to expiry resulted in delta hedging losses for the trader. An obvious question is why anyone would ever sell options? Selling options means that the trader has a theta-positive position and so the value of the option will increase over time. As a result, the challenge for the trader is to ensure that they gain more "rent" from the passage of time than they lose through delta-hedging activities.

3.6.4   Vega

Vega measures a trader's exposure to a change in implied volatility. This should not be confused with gamma, which we argued in Section 3.6.2 was the trader's exposure to actual volatility. Before considering the properties of vega it is worth stepping back to clarify what is actually meant by volatility. Intuitively, it is simply the amount of variability of the returns of a particular asset. The confusion over volatility perhaps emerges as there are a number of different measures:

- *Historical volatility* is a measure of how volatile an asset has been over some past period. It may also be termed "realized volatility".
- *Future volatility* is the degree of expected price volatility over some period. However, at the start of the period this will of course be unknown.
- *Implied volatility* is classically defined as the volatility implied by an observed option price. However, the definition has an unsatisfactory element of circularity. That is to price an option, I need to back out of an observed option price the volatility implied by the premium. However, this leaves the unanswered question as to how the observed option price was calculated – presumably from another option price. So what was the source of that option's implied volatility? As a result, it is perhaps better to redefine implied volatility as "the risk perceived by the market today for the period up until the expiration of a particular option series" (Tompkins, 1994).
- *Historical implied* is a historical record of how implied volatility moved over a period.
- *Forward volatility* is a volatility estimate whose value is known today but applies to some future time period (i.e., the 6-month volatility in 3 months' time).
- *Forecasted volatility* is a predicted measure of volatility.
- *Seasonal volatility* is a measure of volatility that reflects the seasonal aspects of the underlying price.
- *Normalized volatility* is a measure perhaps most commonly seen in fixed income option markets and is calculated by multiplying the implied volatility by the underlying price. So if a bond is yielding 5% and has a 10% yield volatility, this will imply the same expected market movement as 25% yield volatility when yields are 2%. By multiplying the yield on the instrument by the volatility expressed as a percentage, both of these scenarios could be expressed as a normalized volatility measure of five basis points.

Some of the definitions are very similar and so to clarify the issues consider the following example. Since the implied volatility will determine the *price* of the option, a trader's view on the future volatility of the underlying contract will determine the *value* of the transaction. If the trader believes that the future volatility will be less than the implied volatility then there is an argument to suggest that the option is overpriced and so should be sold. Conversely, if implied volatility is low with respect to expected future volatility the option should be purchased. However, future volatility is of course unknown at the start of any period, but the trader could use historical measures and forecasts to make an intelligent estimate.[3]

There is a positive relationship between the value of all European-style options and implied volatility; that is an increase in implied volatility will cause the prices of both calls and puts to rise. This relationship is illustrated in Figure 3.8. There are a number of key points that arise from the diagram:

- The premium of the ITM option includes an element of intrinsic value which explains why the line starts some way up the y-axis.
- The relationship between implied volatility and the ATM option is proportional; a doubling of implied volatility will double the option premium.
- For OTM options, when implied volatility is very low a doubling in its value will cause the option premium to more than double in value.
- Vega is the slope of these lines, which means that it is constant for ATM options (all other things being equal) but will change as implied volatility changes for ITM or OTM strikes.

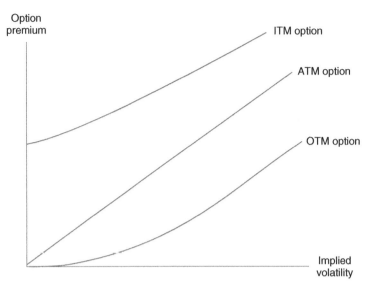

Figure 3.8   Relationship between implied volatility and option premium for options with different strikes.

- Buyers of options (calls and puts) are considered to be vega positive, while sellers of options are vega negative.
- Vega is highest for long-dated, at-the-money strikes, whereas short-dated OTM/ITM strikes will have the lowest vega values.

Vega in three dimensions is shown in Figure 3.9.

A trader can take vega exposure to express a particular view on how the market will evolve. A long vega position implies that the trader believes that implied volatility will increase, whereas a short vega trade expresses the opposite view. However, implied volatility relates to the distribution of spot prices at maturity not current market movements, which are traded using delta and gamma. There is something of a myth relating to vega in that many participants believe that movements in the underlying price will go hand-in-hand with movements in implied volatility. Although this may occur it is not a dependent relationship, since the two market factors are independent variables within an option-pricing framework. If a trader believed a volatile spot price was a temporary phenomenon then there would be no need for them to change their implied volatility quotes. However, if they believed that current market movements may affect the range of at-expiry values for the underlying asset then it is more likely that they will adjust their implied volatility quotes.

Vega-related Greeks

Figure 3.8 shows that for an ATM option vega is a constant but for other strikes will change as implied volatility itself changes. This is captured by the Greek measure "vol gamma" (sometimes called "volga" or "vomma"). Although not shown in the diagram vega will also change as the spot price changes and this effect is captured by "vanna" (sometimes called

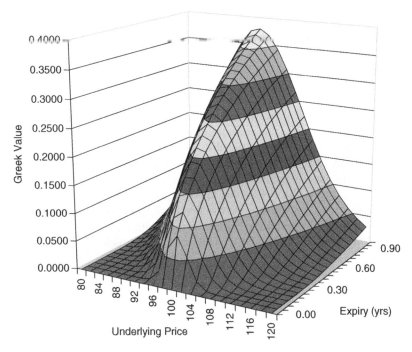

Figure 3.9 Evolution of vega with respect to the underlying price and expiry (option strike = 100).

"dvega dspot"). Readers interested in understanding more about the maths relating to these measures are referred to Haug (2007).

Headline and weighted vega

Anecdotally, in some markets (e.g., equity), traders suggest that when markets crash or become more nervous, the implied volatility of shorter-dated options increases by more than that of longer-dated exposures. When the markets rally, the implied volatilities of shorter-dated options drop more than longer-dated maturities. As a result, some traders make a distinction between "headline vega" and "weighted vega", with the latter seen to be a "truer" measure of exposure to changes in implied volatility. Headline vega is defined as the total vega exposure per maturity in an option portfolio, whereas weighted vega is defined as the total vega exposure per maturity weighted by time in years. To illustrate the concept, suppose a trader is running an option position which has a 3-month vega exposure of £100,000. This can be interpreted to mean that if 3-month implied volatility changes by 1% our option portfolio will gain or lose £100,000. Using the concept of weighted vega, this 3-month exposure would not be the same as a 3-year vega of £100,000:

- The weighted vega for the 3-month position is $£100,000/\sqrt{(3/12)} = £200,000$.
- The weighted vega for the 36-month exposure is $£100,000/\sqrt{(36/12)} = £57,735$.

This indicates that the market risk is concentrated in the shorter-dated maturity and the trader would hedge this exposure accordingly.

3.6.5 Smiles, skews and surfaces

One of the assumptions of pricing options using a Black–Scholes framework is that the implied volatility input is not dependent on strike or maturity – i.e., it is a constant across both these variables. However, this assumption is contradicted by empirical observation. When volatility varies with respect to strike this is referred to as a volatility smile or volatility skew. When volatilities vary according to maturity it is possible to describe volatility as possessing a term structure. Combining these two concepts together, it is possible to derive the concept of a volatility surface. However, in our experience it is common for practitioners to use the terms interchangeably and so we will first of all define our terms. A volatility smile exists where OTM and ITM options are priced using a higher implied volatility input than that used for ATM options. This would typically be seen in markets like foreign exchange (see Figure 3.10).

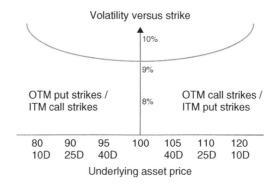

Figure 3.10   Example of volatility smile D = Delta.

If the smile is somewhat lopsided then this is termed a volatility skew. For example, equity index options tend to display a skew to the downside. That is, OTM puts (and ITM calls) are priced at a higher implied volatility than ATM options and OTM calls (and ITM puts). Several reasons have been offered to explain the existence of non-constant volatility. Arguably the most popular reason is the concept of "fat tails"; the occurrence of extreme events is greater than the option model predicts since the underlying distribution does not conform to the classic (lognormal) distribution used in theoretical option pricing (see Figure 3.11).

De Weert (2008) offers a second explanation, which is based on traders' hedging activities. Using the equity market as an example, he points out that as markets crash they tend to become more volatile. For those traders who had sold OTM put options, these options would suddenly tend towards becoming ATM and their gamma exposure would increase. As we showed in Section 3.6.2, delta hedging a short option position in a volatile market will lead to losses as a result of rebalancing the hedge. Since the trader will be aware of this problem, he is more likely to initially price his options with a higher implied volatility to provide him with an extra cushion.

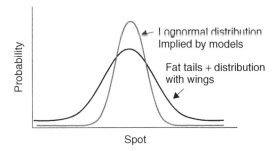

Figure 3.11   Example of fat-tailed distribution relative to lognormal distribution.

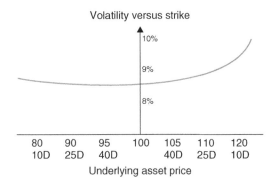

Figure 3.12   Example of volatility skew D = Delta.

The third explanation is simple demand and supply. If a trader expects a rally in the market he may decide to buy OTM calls in anticipation of the event occurring. To finance this purchase he could sell OTM puts which he believes would not be exercised since the market is expected to move in the opposite direction. As a result of the purchase and sale, the implied volatility of OTM calls rises and falls for OTM puts and the market becomes skewed to the upside (Figure 3.12).

Both De Weert (2008) and Tompkins (1994) note that the smile/skew will evolve over time. If we use De Weert's argument that traders' hedging activities will be the driver of the smile/skew, it follows that since gamma is greatest for short-dated, at-the-money options the smile/skew will tend to become more pronounced over time as the potential for delta hedging losses increase.

3.7   VALUE AT RISK

The methods of calculating market risk that we have covered so far could be classified as instantaneous measures of risk; how much would I lose if rates were to suddenly change by one basis point? In the early 1990s many institutions started to develop market risk models that were forward-looking in nature. As a result, a chapter on market risk would not be complete without some coverage of the concept of value at risk (VAR). The theory of VAR has been documented extensively in other textbooks and readers interested in understanding the subject in greater detail are referred to these sources (e.g., Jorian 2009).

Since it is impossible to know what is going to happen in the future, VAR relies on the use of price distributions and their associated probabilities to calculate expected market risk. The three main methods of calculating VAR are:

- Variance/covariance techniques.
- Historical simulation.
- Monte Carlo simulation.

It is beyond the scope of this book to comprehensively discuss the detail of these techniques and their relative advantages and disadvantages. However, to illustrate the concept it is perhaps instructive to refer to published data and understand how the output of the different methods could be interpreted. For example, Barclays uses a daily value at risk (DVAR) measure as the primary mechanism for controlling market risk. They define DVAR as "an estimate, with a given confidence level, of the potential loss which might arise if the current positions were to be held unchanged for one business day. If a confidence level of 98% was applied then daily losses exceeding the DVAR figure are likely to occur, on average, only twice in every one hundred business days".[4] There are a number of points that arise from this definition:

- VAR is only an estimate, does not represent a guarantee and changes on a daily basis.
- In this example the VAR exposure is based on a 1-day holding period, which assumes that a position could be unwound within 24 hours. Some institutions have opted for a more conservative 10-day holding period, which results in an increased VAR measure (all other things being equal) since there is a greater chance of an adverse price change.
- It is possible for losses to exceed the stated number on more than two of every one hundred days.
- A certain confidence limit of 98% equates to a given standard deviation (2.33 in this case). There is no regulatory requirement for banks to measure VAR at a given confidence level, however, the efficacy of each bank's approach is regularly assessed and Barclays notes that the UK regulator – the Financial Services Authority (FSA) – employs back-testing to count the number of days when a loss exceeds the corresponding DVAR estimate measured at the 99% confidence level.

The favoured method used by the bank to calculate DVAR is historical simulation. In their 2008 annual report the bank outlines their three-step approach to the calculation:

1. Every position held by the bank on any given day is revalued to derive a hypothetical profit or loss using 2 years' worth of daily market prices (i.e., approximately 500 profit and loss calculations are derived for every current position).
2. A total profit or loss figure for the bank's entire position for every individual day in the 2-year sample is calculated by summing the individual profits and losses.
3. The DVAR is a given percentile (e.g., 95% or 98%) selected from the 2 years of daily, hypothetical total profits or losses.

Figure 3.13 illustrates the average, high and low DVAR for two asset classes comparing 2008 with 2007. The period was one of great volatility and the VAR numbers reflect this increased turbulence.

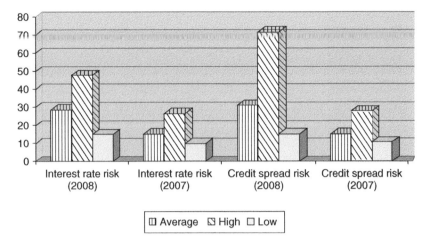

Figure 3.13   Daily value at risk (GBP millions).
Source: Barclays plc 2008 annual report.

4
Expressing Views on the Interrelationships between Products

In Chapter 2 we presented our relative value framework (reproduced below as Figure 4.1) and described some of the mathematical relationships that exist between the different asset classes.

In this chapter we consider the typical types of strategy that are used in the market to express views on the relationships between the different products within the triangle. For example, if we consider the spot–forward relationship using bonds as our underlying asset class the pricing relationship between the two can be expressed as:

$$\text{Forward price} = \text{Spot price} + \text{repo expense} - \text{coupon income}$$

This identity shows there are two variables that influence the forward price (i.e., spot prices and repo rates), so a trader could execute a transaction that would profit from expected movements in one or both of these components.

This chapter will consider a number of trading strategies along the different sides of the triangle but for consistency, we will focus mainly on the fixed income world.

The trades we will analyse are.

Spot–forward
- Bonds and bond futures.

Spot–swaps
- Sovereign bonds and interest rate swaps.

Forwards–swaps
- Bond futures and forward-starting interest rate swaps.

Options
- Directional and volatility strategies.
- Caps/floors and swaptions.

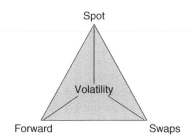

Figure 4.1 A relative value framework.

4.1   THE SPOT–FORWARD RELATIONSHIP

Section 2.4.1 covered the theory of forward bond pricing. The key points of that section were:

- If the coupon on the bond is greater than the repo rate, the bond is said to have positive carry and the forward clean price will be below the spot clean price. It does not mean that the bond is "cheap" and does not imply that bond prices are expected to fall.
- If the coupon on the bond is less than the repo rate, the bond is said to have negative carry and so the forward price will be above the cash clean price.
- The forward price of a bond is influenced by spot bond prices (i.e., movements in the bond's yield) and repo rates.
- An increase in spot bond prices will cause the forward price to rise and vice versa (all other things being equal).
- An increase in repo rates will cause forward prices to rise and vice versa (all other things being equal).
- Over time, the net carry for a forward position of a given maturity will decline but not necessarily on a linear basis. As a result, the forward and cash price for a given future settlement date will gradually converge to be identical at maturity.

One of the more popular techniques in the fixed income market to exploit expected movements in the spot–forward pricing relationship is referred to as "basis trading". This trade is expressed by taking offsetting positions in cash bonds and bond futures as the term "basis" can be thought of as another term for carry. We will illustrate the concept using German Bund futures, but the technique is equally applicable in any sovereign bond futures market.

4.1.1   Bond futures

Futures contracts were introduced in Chapter 1, but here we will focus on the unique features of bond futures. A futures contact was defined as a legally binding agreement on a recognized exchange to make or take delivery of a specific instrument at a fixed date in the future at a price agreed at the time of dealing.

At the time of writing, there are four German government bond futures traded on Eurex, which give an investor exposure to different maturities along the yield curve:

- **Euro-Schatz** – exposure to the $1\frac{3}{4}$ to $2\frac{1}{4}$-year maturity of the yield curve.

- **Euro Bobl** – exposure to the $4\frac{1}{2}$ to $5\frac{1}{2}$-year maturity of the yield curve.

- **Euro Bund** – exposure to the $8\frac{1}{2}$ to $10\frac{1}{2}$-year maturity of the yield curve.

- **Euro Buxl** – exposure to the 24 to 35-year maturity of the yield curve.

Each bond future gives exposure to a range of maturities on the yield curve rather than a single point (see Figure 4.2).

The contract specification for the Bund future is shown in Table 4.1.

The unique property of this futures contract is that there is no underlying instrument with a coupon of 6% that matures between $8\frac{1}{2}$ and $10\frac{1}{2}$ years in the future. The contract was deliberately designed this way to allow market participants the ability to deliver one of a number of pre-specified bonds. The intention was to avoid excessive demand for a

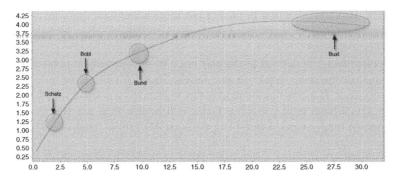

Figure 4.2 The German sovereign bond yield curve with the various bond futures maturities superimposed.

Table 4.1 Contract specification for Bund future

Trading unit	€100,000 nominal value of a notional Bund with a 6% coupon
Settlement	A delivery obligation arising out of a short position may only be fulfilled by the delivery of certain debt securities issued by the Federal Republic of Germany. The seller has the choice over which bond is delivered
Delivery months	March, June, September, December
Delivery date	The 10th calendar day of the respective delivery month
Quotation	Per €100 nominal
Minimum price movement ("tick")	0.01(1 tick = €10)

Source: Eurex.

single bond at a particular date. The exchange states which bonds are part of the so-called "deliverable basket" and for the Bund future maturing in June 2010, they were:

- 3.75% of January 2019
- 3.50% of July 2019
- 3.25% of January 2020

However, as we will try to show later, the exchanges' attempts to make the eligible bonds equally attractive to deliver does not work in reality.

The contract specification outlined in Table 4.1 allows the seller of the future to choose which of the eligible bonds they wish to deliver. But imagine that as the buyer of the future you were delivered €100 nominal of the 3.75% of 2019 when you were expecting a bond with a coupon of 6% as stated in the contract specification. Intuitively, the buyer would only accept this bond at a lower cost. In an attempt to ensure each of the deliverable bonds are equivalent, all bond futures contracts use the concept of a conversion factor (sometimes referred to as a "price factor"), which can be used to calculate the invoice amounts for settlement on delivery date. However, the method used by most exchanges establishes the equivalence in terms of yield rather than price.

The conversion factor is calculated and published by the exchange and remains fixed for the duration of the contract. However, the conversion factor will differ depending on the delivery month. Readers interested in finding out more about how this conversion factor is calculated should refer to the websites of the various exchanges where technical documents can be freely downloaded.

The conversion factor is defined as the unit price of the deliverable bond that will result in a yield equal to the coupon rate on the notional bond for the same value date on the futures delivery date. If a bond in the deliverable basket has a coupon rate that is less than that on the notional bond future, its price factor will be less than one and vice versa.

We can interpret the conversion factors for the June 2010 Bund futures contract as follows:

- The 3.75% of January 2019 has a conversion factor of 0.852328, which means the bond would trade at 85.2328 to yield 6% on 10 June 2010.
- The 3.50% of July 2019 has a conversion factor of 0.828936, which means the bond would trade at 82.8936 to yield 6% on 10 June 2010.
- The 3.25% of January 2020 has a conversion factor of 0.803710, which means the bond would trade at 80.3710 to yield 6% on 10 June 2010.

In addition to creating a degree of equivalence, conversion factors are also used for comparing the price of the futures contract with any individual bond in the deliverable basket. This is because the deliverable bonds have different coupons and maturities to the notional bond future. To make the comparison, either the deliverable bond price or the futures price should be adjusted. When making the adjustment to the futures price, the quoted price for the future is multiplied by the conversion factor. When adjusting the cash price, the quoted cash price is divided by the conversion factor.

Although the aim of the conversion factor is to create a degree of equivalence, the formula used by the exchanges is not perfect and so – to misquote George Orwell – during the trading cycle one bond may become more equivalent than all the others!

4.1.2   The cheapest to deliver

Since there are a range of bonds that could be delivered, the seller will logically select the bond that is cheapest to purchase and deliver into the future. This particular bond is referred to as the "cheapest to deliver" (CTD) and it is from this bond that the futures will take its price. However, we will show later that the CTD could change over the life of the futures contract.

There are a number of different techniques that can be used to identify the bond which is the CTD. The three most common techniques are:

- The lowest converted forward price.
- The highest implied repo rate relative to its actual repo rate.
- The lowest net basis.

In the majority of cases these techniques will all yield the same result but the first technique (lowest converted forward price) is arguably the most popular.

The lowest converted forward price is estimated by calculating the forward price for each bond in the deliverable basket to the delivery date of the future and then dividing it by the conversion factor.

The formula for calculating the forward price of a bond is:

$$FP + FA = SP + SA + [(SP + SA) \times R \times N/360] \tag{4.1}$$

where:

FP — clean forward price

FA = accrued interest at forward settlement

SP = spot clean price

SA = accrued interest at spot settlement

R = repo rate

N = holding period

The formula says that the dirty price of the bond for forward settlement is equal to the spot dirty price plus the cost of financing the position. However, the formula could be restated to take into account that forward prices like spot prices are quoted on a clean basis. As a result, the formula becomes:

$$FP = SP + [(SP + SA) \times R \times N/360 - (FA - SA)] \tag{4.2}$$

Formula (4.2) states that the clean futures price can be derived from the clean spot price, the cost of financing the dirty value of the bond and the accrued interest earned over the holding period.

However, equation (4.2) only derives the theoretical OTC forward price. To derive an equivalent theoretical futures price the equation becomes:

$$FP \times CF = SP + [(SP + SA) \times R \times N/360 - (FA - SA)] \tag{4.3}$$

where:

FP = futures price

CF = the conversion factor applicable to the deliverable bond

If we move the conversion factor to the right-hand side of the equation, the result is termed the converted forward price (i.e., the futures equivalent of an OTC forward price). This is shown in equation (4.4):

$$FP = \frac{SP + [(SP + SA) \times R \times N/360 - (FA - SA)]}{CF} \tag{4.4}$$

This price is also sometimes referred to as the "breakeven" futures price. If a trader could buy the bond at the current spot price and simultaneously sell the future at a price greater than its "breakeven" futures price and hold it to the maturity of the futures, he would be able to lock in an arbitrage profit. Since arbitrage profits are rare, another way of thinking about this is that the seller of the future will choose the bond with the lowest converted forward price at it will minimize his loss by delivering this bond. From this it follows that the trader would logically select the bond with the lowest breakeven futures price and as a result it will be the CTD.

To illustrate the concept of the lowest converted forward price let us consider the three bonds within the deliverable basket. The first step is to calculate the forward price of the bond for delivery on the futures settlement date (10 June 2010 in this case). If we divide this value for each of the bonds by their respective conversion factors, we can derive the converted forward price. These calculations are shown in Table 4.2.

Table 4.2 Calculation of converted forward price

Deliverable bond	Forward price for futures settlement date	Conversion price	Converted forward price
3.75% of January 2019	103.523	0.852328	121.459
3.50% of July 2019	101.408	0.828936	122.335
3.25% of January 2020	99.142	0.803710	123.355

Source: Eurex, own calculations.

Note that the current futures price is 121.48. The breakeven futures calculation for each bond indicates that the 3.75% of 2019 is the CTD, since it would be possible to buy and hold the cash bond at a futures equivalent price of 121.459, while selling the future at 121.48 making two basis points of profit. Some readers may query why the market is allowing an apparent risk-free profit, but note that this calculation does not take into account bid–offer spreads or transaction costs. Delivering either of the two remaining bonds into a short futures position would incur a loss.

The second way of identifying the CTD is by using the concept of the implied repo rate (IRP). This is analogous to the definition of implied volatility used in Chapter 3. The implied repo rate is similar in that it is the funding rate implied in an observed futures price.

Equations (4.1) and (4.2) showed how to calculate the theoretical futures price assuming a given repo rate. However, the actual futures price and all the prices for the basket of deliverable bonds are directly observable and so as a result we can back out of the futures pricing formula the repo rate implied for each deliverable bond. When a trader buys any cash bond, the repo rate represents an expense but a trader selling a bond for future delivery should therefore "earn" the repo rate implied in the sale price. So, taking the two principles together, a trader who buys a bond and simultaneously sells a future would select the asset that has the lowest actual repo cost relative to the highest implied repo earned.

Equation (4.2) derived the FP (the theoretical futures price) given RP (the repo rate). If we now take the observed FP as given, we can "turn this equation around" to derive the RP that is consistent with the actual futures price:

$$IRP = \frac{[(FP \times PF + FA) - (SP + SA)]}{(SP + SA)} \times \frac{360}{N} \tag{4.5}$$

The numerator inside the square brackets is the gross profit made from buying the bond and delivering it into the futures (i.e., shorting the futures at the current futures price). This profit includes capital gain/loss as well as accrued interest on the bond, but excludes the cost of funding the position so it represents a gross profit. The denominator converts this gross profit into a percentage return based on the investment in the cash bond and the fraction outside the square brackets annualizes this rate.

The IRP helps the trader determine which of the deliverable bonds should be the CTD: it's the bond that generates the highest net profit (or lowest loss) from a long cash and carry operation, net of funding costs – i.e., the bond with the highest IRP relative to its actual RP.

If we refer back to the three bonds in the deliverable basket, the implied repo rates are shown as follows:

- 3.75% of January 2019: Actual repo rate = 0.27%; implied repo rate = 0.35%
- 3.50% of July 2019: Actual repo rate = 0.27%; implied repo rate = −1.09%
- 3.25% of January 2020: Actual repo rate = 0.32%; implied repo rate = −2.72%

Using this measure, the 3.75% of January 2019 is the CTD since it is the bond with the highest implied repo rate relative to its actual repo rate. The trader could buy the instrument for spot value and pay a repo rate of 0.27%; selling the future earns the trader a rate of 0.35%, resulting in a positive margin of 0.12%. Once again, it would seem that this presents a riskless profit but bear in mind the caveats we noted earlier in that the quoted repo rates are indicative only. Many practitioners make the assumption that all the bonds could be financed at the same rate and so the CTD is often seen simply as the bond with the highest implied repo rate.

The third way of identifying the bond that is the CTD is that it is the bond with the lowest net basis. We argued earlier [equations (4.1) and (4.2)] that the forward price of a bond is different from that of the underlying instrument because of the implied cost of carry. This difference is also referred to as the gross basis. However, since we are comparing a cash bond with a bond future, we must take account of the conversion factor. So the gross basis is calculated as:

$$\text{Gross basis} = \text{SP} - (\text{CF} \times \text{FP})$$

To illustrate the concept, let us take the 3.75% of January 2019 and use prices for settlement on 16 December 2009:

- The clean spot price = 105.159
- The conversion factor = 0.852328
- The futures price = 121.48

The gross basis is therefore:

$$= 105.159 - (0.852328 \times 121.48)$$

$$= 105.159 - 103.540805$$

$$= 1.618195$$

It is important to realize that all the gross basis captures is the difference between the cash bond and the future at any one moment in time. Suppose a trader was deciding whether it would be worthwhile to buy the bond for spot value (at 105.159), and sell the future (at an adjusted price of 103.540805) hoping that the actual net carry on the position would allow him to recoup the loss on the transaction of 1.618195 (i.e., the theoretical gross basis). At first glance such a strategy should break even as the gross basis should be reflective of the carry on a long bond position. Any profit or loss made on the transaction is termed the "net basis" (sometimes referred to as "value basis" or "basis net of carry"). Net basis is simply the observed gross basis adjusted for the cost of actually carrying the long cash/short futures position to the futures maturity. More formally, it is defined as:

$$\text{Net basis} = \text{Gross basis} - \text{net carry}$$

$$\text{Net basis} = \text{Gross basis} + \text{repo cost} - \text{coupon income}$$

To illustrate the concept we will use the 3.75% of January 2019 and assume a settlement date of 16 December 2009. From the previous computation we calculated a positive gross basis of 1.618195, which we argued would actually result in a cash loss to the trader, ignoring carry, if they were to buy the bond and sell the future. The next step is to calculate the carry from this transaction.

There are 176 days between 16 December 2009 and 10 June 2010. An investor buying the cash bond for this period would earn a coupon of 3.75% on €100 nominal, resulting in accrued income of 1.808219.

The dirty price of the bond for settlement on 16 December 2009 is 108.713795, and the cost of funding this position for the 176 days at a repo rate of 0.27% until the maturity of the futures contract is 0.143502. As a result, the long cash/short futures trade carries positively over the 176-day period. This positive carry is 1.664717 (1.808219 − 0.143502) per €100 nominal. If we insert these values into the equation for net basis, we will arrive at a value of:

$$\text{Net basis} = \text{Gross basis} + \text{repo cost} - \text{coupon income}$$

$$= 1.618195 + 0.143502 - 1.808219$$

$$= -0.046522$$

The interpretation of this net basis figure is often a source of confusion. Using the quoted figures (which are indicative rather than firm quotes), a trader could buy a bond and sell the future to make a profit on the entire trade. The positive gross basis (which represents a price loss from buying the bond and selling the future) is offset by the positive carry, which is greater. The confusion surrounds the fact that the profit (i.e., the net basis) is represented as a negative value. That is, unfortunately, mere market convention. Since the market does not expect such a trade to make money, the value is represented as a positive number, which is interpreted as a loss.

The key learning point is the fact that the CTD is the bond with the lowest net basis; that is, the bond which generates the lowest loss or highest profit from a long cash/short futures position held to maturity. The interpretation of the net basis for the different cash–futures strategies can be summarized as follows.

Long bond/short futures position held to maturity
• Negative net basis is a profit (rare).
• Positive net basis is a loss (more likely).

Short bond/long futures position held to maturity
• Positive net basis is a profit.
• Negative net basis is a loss.

Table 4.3 summarizes the results from the different techniques used to identify the CTD. In all three instances the 3.75% of January 2019 was the CTD.

We have argued that in a "long cash and carry trade" (buy the cash bond, sell the future and hold to maturity), a positive basis would mean that the strategy would realize a loss. However, if the position was executed in reverse (sell the cash bond/buy the future and hold

Table 4.3 Identifying the CTD for the June 2010 Bund future

Bond	Lowest converted forward price	Highest implied repo rate relative to actual repo rate	Lowest net basis
3.75% of January 2019	121.459	0.08% (0.35% − 0.27%)	−0.04
3.50% of July 2019	122.335	−1.36% (−1.09% − 0.27%)	0.69
3.25% of January 2020	123.355	−3.04% (−2.72% − 0.32%)	1.49

to maturity), this positive basis would represent a profit. As a result, it would seem to suggest that such a trade (a "reverse cash and carry") would usually result in a profit. However, recall the bond specification from Table 4.1. It was pointed out that the seller of the future has the choice over which bond would be delivered at maturity. Executing a reverse cash and carry trade on a non-CTD bond such as the 3.25% of January 2020 means that if market conditions remain unchanged, the trader would be delivered the 3.75% of January 2019. As a result, they would have a short position in one bond (3.25% of January 2020) and a long cash position in another (3.75% of January 2019), which is a yield curve spread trade (more on this in Chapter 6). However, it is possible for the cheapest to deliver to change over the life of the future and so the reverse cash and carry trade with a non-CTD bond may be successful if the trader had a particular view on how the yield curve may evolve.

4.1.3   Changes in the cheapest to deliver

One of the consequences of using the conversion factor formula is that all of the bonds will only be equally cheap to deliver if the yield curve is flat and equal to the coupon on the notional future. To illustrate how the CTD could change, it is perhaps convenient to consider a deliverable basket that comprises just two bonds. The two bonds have different DV01s and different maturities.

Figure 4.3 illustrates how the CTD could change over the life of the bond future. As a rule of thumb, if market yields are below the notional coupon on the future, the CTD will tend to track the bond with the lowest DV01 and shortest maturity. This is because as yields fall, the rise in price of this type of bond is relatively small and so will tend to remain the bond with the lowest converted forward price. A rise in yields will push bond prices down with the result that the high DV01 bond will tend to fall by the greatest amount, resulting in the lowest converted forward price. It is only when market yields are identical to the coupon on the notional future that a trader would be indifferent between the two bonds. Indeed, if we refer back to our basket of deliverable bonds with market yields at just over

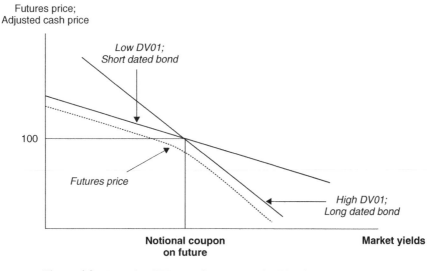

Figure 4.3   How the CTD can change over the life of the bond future.

3.00%, below the notional coupon on the bond future (6%) the bond with the lowest DV01 and the shortest maturity is indeed the CTD. The values were:

- 3.75% of January 2019; DV01 = 0.0803
- 3.50% of July 2019; DV01 = 0.0829
- 3.25% of January 2020; DV01 = 0.0852

As an aside, Figure 4.3 illustrates some other concepts:

- The futures price tracks whichever bond is the CTD. Since the CTD has the lowest converted forward price, this represents the smallest loss (or possibly highest profit) from a "long cash and carry" trade.
- The bond futures price displays negative convexity; a significant fall in yields results in smaller increases in bond prices (to see this compare Figure 3.1 with Figure 4.3).
- Since the seller of the bond future has the right to choose which bond to deliver, they are in effect long an option. As a result, the futures price tracks the bond that is the CTD but trades slightly below this price to reflect the value of this optionality.
- When market yield is equal to the notional yield on the bond the optionality is greatest as both bonds are equally cheap to deliver.

Having established that the CTD could change over the life of the bond futures transaction, what will cause it to change and can this be predicted?

Burghardt *et al.* (2005) suggest a number of factors that could cause the CTD to change:

- The absolute level of yields.
- The slope of the yield curve (if a bond cheapens sufficiently relative to the other deliverables in the basket it will tend to become the CTD).
- If a new bond or note is added to the deliverable basket it may occasionally become the CTD.

Plona (1997) derives a formula that will calculate the change in the yield curve required for another bond to become the CTD:

$$\Delta\text{Yield} = \frac{\left(\dfrac{\text{FDP}_{\text{CTD}}}{\text{Conversion factor}_{\text{CTD}}} - \dfrac{\text{FDP}_N}{\text{Conversion factor}_N}\right)}{\left(\dfrac{\text{DV01}_N}{\text{Conversion factor}_N} - \dfrac{\text{DV01}_{\text{CTD}}}{\text{Conversion factor}_{\text{CTD}}}\right)}$$

where:

FDP = forward delivery price

CTD = cheapest to deliver bond

N = another eligible bond in the deliverable basket

DV01 = change in the clean price for a one basis point change in yield. This is expressed as a negative value and multiplied by 100

If we analyse the three bonds within the deliverable basket using the above formula, we can derive what yield change would lead to a change in the CTD (Table 4.4).

Below is a worked example based on the 3.5% of July 2019:

$$\Delta\text{Yield} = \frac{\left(\dfrac{103.523}{0.852328} - \dfrac{101.408}{0.828936}\right)}{\left(\dfrac{-8.29}{0.828936} - \dfrac{-8.03}{0.852328}\right)}$$

$$\Delta\text{Yield} = \frac{(121.4591 - 122.3351)}{(-10.0008 - (-9.4213))}$$

$$\Delta\text{Yield} = \frac{-0.876}{-0.5795} = 1.511648\%$$

The result means that the 3.50% of July 2019 is likely to become the CTD if yields were to rise by just over 1.5%. This is consistent with our rule of thumb, which suggests that bonds with a higher DV01 will tend to become the CTD when yields rise.

Using this sort of analysis, a trader could execute a trade that may be profitable if he expected the yield curve to move by a particular amount over the life of the bond futures contract.

However, this analysis does not capture the reality of how yield curves move. We will show in Chapter 5 that one of the key themes of fixed income markets is that as yields fall (a market rally) the curve has a tendency to steepen but will tend to flatten as yields rise (a sell off). The concept is illustrated in Figure 4.4, and an illustration of the relative price volatilities is shown in Figure 5.8.

From this it follows that if yields were to fall, the likelihood of CTD switches is reduced as the price of shorter-dated bonds will rise by more than long-term bonds. This will delay the switch in the CTD from the longer to the shorter-dated bond. As yields rise, the price of shorter-dated bonds falls by more than longer-dated bonds. Therefore, the shorter-dated bond is likely to stay as the CTD for longer. This means it is possible to slow down or quicken up the point at which a switch occurs between bonds being the CTD.

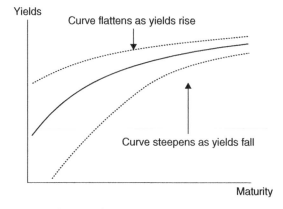

Figure 4.4   Yield curve movements.

Table 4.4   Yield changes required for a deliverable bond to become the CTD

	3.75% January 2019	3.50% July 2019	3.25% January 2020
Forward delivery price	103.523	101.408	99.142
Conversion factor	0.852328	0.828936	0.803710
DV01 (multiplied by 100)	8.03	8.29	8.52
Required yield change to become CTD	Currently CTD	1.51%	1.61%

4.1.4   The yield beta

One way in which these concepts could be captured is to use the concept of a yield beta. This measures the extent to which bonds move against each other. They are defined as "the amount by which a bond's yield is expected to change for a one basis point change in the yield of whichever issue is chosen to be the reference point" (Burghardt *et al.*, 2005). The results obtained in Table 4.4 to predict the change in the CTD could be modified such that the DV01 of the bonds in the deliverable basket is multiplied by the yield beta using the current CTD as the benchmark instrument.

4.1.5   Trading the basis

Within the context of this chapter we are considering the relationship between different sides of the RV triangle. Having spent considerable time looking at the fairly complex concept of bond futures, we can now analyse how to trade the cash–futures relationship. The difference between the cash and the bond futures price was described as the gross basis, and in this section we will look at the technique of basis trading. Earlier in the chapter we defined the gross basis as:

$$\text{Gross basis} = \text{Clean bond price} - (\text{futures price} \times \text{price factor})$$

$$= \text{SP} - (\text{FP} \times \text{CF})$$

where:

SP = spot clean price of the bond

FP = bond futures price

CF = conversion factor of the bond in question

A basis trade is defined as a long (short) position in a bond, normally the cheapest to deliver (CTD), combined with an offsetting short (long) position in the futures. Basis trading can be done with any deliverable bond but for presentation purposes, we shall assume here we are using the CTD.

So by market convention:

- Long the basis = long the cash bond and short the futures.
- Short the basis = short the cash bond and long the futures.

The party that is long the basis profits if the price of the cash bond rises *relative* to the adjusted futures price, and vice versa. If the basis is positive, the party that is long the basis gains if the basis widens and vice versa.

What matters in basis trading is not the absolute level of the cash bond price or the adjusted futures price, but their relative values. So in this sense basis trading is a relative-value play.

It follows that to be successful at basis trading, you have to understand the factors that drive the basis. If the bond has positive carry (i.e., the coupon earned is greater than the funding cost or the bond yield is greater than the repo rate), then the basis should be positive and vice versa. Typically, the yield curve is positive and so is the gross basis and as the yield curve moves, so does the basis. Basis trading has much to do with correctly predicting future changes in the shape and slope of the yield curve, since the gross basis is driven by bond prices (i.e., the long-term segment of the curve) and repo rates (i.e., the short-term part of the curve).

What drives the gross basis?

Suppose the gross basis on the CTD is currently positive, reflecting the fact that the carry on the underlying asset is positive. The gross basis will change in the following manner (all other things being equal) in response to a change in each of the market factors specified below:

- *An increase in repo rate will cause the gross basis to fall* – Higher repo rates increase the cost of funding a cash bond position and therefore require the futures to trade higher. If the gross basis is currently positive, this should reduce its value.
- *A fall in the yield on the CTD bond will cause the gross basis to fall* – This leads to a higher cash bond price, which also increases the cost of funding the underlying position. The futures price should therefore trade higher and the gross basis should contract.
- *A flattening of the curve will cause the gross basis to fall* – This means that long yields fall and short yields (including repo rates) rise. It follows from our two previous arguments that the gross basis should contract.
- *If the CTD bond went on special in the repo market the gross basis would increase* – This means that the specific repo rate on the CTD bond is lower than the rate for general collateral, so it follows from our previous observation on repo rates that the gross basis should expand.
- *The passage of time will cause the gross basis to contract* – The gross basis reflects the net carry on the bond, so as the contract approaches delivery the gross basis should converge to zero.

Basis trading is primarily a way of trading relative yields (the yield on the CTD bond relative to the repo rate) but, as we explained earlier, it also has an element of options trading: you need to assess the amount by which the net basis could widen or narrow as the risk of a change in CTD increases or decreases. Unfortunately, the delivery option is no ordinary option and is difficult to model. With an ordinary option, the underlying instrument is volatile while the strike is fixed. The delivery option on the bond futures involves giving up the CTD, a volatile instrument, for a cash bond which is also volatile. One way of analysing the optionality is to treat this as an example of an exchange option, where we have to take into account not only the volatility of each asset price but also the correlation between them – and correlations are notoriously volatile statistics.

In fact, one could argue that there is not just one but a series of exchange options, as the CTD could potentially be exchanged for any one of the other deliverable bonds. But these options are interdependent because the short's exercise of one of them (by exchanging the current CTD for another bond at the futures expiry) automatically destroys all the others!

Using proprietary options models, traders attempt to determine the options-adjusted fair value basis, i.e., the theoretical value of the net basis after taking into account the fair value of the delivery option. This allows them to determine if the futures contract is fairly priced and therefore whether the futures represents the most effective way to express a view on anticipated market movements. If the option is mispriced it may indicate that basis trading is a more effective way of expressing a view on an anticipated move in the yield curve.

As with any options position, the party that is short the option is exposed to additional risks, for which they receive a premium. In the bond futures market, this option premium is not an explicit cash flow but is reflected in the observed price of the future. In theory, the profit and loss from buying a cash bond, selling a future and holding the position to the maturity of the futures should result in a zero profit and loss. In other words, the net basis should be zero. However, as we have already shown, this is rarely the case and so the net basis must represent the value of the option. So, the net basis can be thought of as the price the buyer of the basis pays for the delivery options and the price the trader selling the basis is getting paid for the delivery options. We noted earlier that a long "cash and carry trade" would result in a positive net basis, i.e., a loss if held to maturity. The magnitude of this loss is the "cost" of the option – the right to choose which bond to deliver.

Certain bond futures such as the UK and US contracts will have a number of embedded options. For example, both of these contracts allow the seller to make physical delivery of the bond on any day in the settlement month rather than just one day. Readers interested in finding out more about these other options are referred to Burghardt et al. (2005).

Since the net basis is normally positive – reflecting the holding of a long option position – the future trades at a discount to its theoretical value, or fair value. The trader who is short the basis pays less for the futures than its fair value because, in buying the futures, they also sell the delivery option to the futures seller. The discount to fair value of the futures price represents the premium earned for selling this option (see Figure 4.3). As we will see shortly, the magnitude of this discount will determine whether the future is fairly valued.

The more volatile the market, the higher the probability that the CTD bond will change – i.e., the shorts will exercise their option to change which bond they choose to deliver. Since the shorts will always deliver the bond that offers them the greatest benefit, the higher the market volatility the higher the delivery risk faced by those who are long the future. Therefore, the higher the premium they expect to earn from being short the delivery option.

Labuszewski and Sturm (2008) restate the different basis trading strategies in terms of their option equivalent (see Table 4.5).

To illustrate the logic of this table, consider once again Figure 4.3. As yields rise above the notional coupon, the longer-dated bond with the higher DV01 has a tendency to become CTD. As yields rise, the price of the bond falls and its basis declines. As yields fall, the price of the bond rises and its basis increases – although it is no longer the CTD. So, looked

Table 4.5 Summary of basis trading positions expressed as option-equivalent exposures

	Long CTD basis – *Long cash bond, short future* (*long the delivery option*)	Short CTD basis – *Short the cash bond, long the future* (*short the delivery option*)
Yields < notional coupon	Long put option	Short put option
Yields = notional coupon	Long straddle	Short straddle
Yields > notional coupon	Long call option	Short call option

at in this way, a position that is short this future (i.e., long the embedded optionality) means that the basis behaves like a call on bond prices.

Valuing the embedded optionality

The valuation of the embedded optionality within a bond futures position is complex. Interested readers are referred to either Burghardt et al. (2005) who provide an intuitive explanation of the process or Veronesi (2010) who illustrates the concept with a worked example. Our aim is to provide our own intuitive explanation.

In Chapter 2 we presented a simplified way of valuing an option on crude oil. For example, Figure 2.12 showed how we could value the option as the present value of the sum of the expected values. The fair value of the option was calculated by overlaying a probability distribution onto a series of expiry cash flow payoffs. This logic is now extended to bond futures, with the principles illustrated diagrammatically in Figure 4.5(a)–(c). Figure 4.5(a) is similar to Figure 4.3, but for ease of illustration looks at the deliverable basket at the maturity of the futures. Yield* is a level of yields equal to the notional coupon on the bond, while current yields are higher than this value.

We argued above that the basis of the longer-dated bond acts like a call option on bond prices, and Figure 4.5(b) shows the relationship between net basis and yield levels, again shortly before expiry. At high yields the longer-dated bond is the CTD and so the net basis is constant and very low in value. At low yields the net basis would increase in value as this bond is no longer the CTD.

In Figure 4.5(c) we can overlay the net basis payoff shown in Figure 4.5(b) with a probability distribution and then use the option pricing principles shown in Section 2.7.1 to calculate the fair value of the net basis on the current CTD – i.e., the fair value of the embedded option.

Suppose that a trader has used an option pricing model to calculate the fair value of the embedded optionality. From this he can calculate the theoretical or fair value of the net basis and compare it to the actual net basis. The buy or sell rules are as follows:

- If the actual net basis > theoretical bet basis, then the basis is trading rich to fair value and should therefore be sold. Richness implies that the future is cheap – the cash price is too high relative to the futures price or the futures price is too low relative to the cash price.
- If the actual net basis < theoretical basis then the basis is cheap, suggesting a long basis trade. A cheap basis implies a rich future – the cash price is too low relative to the futures price or the futures price is too high relative to the cash price.

To illustrate these rules consider the 3.75% of January 2019 used in earlier examples. We calculated the gross basis as:

$$= 105.159 - (0.852328 \times 121.48)$$

$$= 105.159 - 103.540805$$

$$= 1.618195$$

The value of the gross basis includes both the cost of carry and the embedded optionality. Since the repo expense is 0.143502 and the coupon income was 1.808219, the carry totals to a value of −1.664717. Since the cash bond and the carry components have no optionality,

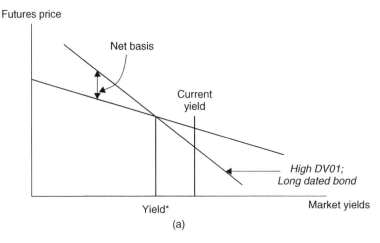

(a)

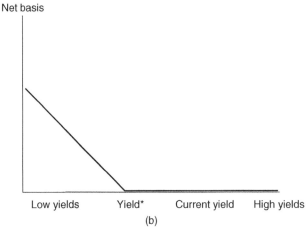

(b)

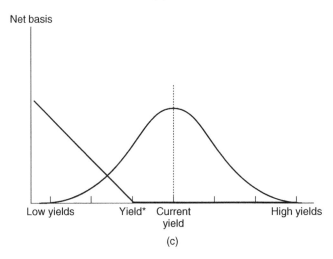

(c)

Figure 4.5   (a) The deliverable basket of bond moments before the expiry of the bond futures contract. (b) The net basis of the long-dated bond from part (a) against yields. (c) The net basis of the long-dated bond from part (a) with an overlaid probability distribution.

the residual value – which is part of the observed futures price – is the embedded option value and is worth –0.04652. Admittedly, this is something of an odd position in that a trader initiating a long basis trade (buy the bond, sell the future, long the delivery option) is actually being paid for buying the option. Suppose, however, the fair value of the option (i.e., the theoretical value of the net basis) had been calculated as +0.01. Holding the price of the cash bond and carry components the same (as they have no optionality), the fair value of the future would have to be about 5.5 basis points lower in order to return a net basis of 0.01 – 103.4843 to be a little more precise. This confirms the notion that the future is rich and the basis cheap, implying buy the basis and in this instance get paid for going long an option!

4.1.6 Implementing a basis trade

Suppose a trader has been monitoring the evolution of the gross basis on the current JUN 10 Year US Treasury Note futures contract. Over the last few months the gross basis has contracted as the growing risk of recession in the USA has driven the Treasury yield curve flatter and flatter. Now, however, with increased military spending, rising commodity prices and a tax-cutting package all happening together, market sentiment seems to be changing and talk of deflation, which some analysts had been warning against earlier in the year, has all but evaporated.

The trader feels that the yield curve is likely to steepen in the coming weeks (as the effects of higher commodity prices begin to filter through the headline inflation figures) and wishes to profit from this view. Moreover, as long yields rise again the trader believes that the CTD could change and this could be reflected in a rise in the net basis as well. The prevailing market data is as follows for settlement on 10 April:

Futures contract	
1st delivery date	2 June
Days to delivery	53
Futures price	105.94 (decimal)
CTD bond	
Coupon	5.00%
Maturity	8-year bond
Yield	5.022%
Conversion factor	0.935858
Clean price	99.84 (decimal)
Accrued (10 April)	0.74586
Accrued (2 June)	1.47790
Repo rate	2.70%

The gross basis on the CTD is:

$$\text{Gross basis} = 99.84 - 0.935858 \times 105.94$$
$$= 0.695$$

The trader decides to buy the CTD and sell the futures in order to profit from a widening of the gross basis while remaining overall market neutral and having no exposure to parallel shifts in the yield curve.

The contract size for the 10 Year US Treasury Note futures is USD 100,000 nominal. The trader is planning to trade USD 100 million nominal of the CTD bonds and now needs to determine how many JUN futures would be needed in order to make the net position market neutral. A newcomer into this market may be forgiven for reasoning that since the trader will buy USD 100 million of a deliverable bond and the futures contract size is USD 100,000, he will need to sell 1,000 futures contracts (= 100,000,000/100,000). Unfortunately, it's not that simple if we want the basis position to be market neutral. The "naïve" approach to hedging suggests the following relationship:

$$\text{Number of futures sold} \times \text{change in the value of one future}$$

$$= \text{Change in value of cash position}$$

This implies a hedge ratio of:

$$\text{Number of futures sold} = \frac{\text{Change in value of target bond}}{\text{Change in value of one future}}$$

This relationship can also be expressed using the DV01 of the bonds:

$$\text{Number of futures sold} = \frac{\text{DV01 of the target bond}}{\text{DV01 of one future}}$$

To calculate the DV01 of the futures contract, recall that its price tracks whichever bond is currently the CTD. Very close to expiry the futures pricing equation tells us that:

$$\text{Futures price} \times \text{conversion factor} = \text{CTD price}$$

And so it follows that:

$$\Delta\text{Futures price} = \Delta\text{CTD/conversion factor}$$

And so:

$$\text{DV01 of futures} = \text{DV01 CTD/conversion factor}$$

As a result, the correct futures hedge is:

$$\text{Number of futures sold} = \frac{\text{DV01 of the target bond}}{\text{DV01 of CTD/conversion factor}}$$

However, this will not be a perfect hedge as it ignores two things:

- The carry prior to delivery as the cash and future may not move on a one-to-one basis.
- The value of the delivery options, which may also vary over time.

Where the position to be hedged is the CTD itself (as in our example), the formula reduces to the following:

$$\text{Number of futures sold} = \frac{\text{Nominal value of the position}}{\text{futures contract size}} \times \text{conversion factor of CTD}$$

If we apply the non-option-adjusted hedging formula, the trader would need to sell 936 contracts ($100m/100,000 \times 0.935858$, rounded).

As an aside, an alternative way of measuring the DV01 of the future acknowledges the existence of the delivery option. As a result, it is common to calculate the option-adjusted DV01 (OADV01). This can be estimated as follows:

- Shock the spot yields on all the deliverable bonds by a small amount such as $+/- 10$ basis points.
- Recalculate which bond would be the new CTD in each of the scenarios as well as its resulting price.
- The OADV01 is the difference between the resulting futures prices in the up and down scenarios divided by the size of the shock.

The following is the market data observed 29 days after the original trade was put on (i.e., for settlement on 9 May):

Futures contract	
1st delivery date	2 June
Days to delivery	24
Futures price	104.10 (decimal)
CTD bond	
Coupon	5.00%
Maturity	8-year bond
Yield	5.2618%
Price factor	0.935858
Clean price	98.25 (decimal)
Accrued (9 May)	1.14641

The gross basis has now moved to a value of 0.827:

$$\text{Gross basis} = 98.25 - 0.935858 \times 104.10$$

$$= 0.827$$

From this we can calculate the profit/loss on the trader's position (Table 4.6).

An alternative way of calculating the results is to express the carry as a percentage of the bond's face value and add this to the change in the basis (Table 4.7).

Back on 10 April, the position had positive carry and so it was possible for the trader to make money even if the basis contracted. We could calculate the "breakeven gross basis"

Table 4.6   Calculation of the profit and loss from a basis trade

	10 April	9 May	Gain/loss (USD)
Clean bond price	99.84	98.25	$(-0.9984 + 0.9825) \times 100m = $ **−1,590,000**
Futures price	105.94	104.10	$(+1.0594 - 1.0410) \times 936 \times 100,000 = $ **1,722,240**
Accrued interest	0.74586	1.14641	$(-0.0074586 + 0.014641) \times 100m = $ **400,552**
Funding cost			$-(0.9984 + 0.0074586) \times 100m \times 0.027 \times$
			$29/360 = $ **−218,774**
Net profit/loss			**+314,018**

Table 4.7 Summary of profit and loss from the basis trade

	10 April	9 May	Change
Gross basis	0.695	0.827	0.132
Accrued interest	0.746	1.146	0.401
Funding cost			−0.219
		TOTALS	0.314

on this position to 9 May – i.e., the level to which the basis could have moved before generating a loss on the position as follows:

$$\text{Net carry to 9 May (as \% of face value)}$$

$$= 0.401 - 0.219$$

$$= 0.182\%$$

So the breakeven gross basis on 10 April

$$= 0.695 - 0.182 = 0.513$$

Having established that the position made a profit, we must ask what change in market factors has brought this about – all other things being equal – between 10 April and 9 May.
The profit could be attributable to one or more factors:

- *The yield curve pivoted anti-clockwise (i.e., it steepened)* – Rising bond yields and/or falling repo rates reduce the cost of funding the bonds, and hence increase the basis. This was what the trader had been expecting.
- *The bond that the trader held was no longer the CTD* – If the bond that is being held is no longer the CTD then there is another bond that is now cheaper and it is dragging the futures price down, relative to the price of the cash bond that is being held.

Since the futures price is driven by the price of whichever bond happens to be the CTD, Figure 4.3 shows that the price behaviour of the futures contract has negative convexity (especially near the inflexion points), whereas the price behaviour of each deliverable bond has positive convexity. So a basis trader who is long the cash CTD bond (i.e., long convexity) and short the bond futures (i.e., long convexity) is therefore net long convexity.

Since the basis trade is constructed to be market neutral (i.e., zero net DV01), this implies that a change in CTD will be beneficial to the long basis trader regardless of whether this happens because yields rose or because they fell!

The reader is justified in wondering if a position that makes money regardless of which way the markets move sounds like a free lunch, which of course it can't be. In fact, the cost of a long basis position is the net basis that the trader has to pay in order to enter into it. This net basis will decay to zero as the futures approach delivery – just like the premium on an option – and it will not be offset by the positive carry on the underlying bond.

So a long basis position will show a net profit regardless of whether yields rise or fall – i.e., it is market neutral and long convexity. This profit is caused by changes in CTD:

- As yields rise, the high DV01 bonds become CTD and push the futures down.
- As yields fall, the low DV01 bonds become CTD and pull the futures back.

In either case, the futures price is pulled down relative to the price of the bonds that we hold, so the basis increases and we make money.

The net payoff profile of this long basis position is similar to that of a long straddle in options trading. Neither of these strategies comes for free: they both incur a premium which decays as the positions approach expiry.

Bond futures – a conclusion

The reader may be reeling at this moment from all the figures and examples presented so far. If it is any comfort, in Schofield's experience, bond futures ranks as one of the most difficult subjects for people to grasp.

To make sure that we stay loyal to our overall theme within the book ("what is the most effective way of expressing a view on anticipated market movements"), we need to consider how a trader may apply their understanding of the net basis. One approach is to decide if directional yield curve movements can be best expressed using basis trades. This can be determined by looking to see if net basis is cheap or rich. Having valued the optionality embedded within the futures price, it should be possible to back out a value for the option's implied volatility. We could then compare it to empirically observed values of volatility to determine if current levels represent a possible trade entry point. Alternatively, the implied volatility could be compared to that observed in either the bond option or swaption market to determine if different values are consistent with each other. An anomaly may represent an opportunity to express a view using one instrument relative to another.

4.2   THE SPOT–SWAP RELATIONSHIP

Over time swaps have become a very popular benchmark for investors and issuers, even for those participants who may never actually deal in the derivatives market. For example, in the European corporate bond market it would be normal to price new issues as a spread to euro swap rates rather than a euro-denominated sovereign yield. This convention arose for a number of reasons:

- Some government bond issues are illiquid, either due to the small issue size or perhaps due to the fact that they are very popular with long-term investors (i.e., pension funds) who will buy the assets with little intention of selling them in the short term.
- Some government bonds are deliverable into bond futures contracts and so the demand for these maturities will make the assets relatively expensive.
- Some bonds may be included in popular indices and so those market participants who are benchmarked against these values may decide to purchase the instrument, forcing its price to increase relative to its theoretical value.
- If a bond is in high demand in the cash market it will go "on special" in the repo market (see explanation in Chapter 1), which again may make the issue relatively expensive.
- There may be excess demand for certain maturities for specific asset and liability management purposes (e.g., pension funds prefer longer-dated assets to help finance their long-dated liabilities).

4.2.1   Understanding swap spreads

Consequently, anyone using swaps as a benchmark will need to understand how swap rates will move. Swap rates, however, can be decomposed further into two components – a sovereign yield of a matching maturity and a swap spread.

The existence of swap spreads can be explained in terms of credit perceptions, but a change in this perception may not be the only factor that will lead to a change in spreads. One explanation for the existence of swap spreads is the relative credit strength of the bank sector with respect to the government sector. If the government is running a budget deficit and borrowing heavily while the private sector is reducing the amount of leverage in their balance sheets, swap spreads should in theory narrow. So conversely, when a government is in surplus and the private sector is borrowing more, then spreads should widen. Recall from Chapter 1 that specific counterparty credit risk for a transaction is accounted for by adjusting the interbank swap rate for a number of influencing factors. So to be clear, the relative credit strength of the banks to the government explains why swap spreads exist but that these spreads are the basis for negotiating the specific credit risk of a particular counterparty.[1]

Since the swap rate is expressed as a government benchmark yield plus a spread, it would be fair to say that the swap spread represents the risk that is unique to the swaps market. As a result, swap spreads can be isolated and trades constructed to exploit expected changes in their value. It is also important to note that swap spreads can be expressed in a number of ways. Since a swap rate is expressed as a benchmark yield plus a spread, it would be reasonable to assume that swap spreads are quoted as a positive number. However, some market practitioners define the swap spread as the benchmark yield *minus* the swap rate, resulting in a negative value. This can become particularly confusing when the market starts to use ambiguous phrases like "tightening", "narrowing" and "widening". For ease of illustration we will define swap spreads as a positive number and explain their subsequent movements in clear language!

Although credit factors can explain the existence of the swap spread, there are a number of other non-credit factors that will lead to changes in its value. Swap spread analysis can become complicated in that spreads may be influenced by a multitude of factors at any one time. For ease of illustration, our analysis assumes that all other factors are held constant.

- **The demand and supply for government bonds** – An increase in the supply of government bonds will result in a fall in prices and a corresponding rise in yields. Assuming that swap rates remain constant then the spread between the two parameters will fall. The opposite should apply for those instances where governments buy back their debt.
- **The perceived creditworthiness of the banking sector** – If there are concerns over the creditworthiness of banks then there may be a "flight to quality" with the increased purchase of government bonds. As a result, yields will fall and LIBOR may increase. Since swap rates are in effect long-dated LIBOR rates they may well increase, causing swap spreads to widen.
- **The shape of the swaps curve** – If the swap curve is very steep, it is advantageous to receive longer-term swap fixed rates and pay short-term LIBOR. This increases the demand to receive fixed, making it relatively "expensive". However, in this context expensive is defined as a fall in rates, i.e., it becomes less attractive to receive fixed. If swap rates fall and government yields are unchanged, then swap spreads will fall. If the curve is flat or perhaps inverted, floating-rate borrowers are more likely to want to pay a fixed rate. By paying fixed and receiving LIBOR in an interest rate swap, the LIBOR cash flow should neutralize their underlying floating borrowing exposure, leaving them a net payer of fixed. As a result of this activity swap rates should increase, removing the relative attractiveness of the strategy and leading to an increase in swap spreads. This relationship is shown in Figure 4.6. The observant reader will note that on certain occasions (i.e., May 2009) the swap spread became negative, implying that the banks were considered a better credit risk than the governments! However, this interpretation needs to be treated with caution. *"A swap rate, irrespective of the tenor, carries the risk of a Libor panel bank defaulting in the*

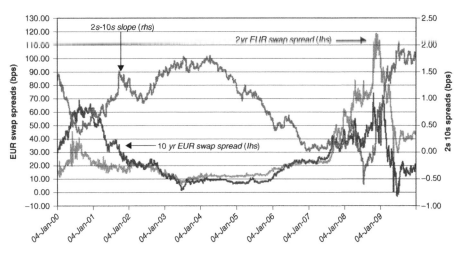

Figure 4.6   The relationship between EUR swap rates and the slope of the swap curve. January 2000–November 2009.
Source: Data sourced from Barclays Capital Live. Used with permission.

next three months as the rate is built on 3m Libor settings. If a Libor panel bank were to default, it would no longer be in the panel and Libor would still be computed based on settings by the remaining banks. The default risk would certainly rise, resulting in a higher Libor setting, but it would still reflect the risk of a Libor panel bank defaulting over the subsequent three months. The tenor of the swap – 5y or 30y – has no bearing on the implicit default risk. A government bond, on the other hand, carries the sovereign risk over the life of the bond. Hence, a negative 30y swap spread simply means that the market perceives the banking system to be healthier over three-month periods than the government over the next 30 years, a possibility that cannot be considered trivial" (Pradhan, 2010).

- **Absolute level and direction of rates** – If swap rates are expected to increase, floating-rate borrowers are more likely to look to pay fixed. Those entities in the market who would normally receive fixed will leave their positions unhedged, with the net result that swap rates will increase. Consequently, swap spreads will tend to increase when rates are trending higher and fall when interest rates are falling generally (see Figure 4.7).

Trading swap spreads

In Section 3.5.3 we considered how swaps could be used to express a view on the steepening or flattening of the swaps curve. Here we will construct a trade that will isolate the swap spread in an attempt to profit from an expected movement. In Figure 4.8 we show the evolution of the 5-year USD swap spread over a 3-month period in 2009.

Figure 4.8 highlights two particular dates that we could use to illustrate (with the benefit of hindsight) how a trader may express a view on movements in the swap spread. Suppose that for settlement on 2 November 2009, the following market rates were observed:

Swap market
- 5-year swap rate $= 2.69\%$
- DV01 $= 4.70$ (scaled by a factor of 100)

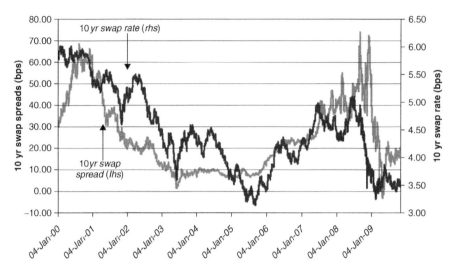

Figure 4.7 Relationship between 10-year EUR swap rates and swap spreads. January 2000–November 2009.
Source: Data sourced from Barclays Capital Live. Used with permission.

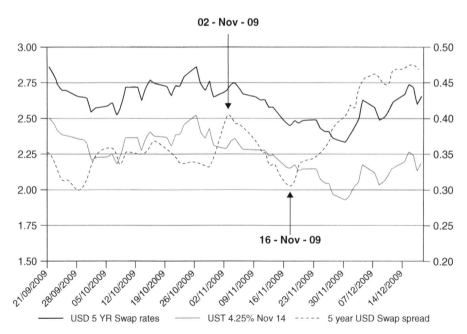

Figure 4.8 Evolution of 5-year USD swap spread (measured on the right-hand axis; September–December 2009).
Source: Data sourced from Barclays Capital Live. Used with permission.

Table 4.8   Summary of transactions required to express a view on the movement of swap spreads

View on swap spreads	Transactions
Spread expected to increase?	Pay fixed on a swap and buy a government bond
Spread expected to fall?	Receive fixed on a swap and short a government bond

UST 4.25% of November 2014

- Clean price = 109.286
- Accrued interest = 1.964 (100 × 4.25%/2 × 171/185)
- Dirty price = 111.25
- Yield to maturity = 2.286%
- DV01 = 4.98
- Repo rates = 0.05%
- Swap spread = 0.404%

The trader feels that the recent increase in the swap spread will reverse and fall back to the short-term levels recently experienced. He decides to express this view by executing a swap against a sovereign bond of the same maturity. Table 4.8 summarizes the relevant transactions.

The trader decides to execute a DV01-neutral trade between the two instruments based on a transaction size of USD 10m. The ratio of the DV01s returns a value of 0.943775 (4.70/4.98) and so the trader decides to short USD 9.5m of US Treasuries against receiving fixed on the swap with a notional of $10m and maturity of 5 years. The short US Treasury position is facilitated by using the repo market. The position is closed on 16 November when the trader believes the spread has fallen sufficiently. The positions are closed out at prevailing market rates:

Swap market
- 5-year swap rate = 2.47%

UST 4.25% of November 2014
- Clean price = 109.852
- Yield to maturity = 2.159%
- Swap spread = 0.311%

The profit and loss on the transaction is:

- Short US Treasury position = $9.5m (109.286 − 109.852)/100 = −$53,770
- Interest earned on cash leg of repo (we have assumed no haircut) = $10,568,750 × 0.05% × 14/360 = +$206
- Coupon paid on cash leg of repo = $9.5m × 4.25%/2 × 14/185 = −$15,277
- Profit and loss on close out of swap position = $10m × (2.69% − 2.47%) × 4.70 = +$103,400
- Total profit and loss = +$34,558

4.2.2   Negative swap spreads

An interesting phenomenon witnessed in the swaps markets from 2008 to 2010 was the existence on a prolonged basis of a negative swap spread (Figure 4.9).

Figure 4.9   Negative 30-year USD swap spreads (January 2008–December 2009).
Source: Data sourced from Barclays Capital Live. Used with permission.

These negative swap spreads were attributed to:

- Increased government borrowing, which caused long-term sovereign yields to rise and swap spreads to decline.
- Increased concerns over sovereign creditworthiness, which caused government bond yields to move in line with increasing sovereign CDS spreads.
- Increased corporate swap activity, which saw entities borrowing on a fixed-rate basis (say by issuing a corporate bond) and then entering into a swap where they receive fixed and pay LIBOR. The increase in demand to receive fixed places downward pressure on swap rates.
- The collapse of Lehman Brothers in September 2008 – banks that had traded with Lehman were forced to replace these transactions or otherwise face potential losses from offsetting transactions.
- As the spread fell, traders with exposures to the shape of the curve were forced to hedge these exposures. Traders who had taken a view that spreads could never go below zero decided to take their losses and unwind spread-widening trades. An example of a spread-widening trade would involve paying the 10-year rate and receiving (say) a 5-year rate. If the trader wished to unwind the position they would need to receive fixed in the 10-year maturity and pay fixed in the 5-year. The pressure to receive fixed placed further downward pressure on swap rates.
- A number of structured notes required hedging as the 30-year spread neared zero.
- Pension funds and insurance companies decided to receive fixed on 30-year swaps rather than commit cash to buy bonds as fears over deflation were being expressed by the market.

In theory, this dislocation should have disappeared very quickly but part of the problem related to concerns over counterparty creditworthiness and many institutions were unable to get internal transaction approval for such longer-dated transactions.

4.3   THE FORWARD–SWAP RELATIONSHIP

The forward–swap relationship could be illustrated by the execution of a swap spread trade using forward rather than spot-starting transactions. The transaction can be constructued using forward-starting swaps and bond futures. If the trader expected the swap spread to fall, they would:

- Sell the bond future at the current quoted price.
- Receive fixed on a forward-starting swap with an effective date equal to the maturity of the bond futures contract and a final maturity equal to the maturity of the bond that is currently cheapest to deliver.

For settlement on 2 November 2009, the following prices were observed in the market:

- CTD US Treasury 1.875% of February 2014
- Current clean price = 99.313
- Yield to maturity = 2.042%
- DV01 = 4.01
- Bond futures price = 116.453
- Futures maturity = December 2009 (US Treasury futures are deliverable on any date during the maturity month and have a nominal coupon of 6%)

The first step is to calculate the yield to maturity implied by the bond future at its current price level. This is the yield to maturity from the maturity of the bond futures to the maturity of the CTD. For ease of illustration we will use the final delivery date of the future (31 December 2009) as the settlement date and the CTD matures on 28 February 2014. Pricing the bond using these parameters, the implied yield to maturity is 1.872%. At the time, a 5-year swap effective in 2 months' time was trading at 2.72%, returning a forward swap spread of 0.848%. Similar to the swap spread example in the previous section, the trader would create a DV01-neutral trade to reflect his view on how the forward swap spread would evolve. This could be unwound at a suitable point in the future after the anticipated spread had moved.

4.4   OPTIONS AND TRADING VOLATILITY

4.4.1   Expressing views on market direction and volatility

In simple terms the objective of trading options is to ensure that more premium is received than paid. From this it follows that a trader needs to understand the different components of an option premium and how it is likely to move. In Chapter 2 we argued that an option's premium comprised intrinsic and time value. The intrinsic value of the option is driven by changes in the underlying market, while the two primary drivers of time value are implied volatility and the passage of time. From this it makes sense to suggest that a trader needs to develop views on expected movements in the price of the underlying asset and its implied volatility (Figure 4.10). It is difficult to have a "view" on time, although there are certain option strategies that will exploit the different speeds at which options decay as a result of the passage of time. Tompkins (1994) develops a simple matrix that captures the different ways in which a trader can express views on directional movements and/or movements in implied volatility. We have adopted a similar approach, but emphasizing one of our key themes – "what is the most effective way to express a particular view on the market?" For purposes of space we have decided to omit a number of strategies (e.g., butterflies and time spreads as well as those that are neutral to both direction and volatility), but we highly recommend the Tompkins text to those readers who wish to analyse these strategies in detail.

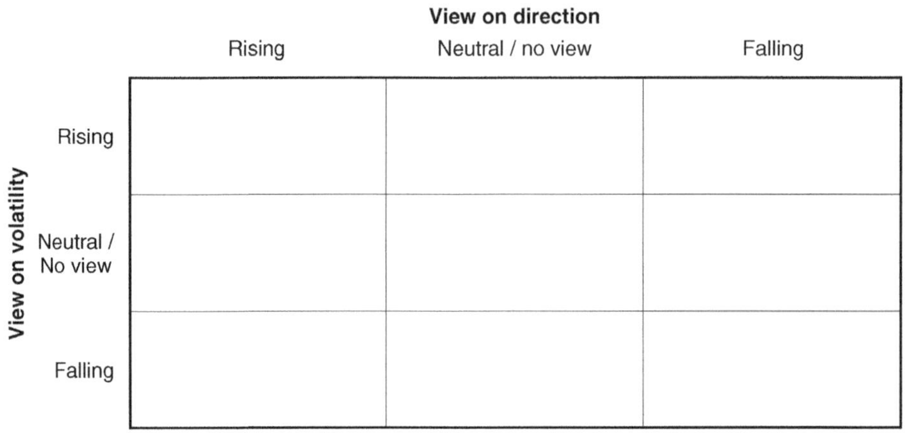
View on direction
Rising
Neutral / no view
Falling
View on volatility
Rising
Neutral / No view
Falling

Figure 4.10 Option-trading matrix for options.

Building-block strategies

The matrix could be populated with the building-block strategies as follows:

- *Buy the underlying asset*: Gives the trader no exposure to implied volatility but the purchase of the asset implies the trader believes that its price will rise.
- *Sell the underlying asset*: No exposure to implied volatility but bearish on price.
- *Buy a call option*: Given the call option has positive vega and positive delta this strategy sits in the "rising volatility, rising price" part of the matrix.
- *Buy a put option*: This position is delta negative and vega positive, suggesting that the trader believes the underlying price will fall and that this will be associated with an increase in implied volatility.
- *Sell a call*: The option position has negative delta and negative vega and so sits in the "falling volatility, falling price" section of the matrix.
- *Sell a put*: The option position has positive delta and negative delta and so sits in the "falling volatility, rising price" part of the matrix.

These positions are represented in Figure 4.11.

Directional strategies

Directional strategies can be constructed using either a single option or combinations of options that are referred to as "vertical spreads". Somewhat confusingly, the market refers to these trades as "call spreads" (to express a bullish sentiment) or "put spreads" (to express a bearish sentiment). Technically, this is somewhat ambiguous as vertical spreads to express bullish views on the market ("bull spreads") can be constructed using either calls or puts. Similarly, bear spreads can be constructed using calls or puts, but as we will see the strategies are not exactly equal.

Figure 4.11   Option-trading matrix for options incorporating the building-block strategies.

Bull spreads
Calls: Buy a low-strike ITM call; sell a high-strike OTM call. A premium is payable and represents the most you can lose.

Puts: Buy a low-strike OTM put; sell a high-strike ITM put. A premium is receivable but represents the most you can make.

Bear spreads
Calls: Sell a low-strike ITM call option; buy a high-strike OTM call. A premium is receivable and represents the most you can make.

Puts: Sell a low-strike OTM put; buy a high-strike ITM put. A premium is payable but represents the most you can lose.

For both sets of strategies where the premium is receivable the "at-expiry" maximum loss is higher and maximum profit lower than those strategies where the premium is payable.

To illustrate the concepts, consider the following examples. We will assume that the spot and forward price is 100 (i.e., no net carry on the position), implied volatility of 20% and 90 days to expiration.

Figure 4.12 illustrates the net payoff from selling a put option at a strike of 99 and buying a put with a strike of 101. The notional amount on both options is 20,000 units of the underlying asset. Using an option pricing model, the initial premium is 20,600. So the maximum profit is the difference between the two strikes less the net premium paid. In this case the maximum profit is 40,000 (101 − 99 × 20,000 units of the underlying asset − i.e., the notional on the option) minus the initial premium of 20,600, which returns a value of 19,400. The maximum loss is the initial premium of 20,600.

The same strategy could have been constructed by selling a call at a strike of 99 and buying a call at a strike of 101. This would have generated an initial income of 19,200,

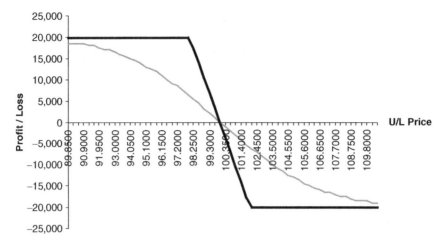

Figure 4.12 Example of net payoff from a "99 – 101 bear spread". Current underlying price is 100. Straight lines illustrate the "at-expiry" profit and loss; curved line represents profit and loss prior to expiry.

which would be the maximum profit on the strategy. The maximum loss if the market had rallied would be 20,800.

From a "Greek" point of view, the bear spread position is initially:

- Mildly delta negative (the delta on the purchased put is slightly greater than that of the sold put).
- Gamma neutral (the sold option is gamma negative, while the purchased option is gamma positive. Given that they have the same maturity and are equidistant from the strike, the gamma exposure is neutral).
- Vega neutral (the sold option is vega negative; the purchased option is vega positive).
- Theta neutral.

As the price of the underlying asset rises or falls beyond both strike prices, the deltas on the options will net to zero. That is, the position will not change in value for subsequent changes in price. Figure 4.12 also illustrates that the time decay does not set in until close to expiry. If the underlying price has fallen, the position will display positive theta as the sold option is dominating. If the underlying price has risen, the position will display negative theta as the purchased will dominate the exposure.

Figure 4.13 shows the "at-expiry" profit and loss for a bull spread constructed from call options. The maximum profit is the difference between the two strikes less the net premium paid.

The bull spread is initially:

- Mildly delta positive.
- Gamma neutral.
- Vega neutral.
- Theta neutral.

Similar to the bear spreads, the deltas will net to zero for large movements in the underlying price. Additionally, time decay will not start to set in until close to maturity and will either be positive or negative depending on how the underlying price has moved.

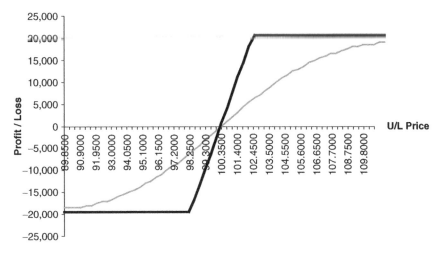

Figure 4.13   Example of net payoff from a "99 – 101 bull spread". Current underlying price is 100. Straight lines illustrate "at-expiry" profit and loss; curved line represents profit and loss prior to expiry.

Table 4.9   Summary of vertical spread trades

	Calls	Puts
Bullish view	Debit strategy *"buy a call spread"*	Credit strategy *"sell a put spread"*
Bearish view	Credit strategy *"sell a call spread"*	Debit strategy *"buy a put spread"*

The analysis can become even more confusing when practitioners talk about buying or selling call or put spreads. If a trader were to construct a bull spread using calls, they would buy a lower-strike option and sell a higher-strike option. However, the counterparty to this structure is therefore selling a lower-strike call and buying a higher-strike call, which is a bear call spread!

One way of clarifying the situation would be to map out the different strategies and whether they involve the receipt or payment of a premium (Table 4.9).

Figure 4.14 shows the position within the trading matrix of the bear and bull spreads illustrated in Figures 4.12 and 4.13, respectively.

Throughout the text our emphasis has been on considering the most effective way to express a particular view on the market. Note that the bull and bear spreads fall into the same category as buying and selling the underlying, respectively. So what are the relative merits? We can analyse this in terms of the upfront payment or receipt and the profit and loss potential.

Scenario: rising price/neutral volatility

Upfront cost/income

- Buying the underlying asset will require the trader to borrow the cost of the asset upfront.
- A bull call spread will require a payment of premium but this will be smaller than buying the asset outright.
- A bull put spread will generate a payment of premium.

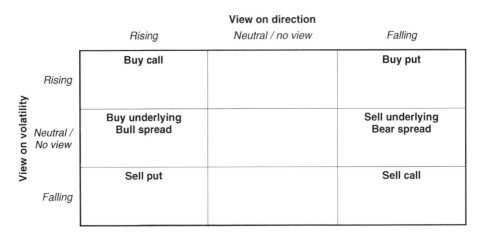

Figure 4.14   Option-trading matrix incorporating directional strategies.

Profit and loss potential
- Purchase of the asset offers unlimited upside or downside.
- Bull spreads have a limited profit and limited loss profile.
- Spreads that involve the receipt of premium have a less favourable at-expiry risk/reward profile.

Scenario: falling price/neutral volatility
Upfront cost/income
- Selling the underlying asset will generate an incoming cash flow equal to the market value of the asset.
- A bear put spread will require a payment of premium.
- A bear call spread will generate a receipt of premium, although less than an outright sale.

Profit and loss potential
- Sale of the asset offers unlimited upside or downside.
- Bear spreads have a limited profit and loss profile.
- Spreads that involve the receipt of premium have a less favourable at-expiry risk/reward profile.

Volatility strategies

Volatility strategies aim to exploit a view on either the implied or realized volatility of an asset. These types of trades can be set up as buying strategies (i.e., volatility will increase) or selling strategies (i.e., volatility will decrease). In addition, there are strategies that will mix an element of directional exposure with a view on volatility.

A classic error of interpretation relates to motivation behind the purchase of a call option. Many people look at this trade in one dimension, arguing it would be appropriate if the trader simply believed that the market would rise. Although this is correct given that the option is delta positive, it will also show a profit and loss from a change in implied volatility (i.e., vega).

Perhaps the classic volatility strategy is a straddle which is constructed as the sale or purchase of a call and a put, typically struck at the money forward with the same strike and maturity. So a trader quoting a volatility bid–offer spread as, say, 10.5% – 10.7% is indicating that at their bid price they will buy an ATM straddle, while their offer represents the price where they will sell the straddle.

The buying volatility position (a long straddle) from a Greek perspective is initially:

- Delta neutral (the positive delta from the purchased call option nets off with the negative delta of the put option).
- Gamma positive (since both options are purchased, the position is "double gamma" positive).
- Vega positive (similar to gamma, both purchased options are vega positive).
- Theta negative (both purchased options display negative theta).

A short straddle (i.e., sell a call, sell a put) is initially:

- Delta neutral.
- Gamma negative.
- Vega negative.
- Theta negative.

Diagrammatically, the net position of a short straddle can be shown as in Figure 4.15.

In this strategy the position is initially delta neutral-ish but the net delta is not exactly zero. If the position is struck at-the-money forward then there will be a small net delta exposure. Some traders select a strike that returns an exact initial zero delta exposure.

Figure 4.15 illustrates that if the underlying price rises, the position will become delta negative (the short call option dominates the exposure) and if the underlying price falls, the position will become delta positive (the short put option dominates the exposure). Neither of the outcomes is desirable and the position will lose money for significant movements in the underling price. As the position approaches expiry it will rise in value due to the positive

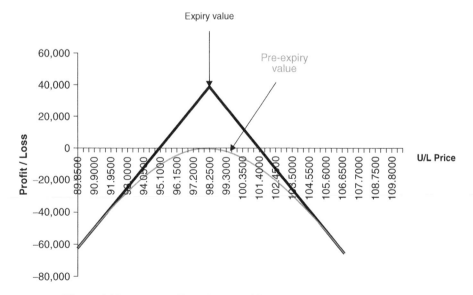

Figure 4.15   Net payoff for short straddle at expiry and prior to expiry.

effect of theta. However, the gamma exposure will also increase, making the profit and loss on the position very sensitive to significant changes in the underlying price. However, the strategy is impacted by both implied and actual volatility. If there is a change in implied volatility but no change in the spot price, then the curved pre-expiry profit and loss profile will rise or fall vertically. If the current spot price changes (actual volatility) then the profit or loss profile will move along the horizontal axis. The profit and loss profile for a long straddle is shown in Figure 4.16. Its position within the trading matrix is shown in Figure 4.17.

However, two popular strategies to exploit the skew/smile are strangles and risk reversals.

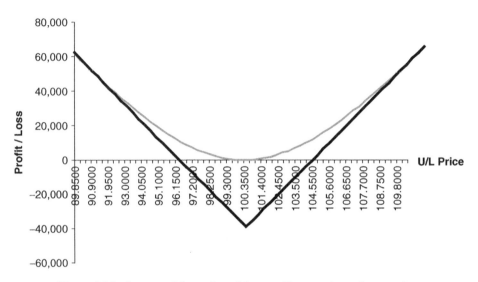

Figure 4.16   Long straddle profit and loss profile at expiry and pre-expiry.

	View on direction		
	Rising	*Neutral / no view*	*Falling*
Rising	**Buy call**	**Buy straddle**	**Buy put**
Neutral / No view	**Buy underlying Bull spread**		**Sell underlying Bear spread**
Falling	**Sell put**	**Sell straddle**	**Sell call**

(Left axis label: **View on volatility**)

Figure 4.17   Option-trading matrix incorporating volatility strategies.

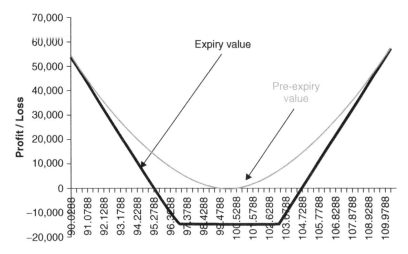

Figure 4.18 The profit and loss profile of a long strangle position.

Strangles are normally quoted for a particular delta value. For example, in the FX market one common quotation is for a "25 delta strangle". So at the bid price the trader will buy a call with the strike set at a level equal to a delta of 25 and buy a put with a strike set also to return a delta of the same value. Since the deltas for the long call and put are positive and negative, respectively, the position is initially delta neutral.

Figure 4.18 shows the net positions of a long strangle, at and prior to expiry. It is the combination of the purchase of a call and a put with the same maturity but with the strikes set out-of-the-money at levels that equate to a 25 delta.

Since both options have a delta of 25, the position is initially delta neutral. Large movements in the underlying price will result in an exposure that is favourable for the direction of the underlying price movement. That is, the position becomes delta positive in a rising market and delta negative in a falling market. However, the position will not show a profit for small price movements. Since both options have been purchased, the position is both gamma and vega positive, but since the options are struck OTM these risks are lower than those of the straddle. This position may show a profit as the options approach expiry since the smile/skew has a tendency to become more pronounced over time.[2] However, the position will lose money as a function of time since both options are theta negative. As the position is struck OTM, the cost is less than a straddle.

The profit and loss profile of a short strangle is shown in Figure 4.19. This is constructed by selling a call and a put with both strikes set at a 25 delta.

The position of the strangles within our option-trading matrix is shown in Figure 4.20.

We can now compare the two volatility strategies in terms of upfront cost/income and the profit and loss potential.

Scenario: neutral price/rising volatility

Upfront cost/income

• Straddle requires a greater initial premium payment than strangle.

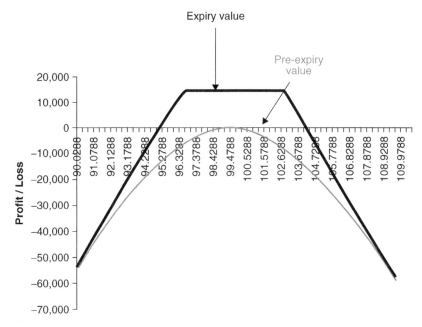

Figure 4.19   The profit and loss profile of a short strangle position.

View on direction

		Rising	Neutral / no view	Falling
View on volatility	Rising	**Buy call**	**Buy straddle** **Buy strangle**	**Buy put**
	Neutral / No view	**Buy underlying** **Bull spread**		**Sell underlying** **Bear spread**
	Falling	**Sell put**	**Sell straddle** **Sell strangle**	**Sell call**

Figure 4.20   Option-trading matrix with strangle exposures added.

Profit and loss potential
- Straddles will break even faster than strangles.
- Profits on both positions are theoretically unlimited (although since prices cannot go negative there is a lower boundary for downside price movements).
- If the market does not move, the straddle will lose more value from time decay than the strangle.

Scenario: neutral price/falling volatility

Upfront cost/income
- Straddle generates the greatest initial premium income.

Profit and loss potential
- Straddles will start to incur losses before strangles.
- Losses on both positions are theoretically unlimited (although since prices cannot go negative there is a lower boundary for downside price movements).
- If the market does not move, the straddle will gain more than the strangle in terms of time decay.

A comparison of the at-expiry profit and loss profiles is provided in Figure 4.21.

The "risk reversal" is a popular options strategy that can be used to express views on how the skew may evolve. Risk reversals measure how much the market is willing to pay for an OTM put against the equivalent OTM call or vice versa. It is usually designed to exploit the change in the spread between the volatility of an OTM call and put.

Suppose the market believed that the underlying price was going to fall. As a result, OTM puts would be in greater demand and so their price in volatility terms would increase. At the same time, traders would seek to finance this purchase by selling OTM calls and so their price in implied volatility terms would decrease. Consequently, the implied volatility for OTM puts rises in relation to OTM calls (see Figure 4.22).

Risk reversals can be used to express a bullish or a bearish sentiment. A bullish risk reversal is used when the trader anticipates a rise in OTM call volatility relative to OTM put volatility as a consequence of an anticipated rise in the underlying price. Typically, it is constructed by the purchase of a 25 delta call and the sale of a 25 delta put. However, the combination of these two options will leave the trader overall delta positive and since this is classed as a volatility trade, he will need to delta hedge this exposure by selling the underlying asset. A bearish risk reversal is used when the trader anticipates a rise in

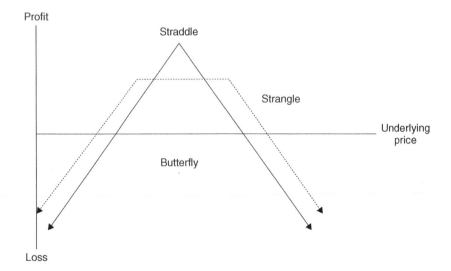

Figure 4.21   Comparison of "at-expiry" profit and loss profile for short straddle and strangle.

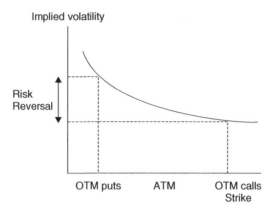

Figure 4.22   Example of risk reversal.

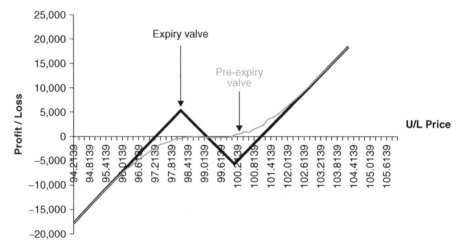

Figure 4.23   The payoff on a bullish risk reversal.

OTM put volatility relative to OTM call volatility as a result of an anticipated downward movement in the underlying price. Typically, it is constructed as the purchase of a 25 delta put and the sale of a 25 delta call with a delta hedge to achieve overall delta neutrality. The strategy is almost (but not exactly) zero premium.

Certain markets, such as foreign exchange, have a "standard" risk-reversal trade which is the 1-month maturity with the options struck at a 25 delta. However, the fixed income market is much more varied, with deltas traded at different levels (e.g., 25 or 50) and with a variety of maturities.

Figure 4.23 illustrates the profit and loss profile for a bullish risk reversal at and prior to expiry.

It is important to note that the strategy is not aiming to benefit from a move in the market price per se, since the position is delta neutral, but rather the change in implied volatility as a result of the anticipated directional move.

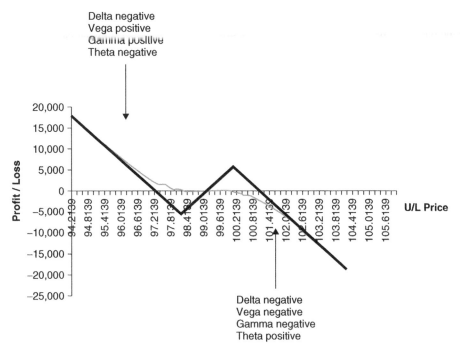

Figure 4.24   Payoff profile of a bearish risk reversal.

The position is initially neutral with respect to all of the Greeks. However, these values will evolve as the underlying price changes. For example in Figure 4.23, if the spot rate increases the position becomes delta positive, gamma positive, vega positive and theta negative. However, if the price of the underlying asset falls, the position becomes delta positive, gamma negative, vega negative and theta positive. This is one reason why the strategy is called a risk reversal; a change in the direction of the underlying price will cause the exposure on the position to reverse in terms of the signs (with the exception of delta).

Similar to the bullish risk reversal, the bearish position is constructed to be initially market-risk neutral. However, a movement in the underlying price will cause one of the option positions to dominate. This can cause the market risk of the profile to change (Figure 4.24).

Risk reversals are quoted on a bid–offer spread basis and so one side of the quote represents a single price for two transactions (i.e., a spread transaction). The quotation follows normal market convention as the bid price is lower than the offer price. The quote will indicate though whether the price is calculated as calls minus puts or puts minus calls. For example, if the quote was given as "0.4/0.5 calls over puts", this would mean that the outright volatility quote for calls is higher than that for the equivalent puts. So at the bid price, dealers are willing to pay a net 0.4% volatility to buy an OTM call AND sell an OTM put. At the offer price the dealers are willing to sell an OTM call and buy an OTM put to earn a net volatility spread of 0.5%. To make the concept clearer, consider the example in Table 4.10. The values have been exaggerated for ease of illustration.

Table 4.10   Constructing a risk-reversal quotation

Option type	25 delta calls	ATM strikes	25 delta puts
Option quote	26.00% − 28.00%	20.00% − 22.00%	23.00% − 25.00%
Interpretation	Buy 25 delta calls at 26.00%	Buy volatility at 20% (i.e., buy ATM calls or puts)	Buy 25 delta puts at 23.00%
	Sell 25 delta calls at 28.00%	Sell volatility at 22% (i.e., sell ATM calls or puts)	Sell 25 delta puts at 25.00%

Table 4.11   Decomposing the risk-reversal quotation

Bid %	Offer %
Will pay away 1% volatility spread to buy a 25 delta call at 26% and sell a 25 delta put at 25%	Will earn 5% volatility spread to sell a delta call at 28% and buy a 25 delta put at 23%

A dealer anticipating an upward movement in the market would quote his risk-reversal trade as "1% − 5% calls over puts". The trader has highlighted that the OTM calls are more expensive than the OTM puts, and indicates to a market user that the trader is anticipating an increase in the underlying market. Risk-reversal bid–offer spreads are constructed by netting off the bid on one side against the offer on the other. A breakdown of the quotation is shown in Table 4.11.

Some volatility strategies will tend to lean in one direction, appearing to be something of a hybrid strategy. There are four strategies that fall into this category of trade: two types of buying trades and two types of selling trades. The four hybrid volatility trading strategies are shown in Figure 4.25.

To get a sense of how these structures are created and their market risk exposure, let us consider the call ratio back spread shown in the upper left-hand quadrant of Figure 4.25. The position is created by selling one call option with a low strike (i.e., an ITM option) and buying two OTM call options with a higher strike. This could be thought of as a bear call spread (i.e., sell a low-strike call and buy a high-strike call) overlaid with the purchase of another high-strike call. This is a "credit" strategy as premium is received at the inception of the transaction. Typically the strike and the maturities for this trade are selected to ensure that the position is initially delta neutral, but the purchased options will tend to dominate initially and so their exposure will resemble the Greeks for a long call option.

The initial value of the Greeks is:

- Delta neutral.
- Gamma positive.
- Vega positive.
- Theta negative.

If the market price rises, the position becomes delta positive and will show a profit. If the market price of the underlying asset falls, then the position will also show a profit but

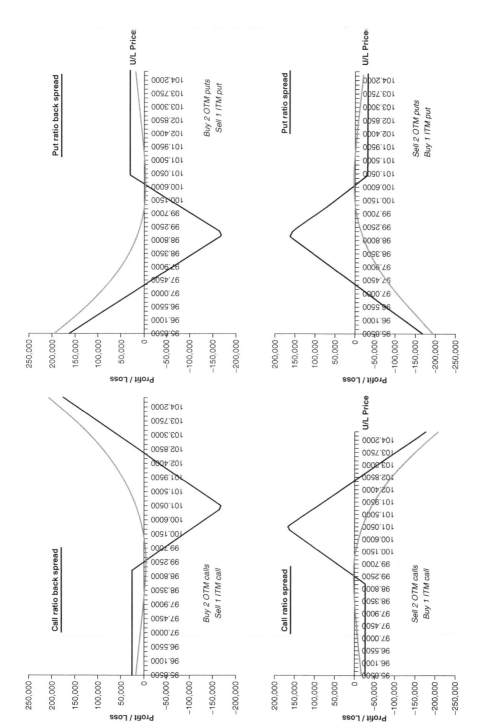

Figure 4.25 Hybrid volatility strategies. The diagram shows the "at-expiry" and pre-expiry (the curved payoff) profit and loss.

| | **View on direction** | | |
	Rising	*Neutral / no view*	*Falling*
Rising	**Buy call** **Call ratio back spread**	**Buy straddle** **Buy strangle**	**Buy put** **Put ratio back spread**
Neutral / *No view*	**Buy underlying** **Bull spread**		**Sell underlying** **Bear spread**
Falling	**Sell put** **Put ratio spread**	**Sell straddle** **Sell strangle**	**Sell call** **Call ratio spread**

View on volatility

Figure 4.26   The option-trading matrix incorporating the hybrid strategies

will become delta neutral. If implied volatility rises, the position will also show a profit. The impact of time on the strategy is dependent on how the underlying price moves prior to maturity. If the underlying price rises, the purchased calls will dominate and the position will display negative theta. However, if the underlying price falls, it is possible for the position to display positive theta due to the impact of the sold option.

Figure 4.26 incorporates these hybrid strategies within the trading matrix.

The ratio back spreads fall into the same box as the call and puts as they have very similar initial Greek exposures. For example, the call option is delta positive, while the call ratio back spread is delta neutral (but will become delta positive if the underlying price rises). The key differences between the strategies are as follows:

- The call option will cost money whereas the call back spread will generate premium income.
- If the market price falls significantly, the premium is lost on the call but the hybrid strategy generates a profit.
- If the market doesn't move, the hybrid strategy will lose more than the call option.

4.4.2   Assessing volatility: cheap or rich?

So far we have considered option strategies within a simple two-dimensional context; how they can be used to express views on implied volatility and/or the direction of the underlying asset. Natenberg (1994) reframes the issue and poses a different question: "given the current volatility climate, what's the right strategy?" This is based on the principle that although implied volatility is used to price an option, its value to a trader is determined by how he expects future volatility to evolve. This relationship could be described as follows:

- *High value, low price?* This suggests that implied volatility is low with respect to expected future volatility. In this scenario the trader would be more likely to be a buyer of options.
- *Low value, high price?* This means that implied volatility is high with respect to expected future volatility. In this scenario the trader would be more likely to be a seller of options.

Of course at the time the trade is initiated, future volatility is unknown but a trader may develop a view on its likely evolution. Natenberg (1994) points out that a trader may wish to consider several factors to assess volatility in order to determine if it is trading "cheap" or "rich" relative to its norm:

- What is the long-term mean volatility of the underlying contract? (Implied volatility tends to be mean reverting.)
- What is the trend in the recent historical volatility?
- What has been the recent trend in historical volatility in relation to the mean volatility?
- Where is implied volatility currently trading and what is its general trend?
- What is the spread between implied and historical volatility?
- What is the general relationship between implied volatility and the underlying price?
- Is the trader considering shorter or longer-term option maturities?
- How stable has volatility been?

Regardless of which method is used to assess volatility there are some general principles that could be followed. These are illustrated below with respect to the trading of swaptions (see Table 4.12).

Table 4.12   Principles for trading swaptions relative to views on volatility

	Implied volatility is rich	Implied volatility is cheap
Bullish on rates (i.e., rates expected to fall)	Sell payers	Buy receivers
Bearish on rates (i.e., rates expected to increase)	Sell receivers	Buy payers

One interesting side note to this analysis is a shorthand formula suggested by Ray (1993):

$$\text{Standard deviation} = \sqrt{\frac{\pi}{2}} \times \text{Mean absolute deviation}$$

Suppose a trader saw an option trading with an annualized implied volatility of 8.68%. This would translate into a 1-month value of 2.51% ($8.68\%/\sqrt{12}$). Inserting these values into the equation and solving for the mean absolute deviation would return a value of two basis points. If the trader believed that on average the asset was going to move by more than $+/-$ 2 basis points over this period, he would consider the option cheap.

4.4.3   Expressing views on volatility of volatility

In the same way as we can trade the volatility of rates it is also possible to trade the volatility of volatility. This is sometimes referred to as "vol of vol" or "volvol". When we trade vega, we are looking at how the premium will change for a change in implied volatility. When we trade volvol, we are considering how vega will change with respect to a change in implied volatility. In Chapter 3 (e.g., Figure 3.8) we introduced the concept of vega-related Greeks and defined vol gamma ("volga", "vomma") as a metric that measured the change in vega for a change in implied volatility. It was argued that vega was constant only for ATM strikes and it is this variability of vega that the volvol strategies attempt to exploit.

The trades needed to execute this view of the market will depend on whether the trader wished to take a long or short exposure to vol of vol.

- Long vol of vol: Long a strangle and short a straddle.
- Short vol of vol: Short a strangle and long a straddle.

There are also some variations on the trade, which involve the purchase/sale of a wide strangle against a sale/purchase of a narrow strangle.

The trade is executed with vega-weighted notional amounts, so the initial net position is vega neutral. In this way we gain exposure to the "wings" of the vol smile. To illustrate the concept, consider a long "vol of vol" position. If implied volatility for the OTM and ITM options increases (i.e., the smile becomes more pronounced), then the position will show a profit. If implied volatility across all strikes changes, then since the position is vega neutral it should not show a significant profit or loss as the gain or loss on one option position will be broadly offset by a loss/gain on the other.

However, the position is not delta neutral and so additionally the trader will need to dynamically delta hedge this exposure.

4.4.4   The relationship between volatility and the underlying asset

In this section we continue our fixed income focus and consider the relationship specifically between interest rate options and their underlying assets.

Caps/floors and swaps

A cap structure is a strip of OTC interest rate call options on a series of forward rates, all traded with a single strike. The cap gives the buyer protection against an agreed index or reference rate such as LIBOR of a stated maturity rising above a pre-agreed strike rate. The term "cap" is the collective name for the component options, which are individually referred to as caplets. The premium payable on a cap structure is simply the sum of the individual caplet premia. A floor gives the holder protection against an agreed reference rate of interest falling below a pre-agreed strike. Again, a floor is a collective name for the component options which individually are referred to as floorlets. The mechanics of the floor are the same as the cap, but the payoff to a holder would only occur if the reference interest rate was less than the strike rate.

There are two approaches to determine if a cap/floor is in-, out-of or at-the-money. Firstly, each individual option (i.e., caplet/floorlet) could be judged with respect to each of the current forward rates for the period that it covers. Using this process would mean that some options will be in-the-money and some will be out-of-the-money. The alternative way of assessing the value of the structure is to consider the "moneyness" of the entire structure. In Chapter 2 we argued that an interest rate swap could be constructed from a series of forward rates using either FRAs or futures. Since a cap/floor is a strip of options on a series of forward rates, there will be a relationship between swaps and caps/floors.

Since cap/floor structures exclude the option for the spot-starting period, it is more accurate to say that their "moneyness" should be assessed relative to a forward-starting swap of equivalent maturity.

This point can be extended further by considering the concept of cap–floor parity. This concept can be stated as follows:

- Buying a cap and selling a floor at the same strike, maturity and notional amount is equal to paying fixed, receiving floating on a forward-starting interest rate swap, where the fixed rate is equal to the strike rate of the two options.

Buy cap + sell floor = pay fixed on a forward-starting swap

- Similarly, selling a cap and buying a floor at the same strike, maturity and notional amount is equal to receiving fixed, paying floating on a forward-starting interest rate swap, where the fixed rate is equal to the strike rate of the two options.

Sell cap + buy floor = receive fixed on a forward-starting swap

Swaptions and swaps

In the same way that there is a relationship between caps/floors and swaps, a similar identity exists for swaps and swaptions ("swaption parity"):

- Buying a receiver swaption and selling a payer swaption at the same strike, maturity and notional amount is equal to receiving fixed, paying floating on a forward-starting interest rate swap, where the fixed rate is equal to the strike rate of the two options.

Buy receiver swaption + sell payer swaption = receive fixed on forward-starting swap

- Selling a receiver swaption and buying a payer swaption at the same strike, maturity and notional amount is equal to receiving fixed, paying floating on a forward-starting interest rate swap, where the fixed rate is equal to the strike rate of the two options.

Sell receiver swaption + buy payer swaption = pay fixed on forward-starting swap

Exploiting the relationship between swaps, swaptions and caps/floors

The relationships established by cap/floor parity and swaption parity would allow a trader to identify if one of the constituent components is mispriced. A trader would simply use the parity relationships to combine products such that the overpriced asset is sold and the underpriced asset purchased.

It is also possible to trade the relationship between caps/floors and swaptions but we need to consider one extra component – correlation.

As the shape of the yield curve evolves, yields at different maturities on the curve do not always move by the same amount or necessarily in the same direction.

One trading perspective views a cap/floor as a basket of options on individual forward rates, whereas a swaption is an option on a basket of rates. A basket of options is more valuable than an option on a basket unless all underlying forwards are perfectly correlated.

The difference in value between a cap and a swaption spanning the same set of forwards provides a measure of the implied correlation between these forwards.

To understand the significance of this statement let us take a side step to briefly analyse basket options. A basket option is a single option that pays off based on the performance of one or more underlying assets. The payoff on a two-asset basket call option is:

Notional × Max (market price of basket at expiry − strike rate of basket, 0)

The strike rate on a basket call option is calculated as follows:

(Strike rate asset A × weight) + (strike rate asset B × weight)

The market price of the basket option at expiry is:

(Expiry price of asset A × weight) + (expiry price of asset B × weight)

Basket options are priced on the premise that within a particular basket there may be offsetting risks. One central concept of finance is that the risk within a diversified portfolio of assets is less than the sum of the individual risks. This means that the correlations between the underlying assets in the basket work as a form of natural hedge.

Estimating the implied volatility of options on the individual components is usually relatively straightforward, as there is often a deep liquid market. However, deriving the implied volatility for a basket option is more involved and so principles of modern portfolio theory have been adapted. The volatility of the basket is given here for a two-asset portfolio:

$$\sigma_{\text{basket}} = \sqrt{\left(w_{x_1}^2 \sigma_{x_1}^2\right) + \left(w_{x_2}^2 \sigma_{x_2}^2\right) + 2 \times \left(w_{x_1} w_{x_2} \rho_{x_1 x_2} \sigma_{x_1} \sigma_{x_2}\right)}$$

where:

$\sigma_{x_1}^2$ = variance of asset 1

$\sigma_{x_2}^2$ = variance of asset 2

$\rho_{x_1 x_2}$ = correlation between asset 1 and asset 2

σ_{x_1} = volatility of asset 1

σ_{x_2} = volatility of asset 2

w_{x_1} = proportion of asset 1

w_{x_2} = proportion of asset 2

The formula shows that one extra component needs to be taken into account when calculating the volatility of a basket, and that is the correlation existing between the different underlying assets. The same formula can be adapted for multiple assets, except there would then be multiple correlations that need to be taken into account. The equation illustrates that as the correlation between the assets tends towards +1, the volatility will increase, which will lead to an increase in the option premium.

As the correlation decreases the assets have a tendency to move in opposite directions. As a result, if one of the assets is ITM, the other may well be OTM. This will reduce the potential payoff and so the premium will fall.

Trading the "wedge"

The implication from analysing basket options is that, all other things being equal, caps/floors (a basket of options) should trade with a higher volatility than swaptions (an option on a basket of short term rates from which the underlying swap derives its value) unless all the underlying forward rates are perfectly correlated. Caps/floors and swaptions are often quoted in the interbank market as straddles. So a bid–offer spread expressed in volatility terms can be interpreted as follows:

Bid	Offer
Buy a cap and buy a floor	Sell a cap and sell a floor
Buy a payer and buy a receiver	Sell a payer and sell a receiver

The transactions would be done with the same strike, maturity and notional amount.

The market uses the concept of the volatility wedge as a measure of the implied correlation amongst short forward rates. The wedge is defined as the volatility of a cap/floor minus the volatility of a swaption. Consequently, an increase in correlation would reduce ("cheapen") the wedge differential due to higher swaption volatility, while a decrease in the correlation would increase ("richen") the wedge.

To illustrate the concept, consider the following intuitive explanation. Suppose some investors are uncertain about the future direction of Central Bank interest rates. They decide that the optimum way to profit from this is to execute the following trade:

- Buy a portfolio of options on short forward rates (i.e., either a cap or a floor).
- Sell a single option on the average of these rates (i.e., a swaption) to partly finance the purchase.

For ease of illustration, let us assume that we are considering four consecutive short-term rates each of which are 5%, with the result that the average of these four rates is also 5%. The investor buys a portfolio of four options, each struck at 5%, while financing this by selling one option on the average of these rates (also 5%).

The trade will pay off if all the short rates are different from the 5% strike but the average remains the same. Suppose that two of the rates fall to 4%, while the other two rates increase to 6%. The average is still 5% and so the short option does not incur any loss. Two components of the portfolio of options will gain, while two will expire worthless. The further the short rates are from each other, the more the portfolio will earn. The profit and loss will therefore be the payoff on the portfolio of options minus the initial outlay.

However, the trade will not pay off if the short rates trend in the same direction. For example, if all the rates increase by 1% the payoff on the portfolio of options will be matched by a payoff on the single option. As a result, the trade will lose its initial outlay.

From this example we can see that the position will display maximum profits when the short rates are negatively correlated. So if Central Bank rate action (i.e., uncertainty over the timing of rate moves and the eventual new steady-state level of interest rates) causes the curve to steepen or invert, the strategy will pay off. Put another way, in this example there should be an outperformance of cap/floor volatility relative to swaption volatility.

From this we could derive a series of trade possibilities:

Correlation expected to decrease?
• Buy cap/floor straddles and sell swaption straddles.

Correlation expected to increase?
• Sell cap/floor straddles and buy swaption straddles.

Figure 4.27 shows the "5 × 10 wedge" (a benchmark point) for the period January 2004 to January 2010. It is worth spending a moment considering the nomenclature used to express these trades. A "5 × 10 wedge" comprises two trades:

• A 5-year option into a 5-year swaption straddle (normally referred to as a 5yr 5yr swaption).
• A 5-year cap/floor straddle which becomes effective in 5 years' time (normally referred to as a 5 × 10 cap/floor straddle using terminology taken from the FRA market).

Typically, cap/floor vols trade above swaption volatilities and so the value of the wedge is normally positive. This means that when correlations increase, the wedge decreases in value due to higher swaption volatility and when correlations decline, the wedge increases due to lower swaption volatility. The wedge is close to flat or par level (i.e., swaption vol is close to cap/floor vol) when correlations are approaching the 100% level.

Figure 4.27 shows that the wedge has experienced negative values for prolonged periods of time, contrary to what the theory would suggest. A negative value for the wedge would suggest an increase in swaption volatility and a correlation in excess of 100%. However, in wedge analysis the correlation analysis is more intuitive than it is formal. As a result, the relationship does not conform to any "no-arbitrage" pricing rules, which is why the implied correlation could be in excess of 100%.[3]

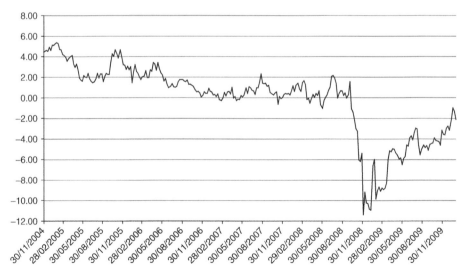

Figure 4.27 The 5 x 10 wedge. Data expressed as basis points per annum, normalized volatility.
Source: Data sourced from Barclays Capital Live. Used with permission.

Swaption triangles

Similar to interest rates there is a term structure for volatility which gives rise to a number of different trading opportunities. Forward volatility is a value for implied volatility known today but which applies to a future time period. In Section 2.3.4 we introduced a way of pricing a forward rate of interest from two spot-starting rates. One way of calculating the forward volatility is presented by Tompkins (1994):

$$\sigma_F = \sqrt{\frac{[(t_L - t_0) \times \sigma_L^2 - (t_S - t_0) \times \sigma_s^2]}{(t_L - t_S)}}$$

where:

σ_F = forward volatility from period t_S to t_L

t_L = number of days from trade date to long-dated option expiry

t_S = number of days from trade date to short-dated option expiry

t_0 = trade date

σ_L^2 = implied variance from trade date to long-dated option expiry

σ_S^2 = variance from trade date to short-dated option expiry

To illustrate the concept, consider the following simple example. Suppose that a 3-month option (90-day expiry) is trading at an implied volatility of 10% p.a. while a 6-month option (180 days) is trading at an implied volatility of 12% p.a. The 3-month forward volatility is:

$$\sigma_F = \sqrt{\frac{[(180 - 0) \times 0.12^2 - (90 - 0) \times 0.1^2]}{(180 - 90)}}$$

$$= 13.71\%$$

A trader could perhaps analyse this value in terms of what he would expect to see based on historical data; a relatively high or low value may indicate a potential trade opportunity. This could be caused by trade flows in the spot market which may cause the forward values to move outside historical norms. To exploit potential movements such as these, the traders would need to execute transactions with different maturities. So if the trader felt that the value of 13.71% was low relative to historical norms they could buy longer-dated options and sell shorter-dated options.

Another popular strategy that is sometimes used in these circumstances is volatility spread trades. Using swaptions as an example, a hypothetical relationship might be the volatility on:

• 3-year options into 2-year swaps ("3yr 2yr") against 2-year options into 3-year swaps ("2yr 3yr"), or perhaps
• 4-year options into 1-year swaps ("4yr 1yr") against 1-year options into 4-year swaps ("1yr 4yr").

Another way of taking advantage is by the use of swaption triangles, which are a combination of three swaptions. Suppose a trader has calculated the forward volatility of options on 2-year swap rates. These are shown in Figure 4.28.

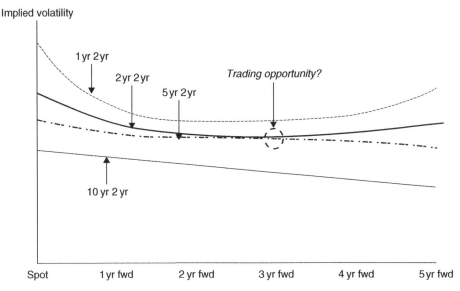

Figure 4.28   Forward volatilities on options on 2-year swap rates.

The figure can initially seem very confusing, since it involves swaption terminology. Take the uppermost curve labelled "1yr 2yr". This curve traces out a series of implied volatility quotes for 1-year options into 2-year swaps. At the far left-hand side of the curve the implied volatility quote is for a spot-starting 1-year option into a 2-year swap. The next point on the curve to the right of this is for the same swaption (1yr 2yr) but starting in 1 year's time. Therefore, the far right of the curve references a 1-year option into a 2-year swap but starting in 5 years' time. So although the maturity of the swap is constant in this case (2 years), we are analysing options of different maturities (1, 2, 5 and 10 years) that start in different forward periods (1, 2, 3, 4 and 5 years' time).

Suppose the trader feels that the "dent" around the 3-year point presents a possible trading opportunity, caused by depressed levels of spot swaption volatility in the 3yr 2yr and 4yr 2yr part of the swaption surface. The trader takes the view that the 2yr 2yr volatility, 3 years forward (circled in Figure 4.28) represents a possible trading opportunity and should increase as volatilities revert to their normal levels. This forward-starting exposure can be exploited by executing the following transactions:

- Buy 3yr 2yr and 5yr 2yr ATM swaption straddles.
- Sell a 3yr 4yr ATM swaption straddle.

This combination of trades is shown in Figure 4.29, and should show a profit if volatilities revert to more "normal" levels.

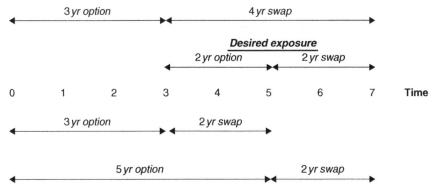

Figure 4.29   Creating a swaption triangle.

5

Identifying Value in Sovereign Bonds

5.1 WHAT IS RELATIVE VALUE?

Traditionally, relative value has been defined in terms of simple "cheap–rich" analysis but, as we argued earlier, this is only one aspect of the concept. Recall our wider definition: *"What is the optimal or most efficient way of expressing a view on an expected market movement?"*

Trades can be looked at either from a macro or a micro perspective. Arguably, traditional "cheap–rich" analysis is a classic example of the micro approach; buy underpriced asset A and sell overpriced asset B. However, most micro trades have a macro element for their rationale. Suppose that we wish to take a view on the market's perception of default risk between two sovereign borrowers as represented by their asset swap spread (ASW). Although this could be executed as a micro trade it will have a macro element as asset swap spreads are directionally related to market levels. We will consider these specific issues later in the chapter.

It is also worth pointing out that relative value trades do not represent "risk-free arbitrage". Many of the problems associated with the financial crisis that started in 2007 were directed at so-called "arbitrage" collateralized debt obligations (CDOs). These instruments took high-yielding assets and applied securitization principles to transform them into investment grade securities. In reality, these instruments merely redistributed credit risk without actually eradicating it. When the underlying high-yield assets failed, the issued securities that referenced these cash flows suffered significant defaults. True arbitrage – where one asset trades at two different prices in the same market – is very rare and will usually be exploited swiftly by market participants.

Having made all of these points, this chapter is largely dedicated to traditional "cheap–rich" analysis within the context of sovereign bonds. The chapter breaks down into three distinct parts. In the first section we consider a variety of yield curve issues. These include:

- Theories of the yield curve.
- How the yield curve moves in theory and practice.
- Factors that influence the shape of the curve.
- How the curve is actually drawn or modelled.

The second section defines a variety of spread measures used to identify value within a population of bonds. The third section focuses on applied techniques used to identify value and highlights some strategies that could be employed to exploit any opportunities that have been identified.

5.2   UNDERSTANDING THE YIELD CURVE

5.2.1   Yield curve formation

The finance literature suggests that there are four main theories to explain the term structure of interest rates. These are usually called the "expectations", "liquidity preference", "preferred habitat" and "market segmentation" hypotheses. For practical purposes, the last three in the list can be thought of as particular cases of the same basic idea, which is that certain market participants (either borrowers of funds or lenders of funds) will cluster around certain specific parts of the yield curve unless they are paid to do otherwise.

The preferred habitat hypothesis, for example, essentially says that market participants will generally prefer one particular maturity bucket and will need to be paid significant yield premiums (in the case of investors) or face significantly lower funding costs (for borrowers) in order to be enticed to move to another maturity bucket. Likewise, the market segmentation hypothesis says that many investors have restrictions regarding where on the curve they can participate. These restrictions arise either from the underlying nature of their business (e.g., pension funds or mortgage banks) or from legal constraints such as the case of money-market mutual funds which have to be invested in very short-dated instruments.

Both of these theories suggest that market participants do not see different parts of the yield curve as perfect substitutes for each other although, of course, there is a subtle difference in that the idea of market segmentation does not actually allow for much switching between maturity buckets while the idea of preferred habitat, at least, allows for borrowers and investors to move along the curve – even if it does require them to be "bribed" to do so.

The liquidity preference hypothesis says that people will move further out on the yield curve but only as long as the inducements (higher investment yields or lower funding costs) continue to increase along with maturity. Again, in a sense, liquidity preference says that there is a need for a "bribe" to move along the curve although, in this case, we at least know that without inducements market participants will tend to crowd the short end. In the other cases, without monetary inducement, market participants will stick with their preferred maturity buckets, which could be the 0y–1y maturities for money-market funds, the 1y–5y maturities for many reserve managers, the 5y maturity for mortgage banks, the 5y–10y maturities for asset managers or the 10y–30y maturities for pension funds (this list is not meant to be exhaustive).

The expectations hypothesis, in contrast, says that the yield curve represents the combined effect of the future interest rate expectations of all market participants. So, for example, if today's 1-year interest rate is 5% and market participants expect that the 1-year interest rate starting this time next year will be 4%, then we can calculate where the 2-year interest rate should be trading, i.e., 4.5%. The 2-year interest rate would give a return of 4.5% per annum for 2 years, for a return of 9% in total (note that we are ignoring compounding for simplicity). A 1-year investment at 5% followed by a 1-year investment at the future expected rate of 4% would also return 9%. This is exactly how it should be, since the 2-year rate is determined by the current 1-year and the expected 1-year rate, in 1 year's time. In the same way, the 3-year rate is determined by the combination of today's 1-year rate, the 1-year rate expected in 1 year's time and the 1-year rate expected in 2 years' time. So, if the 1-year rate expected by the market in 2 years' time is, say, 3% then we can calculate the spot 3-year rate; it is 4%. So, the 3-year interest rate would give a return of 4% per annum for 3 years, for a return of 12% in total (again, we are ignoring compounding for simplicity). A 1-year investment at 5% followed by a 1-year investment at the 1-year future expected rate of 4%, followed by a 1-year investment at the future expected rate in 2 years' time of 3% would also return 12%.

By extension, if we know today's short-term interest rate (the 1-year rate in the example above) and we know the profile of expected short-term rates, then we are able to derive today's yield curve.

Of course, we cannot observe interest rate expectations directly but we can always observe the yield curve. And, as we said above, the yield curve represents the combined effect of the future interest rate expectations of all market participants. So, by some rearranging of equations, we can calculate the market's interest rate expectations from the currently prevailing interest rate structure. So, if we observe that the 1-year interest rate is 5% and the 2-year interest rate is 4.5%, then we can determine that the market's expected 1-year rate in 1 year's time is 4%.

Take a minute to think about this.

If the expectations hypothesis is correct, then we can look at a particular yield curve and determine the profile of future interest rate expectations. This is quite a powerful result. So, when financial commentators tell us that the market is "expecting" interest rates to develop in a certain way, they are actually calculating expected interest rates from the observable yield curve. Not only that, but they are implicitly saying that yield curves are determined by interest rate expectations.

There are a few things to note here. First, to be able to calculate interest rate expectations from a yield curve, one has to believe that other factors (i.e., liquidity preference, market segmentation, preferred habitat) are absent from the yield curve determination. It would be virtually impossible to gauge accurately how much each of these factors impacted the observable yield curve. Who knows, for example, whether preferred habitat effects have a 1bp, a 5bp, a 10bp or even a 20bp effect on yields in the 10-year maturity of, say, the USD interest swap curve. Once one accepts that yield curves are determined not just by interest rate expectations but by other factors also, then one cannot accurately determine interest rate expectations from observed yield curves. Obviously, we can calculate implied forward rates but, and this is very important, these forward rates are not expected rates unless a very stringent assumption holds (i.e., unless yield curves are determined in aggregate solely by interest rate expectations).

Another point to note; even if the expectations hypothesis does hold, how are these expectations determined? Who knows! The expectations hypothesis says nothing about how interest rate expectations are generated (we leave that to the economists), it says only that expectations exist and they determine the yield curve.

In reality, yield curves are determined by all of the factors discussed above. The pure expectations hypothesis does not hold on its own, even if it happens to be the dominant factor at work.

By now, it should be clear that downward-sloping yield curves will tend to imply that market participants expect interest rates to fall over time. By extension, a steep, upward-sloping yield curve will tend to imply that market participants expect interest rates to rise over time. Of course, a gentle, upward-sloping yield curve could imply that interest rates are expected to stay steady but that liquidity preference considerations have pushed longer-dated interest rates higher relative to short-dated interest rates. For example, investors may only be willing to lock up their money in long-term investments if they are paid a premium to do so.

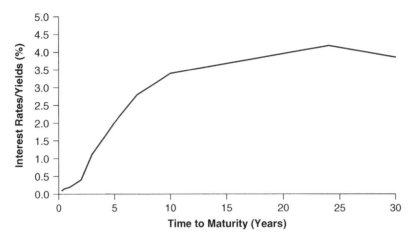

Figure 5.1 Stylized yield curve.

Figure 5.1 is a stylized depiction of a generic yield curve that aims to highlight how some of the factors discussed above impact yield curve shape. Market segmentation effects, for example, have caused money-market investors to crowd into short-dated instruments (zero to 2 years), reducing their yields relative to the rest of the curve. In the 2 to 10-year maturities the curve is steeply upward-sloping, suggesting that market participants expect interest rates to rise over time while, from the 10-year sector onwards, the gently sloping yield curve implies that interest rates are expected to stay more or less stable in the longer term and that liquidity preference effects are the dominant factor determining yield curve shape here. Finally, at the very long end of the curve, preferred habitat effects have caused pension funds to crowd into very long-dated instruments, again reducing yields relative to the rest of the curve.

One word of warning. In reality, the market cannot really be expected to formulate reasonable interest rate expectations much past 5 years ahead. In fact, the more cynical of us would question much past 1 year. So, to pretend that yield curve shapes past the 5-year maturity tell us anything about the profile of interest rate expectations is probably rather fanciful. At the very most, one can say that a certain rate profile is discounted in the curve. Hence, in practice, with regard to the stylized yield curve above, we may wish to say that the steeply upward-sloping yield curve in the 2 to 10-year maturities discounts interest rates rising over time.

Finally, history suggests that economies tend to move in cycles, expanding quickly to begin with, slowing down, then perhaps contracting somewhat, before accelerating again. At the same time, interest rates will be rising and falling in synch with the economy. Consequently, if a market yield curve accurately reflected the pattern of the likely out-turn for interest rates over time, then it should probably discount a cyclical outlook for rates. That seems to be a sensible proposition. Empirically, however, this is rarely the case. Perhaps never, although one probably does not wish to say this just in case one smart reader is able to find such an example. Suffice to say that, in general, yield curves tend to discount rising rates followed by a flat profile. The implication of this is that longer-dated yields are too high relative to the likely out-turn for future interest rates. In other words, investors who are willing to invest in longer-dated instruments will, over time, be paid excess returns. Likewise, borrowers who access longer-dated funds will generally pay over the odds; which is clearly a cost of securing longer-term funds as opposed to having the risk of not being able to roll over short term funding.

5.2.2   How does the yield curve move?

In a series of papers on the yield curve, Antti Ilmanen (1995) argues that there are three main factors that influence the shape of the yield curve: (1) the market's expectations of future rate changes; (2) expected return differentials across bonds of different maturities; and (3) the convexity bias.

Market's expectation of future rate changes

Suppose that the market expects bond yields to increase in the near term. Investors would demand a higher initial yield as any subsequent rise in yields would result in a capital loss. As a result, the yield curve would steepen to a point where the market believed these two effects would be offsetting (i.e., the higher initial return offsets the potential future loss in capital). Ilmanen (1995) argues that the opposite would also apply; if yields were expected to fall then investors would be happy with a lower initial yield as they expect to subsequently enjoy a capital gain. As a result, the yield curve would flatten and possibly invert. He also points out that the market's expectations regarding the future steepness of the yield curve will influence the curve's current degree of curvature. A typical trade that aims to benefit from an expectation that the curve will flatten could be constructed by the sale of a short-dated bond and the purchase of a long-dated bond on a DV01-neutral basis. This position exhibits negative carry and a fully worked example is shown in the appendix to this chapter.

If the curve is expected to flatten then trades designed to exploit this view will generate a profit, which means the initial negative carry has to be at a level where it will exactly match the expected capital gains. As a result, the curve will become more concave – the yield curve will become steeper at the front end than at the long end. Implied forward rates can be used to calculate how much flattening is needed for the trade to break even.

Expected return differentials across bonds of different maturities

The second factor highlighted by Ilmanen is the existence of a risk premium across bonds of different maturities. One of the features of the pure expectations hypothesis is that it assumes that bonds with the same credit quality will have the same expected holding period return. So if an investor held a 2-year and a 1-year bond for 6 months, the return should be identical. The existence of a bond risk premium, however, would violate this principle. This risk premium represents the excess return an investor could earn due to some market factor such as simple demand and supply for a particular asset. Analysing a period from 1970 to 1994 for the US Treasury market, Ilmanen suggests that the risk premia is generally greater for shorter-dated bonds than longer-dated bonds, but does vary over time.

Convexity bias

The third influence on the yield curve is the concept of the convexity bias, which Ilmanen defines as the impact that convexity differences amongst bonds has on the shape of the yield curve. The concept of convexity was covered in Chapter 2, as well as the factors that influenced its value. We argued that positive convexity was a good thing, particularly in periods of high volatility. However, in some sense this outperformance needs to be paid for and so Ilmanen argues that investors will tend to demand a lower yield if the bond is very convex due to the prospect of attractive returns. When the UK government started selling 50-year bonds (e.g., 4.24% of July 2055 was issued in May 2005), there was much discussion in the market about the value of the bond's convexity. Anecdotally, from Bowler's experience it seemed that buyers were more interested in the fact that it had a very high DV01, rather than its convexity properties.

5.2.3   Yield curve movements

In this section we discuss some of the theoretical ways in which a yield curve can move before moving on to consider whether there is any empirical justification. A parallel movement (Figure 5.2) is defined as a situation where yields across all maturities move up or down by the same amount.

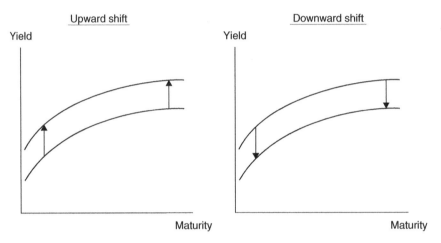

Figure 5.2   Parallel movements in the yield curve.

The movement of a curve from being upward to downward-sloping is termed an inversion, while a downward to upward movement is referred to as normalization (Figure 5.3).

A less pronounced version of inversion and normalization is termed flattening and steepening. A curve flattening is described either as bullish, when it is driven by a fall in long-term rates or bearish, when it is driven by a rise in short-term rates. A steepening curve can also be characterized as being either bullish or bearish. A bullish steepening is driven by a fall in short-term rates and a bearish steepening is driven by a rise in long-term yields. The different permutations are illustrated in Figures 5.4 and 5.5.

The final way of categorizing movements looks at the degree of curvature. A change in the yield curve's curvature will cause it to have a more or less "humped" appearance (Figure 5.6).

5.2.4   How do yield curves actually move?

Generally speaking, there are two popular techniques used to analyse the variability of a complex set of data such as yield curve changes. In multiple regression analysis, the aim is

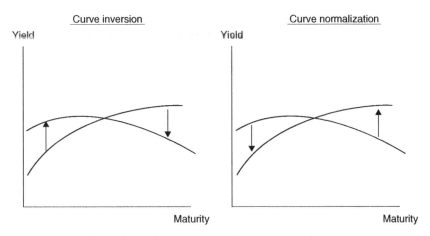

Figure 5.3   Yield curve inversions and normalization.

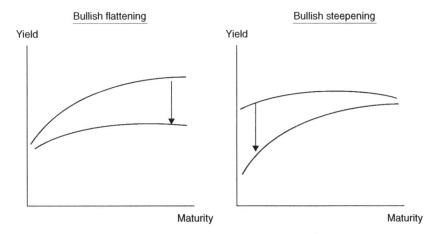

Figure 5.4   Bullish yield curve movements.

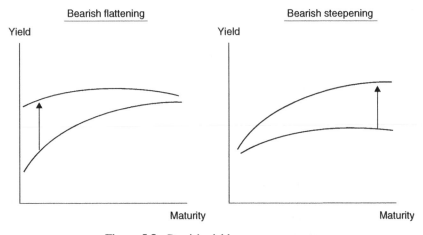

Figure 5.5   Bearish yield curve movements.

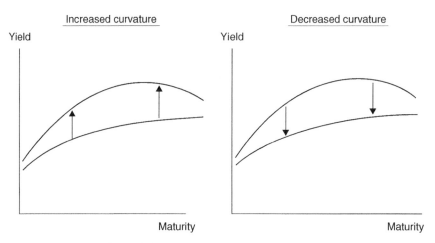

Figure 5.6 Increased and decreased curvature.

to determine a relationship between a dependent variable (such as a particular yield) and one or more independent variables (such as other yields, a yield spread or economic data series). Principal component analysis (PCA) involves examining the relationships amongst all the variables without identifying which variables depend on others. As a result, it only reveals the structure of relationships and doesn't explain any fundamental relationships. PCA aims to reduce a complex set of data into a few components that describe it sufficiently, and also seeks to expose key relationships and opportunities in the data set. Since our overall approach is intuitive in nature, the References provide more sources of information for readers wishing to understand the different techniques in greater detail.

Suppose we are analysing three bonds with maturities of 5, 10 and 15 years. There are only three separate changes that can occur to the shape and position of the curve made up of these bonds over the period in question. The curve could move in parallel, it can steepen between the 5 and 15-year maturities, with the 10-year steepening proportionately and/or it can become more/less convex between the three bonds with the 10-year moving independently. No other movement is possible.

Each of these different curve shifts is independent of the other, and in PCA terminology they are referred to as factors. So, given that we have three ways in which the yield curve can move (parallel movements, steepening, change in curvature), we could label these as factor one, two and three, respectively. Strictly speaking, PCA does not identify each factor and this can only be done subjectively by the analyst interpreting the data.

Moreover, factor three can also be thought of as what is left over after factors one and two have been used to explain the total variability of the data set. It is possible to extend this analysis and argue that with four bonds there will be four factors and that the fourth factor is what is left over after factors one, two and three have been used to explain the variability of the data set. PCA also identifies the relative importance of the different factors. Generally speaking, for a large population of bonds, results from PCA suggest that the first three factors explain over 95% of curve variability.

To illustrate the principles of PCA, let us consider yields on a variety of US Treasury market instruments with a variety of different maturities for the period February 2006 to November 2009. The results are shown in Table 5.1.

Table 5.1 PCA factors for a variety of US Treasury market instruments, February 2006–November 2009

Maturity	Factor 1	Factor 2	Factor 3	Factor 4	Factor 5	Factor 6	Factor 7	Factor 8	Factor 9	Factor 10	Factor 11
1 month	0.04305	0.94419	−0.26929	−0.17876	−0.04374	0.01105	−0.00300	0.00971	0.00441	−0.00388	−0.00244
3 month	0.06852	0.24023	0.29329	0.70039	0.59285	0.05261	0.07731	0.01210	−0.01309	0.00449	0.02168
6 month	0.17519	0.13625	0.39194	0.31869	−0.60510	−0.13188	−0.07049	−0.00660	−0.01159	0.03284	−0.55300
1 year	0.24346	0.09314	0.37041	0.07773	−0.36948	0.09045	−0.06496	−0.01417	0.00552	0.01868	0.79957
2 year	0.36733	0.01283	0.36367	−0.40040	0.20410	0.67710	−0.05131	−0.11340	0.05508	−0.00268	−0.23168
3 year	0.38223	−0.00831	0.15941	−0.23761	0.09222	−0.37474	0.75743	0.21965	0.02870	0.00361	−0.01601
5 year	0.38774	−0.02201	0.01515	−0.13862	0.18926	−0.36988	−0.35458	−0.23477	−0.69005	0.00255	−0.00800
7 year	0.38281	−0.03550	−0.06882	−0.03985	0.14986	−0.36379	−0.34988	−0.23183	0.71755	0.00430	−0.00385
10 year	0.34704	−0.07423	−0.23026	0.09439	0.00368	0.10654	−0.29055	0.84584	−0.02096	0.01034	−0.01859
20 year	0.32630	−0.08606	−0.38756	0.25529	−0.14631	0.20548	0.18703	−0.22868	−0.04496	−0.71959	0.00280
30 year	0.31409	−0.09306	−0.42987	0.24131	−0.11872	0.22342	0.20237	−0.24860	−0.04769	0.69324	0.00693

Data source: US Federal Reserve.

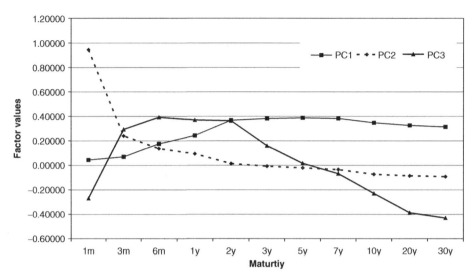

Figure 5.7   Values for PCA factors 1–3 against maturity of the underlying instrument.

Looking at factor one, the factor values (technically known as eigenvalues) from years 2 to 30 are similar in magnitude, so it would be reasonable to say that this is describing the tendency of the yield curve to move in a parallel manner. However, this would also perhaps indicate that the curve is less likely to move in a parallel fashion at the shorter-dated maturities (1 month to 1 year). The values for the second factor decline as maturity lengthen and turn negative from the 3-year maturity point. This could be interpreted as the tendency of the yield curve to steepen (positive values) or flatten (negative values), with the point of rotation being centred on the 3-year maturity. The factor values give some sense of the degree of steepening/flattening you will see between the individual points on the curve. Factor 3 increases initially to the 6-month maturity point and then declines with maturity, turning negative at the 7-year point. This could be interpreted as the tendency of the curve to become more concave in a market rally (a general falling rate environment; as a result, the curve steepens at the shorter maturities and flattens at the longer end) and less concave in a sell-off (rising rate environment). The first three factors are graphed in Figure 5.7.

One interesting point lies in trying to interpret the eigenvalues ("factor values" in Figure 5.7). Despite the fact that PCA makes no attempt to identify or name the different factors, it is market convention to treat the factor values as yield betas. So if the factor value for the 10-year maturity is 0.347 with respect to factor 1, then a one basis point parallel increase in the yield curve will cause the bond's yield to increase by 0.347 basis points.

One of the features of PCA is that it orders the different combinations of variables according to their contribution to the total variance of the data. In Table 5.2 we show the relative importance of these factors.

The key point of the table is that nearly 95% of the total daily yield variation of the bonds within our sample can be explained by factors 1 to 3, which we have postulated are a parallel movement of the curve, a steepening/flattening of the curve and a change in curvature, respectively.

Table 5.2   Yield variance due to each factor

Factor	Variance	Percentage of total	Cumulative percentage
Factor 1	114.64098	74.76%	74.76%
Factor 2	24.10250	15.72%	90.48%
Factor 3	6.72932	4.39%	94.87%
Factor 4	3.89847	2.54%	97.41%
Factor 5	1.79097	1.17%	98.58%
Factor 6	0.76331	0.50%	99.08%
Factor 7	0.60373	0.39%	99.47%
Factor 8	0.32154	0.21%	99.68%
Factor 9	0.18619	0.12%	99.80%
Factor 10	0.16799	0.11%	99.91%
Factor 11	0.13471	0.09%	100.00%

From this we can make a very bold and important conclusion. If you are confident about likely Central Bank activity then, empirically, you will be able to explain most of the likely curve movements. When Central Banks cut rates, curves "rally" (i.e., yields fall/bond prices increase), steepen and become more concave (short end steep, long end flat). When Central Banks increase rates, curves "sell off", flatten and become more convex (short end inverted or flat, long end flat).

Figure 5.8 illustrates this by considering the movement in:

- 2 and 10-year US constant-maturity yields.
- The yield curve curvature as represented as the difference between 30-year, 10-year and 2-year rates. This is measured as the 2 * 10 year rate minus the 2 year rate minus the 30 year rate. A low value represents a convex curve, while a high value represents a concave curve.

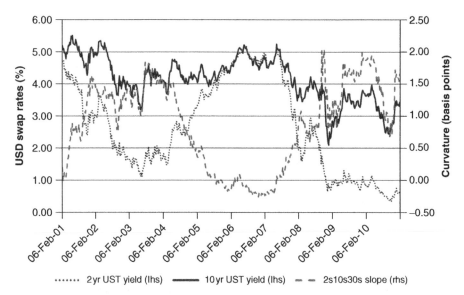

Figure 5.8   2-Year and 10-year yields vs. yield curve curvature. All yields are constant-maturity US Treasury yields (February 2001–February 2011).
Source: Data sourced from Barclays Capital Live. Reproduced with permission.

When the market is "rallying" (falling yields/rising prices), the 2-year rate falls by more than the 10-year rate and the curve becomes more concave as the measure of curvature increases. Equally, when the market "sells off" (rising rates/falling prices), 2-year yields rise by more than 10-year yields and the curve becomes more convex as the measure of curvature decreases. From this we can make the observation that shorter-term rates will usually display greater volatility than longer-term rates.

5.2.5   Yield curve modelling

In this section we consider issues such as which bonds should be included in the sample of bonds used to construct the yield curve and how the observations are joined together when drawing the curve.

The first observation is that our population of bonds for a single yield curve should have the same credit rating. As a result, it would not be possible to mix so-called risk-free sovereign bonds and corporate bonds. Within a population of government bonds some of the bonds will be described as being "on the run", meaning that they are a relatively recent issue and so their price and yield are representative of current conditions. There will be other issues that are "off the run", which are older, maybe less liquid and as a result their yields are arguably less representative of current market conditions. The "on the run" issues are often used as benchmarks by the market, to which they may reference the price of new bond issues with similar maturities.

Not all the bonds in a population will have the same coupon rates, and this may result in the bonds trading at a premium or discount to their face value. Some analysts have a preference for bonds that are trading close to their par value, and so the yield and coupon are similar. High-coupon bonds trading in a low-yield environment will be priced at a significant premium to their par value. Some investors may be discouraged from buying this type of bond due to the fact that as it approaches maturity, its price will drift down towards 100, a situation referred to as "pull to par". No investor will pay a substantial premium to the face value knowing that at maturity they will only receive par. As a result, some analysts will exclude either high-coupon bonds or bonds that are approaching their maturity (e.g., with less than 6 months of remaining maturity). Some issues may be callable, with the issuer having the right to redeem the bond prior to its maturity. This means that the holder of the bond is short a call option and this will impact the yield they receive. As a result, these types of bond are typically excluded.

As a generalization, it may be fair to suggest that analysts have therefore tended to include mainly "on the run" issues and may seek to exclude those bonds whose yields they consider to suffer from some form of distortion. The yield curve is then fitted to pass through these representative observations. It is perhaps because of the degree of subjectivity used in the construction of bond yield curves that some analysts prefer to use swaps as an alternative benchmark. Swap rates are observable and objective and maybe a "better" benchmark to assess value in certain markets.

As a result, a number of bonds within the population of observations will sit off the fitted curve and therefore may be considered – in some sense – to be incorrectly valued.

There are a number of different methods used to fit curves to the selected observations, but there are some basic criteria that need to be applied:

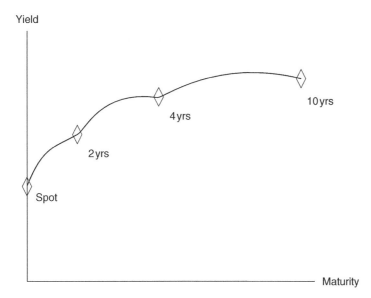

Figure 5.9   The impact of linking four yield curve observations with three cubic equations.

- The curve must be continuous and should not contain any gaps.
- It must pass through all the selected yield observations.
- It must be smooth as any sharpness on the par curve will lead to sudden jumps in forward yields.

One of the most popular techniques to ensure a smooth fitted curve uses the concept of cubic splines. Although the mathematics can be a bit intimidating, we try to present the intuition behind the process.

Suppose we have selected four bonds with different maturities from our sample: spot, 2, 4 and 10 years. The cubic spline technique involves fitting a succession of cubic equations between pairs of observations in order to link them together. Graphically, the initial result might look a little like Figure 5.9.

This is clearly not a continuous smooth curve that links all four points. As a result, we must ensure that the three equations that link each section (spot–2 years, 2 years–4 years, 4 years–10 years) have the same slope and the same degree of curvature at each of the joining points. This will ensure that the forward rates will not jump wildly. The end result should then resemble Figure 5.10.

To achieve the same slope and curvature at each joining point, the equations are differentiated twice. The first derivative ensures the same slope at every observation while the second derivative ensures that the direction of the curves at each joining point is the same.

Every institution will have its own preferred method of modelling the curve, and will also apply its own criteria in the sample selection of the bonds; as a result, there will never be one single curve that will be used by all participants. If two institutions were trying to agree the value of a single transaction, a certain amount of negotiation would need to take place if they were both using their respective curves!

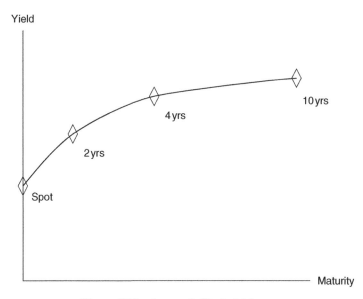

Figure 5.10   A smooth fitted yield curve.

5.3   MEASURES OF SPREAD

5.3.1   Decomposing bond yields

In Chapter 2 we introduced the concept of yield to maturity as a means of measuring the return on a bond. More formally, it was defined as the rate of return an investor would earn if they were to buy the bond at its current price and hold it to maturity. However, it would only be an accurate measure of return if the investor were able to reinvest all of their interim coupons at a rate equal to the original yield.

Although this is a popular measure of yield there are also other measures of value which are used, depending on the type of bond. For example, high-yield issues will typically have an embedded issuer call option that allows the issuer to repay the bond prior to its stated maturity.[1] The yield on the bond to the first possible call date is termed the "yield to call". However, high-yield bonds may have multiple call dates, each with a different strike price. Consequently, an investor could calculate the yield to call for each individual date and the final maturity and by taking the most conservative value (i.e., the lowest derived yield) will have derived the "yield to worst". Each of these methods has their place in fixed income analysis, but they represent absolute measures of yield.[2]

Arguably, it is more common for analysts to decompose yields into constituent components to increase their understanding of the source of their returns. Traditional fixed income analysis usually differentiates between the concepts of "risk-free" and "credit-risky" assets. However, during the financial crisis of 2007–2010 this distinction came under greater scrutiny. In the credit default swap markets for a period in 2008, both the UK and US governments were considered a higher default risk than McDonalds.[3] However, even before the crisis began the European sovereign bond markets had been pricing AAA-rated sovereign debt at different levels depending on the country of issue, largely due to the different perceptions of issuer credit.

Over time, different measures of spread have evolved and to date there is no agreement over which measure is "right". Our aim is to define each of the terms and perhaps identify those measures that are most popular.

Consider the following bond:

Issuer	Ford Motor Credit
Maturity	15 December 2016
Settlement	24 March 2011
Clean price	114.50
Yield to maturity	5.044%
Spread over benchmark	208.50 basis points

According to Bloomberg's YAS screen, the following spread measures were being quoted in basis points:

G-spread	268.50
I-spread	247.7
Basis	−11.8
Z-spread	259.1
ASW	269.3
OAS	280.6
TED	−251.3

Before we consider these measures in detail, Figure 5.11 provides a "big picture" overview of the issues and shows one simple way in which a bond yield could be decomposed.

In simple terms, the foundation of a bond's return is the yield of a government security ("benchmark yield") with the same maturity. The traditional "credit spread" is usually

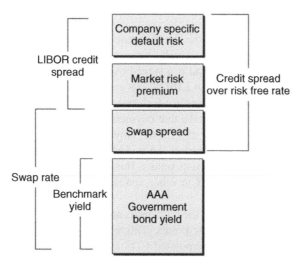

Figure 5.11   Decomposing a bond yield into its component parts.

represented in two ways by systems such as Bloomberg. They may simply measure the difference in yield between the bond and a sovereign issue and a benchmark bond. This benchmark bond may have a very different maturity to that of the bond being analysed. To overcome this, it is possible to use the concept of the G-spread which is simply the difference between the yield to maturity of the bond and that of an interpolated government bond yield.

5.3.2   Swap spreads

We will argue later in the chapter that in certain markets the yields on government bonds may be impacted by a variety of non-economic factors and so over time practitioners have preferred to use interest rate swaps ("the swap rate") as their benchmark pricing tool. As Figure 5.11 illustrates, the swap rate is derived by adding a spread to the government bond yield. The resulting swap rate brings the yield on the instrument to the equivalent interbank credit risk level, which is somewhere between AA and A. One word of caution: the market will often use the phrases "swap rate" and "LIBOR rate" interchangeably, given that they represent a certain level of interbank credit risk. Drivers of swap spreads were analysed in Section 4.2 and so no further analysis is presented here.

However, a specific bond may be considered relatively illiquid (easy to buy but difficult to sell) and so investors may demand a premium to hold the issue – the market risk premium. None of these spreads address the probability that the company will actually default, which could be estimated from say the credit default swap (CDS) market (i.e., the company-specific default risk).

Putting this all together suggests that the traditional notion of a "credit spread" could actually comprise three elements: the swap spread, market risk premium and company-specific default risk. Arguably, it was the realization by the market that traditional credit spread analysis was perhaps too simplistic that led to the development of a number of different spread measures.

5.3.3   CDS spreads

To illustrate the concept, let us consider the difference between the traditional credit spread and the company-specific default risk usually represented by the CDS spread.

Whereas the traditional credit spread is a spread over a government benchmark bond, the CDS spreads are measured relative to LIBOR. To grasp this concept, consider that a bank decides to buy protection on some unspecified asset at a cost of 100 basis points. Since they will have to borrow money to make that payment, the true cost is LIBOR + 100 bps – assuming of course they can finance at LIBOR. However, the CDS market quote assumes that the buyer will finance the purchase of the underlying deliverable obligation at LIBOR and so simply quotes the number of basis points. Having established this method of quoting CDS, the same logic can be applied to other spread measures that we will cover in the following sections.

Reference is sometimes referred to the CDS basis and in the case of the Ford Motor Credit asset this had a value of −11.8 basis points. This is discussed in detail in Section 7.1.1, but Bloomberg define this as the interpolated CDS spread minus the bond's Z-spread (see Section 5.3.6 for a discussion on Z-spreads).

5.3.4   I-spread

The I-spread is defined as the difference between the yield on a cash bond and an interest rate swap rate of the same maturity. So if the yield to maturity on a 5-year bond is say 4.5% and the 5-year swap is 4.00%, then the I-spread +50 basis points. Since a swap can be thought of as a substitute for a fixed income position, then it would be possible to argue that an investor using swaps rather than bonds to express a view on expected market movements is, in this case, earning 50 basis points more than the swap, arguably for the extra degree of credit risk and what we earlier referred to as the market risk premium.

5.3.5   TED spread

Burghardt (2003) points out that in its original form the Treasury Eurodollar (TED) spread was simply the difference between the price of a Treasury bill future and the price of a Eurodollar futures contract. It could therefore be interpreted as a measure of the perceived credit spread between the interbank market (i.e., the value of LIBOR embedded within the Eurodollar quote) and the "risk-free" rate.

The simple TED spread was defined as:

3-month Eurodollar rate *minus* 3-month Treasury Bill rate

He notes that over time this approach was extended and applied to strips of Eurodollar futures. By trading a series of sequential futures, it is possible to create a synthetic zero-coupon LIBOR bond. The yield implied by this instrument could be subtracted from a Treasury note to derive a longer-dated value for the TED spread. When applied to corporate bonds, the TED spread would be calculated as the difference between the yield to maturity of the bond less the implied yield on a strip of short-term interest rate futures of the same currency with a matching maturity. In this context it would be measuring the perceived credit risk between LIBOR and the particular entity being analysed.

5.3.6   Z-spread

One shortcoming of the I-spread was that it only takes into account the difference between bond and swap rates at a single maturity and as such it does not take into account the shape of the entire curve. The Z-spread is the incremental return an investor would earn over the entire zero-coupon curve. This return can be calculated relative to a zero-coupon government bond or a swap curve, although the latter is preferred by systems such as Bloomberg. To calculate the Z-spread, each cash flow on the bond is discounted at a zero-coupon rate plus a fixed spread. The Z-spread is a single value for the fixed spread such that the present value of the cash flows is equal to the observed price of the bond. To illustrate the calculation of a Z-spread, we analyse a 4-year 5.5% annual non-callable corporate bond relative to the zero-coupon LIBOR curve. The associated market rates and cash flows are shown in Table 5.3.

We will assume that the market value of the bond has been observed as 98.8841. However, when using the zero-coupon swap discount factors in Table 5.3 the present value of the cash

Table 5.3 The initial cash flows for calculating the Z-spread for a 4-year non-callable bond

Date	Cash flow	Zero LIBOR rate (%)	Discount factor	Present value of cash flows
1	5.5	4.00	0.961538	5.288462
2	5.5	5.00	0.907029	4.988662
3	5.5	5.50	0.851614	4.683875
4	105.5	5.80	0.798100	84.19955

Table 5.4 The revised cash flows including the Z-spread for a 4-year non-callable bond

Date	Cash flow	Zero LIBOR rate (%)	Discount factor	Zero LIBOR rate + Z-spread (%)	Revised discount factor	Present value of cash flows
1	5.5	4.00	0.961538	4.08	0.960800	5.284399
2	5.5	5.00	0.907029	5.08	0.905650	4.981073
3	5.5	5.50	0.851614	5.58	0.849680	4.673242
4	105.5	5.80	0.798100	5.88	0.795692	83.94551

flows sums to 99.16055. By iteration, it can be shown that adding a fixed spread of eight basis points to the zero-coupon LIBOR curve will return a model price equal to the observed price. This eight basis point spread is the Z-spread. Table 5.4 illustrates the revised figures.

5.3.7 Option-adjusted spread

There is a related measure of spread to LIBOR that also uses a similar iterative technique and is referred to as the option-adjusted spread (OAS). The OAS was originally used to value bonds that were callable and so contained some form of embedded optionality. It is a measure of spread that attempts to eliminate the impact of the option element on the investor's yield. Many practitioners will use the terms OAS and Z-spread interchangeably, but this approach is not strictly correct. The full definition of a Z-spread is zero volatility spread; an option with zero volatility has no value. If we were to apply both methods to a callable bond the Z-spread would assume the call feature is worthless, with the implication that the bond will run to its stated maturity. However, the OAS methodology takes into account the embedded call features and as a result may return a different value.

Suppose we have a 30-year, fixed-coupon bond which can be called after 10 years at par. The buyer of the bond has sold an option to the issuer and so the investor has to be "paid" something in return. To be willing to sell an option embedded within a bond the investor must, therefore, receive a yield premium over and above the yield that an investor would receive for a similar maturity bond without the call feature. To the extent that a Z-spread is a measurement of the distance between the swap curve and the bond's yield curve with no optionality, then the OAS spread will have a bigger magnitude than the Z-spread.

However, there are circumstances where the OAS may be less than the Z-spread. This could arise when analysing shorter-dated callable bonds, where the embedded option's time value is decaying at an accelerated rate. However, the key learning points remain the same – when applying OAS and Z-spread techniques to callable bonds they will normally generate different results. However, when applied to a non-callable bond they should return the same value provided the spread is measured relative to the same underlying curve. Observant readers may note that the OAS and Z-spread for the Ford Motor Credit bond are different. Bloomberg calculate the OAS as the incremental return of the security compared to a benchmark interest rate curve adjusted for embedded options. This would suggest that they are using different underlying yield curves to derive these two values.

5.3.8 Asset swap spread

Over the years both authors have found that asset swaps are generally poorly understood by practitioners, even though they play a central role in the identification of value within the fixed income world. The asset swap spread (ASW) is the incremental return over LIBOR that an investor will earn from buying a fixed-coupon bond and simultaneously entering into an interest rate swap.

In Section 1.7.3 we introduced the basic form of an asset swap and argued that it could be used for a number of reasons:

- The buyer of a fixed-coupon bond may prefer floating cash flows as a match for a particular liability profile.
- Asset swaps can be used to reduce the interest rate risk associated with a particular fixed income exposure.
- They can be used as a way of identifying value in fixed income positions.

In this section we will describe the three main types of asset swap and outline how they are priced.

Yield/yield spread

A yield/yield asset swap structure consists of the purchase of a bond with a simultaneous agreement to pay fixed on a matched-maturity interest rate swap. No consideration is paid to the timings of the individual cash flows on the bond or in the swap, or whether the bond is trading at par or not.

The yield/yield spread is simply the numerical difference between the yield on the bond and the fixed rate on the swap. This is, in effect, the I-spread measure defined in Section 5.3.4. An investor will make money on this transaction if the spread widens, since the bond yield will fall relative to the fixed swap rate.

Par/par

This was the structure described in Section 1.7.3. A bond is purchased at its par value irrespective of its current market price. The fixed rate on the swap is set equal to the coupon on the bond and the timings of both fixed cash flows are set to coincide, to ensure that they have no economic impact on the position. The investor receives LIBOR +/− spread, such that the entire structure is valued as an equitable exchange of cash flows. That is:

$$\text{Present value of the swap} = 100 - \text{dirty price of the bond}$$

The notional on the swap is set equal to the par value of the bond position. The structure that is created is effectively a synthetic floating-rate note, with the magnitude of the spread to LIBOR reflecting the market's perception of the issuer's credit risk. However, it would be

Table 5.5 Cash flows associated with a par/par asset swap for a hypothetical 10-year government bond

Government curve horizontal at:	3.0000%
LIBOR curve horizontal at:	3.5000%
Swap notional:	100.0000
Asset swap spread:	−0.5514%
Bond coupon:	5.0000%

Year	Govt discount factor	Bond coupon	PV of cash flow	Swap discount factor	Fixed swap cash flow	PV of fixed swap cash flow	Forward LIBOR +/− ASW spread	PV of floating swap cash flows
1	0.970874	5	4.8543689	0.966184	−5	−4.83092	2.948633	2.848921
2	0.942596	5	4.7129795	0.933511	−5	−4.66755	2.948633	2.752581
3	0.915142	5	4.5757083	0.901943	−5	−4.50971	2.948633	2.659498
4	0.888487	5	4.4424352	0.871442	−5	−4.35721	2.948633	2.569564
5	0.862609	5	4.3130439	0.841973	−5	−4.20987	2.948633	2.482670
6	0.837484	5	4.1874213	0.813501	−5	−4.06750	2.948633	2.398715
7	0.813092	5	4.0654576	0.785991	−5	−3.92995	2.948633	2.317599
8	0.789409	5	3.9470462	0.759412	−5	−3.79706	2.948633	2.239226
9	0.766417	5	3.8320837	0.733731	−5	−3.66865	2.948633	2.163504
10	0.744094	105	78.1298611	0.708919	−5	−3.54459	2.948633	2.090342

						Fixed		Floating
Dirty price of bond		117.060406		Swap PVs		−41.58303		24.52262
Price minus par		17.060406						
						Net swap PV −17.0604		
	PV of entire structure		0.00000					

incorrect to say that the instrument has no interest rate risk; rather, the combination package has a lower market risk than a single position in the bond. Table 5.5 demonstrates the cash flows associated with a government bond asset swap. For simplicity, we have assumed a flat yield curve for both the bond and the swap markets. This means that mathematically the par, zero and forward rates will be identical. Fixed and floating payments are both assumed to be annual.

In this example we analyse a government bond with a 5% coupon, assuming the yield curve for this asset class is flat at 3%. The flat swaps curve is trading at 3.5%. In columns 2–4 the cash flows associated with the purchase of the bond are set out and indicate that when present valued using a zero-coupon government curve total to a dirty price of 117.06 (to two decimal places). The cash flows associated with the swap are shown in columns 5–9. The investor pays a fixed swap rate equal to the coupon on the bond and all the swap cash flows are discounted at a zero-coupon swap rate. Since the investor is paying par for a bond that is trading at a premium, they have a cash flow advantage of 17.06. However, by subtracting 55.14 basis points from each floating LIBOR payment to the investor – the asset swap spread – this advantage will be lost as the present value of the swap will be − 17.06 basis points. As a result, the asset swap package will be considered an equitable exchange of cash flows. Note that the asset swap spread is negative since the government is considered to be more creditworthy than a bank issuer. If, for some reason, the bond were to become relatively more expensive in the cash market this spread would become more negative (i.e., the investor's return would fall) and would be described as a "widening" of the spread.

This would lead to a situation where bonds had "outperformed" swaps and resulted in the number becoming more negative. If, on the other hand, we had a situation where the spread to LIBOR had moved from, say, LIBOR + 100 bps to LIBOR + 150 basis points, in order to be consistent we would have to describe the situation as a narrowing of the spread.

Market value asset swap

The market value asset swap follows the same principles as the par/par asset swap but does incorporate a number of different features:

- The bond is bought by the investor at the prevailing dirty price rather than par.
- The investor enters into a pay-fixed swap with the fixed rate set equal to the coupon on the bond.
- To ensure that the fixed cash flows on the bond and the swap net out, the notional on the fixed leg of the swap is equal to the par value of the bond.
- The investor receives LIBOR +/− a spread on a notional amount equal to the initial dirty price of the bond. This is the investor's net return and is therefore based on the amount invested.
- At maturity the issuer of the bond repays par to the investor. The investor pays this par value to the asset swap seller and receives the initial dirty price in return. In reality, however, this final exchange between investor and seller is settled on a net basis. As a result the investor will have received LIBOR +/− spread on the dirty value of the bond over the life of the transaction.

The associated cash flows on a market value asset swap using the same government bond as the previous example are illustrated in Table 5.6.

Table 5.6 Cash flows on a market value asset swap (from the investor's perspective)

Government curve horizontal at:	3.0000%
LIBOR curve horizontal at:	3.5000%
Swap notional:	117.0604
Asset swap spread:	−0.4710%
Bond coupon:	5.0000%

Year	Govt discount factor	Bond coupon	PV of cash flow	Swap discount factor	Fixed swap cash flow	PV of fixed swap cash flow	Forward LIBOR +/− ASW spread	PV of floating swap cash flows
1	0.970874	5	4.8543689	0.966184	−5	−4.83092	3.545748	3.425843
2	0.942596	5	4.7129795	0.933511	−5	−4.66755	3.545748	3.309993
3	0.915142	5	4.5757083	0.901943	−5	−4.50971	3.545748	3.198061
4	0.888487	5	4.4424352	0.871442	−5	−4.35721	3.545748	3.089914
5	0.862609	5	4.3130439	0.841973	−5	−4.20987	3.545748	2.985424
6	0.837484	5	4.1874213	0.813501	−5	−4.06750	3.545748	2.884468
7	0.813092	5	4.0654576	0.785991	−5	−3.92995	3.545748	2.786926
8	0.789409	5	3.9470462	0.759412	−5	−3.79706	3.545748	2.692682
9	0.766417	5	3.8320837	0.733731	−5	−3.66865	3.545748	2.601625
10	0.744094	105	78.1298611	0.708919	−5	−3.54459	3.545748	2.513647

			Fixed		*Floating*
Dirty price of bond	117.0604057	Swap PVs	−41.583		29.48858
Dirty price minus par	17.06040567				
PV of end receipt	12.09444255		Net swap PV	−12.0944	
	PV of entire structure	0.0000			

The asset swap spread is now −47.10 basis points. Gale (2006) points out that there is a mathematical linkage between the asset swap spread for market value and par/par swaps:

$$\text{ASW}_{\text{Market value}} = \text{ASW}_{\text{Par/par}} \times \frac{100}{\text{Dirty price}}$$

where:

ASW = asset swap spread

Those readers interested in the proof for this formula are referred to the original paper.

Z-spread asset swaps

In the par/par methodology of pricing asset swaps, the price of the underlying sovereign bond was valued using a single government yield to maturity. When using the Z-spread method to calculate the asset swap spread, a fixed number of basis points is applied to the zero-coupon swap curve until the present value of the bond's cash flows equals the observed market price. At the point where the two prices converge, the number of basis points applied to the zero swaps curve is deemed to be the asset swap spread.

5.4   IDENTIFYING VALUE IN SOVEREIGN BONDS USING ASSET SWAPS

5.4.1   Determining the appropriate benchmark

Value in sovereign bonds is usually expressed as a spread to a particular yield curve, which acts as a benchmark for the analysis. There is no single universally adopted benchmark, but there are three popular choices:

- *Government yield curve* – This curve will usually have an AAA rating but is focused exclusively on bonds, which may experience varying degrees of liquidity. Equally, in identifying bonds that may be mispriced the analyst must have a great deal of confidence in the methodology used to build the curve.
- *Swap curves* – These curves are effectively rated A or AA and offer a very wide range of maturities with deep liquidity. Traditionally, the swap curve has been a popular benchmark as it was seen as a reflection of an institution's cost of borrowing, thereby offering an easy reference point to assess the potential return from trading an asset.
- *EONIA (Euro Overnight Index Average) curves* – These curves are rated AAA and are highly liquid with a wide variety of maturities available. As we showed in Chapter 2 (Section 2.5), these curves are used to value swap transactions whose market value is subject to a counterparty collateral agreement.

EONIA swaps as a benchmark

An EONIA swap is an agreement between two parties to exchange a fixed for floating rate. The floating rate is the compounded average of the daily EONIA fixings for agreed tenor of the swap. The biggest driver of EONIA rates is ECB monetary policy, and an overview of this is presented in Appendix 2.1. This means that the EONIA rate very closely tracks the Central Bank rate and is viewed by the market as having an AAA-equivalent credit risk.

	0m	3m	6m	12m	2y	3y	4y	5y	7y	10y	15y	20y	25y	30y
3m	20.1	23.6	26.1	26.8	28.2	22.6	21.0	19.2	16.5	12.0	7.9	6.9	6.9	6.9
6m	21.9	24.9	26.6	27.7	27.0	23.0	21.0	19.0	16.6	12.0	7.0	7.0	6.0	6.0
1y	24.3	26.0	27.3	28.4	26.5	22.6	21.0	18.8	16.5	12.0	8.0	7.0	7.0	7.0
2y	26.3	27.4	27.6	27.4	24.6	21.8	19.9	18.0	15.6	11.4	7.8	7.0	7.0	7.0
3y	26.4	26.6	26.6	25.9	23.4	20.8	19.1	17.6	14.7	11.0	7.7	7.0	7.0	7.0
4y	25.5	25.6	25.4	24.7	22.3	20.0	18.5	16.8	14.1	10.5	7.5	7.0	7.0	7.0
5y	24.6	24.6	24.4	23.6	21.4	19.4	17.7	16.1	13.5	10.1	7.4	7.0	7.0	7.0
6y	23.7	23.6	23.4	22.6	20.6	18.6	17.0	15.5	13.0	9.8	7.4	7.0	7.0	7.0
7y	22.9	22.8	22.6	21.9	19.9	17.9	16.4	14.9	12.5	9.5	7.3	7.0	7.0	7.0
8y	22.2	22.1	21.8	21.0	19.1	17.3	15.8	14.4	12.1	9.3	7.3	7.0	7.0	7.0
9y	21.4	21.3	21.0	20.3	18.4	16.7	15.3	13.9	11.7	9.1	7.3	7.0	7.0	7.0
10y	20.7	20.6	20.3	19.6	17.8	16.1	14.7	13.4	11.3	8.9	7.2	7.0	7.0	7.0
15y	17.9	17.7	17.5	16.8	15.4	14.0	12.9	11.9	10.2	8.4	7.2	7.0	7.0	6.9
20y	16.0	15.9	15.7	15.1	13.9	12.8	11.8	11.0	9.6	8.2	7.1	7.0	6.9	7.0
25y	14.9	14.7	14.6	14.1	13.0	12.0	11.2	10.5	9.3	8.0	7.1	7.0	7.0	7.3
30y	14.1	14.0	13.8	13.4	12.4	11.5	10.8	10.1	9.1	7.9	7.1	7.0	7.2	7.6

Figure 5.12 Spreads (in basis points) between interest rate swaps and EONIA swaps.
Source: Barclays Capital Live. Reproduced with permission.

Figure 5.12 illustrates a matrix of spreads between euro interest rate swaps and EONIA swaps as of mid-February 2011. The spreads are calculated as interest rate swaps minus EONIA swaps. The columns represent the effective date of the transaction and the horizontal columns show a given maturity. So, the first column shows the spreads between swaps and EONIA for spot-starting swaps with maturities to 30 years. However, the maturities at the shorter end of the curve have the greatest liquidity. Notice that in all instances the spread is positive, implying that the EONIA swaps curve lies below the interest rate swaps curve.

The use of EONIA swaps as a benchmark is increasing, given that during and after the financial crisis that started in 2010 it proved very difficult for anyone to borrow at LIBOR. Additionally, at longer-dated maturities interest rate swap rates were below government bond rates as many banks were unable to obtain credit approval for longer-dated swap transactions. As a result, many analysts are using EONIA rates as a "cheap–rich" guide, looking at the relationship between EONIA and government bond yields on an asset swapped basis.

5.4.2 Term structure of asset swap spreads

Using asset swap analysis to determine if sovereign bonds are trading cheap or rich relative to some notion of fair value has become a popular relative value technique in recent years. By expressing the value of the bond as a spread to LIBOR, the impact of interest rate risk is reduced since the spread is essentially capturing credit-related factors.

Figure 5.13 illustrates the par/par asset swap spreads for a full population of US Treasury bonds against different times to maturity.

The figure shows how a term structure has been fitted around the population of asset swap spreads, with the result that some of the bonds will sit off the curve. At first glance the picture suggests that those bonds that are sitting above the fitted curve are trading "cheap" to fair value; those below the curve are said to be trading "rich" to fair value. However, as we will point out in the next section, further analysis is needed before recommending that particular bonds should be bought or sold.

Another use of asset swaps helps us identify how the market perceives the different credit risks of sovereign issuers that carry the same rating.

Figure 5.14 shows how asset swap spreads for three AAA-rated euro sovereign issuers have evolved over time. The period from about 2003 to 2008 showed how investors largely

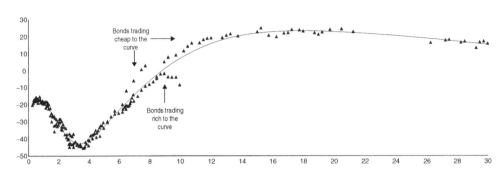

Figure 5.13   Asset swap spreads for the entire population of US Treasury bonds as at 25 November 2009.
Source: Barclays Capital Live. Reproduced with permission.

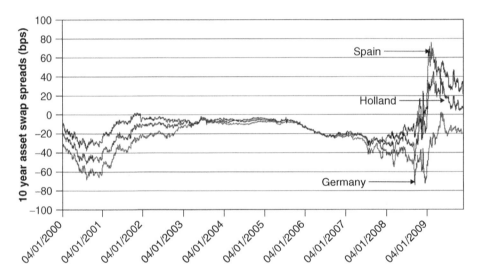

Figure 5.14   10-Year constant-maturity asset swap spreads for Germany, Holland and Spain, 2000–2009.
Source: Data sourced from Barclays Capital Live. Reproduced with permission.

ignored the risks of each individual issuer and spreads generally converged. However, during the credit crisis that followed, spreads moved to reach differentials of about 150 basis points.

Figure 5.15 shows that the asset swaps of most European sovereign AAA issuers trade higher than Germany, suggesting that at first glance the market perceives a higher degree of default risk for Austria, France and the Netherlands.

5.4.3   Assessing value in sovereign bonds

Figure 5.16 gives a snapshot of the Dutch government bond market as of late November 2009. In the first five columns of the matrix the basic details of each bond are highlighted.

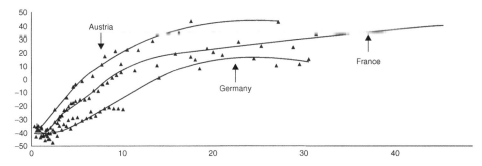

Figure 5.15   Term structure of asset swap spreads for Germany, France and Austria. Data as of 25 November 2009.
Source: Barclays Capital Live. Reproduced with permission.

The remaining columns contain information that may be useful in determining value. One possible approach to identifying value is outlined below:

- Determine the benchmark curve from which value will be assessed. This could either be the government bond curve or the swaps curve (the matrix in Figure 5.16 allows for both).
- Identify those bonds that are trading either rich or cheap to fair value using a particular measure of spread (column 6 in Figure 5.16 shows the par/par asset swap spread which increases with respect to maturity, consistent with the results of Table 5.7). Since the Dutch government is AAA, we would logically expect this spread to trade at a negative spread to LIBOR. From the 8-year maturity onwards, the asset swap spread turns negative and this is a reflection of market segmentation issues noted in Section 5.2.1 – i.e., the tendency of certain participants to cluster around certain maturities of the yield curve.
- Assess the bond's spread relative to those with a similar maturity.
- Identify those bonds whose price movements may be impacted by known market factors. For example:
  - Shorter-dated EUR sovereign bonds may tend to be more expensive as traditionally these are used as Central Bank collateral.
  - In addition, the relative expense of shorter-dated bonds could be explained again by market segmentation issues in that they are held by money market funds, which will have strict liquidity/regulatory limits on what type of instrument they can hold.
  - The bond may be illiquid, could be trading "on special" in the repo market or may be in high demand for delivery into a bond futures contract.

In Figure 5.17 the Bunds trading with 2 and 10-year maturities are all relatively "rich" as they are deliverable into different futures contracts and therefore in demand by the participants.

If a bond is identified as being cheap or rich relative to its peers, the Z-score in columns 7 and 10 can help indicate if it has recently become cheaper or dearer (in this example the Z-score is calculated with respect to a 3-month horizon). Using the Z-score would avoid situations such as buying a bond that is considered cheap only to find it becomes even cheaper.

The Z-score is calculated as:

$$\text{Z-score} = \frac{\text{Current spread} - \text{average spread}}{1 \text{ standard deviation of the spread}}$$

Benchmark Summary for Europe	Coupon	Maturity	Latest Price	Latest Yield	PP Swap Spread	3 M Z-score @ to Swaps	CDS @ Correlation	OAS Govt Spread	3 M Z Score @ to Germany	1 SD in Bps @ to Germany	3M Repo ASK	3 M Carry @ (bps)	3 M Roll Down @ Bund Curve	3 M Roll Down @ to Swap Curve	Size in Billions
Netherlands															
NETHER 5.500% Jul 10	5.5	15-Jul-10	103.001	0.620	-34.6	0.99	-0.4	3.2	1.93	2.5	0.45	10.8	11.9	7.7	10.6
NETHER 4.000% Jan 11	4.0	15-Jan-11	103.470	0.879	-36.5	1.03	-0.0	5.3	3.05	3.6	0.45	12.0	12.0	13.1	12.9
NETHER 5.000% Jul 11	5.0	15-Jul-11	106.205	1.107	-38.3	-1.54	0.2	5.6	0.89	4.1	0.45	12.1	11.4	12.1	15.2
NETHER 2.500% Jan 12	2.5	15-Jan-12	102.365	1.361	-37.6	-2.24	0.5	7.6	-0.05	3.7	0.45	12.2	11.2	11.4	13.1
NETHER 5.000% Jul 12	5.0	15-Jul-12	108.672	1.589	-34.1	-2.10	0.4	9.7	-0.85	3.7	0.45	12.5	10.7	9.6	13.0
NETHER 4.250% Jul 13	4.25	15-Jul-13	107.744	2.007	-26.2	-2.51	0.3	11.9	-0.50	3.5	0.45	12.2	9.2	7.6	16.0
NETHER 3.750% Jul 14	3.75	15-Jul-14	105.961	2.369	-17.6	-2.55	0.3	15.2	0.24	4.6	0.45	11.8	7.3	6.1	13.9
NETHER 2.750% Jan 15	2.75	15-Jan-15	101.022	2.534	-15.0	-2.20	0.3	16.8	0.53	5.4	0.45	11.2	6.4	5.8	8.0
NETHER 3.250% Jul 15	3.25	15-Jul-15	103.130	2.641	-14.0	-1.90	0.4	16.8	0.94	5.7	0.45	11.0	5.4	5.1	14.0
NETHER 4.000% Jul 16	4.0	15-Jul-16	106.643	2.880	-7.4	-1.79	0.3	22.6	0.63	6.6	0.45	10.7	4.3	4.2	12.0
NETHER 4.500% Jul 17	4.5	15-Jul-17	109.407	3.092	-0.4	-1.57	0.3	28.5	0.58	6.4	0.45	10.4	3.8	3.4	12.1
NETHER 4.000% Jul 18	4.0	15-Jul-18	105.456	3.261	2.0	-1.39	0.4	29.5	0.71	6.5	0.45	9.8	3.5	2.8	11.5
NETHER 4.000% Jul 19	4.0	15-Jul-19	104.734	3.412	6.0	-1.04	0.4	30.1	0.97	6.9	0.45	9.4	3.5	2.5	12.7
NETHER 7.500% Jan 23	7.5	15-Jan-23	138.116	3.764	26.9	0.15	0.0	26.4	2.24	5.2	0.45	9.1	3.1	1.8	8.2
NETHER 3.750% Jan 23	3.75	15-Jan-23	99.518	3.796	10.1	0.31	0.0	17.4	2.23	5.5	0.45	8.2	3.1	1.8	6.4
NETHER 5.500% Jan 28	5.5	15-Jan-28	118.436	4.044	22.9	-0.10	0.0	8.9	0.73	1.7	0.45	7.5	0.9	0.5	10.1
NETHER 4.000% Jan 37	4.0	15-Jan-37	98.889	4.067	19.3	1.80	0.2	7.1	1.32	3.1	0.45	5.5	-0.5	-0.3	12.0

Figure 5.16   Sovereign bond cheap/rich analysis (data as of 27 November 2009).
Source: Barclays Capital Live. Reproduced with permission.

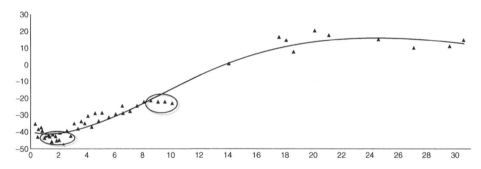

Figure 5.17   German asset swap spreads against maturity (data as of 25 November 2009).
Source: Barclays Capital Live. Reproduced with permission.

The Z-score represents the number of standard deviations that the bond is trading rich or cheap to the chosen average spread measure (par/par asset swap spread in this case). A negative Z-score indicates that the bond is trading rich relative to its 3-month average (even if it appears to be trading cheap to its fair value). A positive Z-score indicates that the bond is trading cheap to fair value. The different shading in this column is used to highlight varying degrees of richness or cheapness. However, this methodology implies a belief that the spread will revert to its average value – i.e., it will display an element of mean reversion. Figure 5.16 also indicates the carry and roll down (columns 13, 14 and 15) that an investor will earn from holding the bond for a specified period (3 months in this

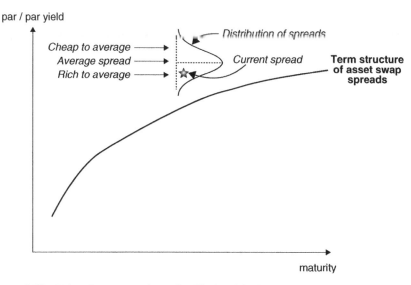

Figure 5.18   Using Z-scores to determine if a bond is cheap or rich relative to the norm.

example). At the time of writing (late 2009), government bond yield curves were relatively steep and Central Banks were expected to hold short-term interest rates at historically low levels for a prolonged period. Consequently, buying a longer-dated bond financed by a repo transaction would generate favourable roll down and carry values. The analyst could select an asset that would generate the most favourable values for these two variables.

In Figure 5.16, the 3.75% of 2023 is trading with a par/par asset swap spread of 11 basis points while its peers (including a bond of the same maturity) have spreads of greater than 20 basis points. The analyst would need to make a judgement as to whether the positive Z-score of 0.31 warrants a purchase decision. Equally, the longest-dated bond (4% of 2037) is cheap as its Z-score of +1.80 indicates it has moved by almost two standard deviations relative to its 3-month average.

Figure 5.18 shows a hypothetical term structure of asset swap spreads with one highlighted observation (shown here as a star) sitting off the curve. With no other point of reference it would be reasonable to suggest that sitting above the curve the asset is cheap relative to fair value. However, if we were to draw a distribution of spreads based on movements over the previous 3 months we would see that it is trading below its average value for the period. As a result, it would be reasonable to suggest that it is trading rich relative to its 3-month average. The analyst would therefore have to make a decision as to whether it is more likely to tend towards its 3-month average (i.e., cheapen) or move back towards the curve (i.e., richen).

Having identified those bonds that contain value, the question is how should one exploit this? This will depend on the types of instrument that the investors are allowed to trade.

- *The bond is trading rich* – If the investor is a non-leveraged account, the simplest strategy might be to sell the bond that is trading rich and buy a cheaper peer bond of a similar maturity that is cheaper. This trade could be unwound when the spreads have reverted to their normal trading range. Leveraged investors (i.e., hedge funds or investment banks) could reverse asset swap the bond. This would involve selling the bond short and receiving fixed in a swap. This swap could be unwound when the spread has reverted to its normal trading range. Another possibility would be to asset swap one of the peer instruments that are trading cheap to fair value.

- *The bond is trading cheap* – This is essentially the opposite of the previous paragraph. Non-leveraged accounts would focus on the cash market while perhaps leveraged accounts would initiate a derivatives transaction.

5.4.4   Forward asset swap spreads

In an asset swap transaction we argued that an investor buys a bond, pays fixed and receives LIBOR plus the ASW on an interest rate swap. The shortcut way of estimating the ASW is to use the following formula:

$$ASW = LIBOR + (bond\ yield - interest\ rate\ swap\ rate)$$

In very simple terms, the position would show a mark-to-market loss if the ASW were to increase, which would occur if the spread between bond yields and interest rate swaps (i.e., the interest rate swap spread) were to increase. This would result from an increase in bond yields and/or a decrease in interest rate swap rates.

In Chapter 2 we considered the notion of a forward as a breakeven value, and it is possible for the same concept to be applied to asset swaps. This will help us identify at what point the position will start to lose money.

There is an additional issue with respect to asset swaps that forward analysis helps overcome. We have assumed that the bond purchase will be financed at LIBOR, but this does not reflect the fact that some bonds can be financed at different repo rates. As a result, it is tempting to think of the "best" or "cheapest" bond as the instrument with the largest asset swap spread. This approach is flawed as it tells you nothing about relative repo rates and therefore the net income to the investor. If the bond is financed using the repo market and the asset is trading "on special", it will have an impact on the overall return. Bonds trading "on special" will often yield less and therefore on an asset swap basis the spread to LIBOR will be lower, making the structure more "expensive". The problem of different repo rates can be accounted for by calculating the forward asset spread. All other things being equal, the asset with the greatest forward asset swap spread would be the logical investment choice.

The forward asset swap spread is today's spread to LIBOR for an asset swap of a given maturity starting at some future date. So we may have a spot asset swap spread for a 10-year transaction of (say) 3-month LIBOR plus 10 basis points. A 10-year asset swap spread 3 months forward could be (say) 3-month LIBOR plus 12 basis points. So in this case an investor executing a spot transaction with a 3-month investment horizon would start to lose money when the asset swap spread moves beyond the forward spread.

Tonge (2001) suggests using the following formula to calculate the forward asset swap spread:

$$Forward\ asset\ swap\ spread = Spot\ asset\ swap\ spread + \frac{(LIBOR - repo) \times time}{forward\ modified\ duration}$$

Let's assume we are analysing two zero-coupon bonds with the same maturity and credit risk, both trading at a price of 10 with the same simple spot asset swap spread. However, the repo market rate for bond A is 0% while bond B is trading at 1%. Logically, an investor would execute the following asset swap transactions:

- Buy bond A and pay fixed on a swap: pay $10 (cash holding goes down), lend the bond in the repo market at 0% (which means borrowing $10 at 0%); investor's cash holding goes up.
- Sell bond B and receive fixed on a swap: receive $10 (cash holding goes up), borrow the bond in the repo market at 1% (which means lending $10 at 1%); cash holding goes down.

As a result, the investor has no net change in their cash position but earns 1% annualized on a $10 deposit; this is free money. The investor has no net duration or maturity mismatch and the associated swap positions are equal and offsetting.

The market will do this trade until bond A richens up and bond B cheapens up to the point where the net expected capital gain from bond B vs. bond A offsets the 1% interest gain. How would an investor know when this has occurred? It is when the forward asset swap spreads are the same. As a result, the forward ASWs let you assess relative ASW spreads without having to go through the rigmarole of looking at repo rates.

We have argued that forward prices (or rates) can be used as breakevens. Let's return to our two bonds and assume that the following spreads are trading:

- Bond A: spot ASW 10 bp, forward ASW 12 bp
- Bond B: spot ASW 10 bp, forward ASW 10 bp

If I buy bond A on an asset swapped basis at 10 bp, I will lose money once the ASW moves above 12 bp. The carry that I make from being able to finance my bond cheaply at 0% is worth 2 bp. If I buy bond B at 10 bp, I lose money as soon as the ASW moves above this level. So, bond A is the cheapest and offers value relative to bond B. Again, the market should buy bond A and sell bond B until the forward ASW spreads are the same. For example, the spreads may evolve as follows:

- Bond A: spot ASW 9 bp, fwd ASW 11 bp
- Bond B: spot ASW 11 bp, fwd ASW 11 bp

However, consider the following case:

- Bond A: spot ASW 9 bp, fwd ASW 9 bp
- Bond B: spot ASW 11 bp, fwd ASW 11 bp

Which is the cheapest? Actually, it is bond B since the investor will earn 11 bp per annum over the life of the ASW. If the investor buys bond A, they will only earn 9 bp per annum over the life of the ASW.

How far forward should you calculate the forward asset swap spread? Basically, as far forward as the traded maturities available in the repo market. If a bond is only special on, say, a 1-month basis but not special on a 3-month basis, then the forward ASW will not show the bond as cheap on a 3-month basis.

5.4.5 Inflation-linked asset swaps

An inflation asset swap is very similar to a nominal bond asset swap in that the end result is a synthetic nominal FRN. An inflation-linked asset swap is the combination of an inflation-linked bond and an inflation swap and as such the inflation component nets out, leaving the investor inflation neutral.

There are two popular inflation-linked asset swaps:

- Par/par – popular in the European markets.
- "Proceeds" asset swaps – what was described earlier as a market value transaction, which is popular in the UK and US markets.

Typically a par/par inflation asset swap would be structured as follows:

- The investor will buy the inflation-linked bond at par, irrespective of its market price.
- The investor enters into an inflation swap where the fixed cash flow will comprise a real yield plus an adjustment to reflect the impact of inflation. The magnitude and timing of the swap cash flows mirror those of the bond.
- However, to value the package we will need an estimate of the future values of inflation as these are required to establish the magnitude of the fixed cash flow payments. Typically, these values are derived from observations of prices in the zero-coupon inflation swap market.[4]
- The investor receives a nominal floating cash flow (e.g., LIBOR or EURIBOR) +/– a spread, with the spread set at a value that ensures the overall package has a net present value of zero.
- At maturity the investor pays the entire redemption amount (uplifted for inflation) to the asset swap seller and they receive back par (although in reality a net payment would be made).

After the collapse of Lehman Brothers in 2008, there was a divergence between spreads to LIBOR obtainable by asset swapping nominal sovereign bonds and those derived from swapping inflation-linked sovereign bonds. Figure 5.19 shows the evolution of nominal asset swap spreads on French nominal bonds (5.75% of 2032) and inflation-linked bonds (3.15% of

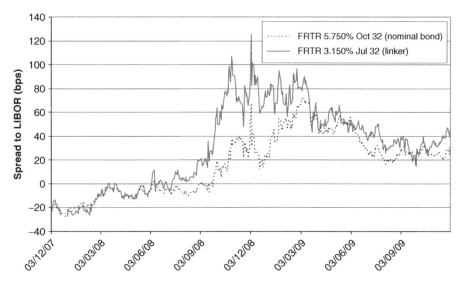

Figure 5.19   Asset swap spreads from nominal and inflation-linked French sovereign bonds. December 2007 to December 2009.
Source: Barclays Capital Live. Reproduced with permission.

2032) from December 2007 to December 2009. The figure shows that the spreads are very close in the early part of the period but diverge significantly in the third quarter of 2008. The difference between the spreads reached a peak of nearly 72 basis points in October 2008. The reason for this "anomaly" was attributed to a number of factors:

- Investors holding inflation-linked bonds sold their holdings and switched into nominal government bonds that were perceived to have greater liquidity.
- Many banks who were holders of inflation-linked bonds as a hedge for their inflation swap exposures sold a large amount of their portfolios for balance sheet management purposes.
- Those participants who already held inflation-linked asset swaps suffered mark-to-market losses as asset swap spreads increased substantially. As the trades were unwound, the increased sale of inflation-linked bonds further depressed their prices.
- As a result, the fall in the price of inflation-linked bonds led to a significant increase in their nominal asset swap spreads compared to those obtained from nominal bonds.

5.5 SUMMARY OF YIELD MEASURES

Spread measure	Definition	How is it measured	Drawbacks
Credit spread	An investor's reward for assuming the potential default of an issuer	Quoted as a number of basis points over the yield of the sovereign benchmark bond. If the benchmark bond is not of the same maturity, the G-spread measures an interpolated value	May overestimate default risk as spread may incorporate other factors such as a liquidity premium or funding risk; suffers from the reinvestment assumption inherent in a yield to maturity measure
Asset swap spread (ASW)	An investor's reward for assuming the potential default of an issuer net of interest rate and funding risk	+/− a number of basis points to LIBOR	May differ in value from credit default swap spread, which is the market's preferred measure of "pure" default risk
Option-adjusted spread (OAS)	An investor's reward for assuming potential default risk, excluding the value of any embedded optionality	Option model required to calculate value	Requires a model and a value for implied volatility of the issuer's yield
Z-spread (zero volatility spread)	The incremental return an investor will earn over the entire risk-free rate assuming zero volatility (i.e., the option is worthless and the bond will not be called); the parallel shift to a benchmark curve required to match the observed price of a bond	A constant number of basis points is then added to each risk-free interest rate such that the derived fair value of the bond is the same as the observed market price	It assumes that the bond will be held to maturity and that spot rates will not change

Spread measure	Definition	How is it measured	Drawbacks
Spread to swaps (I-spread)	An investor's incremental return measured relative to the swap curve	The difference between the yield to maturity of a bond issue and an interest rate swap of the same maturity	Measured at a single maturity point; does not take into account the shape of the curve
Credit default swap (CDS) spread	The number of basis points payable (receivable) to buy (sell) protection against a reference entity suffering an event of default	Model required to calculate value. Based on probability of reference entity defaulting and the loss incurred in the event of default	Some CDS markets (e.g., sovereign names) may suffer from liquidity issues raising the issue as to whether the spread measures the "true" credit risk

APPENDIX 5.1

Curve flattening trade

One popular way of constructing this position is to use bonds with maturities of 2 and 10 years. To ensure that the trade is duration neutral (i.e., the value of the position will not be influenced by a parallel movement in the curve), the trade is constructed with different nominal amounts.

Suppose we believe that the US Treasury curve is expected to flatten and so we decide to implement the view using bonds with a 2 and 10-year maturity. The details of the bonds selected for the flattening trade are given in Table 5.7 (for settlement on 11 November 2009).

The trade is executed by selling USD 10 million of the 2-year and buying USD 2,350,000 (10m × 0.019534/0.082865, rounded) of the 10-year. The actual settlement proceeds are therefore:

- 2-year: USD 10m × 100.361758/100 = USD 10,036,175
- 10-year: USD 2,350,000 × 102.219909/100 = USD 2,402,170

The short 2-year position

The short sale of the 2-year bond is financed by acquiring the asset in the repo market. In this transaction the trader acquires the bond in the repo market, registers it to take full ownership and then sells the asset to fulfil the short leg of the transaction. The proceeds of the short sale are then delivered to the repo counterparty for the agreed term of the transaction. Recall from Section 1.3 that the repo counterparty must redeliver the asset but with interest on cash

Table 5.7 Price data for US Treasury bonds, extracted from Bloomberg.com. Although prices are normally quoted in 32nds, they are shown here in decimal format

Action	Maturity	Coupon	Current price	Yield to maturity	Accrued interest	Dirty price	DV01
Sell	31 October 2011	1%	100.331372	0.83%	0.030387	100.361758	0.019534
Buy	15 August 2019	3.625%	101.353061	3.46%	0.866848	102.219909	0.082865

they have lent at a rate of return of just less than LIBOR. When the bond is reacquired in the open market to settle the second leg of the repo, its price will include a greater amount of accrued interest and so the trader is effectively paying this increase.

The purchased 10-year position

The purchased bond (i.e., the 10-year bond) will earn the accrued interest but the acquisition of the bond will require financing in the repo market. If we assume that the position is held for one week (7 days), LIBOR for the period is 0.25%, the repo rate is executed at LIBOR and the semi-annual coupon period is 182 days, then the associated cash flows are:

Maturity	Bond coupon paid or earned	Financing paid or earned on repo	Carry
2-year	−$3,846.15	+$487.87	−$3,358.28
10-year	+$3,276.44	−$116.77	+$3,159.67

As a result, the position has a slightly negative carry of $198.61 for the 7-day period, or $28.37 per day.

6

Trading the Yield Curve

In this chapter we will cover a number of trading strategies that encompass a variety of maturities along the yield curve. These will include:

- Strategies that attempt to exploit parallel movements in the curve at the short and long end.
- Trades that express views on the steepening and flattening of the curve.
- Trades designed to exploit expected changes in curvature.

In addition, we will consider constant-maturity structures and illustrate their application to express a range-bound view of interest rates.

6.1 TRADING TERMINOLOGY

6.1.1 Long or short?

Yield curve strategies are often riddled with ambiguous jargon and incomplete explanations. At first glance it would appear to be easy to define terms such as "long" and "short", which most people would interpret as bought or sold, respectively. However, the interpretation becomes less intuitive within a fixed income context. Take, for example, the instance where traders talk about being long or short the yield curve. Instinctively, many people think this relates to whether a trader would make or lose money from a rise or fall in yields. However, by convention the phrase is interpreted with respect to price. So if a trader is "long the curve" he will benefit if yields go down since bond prices will rise as a result. Being "short the curve" means he will profit from a rise in yields and therefore a fall in prices. In the same vein, when participants talk about the market "rallying" they actually mean a rise in prices and a fall in yields. Therefore a "sell-off" occurs when prices fall and yields increase. Another popular phrase is when practitioners talk about being long or short duration. A duration strategy refers to the choice of bond maturity such that profits will be maximized (or losses minimized) for an expected movement in interest rates. So if interest rates are expected to fall equally across the curve (i.e., bond prices to rise) then it might make sense to lengthen the net duration of a bond portfolio. A portfolio manager would be faced with a number of different possibilities: they could buy longer-dated bonds, buy bond futures or perhaps receive fixed on an interest rate swap.

6.1.2 Roll down and carry revisited

In Chapter 3 we introduced two vital fixed income concepts, roll down and carry, and we make no apologies for revisiting the concepts again. Both of the concepts can be defined either in price or yield terms (Sadr, 2009). In general terms the carry of a position is defined as the income earned less the expense of holding a position. If carry is expressed from a price perspective, it is the clean spot price minus the clean forward price. From a yield perspective, carry is defined as the forward yield less the spot yield (Sadr, 2009). It is also possible for the roll down on a fixed income position to be expressed in either a price or yield basis. The roll down of a fixed income instrument is the profit or loss from holding a fixed income position due to the passage of time, all other things being held equal. So if the yield curve is upward sloping, a bond will gain in value as it approaches expiry since it will be revalued at successively lower yields. Sadr (2009) defines roll down within a bond context as "*the difference between the spot yield of the bond to the spot yield of another bond whose maturity is shorter by the length of the investment horizon*".

The forward breakeven price (yield) is the price (yield) at which the bond must trade on the forward date in order for a position to break even relative to funding costs. Since the forward price is equal to the spot price plus the net carry, the forward price can be used as a hurdle for the trader to beat. A trader will make money on a long position if they believe that the actual price of the bond at the end of the holding period is greater than the breakeven forward price. Some practitioners (Henderson, 2003; Sadr, 2009) define the breakeven yield to include the roll down of the position. However, forward prices do not take into account roll down as it cannot be guaranteed.

Both carry and roll down will appear on a regular basis throughout this chapter and so a simple example upfront will help focus the reader's thoughts. Suppose that 9-year bonds are yielding 4% and 10-year bonds are yielding 5%. If I buy a 10-year bond with an intended investment horizon of 12 months, then under the assumption that the yield curve does not move, the position will roll down by 8.3 basis points per month ((5% − 4%)/12). One of the strategies we will analyse later in the chapter is a trade that will profit from a steepening of the yield curve. This is constructed by buying a short-dated bond and selling a longer-dated bond. The trade is constructed to be DV01 neutral (i.e., the nominal amounts are chosen such that the DV01 exposure of each position is equal and opposite), so that if the curve were to move in a parallel fashion the trade would show no profit or loss. However, if the trade does steepen as anticipated, the profit per basis point steepening would be equal to the DV01 exposure of a single leg of the trade. Assume the following yields were observed in the market:

6 months	2.00%
18 month	3.50%
1 year	3.00%
2 year	3.80%

We will assume the trader chooses to implement a steepening trade using the 1 and 2-year maturities with an investment horizon of 6 months. At the anticipated close-out date, the two legs would then have a residual maturity of 6 and 18 months. The initial spread between the 1 and a 2-year maturity is 80 basis points, while the spread between the 6-month and 18-month maturities is currently 150 basis points. As a result, assuming the yield curve remains unchanged, the position will have a roll down of 70 basis points. The approximate profit and loss on this trade attributable to its roll down would be 70 basis points multiplied by the DV01 of the position. Another way of looking at the problem is to consider the individual positions. The short 2-year position will roll down by 30 basis points, which will result in a loss. The long 1-year position will roll down by 100 basis points, which will result in a profit. So, in an unchanged yield curve environment the steepening trade will benefit from 70 basis points of roll down.

	0m	3m	6m	12m	2y	3y	4y	5y	7y	10y	15y	20y	25y	30y
3m	0.25	0.40	0.45	0.60	1.43	2.45	3.41	4.09	4.74	5.08	4.93	4.65	4.55	4.42
6m	0.33	0.42	0.47	0.60	1.66	2.60	3.63	4.17	4.70	5.12	4.95	4.67	4.57	4.44
1y	0.40	0.48	0.58	0.87	1.79	2.81	3.69	4.25	4.79	5.09	4.88	4.64	4.53	4.39
2y	0.63	0.78	0.94	1.33	2.29	3.24	3.96	4.41	4.87	5.10	4.84	4.63	4.52	4.38
3y	1.01	1.20	1.39	1.81	2.74	3.57	4.16	4.54	4.92	5.11	4.80	4.62	4.50	4.36
4y	1.45	1.65	1.84	2.26	3.10	3.81	4.31	4.63	4.96	5.09	4.77	4.60	4.50	4.33
5y	1.87	2.06	2.25	2.63	3.37	3.99	4.42	4.70	4.99	5.08	4.75	4.60	4.48	4.30
6y	2.24	2.41	2.59	2.93	3.59	4.13	4.51	4.76	5.00	5.05	4.73	4.59	4.47	4.27
7y	2.54	2.70	2.86	3.16	3.75	4.24	4.58	4.80	5.01	5.02	4.72	4.58	4.46	4.23
8y	2.79	2.93	3.07	3.36	3.89	4.33	4.64	4.84	5.01	4.99	4.71	4.57	4.44	4.20
9y	2.99	3.12	3.25	3.51	4.00	4.40	4.68	4.86	5.00	4.96	4.69	4.56	4.42	4.17
10y	3.16	3.28	3.40	3.64	4.09	4.46	4.71	4.87	4.98	4.93	4.68	4.55	4.40	4.13
15y	3.66	3.75	3.83	4.00	4.32	4.57	4.74	4.84	4.90	4.84	4.63	4.48	4.27	3.97
20y	3.85	3.92	3.98	4.12	4.38	4.58	4.72	4.80	4.84	4.78	4.57	4.38	4.14	3.86
25y	3.94	4.00	4.05	4.17	4.40	4.58	4.69	4.76	4.79	4.72	4.49	4.28	4.04	3.79
30y	3.98	4.04	4.09	4.20	4.40	4.56	4.66	4.72	4.74	4.65	4.40	4.19	3.96	3.74

Figure 6.1 Spot and forward-starting swap rates. (Effective dates are read vertically, tenors are read horizontally; a 5-year swap starting in 12 months' time is quoted at 3.66%.)
Source: Data sourced from Barclays Live. Used with permission.

Consider the swap quotes in Figure 6.1. Suppose that the trader puts on a steepening trade between the 5-year and 10-year maturities with a 12-month investment horizon, at which point the individual legs of the trade would have residual maturities of 4 and 9 years. If the current spot rates for 5 and 10-year maturities are 2.77% and 3.85%, respectively, the spot-starting spread would be measured as 108 basis points. Figure 6.1 shows that the 4-year and 9-year rates, 1 year forward, were 3.37% and 4.29% – implying a forward spread of 92 basis points; a difference of 16 basis points from the spot spread.

At the observed level of rates the DV01 of a spot 5-year position per $10m notional is $4,696, while the DV01 of a 10-year position with a $10m notional is $8,446. We could structure a DV01-neutral trade using the ratios of the two DV01s (1.80) such that a 5-year position of $10m would require the 10-year position to be $5.5m (rounded). The carry relating to the trades would be positive and is shown in Table 6.1.

With a steepening position the transaction will show a profit if the spread increases above the spot-starting value of 108 basis points. However, since the position carries positively, the curve can flatten a little before the trader loses money. We have shown previously that forward rates are breakevens and that the forward spread (4s9s, 1 year forward) has a spread of 92 basis points – the curve can flatten by this amount before the cushion of positive carry is eroded.

Table 6.1 Net carry on a DV01-weighted 5s10s steepening trade. The LIBOR cash flows are calculated on an actual/360-day basis

Maturity	Fixed	12M LIBOR (0.55%)	Total
5-year Receive fixed at 2.77% $10,000,000	$277,000	($55,764)	$211,236
10-year Pay fixed at 3.85% $5,500,000	($211, 750)	$30,670	($181,080)
			$40,156

Table 6.2   Summary of carry and relationship between forward and spot spreads for steepening and flattening positions

Position	Forward spread > spot spread	Forward spread < spot spread
Steepening trade (receive short-dated fixed, pay long-dated fixed; DV01 weighted)	Position carries negatively; curve must steepen by more than the negative carry for trade to be profitable	Position carries positively; curve can flatten by the difference in the spread before the trade loses money
Flattening trade (pay short-dated fixed, receive long-dated fixed; DV01 weighted)	Position carries positively; curve can steepen by the difference in the spread before the trade loses money	Position carries negatively; curve must flatten by more than the negative carry for trade to be profitable

If carry on the flattening/steepening position was unknown, it could be deduced from the spot and forward spreads. If the spot spread between the two maturities for a steepening trade was 100 basis points, then the trade will show a profit if this value were to increase. The forward spread tells us the point from which the trade will show a profit as it is a breakeven number. So if the forward spread at the start of the trade was 120 basis points, the trade will only make money once the spread has increased by 20 basis points. From this we can deduce that the strategy must carry negatively until this breakeven spread is reached.

The carry position on steepening and flattening positions is summarized in Table 6.2.

6.2   TRADING THE SHORT END OF THE YIELD CURVE

6.2.1   Money-market loans and deposits

One of the simplest ways to express views on expected movements in the short end of the yield curve is through the use of simple money-market loans and deposits. For example, if a trader believed that interest rates were going to rise they could borrow a sum of money for an agreed maturity and very shortly thereafter relend the cash if the market has moved as expected. If the curve is upward sloping, another strategy would to borrow on a rolling short-term basis (say overnight) and lend for a longer maturity (say 1 month) in anticipation that overnight rates would remain low or would fall.

6.2.2   Interest rate futures

It may be preferable to execute yield curve trades using derivatives as, unlike money-market transactions, they do not require any substantial initial outlay of cash.

Eurodollar futures specification

One alternative way to express views on short-dated interest rates would be to use short-term interest rate futures (STIRs). These are exchange-traded futures contracts that lock in an interest rate for a future time period. For example, the specification for the Eurodollar futures contract is outlined in Table 6.3.

A common transaction is a spread trade, which aims to exploit a differential between related prices or rates. If the market moves as expected (i.e., the differential increases or decreases), the transaction will show a profit irrespective of any directional price movement.

Table 6.3   Contract specification for a Eurodollar future

Underlying instrument	Eurodollar time deposit having a principal value of USD 1,000,000 with a 3-month maturity
Price quote	Quoted in IMM 3-month LIBOR index points or 100 minus the rate on an annual basis over a 360-day year (e.g., a rate of 2.5% shall be quoted as 97.50). 1 basis point = 0.01% = $25
Tick size	One-quarter of 1 basis point (0.0025% = $6.25 per contract) in the nearest expiring contract month; one-half of 1 basis point (0.005% = $12.50 per contract) in all other contract months
Contract months	March, June, September, December – extending out 10 years plus the four nearest serial expirations
Last trading day	The second London bank business day prior to the third Wednesday of the contract expiry month
Final settlement	Expiring contracts are cash settled to 100 minus the British Bankers' Association survey of 3-month USD LIBOR on the last trading day

Source: CME group.

Spread trades are seen as having a lower market risk than a single (a so-called "outright") position.

There are a number of different participants in the market who would be interested in such spread relationships. Some examples are:

- **Long-term hedgers who are rolling over positions** – This may include traders who are hedging interest rate swap exposures using short-term futures which will need to be rolled over.
- **Hedgers faced with basis risk** – An example of basis risk is where there is a mismatch in the maturity of an underlying exposure and the hedge used to protect the position.
- **Traders rolling over their exposures** – Here a trader may wish to take an ongoing view on, say, 3-month rates and so will continually roll over their short-term exposures.
- **Traders expressing views on the evolution of rates in different currencies** – For example, a trader may believe that USD and EUR rates of a given maturity may converge or diverge.

It is common for traders to talk about "buying" or "selling" the spread and since this terminology can sometimes be ambiguous, we define it as follows:

- **Buy the spread** – differential will become more positive or less negative.
- **Sell the spread** – differential will become less positive or more negative.

The futures market may also use the phrases "buy the curve" (buy nearby futures, sell longer-dated futures in an expectation that the curve will steepen) and "sell the curve" (sell the near-dated contract, buy the longer-dated contract in expectation that the curve will flatten or invert). This terminology may seem inconsistent with that used in Section 6.1, but this is because we are referring to futures prices rather than rates.

There are a number of different popular spread trades that are available.

Short-end curve steepening/flattening

Suppose a trader believes that the short end of the yield curve will steepen. As a result, he expects that the interest rate differential between the near-dated and the far-dated contracts will become more positive. Assume the following prices were observed in the Eurodollar futures market:

Maturity	Price	Implied forward rate
April	99.680	0.320%
September	99.425	0.575%
Spread		0.255%

A steepening of the forward yield curve would imply that longer-term rates would rise relative to shorter-term rates; because of the inverse nature of the futures price quotation, this would imply that longer-dated futures prices would fall relative to shorter-dated prices. The trader "buys the spread" by purchasing the short-dated contract and selling the longer-dated contract. The spread between the two contracts is initially $99.6800 - 99.425 = 0.255$. Let us analyse the profit and loss on the transaction a week later under two different hypothetical scenarios.

Scenario #1

Maturity	Futures price	Implied forward price
April futures	99.6500	0.35%
September futures	99.325	0.675%
Spread		0.325%

Loss on April futures contract = 3 basis points

Profit on September futures contract = 10 basis points

Net profit = 7 basis points

Even though both futures prices fell, the spread between the two maturities increased to 32.5 basis points from its original value of 25.5 basis points. The trade realized a profit as the price of the September contract fell by more than the price of the April contract – i.e., forward rates for September increased relative to April.

Scenario #2

Maturity	Futures price	Implied forward rate
April futures	99.8000	0.20%
September futures	99.50	0.50%
Spread		0.30%

Profit on April futures contract = 12 basis points

Loss on September futures contract = 7.5 basis points

Net profit = 4.5 basis points

Even though both futures prices increased, the spread increased to 30 basis points. The trade realized a profit as the price of the April contract increased by more than the price of the September contract – i.e., forward rates for April fell relative to September, leading to a steepening in the curve.

Exploiting short-end curve anomalies

Suppose the following Eurodollar futures prices have been observed:

Maturity	Futures price	Implied forward rate
March	99.67	0.33%
June	99.54	0.46%
September	99.49	0.51%
December	98.87	1.13%

The trader believes that the September price appears to be too high (forward rate is too low) compared with the adjacent months. He believes that the actual 3-month rate in September will be higher than that currently implied by futures prices. The trader would then be faced with a number of options:

- Sell the September contract.
- Buy the June/September calendar spread at five basis points (this will lose money if the curve pivots in a clockwise direction).
- Sell the September/December calendar spread at 62 basis points (this will lose money if the curve pivots in an anti-clockwise direction).

Another possibility is to execute a butterfly spread. This is a trade that involves the execution of futures with three different maturities. In one sense it could be thought of as two calendar spreads with a common middle contract. In this version of the transaction the trader:

- Buys June @ 99.54
- Sells September @ 99.49
- Buys December @ 98.87

The trade will pay off if the perceived September price anomaly corrects itself. That is, if the price of the contract falls relative to the two neighbouring maturities from a pivot in the yield curve.

Short-end cross-market spreads

A trader believes that the spread between two futures contracts denominated in different currencies understates the expected interest rate differential. The relevant market prices are:

Futures maturity	Futures price	Implied forward rate
December Eurodollar futures	99.205	0.795%
December EURIBOR futures	98.84	1.16%
Differential		0.365
EUR/USD		€1 = $1.3740

Note: For every basis point movement in the EURIBOR contract a single future will change in value by €25.

In order to structure the trade correctly, it is important to take account of the exchange rate between the currencies. Since the Eurodollar futures contract will gain or lose $25 per basis point movement, this is equivalent to €18.20 at current exchange rates and so the transaction should be weighted by a ratio of 1.37 (€25/€18.20). Since the Eurodollar contract is less sensitive in euro terms to a basis point change in interest rates, the trader can execute more of these contracts. So to exploit a potential increase in the interest rate spread (a fall in the spread of futures prices), the trade could be structured as:

- Buy 137 Eurodollar futures @ 99.205
- Sell 100 EURIBOR futures @ 98.84

The position could then be reversed at a profit if the market moves as expected.

Table 6.4 summarizes the required transaction to exploit an expected change in the spread between two interest rates.

Table 6.4   Summary of spread trading transactions

Expectation	Lower-yielding contract	Higher-yielding contract
Spread to narrow	Sell	Buy
Spread to widen	Buy	Sell

Short-term Central Bank rates vs. LIBOR

As a result of the financial crisis that started in 2007, a number of previously stable price relationships began to decouple. One of these relationships was the spread between short-term Central Bank rates and LIBOR. Suppose a trader believed that the spread between the overnight Fed Funds rate and 3-month LIBOR was expected to widen, then one way to express this view would be to buy Fed Fund futures and sell Eurodollar futures.

6.2.3   Interest rate swaps

Basis trading

From about 2007 onwards the "3s6s basis" – which measures the difference between 3-month and 6-month interbank interest rates – changed from being a very stable relationship to one that displayed considerable volatility. This was attributed to the seizing up of the wholesale money markets. Initially this volatility was confined to short-term money-market rates as well as short-dated forward-starting maturities out to about 2 years (i.e., a 3 or 6-month rate, 12 months forward). However, by late 2009 this volatility had extended into very long-dated forward exposures such as the 30-year forward 3s6s basis. This increased volatility gave rise to a number of different basis trading strategies.

The expectation that the spread would widen could be expressed in the following ways.

Interest rate swaps   Pay fixed and receive 6-month LIBOR on an interest rate swap of a given maturity combined with an offsetting position of the same maturity which would be a receive fixed, pay 3-month LIBOR transaction. With this position the trader would need to be confident that the spread between the short-term rates ("the basis") would increase by more than the bid–offer spread that was paid to enter into the two swaps.

Single-currency basis swap   Enter into a single currency basis trade paying 3-month LIBOR and receiving 6-month LIBOR. However, one of the legs of this type of "floating/floating" swap transaction would trade with a spread to ensure that at inception it is an equitable exchange of cash flows. This spread represents the price of the transaction and so the expected movement in the 3s6s basis would need to be greater than this value.

These types of strategy could also be executed on a forward basis which would automatically widen the range of trading possibilities.

Several explanations were proffered to explain the increase in the longer-dated basis relationship:

- An increase in the basis at the short end of the curve should have a ripple impact on the basis at the longer end of the curve.
- Banks became subject to new liquidity regulations that required them to finance longer-dated assets with longer-dated borrowings. This increase in the maturity of the banks' liabilities had an influence on the shape of the forward curve.
- Hedging activity on the back of longer-term corporate debt issuance.

Banks also made money from the increase in the basis as a result of client activity. Many banking clients bought government bonds in asset swap format, where they paid fixed and received 3-month LIBOR (plus or minus a spread) on the swap component. To hedge this exposure the banks would enter into an offsetting swap where they would pay fixed and receive 6-month LIBOR. As the 3s6s basis increased, they were able to realize substantial profits. However, not all institutions were as lucky. Some reports suggested that corporate hedging activities may have resulted in positions that would only be profitable if the spread decreased. For example, a popular way of hedging a bond issue would be for a corporate to issue a fixed-rate bond and then enter into a receive fixed/pay floating interest rate swap. Typically the floating-rate leg would be referenced to 3-month LIBOR. To hedge this exposure some banks may have opted to execute a receive fixed/pay floating swap with the LIBOR leg referenced to 6-month maturities. In this case a widening of the basis would have resulted in a loss on the LIBOR legs of the swaps.

FRAs vs. EONIA trades

In Chapter 5 we noted that there was increased use of EONIA rates as a benchmark within financial markets. This is because EONIA rates closely track Central Bank rates and are therefore regarded as being approximately equal to an AAA-rated level of credit exposure.

We also noted in Chapter 1 that the FRA market was in essence a single-period swap. As a result, the FRA–EONIA spread is interpreted as the market's changing perceptions of the credit risk of the government sector with respect to the banking market. In order to express a view on this relationship, a trader would need to execute an overnight index swap (OIS) against an FRA. However, since the FRA market is forward-starting, the OIS would need to have a similar maturity. Suppose that a trader believed that the market's perception of the banking system's creditworthiness relative to the government market would deteriorate. This would translate into an increase in the FRA–EONIA spread. To exploit this expected movement the trader could:

- Receive LIBOR and pay fixed in an FRA.
- Pay compounded floating and receive fixed on an OIS of the same maturity.

It is also possible to express this view using futures contracts. For example, the EONIA/EURIBOR intercontract futures allows a trader to express a view on the spread with a single trade. For example, buying the spread would result in the trader receiving one long EONIA futures position and being granted a short EURIBOR futures position.

6.2.4 Options on single-period short-term interest rates

It is also possible to express views on short-term interest rate movements using options referenced to single forward periods. Arguably the most popular type of option that would fall into this category would be an option on an exchange-traded interest rate future. In order to avoid repetition of material already covered, interested readers are referred back to Chapter 4, which covered option trading strategies in some detail.

6.3 TRADING THE SLOPE OF THE YIELD CURVE

In this section we consider a variety of strategies that aim to profit from a change in the slope of the yield curve. These trade ideas either span the entire length of the curve or just focus on expected slope movements within a relatively narrower range of maturities.

6.3.1 Short-term interest rate futures vs. bond futures

One trade that spans the entire length of the yield curve involves trading STIRs against bond futures. In this example, we will use the same Bund future introduced in Chapter 4. The trader has identified that the yield spread between the near-dated STIR futures contract and the Bund future has widened considerably over recent times (i.e., the yield curve has steepened on a forward basis). However, he expects that the curve will flatten and so to express this view the trader sells the STIR future and buys Bund futures. Both futures contracts have the same expiry and to protect against a parallel movement in the curve will be constructed to be DV01 neutral. The current market prices for the two products are:

June EURIBOR future	99.75
June Bund future	121.48

The EURIBOR future will change in value by €25 for every basis point change in the forward rate. From Chapter 4, the Bund that was cheapest to deliver (the 3.75% of January 2019) had a DV01 of 8.03 (per 10,000 nominal). This DV01 is divided by the Bund's conversion factor (0.852328) to return an adjusted DV01 value of 9.421256 (8.03/0.852328). Since the Bund future has a notional contract size of €100,000, this DV01 figure would equate to a monetary value of €94.21. Hence the number of EURIBOR futures per Bund future is 3.77 (€94.21/€25); since the EURIBOR future has a lower DV01, the trader should execute a greater number of these relative to the Bund futures. So, if we assume that the trader buys 100 June Bund futures, he should sell 377 EURIBOR futures to ensure the position is DV01 neutral.

Suppose that 1 week later the curve has flattened as expected and short-term rates have risen relative to long-term rates. The new prices observed in the market are:

June EURIBOR future	99.51
June Bund future	120.88

The profit and loss on the position are therefore:

$$\text{Profit on EURIBOR future is 377 contracts} \times 24 \text{ basis points} \times €25 = €226{,}200$$

$$\text{Loss on Bund future is 100 contracts} \times 60 \text{ ticks} \times €10 = €60{,}000$$

$$\text{Overall profit on the transaction is therefore } €166{,}200$$

6.3.2 Fed Funds futures vs. interest rate swaps

In the last example, the trader was taking a view between short-term interbank futures and long-term government rates. In a similar vein, a trader could take a view between short-term government rates and long-term interbank rates. One way of expressing this particular view would be to execute a DV01-neutral trade between US Fed Fund futures and a forward-starting interest rate swap with an effective date to match the maturity of the futures. For example, if the trader believed that the curve would steepen, resulting in an increase in the yield spread between the two instruments, then they should pay fixed on the forward-starting swap and buy the short-dated futures contract.

6.3.3 Bonds and swaps

In this section we illustrate how views on expected yield curve movements could be expressed using bonds. Steepening trades can also be constructed using interest rate swaps and an example of this is shown in Section 3.5.3.

We start with a single transaction and then gradually increase the complexity. We make a number of simplifying assumptions for ease of illustration:

- Investment horizon = 92 days.
- All of the bonds will pay coupons annually, and we will assume that the current settlement date is also a coupon payment date so there is no accrued interest.
- All of the bonds are currently trading at par.

- The bond day basis will be actual/actual.
- A money-market day basis of actual/360.
- 3-month (92-day) repo rate is 0.25%.

We will analyse each transaction in terms of:

- Sources of profitability.
- Carry.
- Roll down.

5-year "bullet" trade

In this transaction the trader buys €10m of the 5-year bond and finances it for 92 days in the repo market. The details of the bond are:

- Price = 100.00
- Coupon and yield = 2.77%
- DV01 = 0.046099

The first step is to calculate the carry on the position.

Coupon income
$$€10,000,000 \times 2.77\% \times 92/365 = +€69,819$$

Repo expense
$$€10,000,000 \times 0.25\% \times 92/360 = -€6,389$$

Over the 3-month horizon the position carries positively to the tune of €63,430. We could use this information to calculate the 3-month forward price of the bond, which would allow us to calculate the breakeven on the position. Since the position carries positively, this acts as a buffer against a potential fall in price/rise in yield. As a result, we can derive the forward breakeven price as the spot price less this positive carry element:

$$€10,000,000 - €63,430 = 9,936,570 \text{ or } 99.3657$$

This price implies a yield to maturity (for settlement in 3 months' time) of 2.91%, a difference of 14 basis points from the current yield. So, if the trader were able to sell the bond in 3 months' time at 99.3657, then his overall profitability on the transaction would be zero. From this it follows that he will make a loss at any yield greater than 2.91% or any price less than 99.3657. As a result, this strategy (sometimes referred to as "riding the curve") is based on the trader's view of how yields will actually evolve relative to the implied forward yield of 2.91%.

Sadr (2009) points out that carry on a bond position can be expressed in either price or yield terms. Price carry is:

$$\text{Spot clean price} - \text{forward clean price}$$

Yield carry is:

$$\text{Forward yield} - \text{spot yield}$$

"If the yield carry is positive, then one can buy the bond spot, finance it in repo to the forward date, and as long as its actual yield on the forward date is lower than the forward yield, one can close out the position by selling the bond for a net profit."

He also presents a very useful shortcut method of estimating the approximate yield carry:

$$\left(\text{Spot yield} - \text{repo rate} \times \frac{365}{360} \right) \times \frac{\Delta T}{\text{DV01} - \Delta T}$$

where ΔT is defined as the length of the holding period in years. In his text, Sadr grosses up the DV01 by a factor of 100, which is common practice in the market. So if we were to apply this formula to our previous example, the yield carry approximation is:

$$\left(2.77\% - 0.25\% \times \frac{365}{360} \right) \times \frac{0.25}{4.6099 - 0.25} = 0.1443\%$$

which is close to our earlier calculation of 14 basis points.

To calculate the 3-month roll down on the position, the bond is repriced using the current yield of bonds with a residual maturity of 4.75 years. Let us assume that the 4-year rate is 2.35%, which is 42 basis points lower than the 5-year rate. From this we will assume that bonds with a maturity of 4.75 years are currently trading about 10.5 basis points (42 bp/4) below the 5-year rate. If we were to price this bond with a residual maturity of 4.75 years at a yield of 2.665%, we would derive a price of 100.455674. This would mean that the holder of the bond would now enjoy a roll-down profit of €45,567.

As a result, we can see that the position carries positively and also enjoys positive roll down.

2s10s Steepening trade

As the name suggests, this transaction is designed to profit from a steepening of the yield curve and is constructed as a combination of long and short positions in different maturities. By convention, the trade is also constructed to be duration neutral in order to protect the investor against parallel yield curve movements. The nominal positions of each bond are selected according to the ratio of the bonds' DV01s. The shorter-dated bond will have a lower DV01, so the position will be larger in nominal terms than the longer-dated bond.

Long position in 2-year bond
- Price = 100.00
- Coupon and yield = 1.2%
- DV01 = 0.019646
- Nominal = €10 m

Short position in 10-year bond
- Price = 100.00
- Coupon and yield = 3.85%
- DV01 = 0.081718
- Nominal = €2.4m

The nominal amount of the 10-year position has been rounded, since it may be difficult for a trader to execute a deal in an "odd size" in the market.

As a result, both positions have about the same DV01 exposure:

$$\frac{10,000,000}{100} \times 0.019646 = €1,965$$

$$\frac{2,400,000}{100} \times 0.081718 = €1,961$$

As before, the first step is to calculate the carry on the entire position.

2-year position
Coupon income

$$€10\,\text{m} \times 1.2\% \times 92/365 = +€30,247$$

Repo expense

$$€10\,\text{m} \times 0.25\% \times 92/360 = -€6,389$$

Net carry on 2-year is +€23,858

10-year position
Coupon expense

$$€2,400,000 \times 3.85\% \times 92/365 = -€23,290$$

Repo income

$$€2,400,000 \times 0.25\% \times 92/360 = +€1,533$$

Net carry on 10-year is −€21,757

The combined position carries positively over the 3-month period to a total value of +€2,101.

Since the yield curve is upward sloping, the roll down on the position can be calculated by revaluing the instruments at lower yields and shorter residual maturities.

If 1-year yields are 0.55% and 2-year yields 1.20%, then again we will assume that over the course of 12 months the 2-year position would roll down by a total of 0.65%. Therefore, over a quarter of a year we may roughly expect the roll down to be about 0.16%. As a result, we can recalculate the price of the bond with a maturity of 1.75 years and a yield that was 0.16% lower (i.e., 1.04%). This returns a bond price of 100.274557, so the long 2-year position shows a profit of +€27,455.

At the 10-year maturity the curve is not as steep and so following a similar procedure as before, we assume a roll down of 0.035%. As a result, the price of a 9.75-year bond at a yield of 3.815% is 100.266987. Having shorted €2.4m at a price of 100.00, the new higher price of the bond generates a loss of €6,408. The roll down on the combined position is therefore +€21,047.

As a result, we can say this position enjoys both positive carry and roll down. If the curve moves in a parallel fashion the profit on the one side of the trade equals the loss on the other, as both legs possess the same DV01; the overall profit is therefore zero. However, the trade will make a profit if the yield curve steepens irrespective of whether overall rates rise or fall. If the curve steepens while rates increase, the loss on the 2-year position is less than the profit on the 10-year position, since both bonds have about the same DV01.

Therefore, the net profit will be approximately €1,963 for every basis point of steepening. If the curve were to steepen while rates decrease, then the profit on the 2-year position will be more than the loss on the 10-year, since both sides have the same DV01. Again, the net profit will be approximately €1,963 for every basis point of steepening. If the curve were to flatten, the trade would make a loss.

It is also worth mentioning that the market will often express roll down and carry in terms of basis points with respect to the cash-equivalent value of the DV01. This is useful when the nominal amounts are different but the risk in DV01 terms is the same. So, if a trader expected a position to display a total of 15 basis points of roll down and carry and had constructed the steepener with a risk of €100,000 per basis point, this would equate to a roll down and carry of €1,500,000.

A flattening trade can be constructed using the same principles, with the position showing a profit if the curve were to flatten.

6.3.4 Conditional curve trades

An unconditional curve trade involves the use of swaps to express views on the evolution of the yield curve slope. If swaptions are used for the same purpose, the trades are referred to as conditional curve trades.

Before we consider how these trades are constructed, let us consider some of the conventions of quoting swaptions. Generally speaking, swaptions can be quoted as:

- Percentage ("lognormal") volatility.
- Normalized volatility (i.e., underlying yield multiplied by lognormal volatility).
- Basis points upfront.
- Cash amount upfront.

A snapshot of USD lognormal volatilities is shown in Figure 6.2.

The matrix highlights two different trading opportunities. Reading down each column shows there is a term structure of option volatility. As with any term structure, transactions could be constructed to express views on its expected evolution. Reading along each line

	3m	6m	1y	2y	3y	4y	5y	6y	7y	8y	9y	10y	15y	20y	25y	30y
1m	88.5	96.4	100.2	75.3	72.6	57.8	51.3	43.4	37.3	34.3	31.9	29.8	25.0	23.6	22.9	22.4
3m	70.3	77.4	74.9	68.5	66.5	54.0	48.7	42.1	37.1	34.5	32.3	30.5	25.9	24.4	23.8	23.3
6m	80.1	87.8	81.0	72.7	64.7	52.8	47.5	41.6	37.1	34.6	32.6	30.9	26.3	24.8	24.2	23.7
12m	96.0	97.0	83.4	67.9	55.8	46.5	41.9	37.9	34.7	33.0	31.5	30.2	26.3	24.9	24.4	24.0
2y	74.5	69.9	62.3	50.1	41.9	37.2	34.3	32.3	30.5	29.4	28.4	27.5	24.6	23.5	23.2	22.8
3y	47.5	44.8	40.9	36.3	32.9	30.7	29.3	28.2	27.2	26.6	26.1	25.5	23.3	22.5	22.2	22.0
4y	34.8	33.6	31.4	29.5	27.9	26.9	26.1	25.4	24.9	24.5	24.1	23.8	21.9	21.3	21.1	20.9
5y	29.9	29.1	27.6	26.3	25.4	24.8	24.3	23.9	23.4	23.1	22.9	22.6	20.9	20.4	20.2	20.0
7y	24.7	24.2	23.4	22.8	22.4	22.1	21.8	21.6	21.3	21.2	21.1	21.0	19.6	19.2	19.1	19.0
10y	21.3	21.0	20.6	20.1	19.8	19.6	19.5	19.5	19.4	19.4	19.3	19.3	18.0	17.5	17.6	17.6
15y	19.2	19.0	18.5	18.1	18.1	18.0	17.9	17.9	17.9	17.9	17.8	17.8	16.6	16.2	16.4	16.5
20y	18.0	17.8	17.5	16.9	16.7	16.6	16.5	16.5	16.5	16.5	16.6	16.6	15.6	15.5	15.7	15.9
25y	18.0	17.8	17.5	16.8	16.6	16.5	16.5	16.6	16.6	16.7	16.8	16.9	16.3	16.4	16.6	16.7
30y	18.1	17.9	17.4	16.6	16.5	16.5	16.5	16.6	16.8	17.0	17.2	17.3	17.1	17.2	17.3	17.4

Figure 6.2 Lognormal volatilities for USD swaptions. Option maturities are read horizontally, swap tenors are read vertically, so the implied volatility of a 1-year option into a 5-year swap is 37.4%. *Source:* Barclays Capital Live. Reproduced with permission.

Table 6.5 Matrix of conditional curve trades

	Steepeners	Flatteners
Bullish	Buy receiver on shorter-dated swap maturity. Sell receiver on longer-dated swap maturity	Sell receiver on shorter-dated swap maturity. Buy receiver on longer-dated swap maturity
Bearish	Sell payer on shorter-dated swap maturity. Buy payer on longer-dated swap maturity	Buy payer on shorter-dated swap maturity. Sell payer on longer-dated swap maturity

suggests yield curve trades on the underlying swap market using options of a given maturity. The latter type of trade is called a conditional curve trade.

Conditional trades are characterized by two features:

- Whether they are bullish or bearish.
- Whether they are expressing a view on the curve steepening or flattening.

The matrix in Table 6.5 illustrates the different ways in which the curve could evolve and the appropriate trades used to express a particular view.

Typically, the trades would be structured to be zero cost and DV01 neutral. Consider the bearish flattening trade, constructed using two swaptions for value 7 April 2010:

- Buy a payer on a shorter-dated swap maturity: a 1-year option into 1-year swap (strike of 1.86%).
- Sell a payer on a longer-dated swap maturity: a 1-year option into 5-year swap (strike of 3.66%).

The long payer position will be exercised if 1-year swap rates rise above the strike similarly the short payer position will be exercised against the holder if longer-dated swap rates rise above the strike. So the trader would like the shorter-dated swap rate to rise by more than any rise in the longer-dated maturity. This is consistent with the description of a bearish flattener outlined in Figure 5.5.

Referring to Figure 6.1, suppose the spot-starting spread between 5-year and 1-year swaps is calculated as 222 basis points (2.77% − 0.55%) while the same spread 1 year forward is calculated as 180 basis points (3.66% − 1.86%). Two common approaches to structuring the trades involve positioning the strikes at-the-money forward (ATMF) or at a level that equates to a 25 delta exposure.

The notional on one of the legs is fixed at a given level (i.e., USD 100m on the "back" swaption – the position with the longer-dated swap component), while the "front" notional is set such that the structure is DV01 forward swap neutral; that is, if both options are exercised at maturity the resulting position would be immune to parallel movements in the yield curve. Having set the notional amounts, the premium can be determined; alternatively, a zero-cost position could be derived by changing the strikes. When determining the zero-cost levels, it is common that the front leg strike is varied, while the back leg strike remains fixed.

For value on 7 April 2010, a conditional flattener trade constructed using USD payer swaptions of 12 months in maturity and swap maturities of 1 and 5 years would have been structured as follows in order to be DV01 neutral on a forward basis:

1-year option into a 1-year swap	USD 465.7m
1-year option into a 5-year swap	USD 100m

The ATM forward spread between the two underlying swaps was actually 179.64 basis points although we rounded it to 180 basis points but the strike of the "front" contract was moved slightly away from the underlying swap rate to give a forward spread of 179.73 basis points. This ensured that the transaction was zero cost. The position was initially delta positive ($2,806), virtually gamma neutral (−$7), vega negative (−$33,594) and theta positive ($74).

6.3.5   Identifying slope trades using swaptions

Swaptions can also be used to identify curve trading opportunities. Suppose we observe the following normalized swaption volatilities (expressed as annual basis points):

- 1-year into 5-year swaption: 117.414
- 1-year into 10-year swaption: 111.901

These values can be interpreted to suggest that the market implies that the short end of the swap curve will be more volatile than the long end. To identify if the current values represent a possible trade opportunity, the first stage is to calculate the current ratio of the two values. This returns a value of 0.953046 (111.901/117.414). The next stage is to run a single-factor regression using, say, 12 months of data.[1] The form of the equation would be:

$$\Delta y_{10} = \alpha + \beta \Delta y_5 + \varepsilon_t$$

The value derived for beta could be compared with the current ratio of implied volatilities to determine if prevailing values may offer a suitable entry point.

Figure 6.3 shows a line of best fit.

A line of best fit returned an intercept value of 0.0015 and a slope (i.e., beta value) of 1.0512. This can be interpreted as saying that for every one basis point change in the 5-year yield, the regression equation predicts a change in the 10-year yield of 1.0512 basis points.

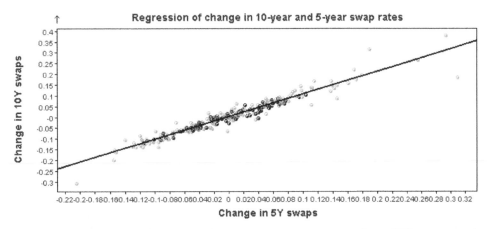

Figure 6.3 Regression results on change in 10-year USD swap rates on 5-year USD swap rates for the period 29 April 2009–30 April 2010.
Source: Data sourced from Barclays Capital Live. Reproduced with permission.

The regression equation suggests that over the past 12 months the most volatile part of the curve has actually been the long end, which is not what we would expect. For example, in Chapter 5 we argued that short-term rates are more volatile than longer-term rates (see, for example, Figure 5.8). So, from this we could conclude that the current ratio of implied volatilities is implying that the curve is expected to revert to more normal behaviour going forward than it has in the recent past.

However, different traders may have alternative views on how they think the curve will move going forward. If they believe that the short end of the curve will be anchored and the long end will continue to be volatile, this would suggest the trader believes the current swaption volatilities are "wrong". So perhaps a suitable strategy in this case would be to buy the 1-year option into a 10-year swap and sell the 1-year option into a 5-year swap.

6.3.6 Volatility and the level of interest rates

General relationship

Although not always empirically perfect, there should be an inverse relationship between percentage (i.e., lognormal) volatility and level of rates. This is shown in Figure 6.4(a) (as a time series) and 6.4(b) (as a scattergraph with a line of best fit).

In some respects this relationship is necessary so that the basis point (i.e., normalized) volatility makes sense. Recall from Chapter 3 that normalized volatility was defined as:

$$\text{Normalized volatility} = \text{Yield} \times \text{lognormal volatility } (\%)$$

Consider the implications of two scenarios where the inverse relationship between lognormal volatilities and rates did not hold. In an environment with low interest rates and low implied volatility, normalized volatility would be extraordinarily low, suggesting that the market was expecting very little movement in rates. Conversely, at high interest rates and therefore high implied volatility, normalized volatility would be high, suggesting that the market was expecting substantial rate movements. But empirically this is not the case, as rates are generally just as volatile in basis point terms when they are low as when they are high. These relationships are illustrated using simple numerical examples in Table 6.6.

Demand and supply for volatility

When curves are steep, which is generally associated with a low-rate environment, there is an incentive to buy receiver swaptions, which pushes implied volatility higher. This is because in normal market conditions the curvature tends to be more pronounced, such that the short end is very steep and the back end is much flatter. In this case there may be more reason to buy receivers in the 2 to 5-year swap maturity range rather than, say, the 10-year swap maturity. Even though rates are low, the steepness of the curve means that the forward rates are high and so the carry and roll down from the underlying swap is favourable. In these circumstances there is little incentive to buy payers or to sell receivers. However, is there an incentive to sell payers? Possibly, although the risk/reward from buying receivers with steep curves and high forward rates is better than that from selling payers. So, in this scenario one would expect there to be a net demand for volatility.

On the other hand, there could be a supply of volatility as insurance companies and retail investors hunt for an enhanced return in a low-yield environment. These investors

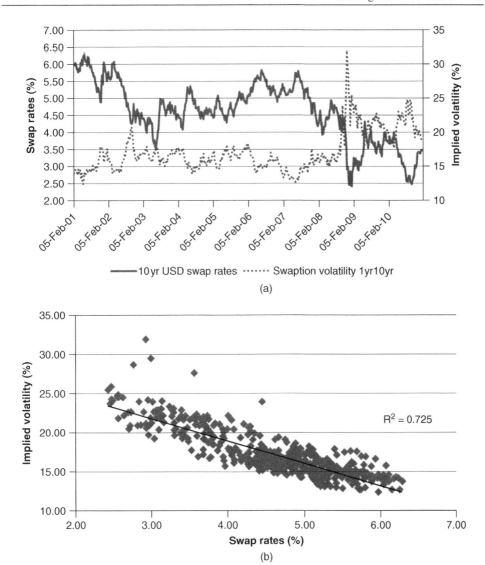

Figure 6.4 (a) Swaption volatility vs. swap rates. (b) Scattergraph of swap rates against implied volatility with line of best fit.
Source: Data sourced from Barclays Capital Live. Reproduced with permission.

Table 6.6 Relationship between yield, lognormal volatility and normalized volatility

Scenario	Yield	Volatility	Normalized volatility (bps)
Low yields, low volatility	1%	2%	2
Low yields, high volatility	1%	15%	15
High yields, high volatility	10%	15%	150
High yields, low volatility	10%	1.5%	15

will buy structured products with an embedded short volatility position, i.e., they are net sellers of options. So the net impact will depend on whether the demand from long receiver positions outweighs the supply of volatility from structured products. So even if sellers of volatility outnumber buyers, it should not fundamentally offset the full impact of the traditional inverse relationship between implied volatility and the level of rates.

6.4   TRADING THE CURVATURE OF THE YIELD CURVE

6.4.1   An overview of butterfly spreads

One of the most popular fixed income trades used to express curvature views is the butterfly spread. This trade can be executed using either bonds or swaps and we will consider both of these approaches in this section.

The essence of the trade is to express a view that a particular segment of the curve is mispriced. For example, a trader may consider that the 5-year swap rate is trading high relative to the adjacent maturities. A simple swap trade that would profit from this view would be to receive fixed on the swap and hold the position until rates have reverted back to their perceived "fair value". However, this type of "outright" trade will have a relatively large market risk, which may be unacceptable. To offset this risk, the trader could take an opposing position in a shorter-dated maturity. However, the combined trades would be exposed to changes in the slope of the curve. To overcome this problem a third longer-dated trade could be added, which would have an opposite exposure to the target 5-year maturity. The result will be a butterfly trade where the mispriced rate (5 years) has been isolated by executing two offsetting trades placed either side of the maturity.

The logic of a butterfly trade is illustrated in Figure 6.5.

There are no set rules as to which maturities the trader should select to express their view, but there are certain maturities that are more popular than others. Examples of trades include:

- 1y–2y–3y
- 2y–3y–5y
- 2y–5y–10y
- 5y–10y–15y

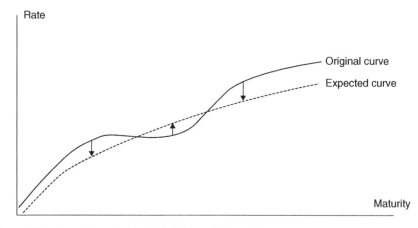

Figure 6.5   Butterfly trade; the kink in the middle of the curve is expected to correct itself.

It is also possible to execute all of these trades on a forward-starting basis, e.g. a 5y–10y–15y trade effective in 3, 6 or 12 months' time.

If the trader believed that the 5-year rate was too high, he would receive fixed in the 5-year maturity ("the belly") and pay fixed on two adjacent maturities ("the wings"). Equally, if the trader believed that the 5-year rate was too low, he would pay fixed on the belly and receive fixed on the two adjacent wings. There are a number of ways in which the trade can be constructed (see, for example, Grieves, 1999), but arguably the most popular techniques are:

- Cash and duration neutral.
- 50/50 weightings.
- Regression-based weighting.
- PCA weightings.

By structuring the trade to be cash and duration neutral, the trader is protected against small parallel shifts but not against a steepening or flattening of the curve. As the name suggests, the advantage of this transaction is that it does not require financing. A 50/50 weighted trade is where the trader will execute the trade with 50% of the interest rate exposure in each wing of the trade. A consequence of this approach is that the transaction is not cash neutral but offers protection against both parallel and slope movements. A shortcoming of both these techniques lies in the use of the DV01 measure to weight the trades. DV01 represents a position's risk exposure for a given change in yields. So DV01 neutrality will only be effective if the curve does move in a parallel fashion. Regression analysis recognizes that yields of different maturities do not always move by the same amount. For example, since shorter-term rates tend to be more volatile than longer-term rates, we may reasonably expect the shorter-dated wing to move by a greater amount than the longer-dated wing. However, this technique is not without its own shortcomings in that the regression coefficients are not stable. As a result, some practitioners prefer to weight the trades based on the results of PCA, the basics of which are outlined in Chapter 5.

6.4.2   2s5s10s Butterfly trade using bonds

If the trader believed that the 2 and 10-year yields were to increase and 5-year yields were expected to fall, a butterfly trade could be constructed by "selling the wings" (i.e., the 2 and 10-year bonds) and "buying the belly" (i.e., the 5-year position).

Cash and duration neutral

To construct a "proceeds-matched" butterfly we need to satisfy a number of criteria. The first equation (6.1) requires the trade to be proceeds matched:

$$\text{Nominal}_M \times \text{Dirty price}_M = \text{Nominal}_S \times \text{Dirty price}_S + \text{Nominal}_L \times \text{Dirty price}_L \quad (6.1)$$

The second equation (6.2) requires the risk of the belly to be equal to the risk of the wings:

$$\text{Nominal}_M \times \text{DV01}_M = \text{Nominal}_S \times \text{DV01}_S + \text{Nominal}_L \times \text{DV01}_L \quad (6.2)$$

The trader would first need to determine the nominal value of the belly and then solve for the short and long-dated positions. The next step would be to determine the nominal value of the short-dated position by expressing the first identity (6.1) in terms of the long-dated nominal:

$$\text{Nominal}_L = \frac{\text{Nominal}_M \times \text{Dirty price}_M - \text{Nominal}_S \times \text{Dirty price}_S}{\text{Dirty price}_L} \tag{6.3}$$

This can then be substituted into equation 6.2 and rearranged to solve for the nominal value of the short-dated nominal position:

$$\text{Nominal}_S = \frac{\text{Nominal}_M \left(\text{DV01}_M \times \text{Dirty price}_L - \text{DV01}_L \times \text{Dirty price}_M \right)}{\text{DV01}_S \times \text{Dirty price}_L - \text{DV01}_L \times \text{Dirty price}_M} \tag{6.4}$$

Once the nominal value for the short-dated position has been determined, the longer-dated nominal can be determined using identity (6.3).

50.50 risk weighting

The 50:50 approach to the construction of the trade is based on two principles. The overall position has no outright risk, which means that the total risk weight of both wings should equal the risk weight in the bond. This requires the following condition to apply:

$$\frac{\text{Nominal}_M}{100} \times \text{DV01}_M = \frac{\text{Nominal}_S}{100} \times \text{DV01}_S + \frac{\text{Nominal}_L}{100} \times \text{DV01}_L \tag{6.5}$$

where S is the short maturity, M the medium and L the long.

The second consideration is to make the position immune from a pivot or rotation of the yield curve. This is done by making the risk weight equal in both wings. That is:

$$\frac{\text{Nominal}_S}{100} \times \text{DV01}_S = \frac{\text{Nominal}_L}{100} \times \text{DV01}_L \tag{6.6}$$

To ensure that both of these conditions are met, we choose nominal amounts such that:

$$\text{Nominal}_S = \frac{1}{2} \times \text{Nominal}_M \times \frac{\text{DV01}_M}{\text{DV01}_S} \tag{6.7}$$

$$\text{Nominal}_L = \frac{1}{2} \times \text{Nominal}_M \times \frac{\text{DV01}_M}{\text{DV01}_L} \tag{6.8}$$

For consistency, we will use the same rates as introduced in Section 6.3.3.

Short position in 2-year bond
- Price = 100.00
- Coupon and yield = 1.2%
- DV01 = 0.019646
- Nominal = €11,700,000

Long position in 5-year bond
- Price = 100.00
- Coupon and yield = 2.77%

- DV01 = 0.046099
- Nominal = €10,000,000

Short position in 10-year bond
- Price = 100.00
- Coupon and yield = 3.85%
- DV01 = 0.081718
- Nominal = €2,800,000

In the above positions we have rounded the DV01-weighted nominal values of the positions, but the full calculation is shown below. We select €10,000,000 for the 5-year ("M") position:

$$\text{Nominal}_S = \frac{1}{2} \times \text{Nominal}_M \times \frac{\text{DV01}_M}{\text{DV01}_S} = \frac{1}{2} \times 10,000,000 \times \frac{0.046099}{0.019646} = 11,732,413$$

$$\text{Nominal}_L = \frac{1}{2} \times \text{Nominal}_M \times \frac{\text{DV01}_M}{\text{DV01}_L} = \frac{1}{2} \times 10,000,000 \times \frac{0.046099}{0.081718} = 2,820,614$$

To analyse the sources of profitability, we can first of all calculate the carry on the entire position.

Carry on the short 2-year position
Coupon expense
$$€11,700,000 \times 1.2\% \times 92/365 = -€35,388$$

Repo income

$$€11,700,000 \times 0.25\% \times 92/360 = +€7,475$$

Net carry is therefore $-€27,913$

Carry on the long 5-year position
Coupon income
$$€10,000,000 \times 2.77\% \times 92/365 = +€69,819$$

Repo expense

$$€10,000,000 \times 0.25\% \times 92/360 = -€6,388$$

Net carry is therefore $+€63,431$

Carry on the short 10-year position
Coupon expense
$$€2,800,000 \times 3.85\% \times 92/365 = -€27,172$$

Table 6.7 Roll-down calculations for butterfly position

Original bond maturity	Nominal position	Estimated 3-month roll down	New yield	Price at shorter maturity and lower yield	Profit/loss on position
2 year	11,700,000	0.16%	1.04%	100.274557	−€32,123
5 year	10,000,000	0.105%	2.665%	100.455674	+€45,567
10 year	2,800,000	0.035%	3.815%	100.266987	−€7,475

Repo income

$$€2,800,000 \times 0.25\% \times 92/360 = +€1,789$$

Net carry is therefore − €25,383

The total net carry on the combined positions is + €10,135.

The roll-down profit and loss is calculated as shown in Section 6.3.3. The bond is revalued assuming no change in the yield curve but with a shorter maturity, which is reduced by the magnitude of the particular investment period. For consistency, we can use the estimated roll-down values used in the previous examples and show the profits and losses in Table 6.7.

As a result, the net roll down on this position is positive and equal to €5,969.

So in this example, the butterfly trade will show a profit if the "kink" in the yield curve corrects itself; this would manifest itself as a fall in the 5-year yield relative to the 2 and 10-year yields. If the opposite occurs then the position will lose money. The position is immune from a parallel movement in the yield curve as well as a rotation around the 5-year maturity. The position carries positively and also enjoys positive roll down.

6.4.3 2s5s10s Butterfly trade using swaps

Consider the matrix of spot and forward-starting USD interest rate swaps shown in Figure 6.1 (reproduced as Figure 6.6 for ease of reference).

	0m	3m	6m	12m	2y	3y	4y	5y	7y	10y	15y	20y	25y	30y
3m	0.25	0.40	0.45	0.60	1.43	2.45	3.41	4.09	4.74	5.08	4.93	4.65	4.55	4.42
6m	0.33	0.42	0.47	0.69	1.55	2.59	3.53	4.17	4.79	5.12	4.95	4.67	4.57	4.44
1y	0.40	0.48	0.58	0.87	1.79	2.81	3.69	4.25	4.79	5.09	4.88	4.64	4.53	4.39
2y	0.63	0.78	0.94	1.33	2.29	3.24	3.96	4.41	4.87	5.10	4.84	4.63	4.52	4.38
3y	1.01	1.20	1.39	1.81	2.74	3.57	4.16	4.54	4.92	5.11	4.80	4.62	4.50	4.36
4y	1.45	1.65	1.84	2.26	3.10	3.81	4.31	4.63	4.96	5.09	4.77	4.60	4.50	4.33
5y	1.87	2.06	2.25	2.63	3.37	3.99	4.42	4.70	4.99	5.08	4.75	4.60	4.48	4.30
6y	2.24	2.41	2.59	2.93	3.59	4.13	4.51	4.76	5.00	5.05	4.73	4.59	4.47	4.27
7y	2.54	2.70	2.86	3.16	3.75	4.24	4.58	4.80	5.01	5.02	4.72	4.58	4.46	4.23
8y	2.79	2.93	3.07	3.36	3.89	4.33	4.64	4.84	5.01	4.99	4.71	4.57	4.44	4.20
9y	2.99	3.12	3.25	3.51	4.00	4.40	4.68	4.86	5.00	4.96	4.69	4.56	4.42	4.17
10y	3.16	3.28	3.40	3.64	4.09	4.46	4.71	4.87	4.98	4.93	4.68	4.55	4.40	4.13
15y	3.66	3.75	3.83	4.00	4.32	4.57	4.74	4.84	4.90	4.84	4.63	4.48	4.27	3.97
20y	3.85	3.92	3.98	4.12	4.38	4.58	4.72	4.80	4.84	4.78	4.57	4.38	4.14	3.86
25y	3.94	4.00	4.05	4.17	4.40	4.58	4.69	4.76	4.79	4.72	4.49	4.28	4.04	3.79
30y	3.98	4.04	4.09	4.20	4.40	4.56	4.66	4.72	4.74	4.65	4.40	4.19	3.96	3.74

Figure 6.6 Mid-market USD interest rate swap rates.
Source: Barclays Capital Live. Reproduced with permission.

The horizontal maturities represent the tenor of a given swap, while the vertical maturities represent the effective date. So the 5-year spot-starting swap rate is 2.77%, whereas the 5-year swap rate effective in 3 years' time is 4.76%.

Butterfly trades are quoted on a bid and offer basis and the easiest way to illustrate the conventions is to use the 50:50 weighting approach. Using this approach the butterfly spread is essentially twice the rate on the belly minus the wings. So a "2s5s10s" butterfly spread is (2 × 5-year – 2-year – 10-year)/2. An alternative way of constructing the quote would be 5-year – (0.5 × 2-year) – (0.5 × 10-year). However, the language used to describe the spread may initially seem counterintuitive. For example, abnormally high spread values may indicate that the belly is "cheap" (i.e., expected to fall) relative to the wings, while very low values indicate that the belly is "rich" (i.e., expected to rise) relative to the wings. However, this approach is perhaps too simplistic. To be consistent with the "cheap/rich" analysis seen in other fixed income contexts, value should be assessed relative to some measure such as a Z-score (see Section 5.4.3).

An example of such an analysis is shown in Figure 6.7. The figure shows the three most commonly used techniques to construct butterfly spreads. Each of these will be considered in the following sections. To illustrate how to interpret the data, let us consider the butterfly spread constructed using regression techniques referenced to the 10, 20 and 30-year maturities. The "weights" column indicates the trade size for the three legs of the transaction while the "spread" column indicates the current value of the spread.

Figure 6.8 shows how the spread has evolved over a 60-day period and shows that it is currently at an extreme which is reflected in the value of the current "Z-score" column in Figure 6.7.

Whatever value is derived for the butterfly spread, it is quoted on a bid–offer basis. So if the mid quote is 6 basis points, the trade may be offered as 4 bps bid, 8 bps offered. So if a trader (i.e., a price taker) believed that the 5-year maturity was to fall, which would result in a fall in the butterfly spread, they would take the bid price. At the bid side of the quote the price taker is receiving the 5-year rate and paying the fixed rate on the two wing transactions. Sometimes the market may describe this movement in the 5-year rate as an "outperformance". This is because the trader treats the change from a bond perspective. In that context a fall in the 5-year rate would lead to an increase in prices. Likewise, if the trader thought that the 5-year rate would increase ("underperform"), this can be interpreted

	PCA Bfly (Changes)			50/50 Bfly		Regression Adj. Bfly (Levels)		
Bfly	Weights	Spread	Z-Score	Spread	Z-Score	Weights	Spread	Z-Score
2 - 3 - 5	1.05 - 1 - 0.20	2.12	1.58	-19.80	1.53	0.74 - 1 - 0.44	-29.06	0.50
2 - 4 - 7	0.92 - 1 - 0.39	-4.88	1.64	-0.14	1.95	0.66 - 1 - 0.66	-67.66	0.44
3 - 4 - 5	0.55 - 1 - 0.48	-0.51	1.68	3.69	1.89	0.49 - 1 - 0.56	-10.81	0.37
3 - 5 - 7	0.49 - 1 - 0.58	-9.40	1.59	15.96	1.80	0.43 - 1 - 0.68	-31.62	0.09
2 - 5 - 10	0.88 - 1 - 0.48	-14.57	1.58	16.93	1.87	0.72 - 1 - 0.78	-111.55	-0.03
3 - 5 - 10	0.72 - 1 - 0.41	-13.95	1.43	-12.21	1.83	0.70 - 1 - 0.53	-56.29	-0.45
4 - 5 - 10	0.80 - 1 - 0.25	-8.14	1.01	-38.52	1.64	0.81 - 1 - 0.28	-20.15	-0.77
5 - 7 - 10	0.55 - 1 - 0.48	-0.11	-0.01	4.80	1.28	0.53 - 1 - 0.51	-8.97	-1.43
4 - 7 - 10	0.44 - 1 - 0.62	-4.59	0.53	27.42	1.31	0.41 - 1 - 0.69	-23.07	-1.12
7 - 10 - 15	0.48 - 1 - 0.54	-3.79	0.06	5.81	0.59	0.50 - 1 - 0.51	-0.77	-0.14
5 - 10 - 30	0.54 - 1 - 0.54	-3.45	-0.03	26.66	0.92	0.68 - 1 - 0.42	14.30	-1.03
10 - 12 - 15	0.51 - 1 - 0.49	-0.98	0.47	0.76	1.24	0.56 - 1 - 0.44	2.04	-0.13
10 - 15 - 30	0.53 - 1 - 0.48	4.01	-0.20	9.25	0.61	0.62 - 1 - 0.39	10.07	-3.13
10 - 20 - 30	0.28 - 1 - 0.73	5.26	-1.40	24.71	-1.94	0.32 - 1 - 0.68	10.12	-3.26
15 - 20 - 25	0.42 - 1 - 0.58	2.21	-2.88	4.23	-1.88	0.39 - 1 - 0.60	2.84	-2.61
20 - 25 - 30	0.35 - 1 - 0.65	0.50	0.68	1.62	-1.05	0.40 - 1 - 0.60	1.60	0.32

Figure 6.7   Cheap/rich analysis of butterfly spreads constructed using interest rate swaps.
Source: Barclays Capital Live. Reproduced with permission.

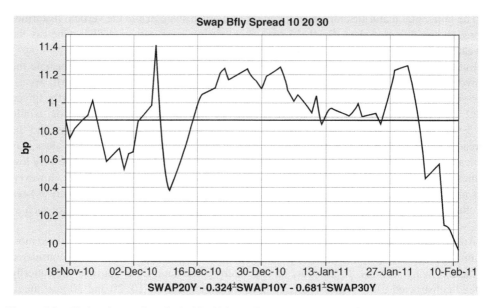

Figure 6.8   60-day time series of 10–20–30 butterfly spread constructed using interest rate swaps. *Source:* Barclays Capital Live. Reproduced with permission.

Table 6.8   Butterfly spread quoting conventions

	Bid	Offer
Quote	4 basis points	8 basis points
Action and motivation	Buy spread (spread expected to rise)	Sell spread (spread expected to fall)
Swap trades	Pay the belly, receive the wings	Receive the belly, pay the wings
Bond trades	Sell the belly, buy the wings	Buy the belly, sell the wings

to mean that the spread will rise so the trader takes the offered quote. In this instance the trader would be paying the 5-year rate and receiving fixed on the two wing transactions.

A market maker would quote a butterfly spread as shown in Table 6.8.

The evolution of the butterfly spread in EUR on a spot or forward-starting basis for a 12-month period in 2009–2010 is illustrated in Figure 6.9.

50:50 weighting

A 50:50 weighted butterfly trade would be quoted and constructed as follows:

	Rate	DV01 (per $10m)
2-year swap rate	1.20%	$1,971
5-year swap rate	2.77%	$4,696
10-year swap rate	3.85%	$8,446

$$2.77 - (0.5 \times 1.20) - (0.50 \times 3.85) = 24.5 \text{ basis points}$$

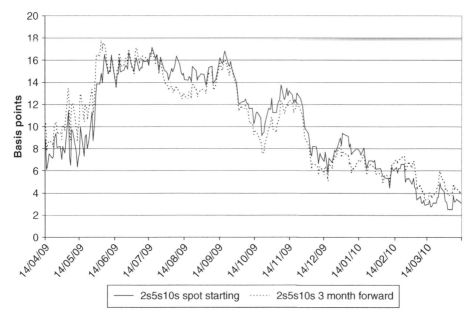

Figure 6.9   The 2s5s10s butterfly spread in EUR on a spot and 3-month forward-starting basis, April 2009–April 2010.
Source: Data sourced from Barclays Capital Live. Reproduced with permission.

The 50:50 weighting approach means the butterfly trade has no exposure to parallel movements in the yield curve, since the total risk weight in the "wings" should be equal to the risk weight in the "body". However, for every 1 basis point non-parallel movement in the yield curve the position would gain or lose \$4,696. This approach is similar to that used in the previous section, when the trade was constructed using bonds.

To derive the relative notional amounts we must solve the following equation:

$$\text{Nominal}_M \times \text{DV01}_M = \text{Nominal}_S \times \text{DV01}_S + \text{Nominal}_L \times \text{DV01}_L \tag{6.9}$$

where S is the short maturity, M is the medium maturity and L the long maturity.

It is also possible to hedge the position against "pivot" risk – the risk that the curve may rotate. This is achieved by making the risk weight equal in both of the wings:

$$\text{Notional}_S \times \text{DV01}_S = \text{Notional}_L \times \text{DV01}_L \tag{6.10}$$

To meet both of these conditions we can choose notional amounts such that:

$$\text{Notional}_S = \frac{1}{2} \times \text{Notional}_M \times \frac{\text{DV01}_M}{\text{DV01}_S} \tag{6.11}$$

$$\text{Notional}_L = \frac{1}{2} \times \text{Notional}_M \times \frac{\text{DV01}_M}{\text{DV01}_L} \tag{6.12}$$

So if we substitute the values for the DV01s presented above we can derive the following trade sizes. We will assume that the notional of the 5-year maturity is EUR 10m:

$$\text{Notional}_S = \frac{1}{2} \times 10,000,000 \times \frac{4,696}{1,971} = 11,912,734$$

$$\text{Notional}_L = \frac{1}{2} \times 10,000,000 \times \frac{4,696}{8,446} = 2,780,014$$

Suppose a trader has analysed the recent price movement shown in Figure 6.8 and believes that the spread will increase and so decides to execute a spot-starting butterfly trade to reflect this view. He pays fixed on the 5-year maturity and receives fixed on the 2 and 10-year maturities. Suppose that shortly after implementing the trade the swaps curve increases by 10 basis points across all maturities. To illustrate the impact of the yield curve movement, we will use the exact DV01-adjusted notional amounts, whereas in reality the trader would round the size of the trades for ease of deal execution. The profit and loss on the three positions are given in Table 6.9.

From Table 6.9 we can see that the butterfly structure is immune to small parallel movements in the yield curve. Consider what would happen if the curve were to pivot about the 5-year point. Let us say that the 2-year rate falls and the 10-year rate rises by the same amount but the 5-year rate remains unchanged. The 2-year receive fixed position would show a profit, while the 10-year receive fixed position would result in a loss. Since the DV01 exposures are equal then ignoring any profit or loss effect from the passage of time, the position would not gain or lose any money.

From this same information we can see that the trade will show the greatest profit if the 5-year rate rises and the 2 and 10-year rates fall. For example, suppose that shortly after the trade was placed the rates moved to the following values:

2-year swap rate	1.10%
5-year swap rate	2.87%
10-year swap rate	3.75%

The new spread quote would be:

$$2.87 - (0.5 \times 1.10) - (0.50 \times 3.75) = 44.5 \text{ basis points}$$

This would represent an increase in the spread of 20 basis points so the approximate profit and loss could be estimated using the DV01 of the position for a change in the spread. In this case the profit would be \$93,920 (20 basis points $\times$ \$4,696).

The shortcoming of using a 50:50 technique lies in the observation that yields of different maturities will have different volatilities and are not perfectly correlated. So the assumption

Table 6.9 The profit and loss from a 2s5s10s swap butterfly

Maturity	Pay or receive fixed	Notional (EUR)	DV01 (EUR per notional)	Profit and loss for 10 basis point parallel move in curve
2 year	Receive	11,912,734	2,348	(23,480)
5 year	Pay	10,000,000	4,696	46,960
10 year	Receive	2,780,014	2,348	(23,480)

that the yields will move in a parallel fashion and by the same magnitude does not always hold. Regression and PCA techniques incorporate information about how the yield curve will actually move.

Regression weighting

The second weighting method we will consider is that of regression weighting. Linear regression creates a line of best fit and helps to predict how a change in one yield (i.e., the 5-year yield) can be predicted with reference to changes in other yields (in this case the 2 and 10-year yields). In this technique the trader runs a regression of changes in the 5-year rate (Δy_5) on changes in the 2-year (Δy_2) and 10-year rate (Δy_{10}) over a sample period. The form of the regression equation in this instance would be:

$$\Delta y_5 = \alpha + \beta_2 \times \Delta y_2 + \beta_{10} \times \Delta y_{10} + \varepsilon_t$$

Using regression terminology there are two independent variables – the change in the 2 and 10-year rates – while the change in the 5-year rate is termed the dependent variable. The α term represents the intercept, which Tuckman (2002) argues is often close to zero when regressing changes on yields on each other and so is therefore ignored. The two β terms are slopes of the best fit line and are used to calculate the hedge ratios for the trade. The term ε represents an error term and can be thought of as the magnitude of the actual change in the dependent variable that is not captured by the different components on the right-hand side of the equation.

Suppose for value on 8 April 2010, regression analysis on the USD swap market derived an intercept close to zero and coefficients of 0.61 and 0.62 for Δy_2 and Δy_{10}, respectively. We can restate the equation as:

$$\Delta y_5 = 0.61 \times \Delta y_2 + 0.62 \times \Delta y_{10}$$

So if both the 2 and 10-year yields move by 5 basis points, we would predict a change in the 5-year rate of:

$$\Delta y_5 = 0.61 \times 5 + 0.62 \times 5$$

$$= 3.05 + 3.01$$

$$= 6.06 \text{ basis points}$$

The two β coefficients can then be used to calculate the butterfly spread as:

$$5\text{-year} - 0.61 \times 2\text{-year} - 0.62 \times 10\text{-year}$$

So, using the swap rates from the previous example the spread now becomes:

$$2.77 - 0.61 \times 1.20 - 0.62 \times 3.85 = -34.9 \text{ basis points}$$

In this example the position in the 5-year swap is hedged with 61% of its DV01 in the 2-year maturity and 62% of its DV01 in the 10-year maturity. In this case a 10 basis point parallel movement in the yield curve will not result in a zero profit and loss position. So it could be said that this method hedges the butterfly against typical rather than parallel curve movements.

PCA

The third technique we will consider is PCA, the basics of which were outlined in Chapter 5. One way in which PCA can be used to identify trading opportunities is to monitor the value of factor 3. When this factor reaches a particularly high or low level for a particular set of bonds, it indicates that the yield curve is displaying unusual curvature given the yield level and steepness of the curve. The focus is on factor 3 because it reflects irregularities in curvature between the three positions that would go to make up a butterfly position. So to identify opportunities the trader could derive a butterfly spread value using the values of factor 3 over a predefined period.

To calculate the appropriate weights for each leg of the transaction the trader would need to conduct some form of PCA similar to that shown in Table 5.1. The justification for using these values is that by convention the market interprets these values as yield betas; the extent to which bonds move relative to each other.

The values for factor 3 can be used to structure the butterfly trade so that it is hedged against shifts in factor 1 and factor 2, leaving exposure only to factor 3, which captures the anomalous curve shape. The following pair of equations expresses these hedges mathematically; the profit/loss on the wings of the butterfly from shifts in factor 1 and factor 2 should offset the loss/profit on the belly.

$$\text{Notional}_{5yr} \times \text{DV01}_{5yr} \times \text{F1}_{5yr} = (\text{Notional}_{2yr} \times \text{DV01}_{2yr} \times \text{F1}_{2yr})$$

$$+ (\text{Notional}_{10yr} \times \text{DV01}_{10yr} \times \text{F1}_{10yr}) \qquad (6.13)$$

$$\text{Notional}_{5yr} \times \text{DV01}_{5yr} \times \text{F2}_{5yr} = (\text{Notional}_{2yr} \times \text{DV01}_{2yr} \times \text{F2}_{2yr})$$

$$+ (\text{Notional}_{10yr} \times \text{DV01}_{10yr} \times \text{F2}_{10yr}) \qquad (6.14)$$

where:

F1 = factor value relating to factor 1

F2 = factor value relating to factor 2

The two equations can then be solved for the two unknowns (i.e., the notional amounts on the two wing positions) by choosing a transaction size for the belly and substituting in the DV01s and the F1s and F2s in the two equations. These weightings will ensure that the trade has a profit or loss performance that closely tracks the changes in factor 3, with the proviso that the yield curve continues to behave as it did during the historical period on which the PCA was based.

For value on 8 April 2010, PCA (using the entire curve structure and covering a 4-year period) suggested weights for the swap notional amounts of -0.42 and -0.54 for the 2 and 10-year maturities, respectively. This would return a butterfly spread of:

$$2.77 - 0.42 \times 1.20 - 0.54 \times 3.85 = 18.7 \text{ basis points}$$

Table 6.10   Nominal positions on a butterfly trade using PCA factor weightings

	2 year	5 year	10 year
Notional amount	−42m	+100m	−54m
DV01 based on notional amount	$8,278	$44,696	$45,608

So, a USD 100m notional for the 5-year belly would be associated with a 2-year notional of USD 42 million and a 10-year notional of USD 54 million. Table 6.10 shows the weightings and the DV01 exposure.

Although there are a number of ways of identifying a suitable entry point, a trader may wish to enter a trade when the Z-score[2] of the third factor reaches a certain level while the exit point could be established when the Z-score decreases to a predetermined level.

6.4.4   Forward and spot spreads and carry

In Table 6.2 we showed how the forward spread could be used to determine the carry on a steepening/flattening trade. Using the same logic we could derive a similar set of rules for butterfly trades.

Consider the long 2s5s10s butterfly trade analysed in Section 6.4.2. In that example we illustrated that this long spread position enjoyed positive carry. The spot rates for this trade were 1.20%, 2.77% and 3.85% for the 2, 5 and 10-year positions, respectively. This returned a spot butterfly spread of 24.5 basis points. Using the rates in Figure 6.1, the 12-month forward prices for 1, 4 and 9-year positions were 1.86%, 3.37% and 4.79%, respectively, which returns a forward butterfly spread of 4.5 basis points. Since the trade must profit if the spread were to increase from its initial value, the lower forward breakeven rate suggests that the position will only realize a loss if the spread were to fall by 20 bps. For this condition to hold the position must enjoy positive carry. Table 6.11 shows the relationship between spot and forward butterfly spreads and the associated carry.

Table 6.11   Summary of carry and relationship between forward and spot spreads for butterfly spread trades

Position	Forward spread > spot spread	Forward spread < spot spread
Buy the butterfly spread	Position carries negatively; spread must increase by more than the negative carry for trade to be profitable	Position carries positively; spread can decrease by the amount of the carry before the trade loses money
Sell the butterfly spread	Position carries positively; spread can increase by an amount equal to the carry before the trade loses money	Position carries negatively; spread must fall by more than the negative carry for the trade to be profitable

6.4.5   Volatility and yield curve slope and curvature

Since curves historically tend to steepen and become more concave (short end steep, long end flat) in market rallies and become more convex (short end inverted or flat, long end flat)

in market sell-offs, there should be a direct relationship between level, slope and curvature. Generally speaking, when rates are high we would expect low percentage ("lognormal") volatility. But when rates are high the yield curve tends to flatten and possess less curvature. From this we can conclude that if one finds a good relationship between the level of rates and the implied volatility, then there should also be a relationship between implied volatility, yield curve slope and curvature.

Consider Figure 6.10(a,b), which shows the relationship between levels of implied volatility and the slope of the curve as a time series (a) and as a scattergraph (b). We established in Figure 6.4(a) that there was an inverse relationship between implied volatility and the level of rates; as rates fell lognormal volatility increased and vice versa.

We have also argued that as rates fall the yield curve will steepen. This means that the spread between 2 and 10-year rates increases if measured as the 10-year rate minus the 2-year rate. This relationship is confirmed in Figure 6.10(b).

Figure 6.10(c,d) analyses the relationship between volatility and the curvature of the yield curve. As rates fall we have argued that the curve becomes more concave (steep short end, flat long end). This means the 2s10s30s spread (defined here as 2 * 10 year minus the 2 year minus the 30 year) will increase. This positive relationship between volatility and the yield curvature is shown in Figure 6.10(d).

As in all aspects of finance, relationships will not always hold and so occasionally the data may not fit our general observations. The analyst would need to consider if the period chosen is unusual; an example might be the monetary conditions that prevailed from late 2008 onwards when short-term interest rates were held at very low levels by Central Banks for a prolonged period in addition to the policy of quantitative easing. This brought about scenarios not normally experienced, such as yield curves being more volatile in the longer maturities than in shorter maturities. Also, with short-term interest rates on hold, actual volatility declined substantially and this dragged down implied volatility, which has meant the expected inverse relationship between volatility and the level of rates did not always exist.

6.5   VOLATILITY, CURVATURE AND SKEW

Although there is not much publically available data to prove it, anecdotally traders tend to accept there is a relationship between yield curve curvature and implied volatility skew. When the curve is very concave (short end steep, long end flat), then there tends to be increased demand for OTM payers on long-dated swap tenors. The rationale is that participants may believe that the long end of the curve will steepen, driven principally by a rise in long-term rates. A similar argument could be constructed for convex curves, where the short end is inverted/flat and the long end is also flat. This would encourage traders to buy OTM receivers on the expectation that rates would fall. This could apply to both long and short-term swap maturities since changes in yield on different points of the curve are highly correlated. However, when short-term rates are high and the short end of the curve is steeply inverted or flat, forward rates will be steeply declining for shorter-dated maturities. So the strikes on receivers for shorter-dated swap maturities may be unattractive relative to those for longer-dated swap maturities.

So, skew tends to be higher in absolute terms when curves are very convex or very concave and lower when the curvature is less pronounced.

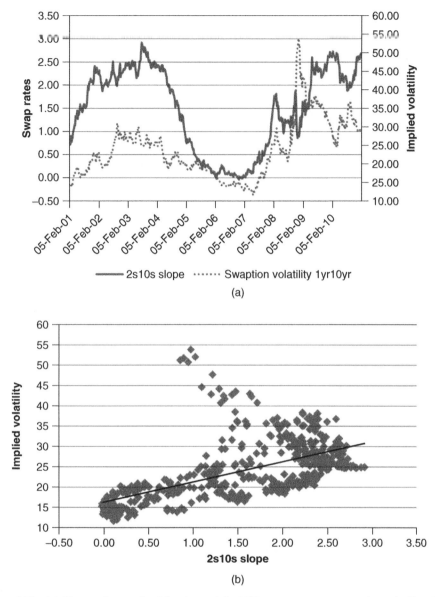

Figure 6.10 (a) Time series graph of the slope of the USD swap curve vs. swaption volatility. 2s10s slope is defined as 10-year swap rate minus 2-year swap rate. (b) Scattergraph of the slope of the USD swap curve vs. swaption volatility. 2s10s slope is defined as 10-year swap rate minus 2-year swap rate. (c) Time series graph of the curvature of the USD swap curve vs. swaption volatility. 2s10s30s spread is defined as 2 * 10 year swap rate minus the 2 year swap rate minus the 30 year swap rate. (d) Scattergraph of the curvature of the USD swap curve vs. swaption volatility. 2s10s30s spread is defined as 30-year swap rate minus 10-year swap rate minus 2-year swap rate.
Source: Data sourced from Barclays Capital Live. Reproduced with permission.

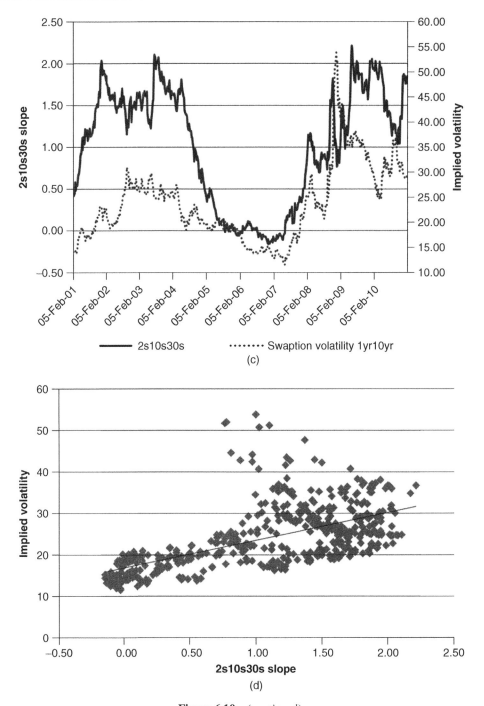

(c)

(d)

Figure 6.10   (*continued*)

6.6   CONSTANT-MATURITY PRODUCTS

6.6.1   Product definitions

In recent years there has been increasing interest in constant-maturity products. A constant-maturity derivative takes its value from a rate of a given maturity that does not change throughout the life of a deal. If we take a conventional interest rate swap of a given maturity – say 5 years – then after 1 year the position takes its value from 4-year rates having "rolled down" the curve. However, a constant-maturity swap (CMS) will have one leg referenced to a given swap maturity that will not change. In their most basic form a constant-maturity swap will consist of a floating/floating structure. The value of one leg will be reset each period to take the value of a fixed-swap maturity – again, say, 5 years. The other floating leg will reference to LIBOR of a given maturity plus or minus a spread. The spread is in effect the price and is set at a level that ensures the net present value of the structure at inception is equal to zero. If the curve is positive in shape we would expect the spread to be positive, while an inverted curve will result in a negative spread. Another feature of this type of swap is that the referenced constant-maturity rate does not have to be the same as the maturity rate of the swap. So although it is perfectly possible to have a 5-year swap referenced to the 5-year constant-maturity rate, it is also possible to have a 2-year swap referenced to, say, the 5-year constant-maturity rate. If an investor were to enter into a "CMS receiver" (receiving the CMS rate paying LIBOR plus a spread), this would imply an expectation of a steepening swaps curve. A "CMS payer" would suggest a flattening view as the investor would pay the CMS rate and receive LIBOR plus a spread. An illustration of CMS bid–offer quotes is shown in Table 6.12. The quotes represent the number of basis points that would be applied to the LIBOR leg of the transaction.

The CMS swap rate is reset at agreed time intervals, usually on a quarterly basis for maturities of up to 3 years and semi-annually thereafter. The CMS fixing is usually determined by reference to a panel of bank quotations.

So in the market parlance a "5-year CMS 10-year" means a swap transaction of 5 years' maturity referenced to the 10-year CMS rate. Typically the counterparty will receive or pay 3-month LIBOR.

There is an alternative way of quoting CMS swaps which still ensures that the transaction is equitable and that is by means of a participation. In this case the LIBOR leg does not attract a spread with the adjustment being applied to the CMS component. The following termsheet illustrates the principle:

Currency	EUR
Maturity	10 years
Party A pays:	92% x EUR CMS10
Party B pays:	12-month EURIBOR set in advance
EUR CMS 10	10-year EUR swap rate, set in advance
Frequency and basis	Annual, 30/360

In this trade the CMS receiver will profit when the curve stays steep as the CMS 10 payout will exceed the EURIBOR floating rate. Hence this would represent an advantage for investors who want to receive a floating rate but at the same time would like to achieve a return greater than money-market rates.

Table 6.12   Quotes for CMS swaps (quotes are illustrative)

Swap maturity	2-year CMS index	5-year CMS index
5 years	12.2–12.7	29.4–30.4
10 years	20.2–21.4	38.7–39.9
15 years	20.7–21.9	34.6–36.5
20 years	20.5–22.0	31.9–34.2
30 years	19.7–21.7	27.6–30.8

Although we have analysed swaps as our introduction to the suite of constant-maturity products, there are also a number of other structures. CMS caps and floors will resemble conventional cap and floor structures, but the main difference is that they will reference a swap rate rather than an underlying LIBOR rate. A popular instrument used in structured products is CMS spread options, which allow the holder to express a view on the difference between swap rates of different maturities – i.e., whether the curve will steepen or flatten.

6.6.2   CMS product pricing

The pricing of CMS products can be quite involved and so to be consistent in our coverage we will approach the issue intuitively.

One popular technique used to price instruments is referred to as "static replication". This technique aims to replicate the payoff on an instrument by combining other related instruments that take their value from the same underlying asset. The cost incurred in creating the replicating portfolio is therefore the price of the instrument.

One pricing approach starts by pricing CMS options and attempts to replicate their payoff using receiver and payer swaptions. Once priced, the CMS options can then be used to value a constant-maturity swap using the principles of put–call parity. Put–call parity, when applied to conventional interest rate options, states that the purchase of a cap and the sale of the floor with the same strike, notional amount and maturity will be equal to a forward-starting swap with a fixed rate equal to the strike of the options.

One of the complicating factors when adopting this pricing approach is that the payoff from any CMS caplet is linear but the payoff from a replicating swaption is concave. The concavity results from the fact that when the option expires, the payoff will be expressed as a percentage interest rate applicable for the entire period of the underlying swap. Suppose the swaption payoff was, say, 0.5% p.a. on a notional of $100m for a period of 5 years. The value of this payment in cash terms is.

Expiry payoff of payer swaption

Max(swap rate at expiry − strike rate, 0) × DV01 × notional amount

Expiry payoff of receiver swaption

Max(strike rate − swap rate at expiry, 0) × DV01 × notional amount

Chapleton *et al.* (2007) argue that a CMS caplet can be replicated by buying a series of payer swaptions at successively higher strikes, while a CMS floorlet can be replicated by buying a receiver swaption at the strike equal to the strike of the floorlet and selling receiver swaptions with lower strikes. The trader would need to make a judgemental decision as to how many of these swaptions were actually required. Chapleton *et al.* (2007) argue that the notional amounts of the replicating swaptions will differ and that the hedging swaption with the strike equal to the CMS option will be significantly larger than the remaining swaptions.

They then argue that put–call parity at maturity will yield the following result:

$$+\text{Caplet}_{\text{cms}} - \text{floorlet}_{\text{cms}} = \text{Underlying CMS rate} - \text{strike}$$

From this they set the strike equal to the forward swap rate and take expected values to derive the following identity:

$$\text{Expected CMS rate} = \text{Forward swap rate} + \text{caplet}_{\text{cms}} - \text{floorlet}_{\text{cms}}$$

From this they argue that a single CMS payment could be replicated by a forward-starting swap and a long position in an out-of-the-money payer and receiver swaptions (i.e., a swaption strangle). They also argue that in a perfect replicating portfolio there is no need for the at-the-money swaptions as they should cancel each other out.

One of the implications of this approach is that the payoff on the replicating portfolio is non-linear while the payoff on the cap and floor is linear. It is common for practitioners to adjust the forward swap rate upwards to reflect this difference in convexity. There are a number of different approaches to calculating this convexity adjustment, and interested readers are referred to sources such as Sadr (2009) or Chapleton *et al.* (2007) for further discussion.

6.6.3 CMS sensitivities and impact on market

While a regular interest rate swap will have exposure to parallel movements in the swap curve, CMS swaps are relatively insensitive to this type of movement. They are more sensitive to steepening or flattening of the curve. Perhaps the easiest way to conceptualize the market risk is to view the position as a combination of two floating-rate note positions and so the duration will be less than a fixed income security of equivalent maturity (see Chapter 3). If there was a sudden increase in demand for CMS products then this would require hedging by the structuring bank. We also pointed out that CMS products were widely used in structured products and so in a similar vein if there is substantial investor interest, the issuing banks would be required to implement some form of hedge. In both of these cases we can conclude that a change in CMS activity will have an impact on long-dated swaption volatility.

6.6.4 Applications of CMS products

From a view-driven perspective, CMS trades can be used to express views on movements in the swap curve. For example:

- *Trader believes that the rate for a particular maturity is too high* – Receive the CMS rate for that maturity and pay LIBOR. If the rate declines, the position is closed out by paying the now lower CMS rate and receiving LIBOR.

- *Trader believes that the curve will flatten* – Similar to the previous example, the trader receives the longer-dated CMS rate and pays LIBOR.
- *Trader believes the curve will steepen* – Pay the CMS rate and receive LIBOR; after curve movement, close the position out by reversing the trades.

One of the reasons that CMS products are popular is that they offer investors the possibility to maintain a constant-duration exposure. CMS structures have been popular among insurers and pension funds that use them as an asset–liability management tool to hedge annuities and guaranteed payments to policy holders.

6.7   STRUCTURED PRODUCTS – RANGE ACCRUALS

Structured products are bespoke financial structures that are "engineered" by combining features of vanilla and exotic products to achieve a desired payoff profile for issuers and investors. They are usually sold in two formats: as an OTC swap or in note format. The OTC swap format is regularly used by corporates, who use the structures for liability management tools to reduce their borrowing costs. However, we will consider transactions that are packaged as bonds to attract the investor client base.

A callable range accrual swap (sometimes referred to as range/corridor swaps) pays the investor a coupon which only accrues if an agreed index meets a predefined condition stated at the outset of the transaction. The coupons are multiplied by an accrual factor, commonly expressed as n/N, where:

n = number of days where the underlying sets within specified ranges

N = number of days in the coupon period

In terms of a payoff profile the investor has an exposure which is the same as a strip of digital options that expire on a daily basis. The investor enjoys an enhanced yield as they have sold a package of options. The structure is illustrated in Figure 6.11.

One example of a structured note referenced to CMS rates is the Atlantic Range Accrual note:

Currency	EUR
Maturity	10 years
Coupons	EUR CMS $10 + 0.10\% \times n/N$
EUR CMS 10	10-year EUR swap rate, set in advance
n	Number of days when 3-month USD LIBOR is less than or equal to 7.50%
N	Number of days in the coupon period
Frequency and basis	Annual; 30/360

The structures can be designed with either fixed or floating coupons. So, in the case of a fixed-coupon structure the investor will be paid (say) 5.30% for every day that an agreed interest rate index fixes within an agreed range. A floating-rate structure may pay a coupon referenced to a particular interest rate index such as EURIBOR plus a fixed spread, the latter being in effect the premia receivable from the sale of the daily digitals. Again this

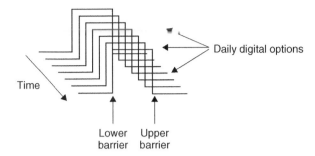

Time

Daily digital options

Lower   Upper
barrier   barrier

Figure 6.11   Example of digital range accrual note.

coupon would only accrue based on the conditionality written into the contract. Although Figure 6.11 shows the reference index accruing within a particular range, it is also possible for the range to be specified as either above or below a given value.

It is normally the issuer that has the right to call the note, typically on each of the coupon payment dates. Since the investor is short the call this further enhances their return.

The magnitude of the yield enhancement is also a function of where the barriers are placed. The more out-of-the-money the barrier with respect to the forward rate, the lower the yield enhancement.

7

Relative Value in Credit

This chapter divides into four main sections. In the first part we apply our relative value framework to analyse the relationships between cash, forwards, swaps and volatility within a credit context. The second, third and fourth parts of the chapter consider our relative value question: "*What is the optimal way to express a particular view on the market?*" These sections address the question in a number of ways with respect to the following themes:

- Credit term structures.
- Single-name credits.
- A portfolio of credits.

In terms of products we will consider the following instruments:

- Bonds.
- Single-name and index credit default swaps (CDSs).
- Asset swaps.
- Credit-linked notes (CLNs).
- Options on CDSs ("credit swaptions").
- Total return swaps.
- Index tranche products.

The basics of bonds, credit default swaps and asset swaps were covered in Chapter 1, and so this knowledge will be assumed. In order to make the chapter manageable in terms of size, we have deliberately omitted products which often fall under the "structured credit" umbrella – such as collateralized debt obligations.

7.1 APPLYING THE RELATIVE VALUE TRIANGLE TO CREDIT

7.1.1 The bond–credit default swap relationship

Single-name CDS basis

In Chapter 5 we defined and analysed the different measures of traded credit spread. Although each measure was slightly different, arguably the most popular measure of traded credit risk in cash bonds is the Z-spread ("zero volatility spread" – see Section 5.3.6). The Z-spread was defined as "*the incremental return an investor would earn over the entire zero-coupon curve*". The Z-spread can be measured relative to either the zero-coupon curves for government bonds or swaps. The Z-spread is calculated by discounting each cash flow on the instrument at an appropriate zero-coupon rate for that maturity plus a fixed spread. The Z-spread is the single value for the fixed spread such that the present value of the cash flows equals the observed price of the bond.

The CDS spread is interpreted by the market as the "true" measure of an issuer's potential risk of default. Although never explicitly stated, it is taken to be an issuer's credit spread relative to the LIBOR curve (O'Kane and Sen, 2004).

Since the Z-spread and the CDS spread attempt to capture the credit risk of a given reference entity, one would reasonably expect their values to be the same. However, empirically this is not the case and as a result the relationship between the two (the CDS basis) is actively traded. By convention, the CDS basis is defined as:

CDS spread minus Z-spread

An alternative way of expressing this basis is to substitute the issuer's asset swap spread (sometimes referred to by its acronym of ASW) for the Z-spread. Recall that asset swapping a bond converts a fixed income instrument into a synthetic floating-rate note. The resultant spread to LIBOR on the floating leg is interpreted as the market's perception of the issuer's credit risk, assuming the bond is trading at par. If the asset swap spread is used, the CDS basis is redefined as:

CDS spread minus asset swap spread

An example of the CDS basis over time is given in Figure 7.1.

Intuitively one might expect the basis to be always positive. In other words, although a bond investor would earn a return linked to the issuer's creditworthiness, the cost of insuring this position against an event of default should logically exceed this return. If the basis were negative, a trader who bought the bond and bought default protection would enjoy the proverbial "free lunch". Suppose that the Z-spread on a bond is 20 basis points while the CDS spread on the same reference entity is 15 basis points. This would result in a negative basis of 5 basis points. Not only is the trader protected against the default of the reference entity, but they are still making a return which primarily derives its value from the market's perception of the issuer's credit risk.

Since negative basis scenarios do exist, the obvious question that arises from this is why? One starting point is to realize that the two markets will attract different participants who

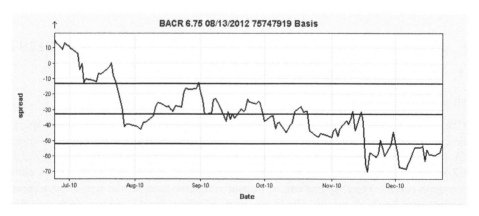

Figure 7.1   CDS basis for 6.75% 2012 issued by Barclays Bank plc. Data covers period June–December 2010.
Source: Barclays Capital Live. Used with permission.

may react at different speeds to new information. The CDS market will largely be dominated by investment banks and hedge funds, which are more likely to react swiftly to changes in the perceived creditworthiness of a particular reference entity. However, the cash bond market will probably be dominated by "buy-and-hold" participants such as pension funds and insurance companies, who may not react as quickly.

O'Kane and McAdie (2004) suggest a number of different reasons for the existence of the CDS basis by analysing situations where the CDS spread could either be larger or smaller than the asset swap spread. They suggest the following reasons.

Why the CDS spread could be greater than the asset swap spread:

- For those protection buyers who wish to effect physical delivery as part of the auction process, the terms of the CDS transaction allow for the delivery of one asset from a basket of eligible assets. This means there is a possibility that the components of the basket may be trading at different prices. This gives rise to a delivery option similar to the "cheapest to deliver" concept considered in Chapter 4. Since the buyer of protection has the right to choose which bond to deliver, this option will cause the CDS spread to be greater than the asset swap spread.
- Depending on the terms of the CDS, an event of default could be triggered by a restructuring. Although this may constitute a credit event for the CDS, it does not constitute a default on the underlying asset. Since this presents an extra risk for the seller of protection, they may demand a higher spread.
- The CDS market tends to trade with greatest liquidity in the 3, 5, 7 and 10-year maturities. Away from these maturities, CDS bid–offer spreads will be wider.
- Since it can be relatively difficult to short a corporate bond in the physical bond markets, default swaps offer an easier way to express a view and so may trade with a higher spread.

Why the default spread could be less than the asset swap spread:

- If banks finance physical bond purchases at a positive spread to LIBOR, their overall return from owning a particular bond will be lower. In this case, selling CDS protection may seem a relatively more attractive transaction. If there is increased pressure to sell CDSs, spreads will tend to fall.
- Buying protection using a CDS results in two sets of credit exposures: that of the reference entity and that of the CDS seller. If the reference entity and the protection seller are considered to be correlated from a default perspective, the CDS spread may fall. This high-default correlation suggests there is an increased probability that a default in the reference entity will cause the protection seller to default. As a result, the CDS protection is seen as being less valuable.
- If there has been significant issuance of structured credit products which reference CDS contracts, the excess of protection sellers will drive CDS spreads down.
- Some CDS maturities are more liquid than the underlying bond market.
- If a credit event is declared, basis traders holding the bond in the form of an asset swap are left with a residual interest rate swap position, which will need to be unwound. To compensate for potential losses that could result from unwinding this exposure, they may demand a higher asset swap spread.

From a trading perspective it is common to talk about "long" or "short" basis trades:

- *Long basis trade* – Buy a bond (or receive LIBOR plus a spread in an asset swap), buy default protection.
- *Short basis trade* – Short a bond (or pay LIBOR plus a spread in an asset swap), sell default protection.

Note that a short basis trade is not the same concept as a negative CDS basis!

CDS indices

One of the areas of significant growth in credit derivatives has been the development of credit derivatives referenced to a portfolio of names. There are a number of credit portfolio products traded in the market: nth-to-default structures; tranche products; collateralized debt obligations, to name but a few. In this section we will focus on index CDSs. Figure 7.2 highlights some of the more popular credit indices.

Like any index, the quoted number could be interpreted as a measure of the health of a particular sector or market as a whole. However, credit indices are also tradable OTC credit products with defined maturities and features similar to single-name default swaps. When one sees the word "index" it is tempting to think that this is just one number that is quoted on an ongoing basis, similar to an equity index. However, since they are CDS contracts with fixed maturities (typically 3, 5, 7 and 10 years), there will be an index value for each of these different maturities (see Figure 7.3). We will also show that a new index is issued every 6 months and so for any given maturity there will be a number of quotes relating to the different series that are currently being traded.

The indices are referenced to a portfolio of credit default swap names rather than a portfolio of cash bonds. The single-name CDS contracts eligible for inclusion in the indices are fixed every 6 months on or around 20th March and September, which are referred to as

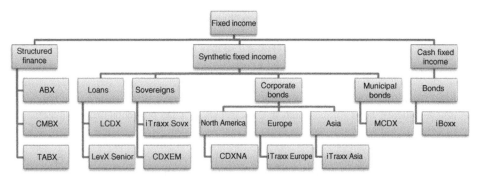

Figure 7.2   Family of credit indices.
Source: Markit.

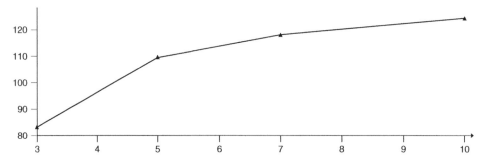

Figure 7.3   Credit term structure of iTraxx Main series 14. Data as of 24 December 2010.
Source: Barclays Capital Live, reproduced with permission.

the "roll dates". The constituent members of the index are selected according to a prede-termined set of rules. For example, the iTraxx Main Index comprises 125 equally weighted investment grade names with the highest trading volumes over the previous 6 months. The constituent names remain unchanged through the life of the trade except in the event of default, in which case the name is removed from the index.

In actuality, a contract's maturity will be slightly longer than its stated tenor. So a new 5-year contract created on 20th March of a particular year will mature on 20th June, 5.25 years later. Each new contract created on a particular roll date is referred to by a consecutive number, e.g. series 1, series 2 and so on.

The purpose of revising the composition of the index every 6 months is to preserve the credit quality of the stated portfolio which participants are trading. As a result, the market refers to the "on the run" series, which is the most recent portfolio of names and the "off the run" series, which are all of the older issued indices.

In order to ensure that they have exposure to the latest components of the index, CDS index participants tend to continually roll their exposures. So if protection is bought or sold on the current series of a particular index with a maturity of 5.25 years, then when the new index is published 6 months later the participant will terminate the existing contract and enter into the new series. It is important to note that participants are not obliged to roll these contracts but anecdotally the majority choose to do so. Since the contracts can be unwound at any time, a payment is made between the counterparties to settle the difference between the fixed-coupon and par spreads at the time of termination. Since rolling between contracts is an exceptionally popular trade, market makers now offer a single transaction to facilitate this.

A market maker would quote the trade as in Table 7.1.

If the market maker were to quote "7/7.5", this could be interpreted to mean they would pay a net amount of 7 basis points to "buy the roll" but would wish to receive a net amount of 7.5 basis points to "sell the roll".

The indices trade on a fixed-coupon basis similar to the single-name CDSs. The coupon payments will match the frequency and maturity of those on the underlying CDS contracts and so pay quarterly coupons on 20th March, June, September and December. As per the single-name contract, the indices will involve an upfront payment or receipt at the start of the transaction to ensure that the contract is considered equitable.

In the event of default, the protection seller pays the protection buyer an amount equal to:

$$\text{Notional amount} \times (100\% - \text{recovery value})$$

It would be at this point that single-name CDS contracts would terminate, but index trades continue until either all of the names have defaulted or until the contract matures. After the

Table 7.1 Quotation conventions for credit index roll trade

Buy the roll	Sell the roll
Buy protection on shorter-dated series	Sell protection on shorter-dated series
Sell protection on longer-dated series	Buy protection on longer-dated series

default of a particular reference entity, the notional amount of the contract is then reduced by 100% of the weight of the defaulted name. Take the iTraxx Main, which is constructed as 125 equally weighted investment grade names. Each of the names contributes 0.8% to the index, so the default of one name on a €10m contract will reduce the notional amount by €80,000.

The index CDS basis/skew

We have shown that a credit default index is simply a basket of single-name credit default swaps. Logically, it should follow that the fair value of the index can be derived by observing the individual CDS spreads. However, like most markets the relationship is not perfect and does not always hold. As a result, it presents an opportunity for a trader to make some money. The difference between the value of the constituent names in an index and the index value itself has been termed the "basis" or the "skew". Typically, the basis is defined as:

$$\text{CDS index skew} = \text{Market index spread} - \text{intrinsic index spread}$$

Rennison *et al.* (2008) argue that factors such as higher trading volumes on credit indices relative to the single-name constituents will tend to increase the value of the basis.

The skew cannot be calculated by simply adding up the par spreads of the constituent single-name CDS (i.e., the intrinsic index spread) and subtracting it from the market index spread. This is because account has to be taken of the upfront cash flows payable or receivable on all the constituent contracts.

An arbitrage opportunity occurs when the cash flows on the index and the replicating trades are not equal. Presented more formally, an arbitrage opportunity would occur when the following equality does not hold:

$$\left(\text{Spread}_{\text{market index}} - \text{Coupon}\right) \times \text{PV01}_{\text{index}} = \sum_{i=1}^{n} \left(\text{Spread}_i - \text{Coupon}\right) \times \text{PV01}_i$$

Executing the arbitrage trade could be quite involved, depending on the chosen index. If the trade was based on the iTraxx Main Index, the trader would need to execute 125 single-name contracts to replicate the index. As a result, traders tend to prefer those indices which have a smaller number of components. This has led to the increase in liquidity of the HiVol and Crossover indices, which are sub-indices of the North American CDX product. The skew is typically widest when the market is most volatile, but for the arbitrage trader this opportunity may not be as promising as it sounds, since bid–offer spreads may be at their widest.

7.1.2 The forward–swap relationship

In Chapter 4 we considered in some detail the relationship between cash bonds and bond futures. There is no equivalent corporate bond future and so this relationship is difficult to trade. However, credit default swaps can be used to express views on how CDS spreads are expected to evolve with respect to their implied forward values. So in effect they allow investors to express a view on the perceived future default risk of a company.

Suppose a trader is looking to express a view on the potential default of a large European manufacturing company. They decide to execute the following trades:

- Buy €100m 10-year protection.
- Sell €100m 5-year protection.

This trade expresses a forward-starting bearish view on the reference entity's CDS spread for a 5-year period in 5 years' time. If the position is held until the end of the shorter-dated contract, the performance of the transaction would be a function of the spot par spread that prevailed at that time. So in the above example, the position will show a profit in 5 years' time if the par 5-year spread is greater than the initial implied forward par spread.

The calculation of the forward spread involves some mathematics but can be expressed in terms of expected losses (Rennison *et al.*, 2008):

Expected loss over forward time period

= Expected loss over longer-dated period − expected loss over shorter-dated period

Suppose we were trying to calculate the 5-year forward in 5 years' time. We could use the spreads (S) and the applicable PV01 values to calculate the forward spread:

$$S_{5,5} \times \text{PV01}_{5,5} = (S_{10} \times \text{PV01}_{10}) - (S_5 \times \text{PV01}_5)$$

If we were to rearrange the formula to solve for the 5-year spread, 5 years forward the result would be:

$$S_{5,5} = \frac{(S_{10} \times \text{PV01}_{10}) - (S_5 \times \text{PV01}_5)}{\text{PV01}_{10} - \text{PV01}_5}$$

The numerator represents the expected loss of the position, whereas the denominator represents the position's expected market risk.

At this point we could make the following initial conclusions:

- A forward purchase will benefit from a spread widening or curve steepening. It is a bearish trade on the reference entity but is "cheaper" than simply buying outright spot-starting protection as the short protection leg subsidizes the long protection leg.
- A short forward protection will benefit if the spread between the two maturities falls and/or the curve flattens. Since the notional amounts are equal, it is default neutral until the expiry of the shorter-dated transaction.

We will make the following assumptions:

- The trades are executed using Standard European Corporate terms.
- The reference entity is trading at a fixed coupon of 100 basis points.
- Par CDS spreads (i.e., those that would prevail in the absence of the fixed-coupon format) are higher than the ongoing 100 basis point fixed coupon. For illustrative purposes let us assume the 5-year par spread is 210 basis points while the 10-year par spread is 225 basis points.
- The 10-year position requires 9.5% upfront, while the 5-year position trades with 5.0% upfront.

Since the par CDS spreads are greater than the fixed coupon, the 10-year protection buyer will make a payment of 9.5% while the short 5-year protection position will enjoy an upfront receipt of 5.0%. On the notional of €100m this will equate to a cost of 4.5% to the trader.

From an ongoing cash flow perspective, once the upfront cash flow has been settled there will be no further exchanges of cash for the first 5 years. This is due to the fact that the magnitudes of the coupon payments are equal.

Arguably there are three potential sources of profit and loss for this trade:

1. Carry from the coupon payments.
2. "Pull to par".
3. Funding of the upfront payment.

For the first 5 years there is no carry on the trade from coupon payments, since they are equal and opposite. The "pull-to-par" effect is the mark-to-market effect due to time decay. The long 10-year position will decay negatively as a reversing short position will be done at a lower rate if the credit curve remains positive. The 5-year position decays positively at a faster rate given its shorter maturity, as the position could be reversed by buying protection at a lower rate. Since the trade requires an initial outlay of funds there will be a financing requirement, which of course represents a cost. However, for the first 5 years the profit and loss on the trade will be virtually zero as the pull-to-par profits and funding costs will largely offset each other.

From the period 5 to 10 years the trade will carry negatively as the short position will have expired, the 10-year leg will experience negative decay and the trader will still be funding the upfront payment.

At first glance it would appear as if this trade would not suffer as a result of a credit event (sometimes termed "jump to default" risk), since the notional amounts are equal. As such, the trader would pay and receive 100% less the agreed recovery rate. However, if a credit event is declared shortly after the position is implemented, although there would be no loss on the trade's notional values, the upfront payment of 4.5% (€4.5 million) is lost.

7.1.3   Volatility

Basic terminology

Options on credit default swaps allow investors to express views on the direction of credit spreads and/or their volatility. Since they are options on swaps, the convention is to refer to the structures as either "payers" or "receivers". The buyer of a payer swaption has purchased the right to pay a CDS spread at a specific strike rate – i.e., they purchased the right to buy protection. This means that the payer will be in-the-money if spreads are greater ("wider") than the strike at the expiry. It can be thought of as a call on credit spreads. A long receiver position gives the holder the right to sell protection at a specific spread level. This option will be in-the-money if spreads are lower ("tighter") than the strike at expiry. It can be thought of as a put on spreads.

A summary of the payoffs is shown in Figure 7.4.

Calculating expiry payoffs and breakevens

As Table 7.2 suggests, the payoff at the maturity of the option is only partially based on the difference between the spread and the strike. The calculation of the settlement amount will also be a function of the contract's risky PV01 at the expiry of the option. Suppose that an investor has bought a 6-month option on a 5-year index CDS with a strike of 50 basis

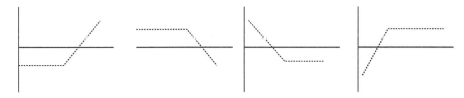

Figure 7.4 At expiry payoffs for long payer, short payer, long receiver and short receiver, respectively.

Table 7.2 Summary of credit default options

Type of option	Buy a payer (long call on credit spreads; long put on credit quality)	Sell a payer (short call on credit spreads; short put on credit quality)	Buy a receiver (long put on credit spreads; long call on credit quality)	Sell a receiver (short put on credit spreads; short call on credit quality)
Description	Purchase the right to buy protection	Sell the right to buy protection	Purchase the right to sell protection	Sell the right to sell protection
Action if exercised	Buy CDS protection at strike	Sell CDS protection at strike	Buy CDS protection at strike	Sell CDS protection at strike
Market view	Bearish on the credit	Stable/bullish on the credit	Bullish on the credit	Stable/bearish on the credit
Option premium	Paid upfront	Received upfront	Paid upfront	Received upfront
Maximum gain	(Spread − strike) × forward risky PV01 − premium	Upfront premium	(Strike − spread) × forward risky PV01 − premium	Upfront premium
Maximum loss	Upfront premium	(Spread − strike) × forward risky PV01 − premium	Upfront premium	(Strike − spread) × forward risky PV01 − premium

points. At maturity the index is trading at a par spread of 60 basis points and so the option is 10 basis points in-the-money. However, the intrinsic value of 10 basis points per annum and since the underlying CDS contract has a maturity of 5 years, this can be converted into a monetary value by multiplying by the risky PV01 (see Section 3.3.6) that prevails at the option's expiry. Suppose that at the option's maturity the risky PV01 of the underlying CDS is 4.2, then the dollar value of the 10 basis point per annum intrinsic value based on a \$10 million notional is \$42,000 (\$10m × 0.10% × 4.2).

From this we could summarize the expiry option payoffs:

$$\text{Long a payer option} = \text{Max}(\text{CDS par spread at expiry} - \text{strike}, 0) \times \text{risky PV01}$$

$$\text{Long a receiver option} = \text{Max}(\text{strike} - \text{CDS par spread at expiry}, 0) \times \text{risky PV01}$$

Because the payoff is multiplied by the risky PV01, the hockey stick-shaped expiry payoffs are not exactly linear and do possess an element of curvature. There is a shortcoming in expressing the option payoffs in this manner as they do not recognize the fact that the indices will trade with a fixed coupon. Suppose we have a payer option with a strike of 120 but where the underlying index has moved to 125 basis points at expiry. At the option's expiry the holder will exercise and buy protection at the strike rate of 120 but would have to pay 20 basis points upfront since this spread is above the 100 basis point fixed coupon. Had they not done the option, a long protection position at the prevailing market level of 125 basis points would require an upfront payment of 25 basis points. The at-maturity payoff expression that allows for the fixed coupons is:

$$\text{Max}[(\text{spot par spread} - \text{fixed coupon}) \times \text{PV01}_{\text{spot}}$$
$$- (\text{strike} - \text{fixed coupon}) \times \text{PV01}_{\text{strike}}, 0]$$

where $\text{PV01}_{\text{spot}}$ and $\text{PV01}_{\text{strike}}$ are the PV01s calculated assuming par spreads were trading at the spot and strike levels, respectively.

The calculation of a credit swaption's breakeven is not as straightforward as it may seem. Consider our 6-month index option referenced to a 5-year underlying. We will assume the premium is 30 basis points and the risky PV01 of the underlying asset is 4.2. These values suggest breakeven occurs when the position generates a profit of 30 basis points. However, this would occur when the underlying spread has moved by 7.14 basis points (30/4.2) from the strike.

Features of credit swaptions

- Anecdotally, options on indices are more popular than single names. CDS options are traded on the following indices: CDX Investment Grade; CDX High Yield; iTraxx Main; iTraxx Crossover; iTraxx Japan.
- Greatest liquidity is in the iTraxx Main and the CDX Investment Grade indices, where the typical trading size will be €250m and $250m, respectively.
- Since credit indices roll every 6 months, liquidity in CDS options is concentrated in shorter-dated maturities ranging from 1 to 6 months.
- Options are usually referenced to 5-year CDS maturities.
- They are typically European in style and expire on the standard CDS roll dates.
- Anecdotally, there is greater demand to buy options than to sell, which tends to keep premiums relatively high.
- The options are typically physically settled rather than cash-settled. That is, the option buyer will enter into a CDS to either buy or sell protection.

Pricing credit swaptions

CDS options are priced using the mid-market par spread of the underlying index. The premiums are quoted in basis points of notional payable on an upfront basis. CDS options are also traded with an assumed delta exchange. That is, the buyer of a payer option will agree to sell protection on the underlying index for a notional amount determined by the delta of the CDS option.

The implied volatility of a credit index option can be thought of as the perceived future volatility of the credit index which justifies the price paid for the option (Willemann and

Bicer, 2010). The authors also suggest three ways in which to evaluate the relative richness or cheapness of a credit option:

1. *Comparison of implied volatility against realized volatility* – Here the trader compares the volatility priced into an option relative to a comparable value over some historical period. An example would be to compare 3-month implied volatility with historical 3-month realized volatility.
2. *Comparison of implied volatility against realized daily spread moves* – The trader can convert an implied volatility into a daily equivalent spread change by applying the following useful shortcut formula:

$$\text{(Annual implied volatility} \times \text{spot price)}/16$$

The denominator is the approximate value of the square root of the number of trading days (usually taken to be 250) in a year. So if the implied volatility is observed as 90% and the index is trading at a spread of 110 basis points, this would translate approximately into a daily spread move of about 6.2 basis points. This expected movement could then be compared to observed movements in the spread.
3. *Comparison of implied against realized spread ranges* – The trader could take the premiums quoted for straddles of a given maturity and then work out at what index levels the positions would break even. This breakeven range could be compared to similar historical values. In addition, the frequency with which spreads have increased or decreased beyond these levels for the same maturity on a historical basis may aid the evaluation process.

Credit events

Table 7.3 summarizes what would happen to single-name credit default swaptions if a credit event is declared.

The exact settlement procedure upon the occurrence of a credit event will depend upon the maturity of the option. Suppose a credit event on one of the constituent names within the underlying index is declared but the auction to determine the recovery rate is scheduled for after the option's expiry. When the option is exercised, the underlying will comprise the index with the defaulted name. If the auction is before the option's expiry the underlying index will be delivered without the defaulted name. In this case, if the option is subsequently exercised the buyer of a payer and the seller of a receiver will receive loss payments based

Table 7.3   Summary of consequences for credit options if a credit event is declared

Buy receiver	Buy payer
Not exercised; premium lost	*Exercised*
(Exercise would result in short protection position requiring payment of 100% less recovery rate)	(Exercise would result in long credit protection position; would receive 100% less recovery rate)
Sell payer	Sell receiver
Exercised against seller	*Not exercised against the seller*
(Exercise results in short credit protection position for option seller. Would have to pay 100% less recovery rate)	(Exercise would require option buyer to sell protection which would require a payment of 100% less recovery rate)

on the recovery rate. Therefore, the decision to exercise will be effected by the potential loss payment to be paid or received upon exercise.

Options on single names will have a "knock-out" or "knock-in" feature. If the CDS option has a knock-out feature it will terminate if there is a credit event before the option's expiry date. It is also possible for the transaction to trade with a knock-in feature. This will result in the option being exercised automatically if a credit event is declared before the option's expiry date.

It is important to realize that options on CDSs only provide protection against spread rather than default risk, which would be of concern for a long payer position. At the point where a reference entity suffered an event of default, the long payer position would be in-the-money but the knock-out feature would extinguish the trade, leaving them with no position. To get around this problem the option holder could pay for default protection until the expiry of the option.

Index options do not have the knock-in and knock-out features. Holders of options on indices will wait until the option's expiry date to decide if exercising the basket is economical. Suppose that an entity has bought a payer on an index and one name defaults prior to expiry. If they exercise the option they will be a protection buyer on the remaining names within the index as well as the defaulted name. An investor who exercises a receiver is short protection on both the index and the defaulted name.

It is not always obvious whether an option should be exercised. Suppose a long payer option is struck on an index at 50 basis points. At expiry let us assume that one name has suffered a credit event but the index is trading at 45 basis points. Even though the strike is greater than the current market price, the holder may still exercise the option. This is because the cost of buying protection on the name that suffered a credit event may be considerably greater than the five basis point difference between the spread and the strike.

Applications of credit swaptions

In terms of applications, all of the generic option trading strategies considered in Chapter 4 could be applied within a credit context. However, we consider a number of strategies that are more specific to the credit markets.

Expressing views on credit quality – An example of this would be to buy OTM receivers on a high-yield index while selling OTM payers on investment grade names. The size of each leg is such that overall the strategy is zero premium. This would imply a view that the trader believes that in an environment where credit spreads are increasing, the high-yield index will "underperform" the investment grade names. This means that although both sets of spreads will increase, high-yield spreads would not increase as much as investment grade spreads. This trade is sometimes called a "compression" trade – where spreads of all credit ratings will tend to "bunch" together.

Credit swaptions can also be used to express directional views on reference entities. Taksler (2004) notes that buying a payer swaption is often an expensive way to short a credit. Unlike many options where the premium is usually a fraction of the underlying price, the premium on a payer swaption may be greater than the cost of buying protection. In this case the purchase of a payer swaption might be more appropriate if the investor believed that the credit quality of the underlying would improve (with the result that the option would expire worthless) but they couldn't afford for their view to be wrong (in which case they would exercise their option).

Expressing views on regional differences – Perhaps a trader believes that the CDX Investment Grade index will outperform the iTraxx Main. This could be achieved by selling receiver swaptions on the iTraxx Main and then using the proceeds to finance the purchase of receiver swaptions on CDX Investment Grade. For example, the iTraxx Main position will lose money if spreads fall but the CDX position will make money.

Expressing views on cross-asset class performance – If the trader believed that, in a market rally, equity would outperform credit then a possible trade would be:

- Sell receivers on a credit index.
- Buy calls on an equity index.

The credit receivers would lose money if credit spreads decline (as may be expected in an equity market rally) but again, since it is an outperformance trade the position should show a profit courtesy of the performance of the call option.

7.2   EXPRESSING VIEWS ON THE CREDIT TERM STRUCTURE

In Chapter 6 we considered a number of yield curve strategies such as steepening, flattening and butterfly trades. In this section we analyse the same structures within a credit context.

7.2.1   Steepening/flattening trades

Since CDSs exhibit a term structure, views could be expressed on possible steepening or flattening scenarios. An example of a credit term structure for a single-name reference entity is shown in Figure 7.5.

These will typically be constructed to be "duration neutral", so that they are protected against parallel movements in the curve. For ease of illustration, we will use the same figures presented in Section 7.1.2. In that example the par CDS spreads for the reference entity were different from the fixed coupon of 100 basis points. Since par spreads were greater than the fixed coupon, an upfront adjustment was required to make trades equitable. To calculate this value we need to derive the notional values of each leg of the trade. We will assume that the DV01 of the trade has been calculated as 4.5 and 7 for the 5 and 10-year maturities, respectively (the values are illustrative). The ratio of the DV01s returns a hedge

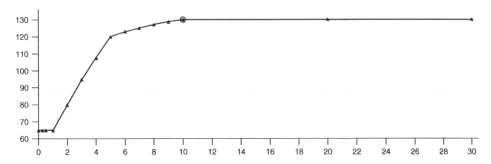

Figure 7.5   Credit term structure for Barclays Bank plc CDS spreads. Data as of 24 December 2010. *Source:* Barclays Capital Live. Reproduced with permission.

ratio of 1.56 and so, based on a notional amount of €100m for the 10-year transaction, we would require a 5-year notional with a value of €156 million. Since a steepening trade implies that longer-term spreads will increase by more than shorter-term spreads, the trader will need to buy 10-year protection and sell 5-year protection.

Based on these notional amounts the upfront payment and receipt are as follows.

Long 10-year protection position

$$€100m \times 9.5\% = -€9,500,000$$

Short 5-year protection position

$$€157m \times 5\% = €7,850,000$$

Net payment will be $-€1,650,000$

Since the notional amounts are not equal the coupon cash flows will not cancel, with the result that the position will exhibit an element of carry.

Long 10-year protection position

$$€100m \times 1\% = -€1m$$

Short 5-year protection position

$$€157m \times 1\% = €1.57m$$

The carry attributable to the coupon will be €570,000 in favour of the trader. However, the total carry on the trade would also need to take into account the fact that the upfront payment will require financing. Assuming the position is not terminated early, then after 5 years the short protection position would mature and the position would carry negatively courtesy of the long 10-year position.

The "pull-to-par" effect measures the profit or loss due to the passage of time, all other things being equal. Take the long 10-year protection position where there is a requirement to make a payment of €9.5m, due to the fact that the par spread of 225 basis points is higher than the fixed coupon. An alternative way to view the pull-to-par effect is to treat the position as an equivalent bond and express the price of the CDS in bond-equivalent terms. Suppose that the 5-year CDS is trading at a price of 95.47, while the 10-year is trading at 91.01 (the prices are illustrative).

Recall that on this trade the buyer of 10-year protection is short the credit, which means that the leg is economically equivalent to being short the bond. As a result, the bond will gradually increase in value towards par as it approaches maturity. For a short bond position this would represent a mark-to-market loss. However, there is a positive pull-to-par effect on the 5-year maturity which initially outweighs that of the 10-year leg. Once the 5-year leg has expired, the position will experience a negative pull to par courtesy of the 10-year position.

Although there are many ways to define pull to par, Rennison *et al.* (2008) suggest the following formula:

$$\text{Pull to par} = (\text{Par spread} - \text{fixed coupon}) \times \Delta\text{PV01 of par spread}$$

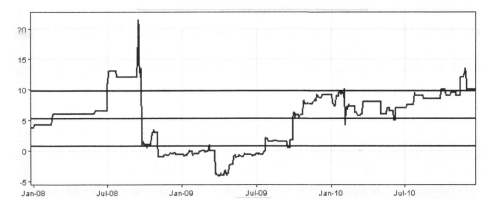

Figure 7.6 3–5–7 CDS butterfly spread for Barclays Bank plc. Data covers a 3-year period from December 2007–2010.
Source: Barclays Capital Live. Reproduced with permission.

Since the DV01 exposures of the position are equal – €70,000 – then the position will enjoy a profit equal to this amount per basis point of steepening. Since the notional amounts are not equal, however, an event of default will have a net impact on the position. The trader has sold €57 million more protection than he has bought and so the loss is:

$$€57m \times (100\% - \text{recovery value}) + \text{initial upfront payment}$$

7.2.2 Butterfly trades

The fundamental principles of butterfly trades were covered in Section 6.4.1. Suppose a trader wished to express a view on the curvature of three popular CDS maturities: 3, 5 and 7 years. An example of a CDS butterfly spread between 3, 5 and 7-year maturities for a particular single-name reference entity is shown in Figure 7.6.

The trader believes that the 5-year spread ("the belly") is too high relative to adjacent maturities ("the wings"). As a result, he buys 3 and 7-year protection and sells 5-year protection. Leeming and Hagemans (2009) argue the resultant exposures for such a trade are:

- *Mark-to-market sensitivity* – Like their fixed income equivalent, the trades are designed to be neutral against parallel movements in the curve as well as rotations around the maturity of the "belly". As a result, the profit and loss on the position for a change in the butterfly spread is:

  $$\text{Notional amount of belly} \times \text{DV01 of belly} \times \text{change in spread}$$

- *Default risk* – If a credit event is declared, this is calculated as:

  $$\text{Sum of notionals} \times (100\% - \text{recovery rate}) + \text{sum of upfront payments}$$

- *Time decay* – Broken down into three subcomponents:
  - *Carry*, the net coupon earned or paid.
  - *Pull to par*, the profit or loss due to the amortization of the upfront payment to zero over the life of the trade.

- *Roll*, where – as the definition of pull to par assumes that the par spread of the reference entity does not change over the life of the transaction – the concept of roll accounts for the fact that the credit spread rolls down the curve (or up depending on the shape of the term structure) and so is defined as the mark to market due to the resulting change in credit spreads.
- *Breakeven* – The amount by which the spread must move for the position to break even.

7.2.3 Convexity

In Section 3.3.6 we considered the market risk of credit instruments and introduced the concept of PV01 and DV01. Rennison *et al.* (2008) define the metrics as follows:

- PV01 is the effective duration of a CDS contract adjusting for default risk.
- DV01 is the profit and loss sensitivity of a CDS contract to parallel curve shifts (also sometimes referred to as "CS01" or "credit spread 01").

In this section we introduce and illustrate the concept of convexity within the context of default swap contracts. We define convexity as a change in the DV01 for a change in the CDS spread. This is important for trades with two legs (e.g., steepening or flattening trades) as the ratio of notionals will change as the spreads change – resulting in an over- or under-hedged trade. Rennison *et al.* (2008) suggest that as a rule of thumb, any profit or loss scenario that involves a 5-year spread change of more than 100 basis points would need to take into account convexity.

Table 3.2 outlined the calculation of the PV01 of a trade and from this it can be seen that if the spread on a CDS contract increases, the survival probability falls and so the discounted value of the cash flows must decrease. This results in both a lower PV01 and DV01.

To illustrate the impact of convexity, consider the following example. Suppose we have traded a 5-year CDS, where we have bought $10m of protection at a quoted spread of 1.6%. Using a CDS calculator, the DV01 at inception is calculated as $4,114. That is, we will lose $4,114 for every one basis point change in the spread for this $10m position. Suppose the CDS curve increases instantaneously by 1%. Given the mathematics of discounting cash flows, the profit on the trade will not be 100 times the initial DV01 (i.e., it will not be $411,400) and is in fact $396,087. From this we can conclude that a long protection position displays negative convexity (profits from a spread widening decelerate) while a short protection position displays positive convexity (losses from a spread widening decelerate).

Rennison *et al.* argue that the impact of convexity on steepening and flattening trades is not straightforward and will be impacted by:

- The type of trade (steepening vs. flattening).
- The tenor of the trade.
- The notional amounts.

From this they derive two rules of thumb:

1. *A flattening trade will display positive convexity* – The profits from a given flattening of the curve will be greater than the losses incurred from the same magnitude of steepening.
2. *A steepening trade will display negative convexity* – The gains from a steepening move are less than the losses incurred if the curve were to flatten by the same amount.

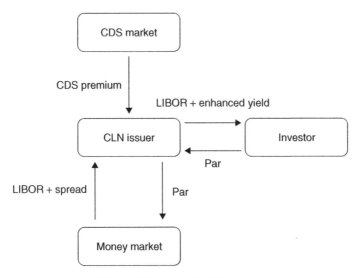

Figure 7.7   A credit-linked note.

7.3   EXPRESSING A VIEW ON A SINGLE REFERENCE ENTITY

In this section we consider one of the questions central to the relative value approach: *"What is the most effective way to express a view on the underlying asset?"* However, before we consider relative value for single-name reference entities, we include a short note on the main features of credit-linked notes.

7.3.1   Credit-linked notes

A single-name credit-linked note (CLN) is a synthetic funded security that gives credit exposure to a particular reference entity. They are intended to be a "buy-and-hold" security as the secondary market for these instruments is normally thin. In its most basic form the CLN will resemble a floating-rate note where the investor will pay par and receive LIBOR plus an enhanced spread until either the note's maturity or the default date of the reference entity.

Figure 7.7 illustrates one way in which a CLN could be constructed. The investor pays par to the CLN issuer, who deposits the money to earn a return based on their normal money-market activities – assumed here to be LIBOR. At the same time the CLN issuer sells CDS protection on the agreed reference entity with a maturity equal to the CLN. The CLN issuer will pay an enhanced yield to the investor, which will comprise a LIBOR component (financed by the money-market deposit) and an enhanced yield (essentially the premium on the short CDS position).

There may be a number of reasons why a client would choose to buy a CLN:

- They will receive an enhanced rate of return.
- Cash bonds in the reference entity may not be available or liquid.
- The instrument can be customized with respect to maturity, currency, coupon or recovery rates.

- An investor may prefer a CLN over a bond if the reference entity is trading with a positive CDS basis (i.e., the CDS spread is higher than the credit spread on the underlying asset) and if the issuer of the note has a high funding spread.

These structures will present the investor with two sets of default risk. If the reference entity has not defaulted by the maturity of the note, the investor will receive back par. However, if the reference entity suffers a credit event the investor will receive back their investment less the CDS auction recovery rate and no further coupons will be received. This means that the investor's maximum loss is 100% of their investment.

The second source of credit risk is the default of the CLN issuer. This will lead to the termination of the CLN irrespective of the performance of the reference entity. The investor will then rank pari passu with other senior unsecured investors for their claim against the issuer.

Figure 7.8 shows the cash flows in the event of a credit event being declared on the reference entity. The CLN issuer will terminate the money-market deposit early, incurring a break fee and settling any mark-to-market gains or losses related to changes in their funding spread. The CLN issuer will then settle the cash flows associated with the CDS based on the amount announced via the auction process. The investor is then paid the residue of the remaining cash. Since the investor can never lose more than 100% of the sums invested, if the reference entity were to default with zero recovery rate and the sums received under the money-market deposit were less than 100%, then the CLN issuer would have to finance the shortfall to the CDS protection buyer. The opposite would also apply in that the investor cannot benefit by more than 100% of the amount invested in the event of default. As a result, it is theoretically possible for the CLN issuer to make a profit if the following conditions occur:

- The reference entity suffers an event of default and the recovery value is high.
- The issuer's creditworthiness improves, resulting in a mark-to-market profit when unwinding the money-market deposit.

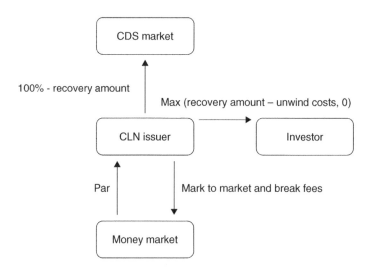

Figure 7.8   Cash flows associated with a credit event being declared on the reference entity.

Although a CLN may appear to be similar to a bond, there are a number of differences worth noting:

- *Restructuring* – If the CLN includes restructuring as a credit event, it will mean that the investor will receive back the recovered amount less any deposit break costs. With a physical bond holding the investor would simply receive the restructured bond flows.
- *Debt buy backs* – In the event of a company buying back all of its own debt, physical bond holders would receive an agreed repayment amount. However, since this is not defined as a credit event the CLN and the underlying CDS will continue to pay out until the scheduled maturity.
- *Issuer default risk* – The investor is exposed to the default of the issuer. In this case the investor will receive the recovery rate on the underlying deposit and will have no further exposure to the reference entity.
- *Recovery rate* – In the event of a default by the reference entity, a physical bond holder could choose to sell their holding or hold until the bankruptcy practitioners have determined the amount to be recovered, which could take several years. The amount recovered in a CDS transaction will be determined by the auction process that will take place shortly after the event of default has been declared. The different processes could result in different cash flows.
- *Secondary market liquidity* – It is unlikely that any secondary market in the instrument will enjoy much liquidity. As such, these instruments are more appropriate for buy-and-hold investors.

When determining the spread to LIBOR, it may be tempting to think that the investor would simply earn the spread to LIBOR on the underlying deposit as well as the CDS premium. However, there is also a subtle correlation issue that needs to be taken into account. Recall that the issuing bank could incur a loss on the structure in the following scenario:

- The reference entity defaults with 0% recovery.
- Funding spreads for the CLN issuer increase, resulting in a reduced principal amount from terminating the underlying deposit.

If the issuing bank believes that their funding spread and the potential default of the reference entity are positively correlated, they may seek to reduce the coupon they pay to the investor in anticipation of potential future losses. However, from the investor's perspective this positive default correlation increases their overall default risk and so they would logically demand a higher coupon.

Consider the following hypothetical example:

Reference entity's 5-year asset swap spread	300 basis points
Reference entity's 5-year CDS spread	250 basis points
Issuer's funding spread to LIBOR	100 basis points
Issuer's 5-year CDS spread	75 basis points

The maximum coupon payable on the CLN would be the sum of the reference entity's CDS spread (250 basis points) plus the issuer's funding spread to LIBOR (100 basis points) – i.e., 350 basis points. However, it may be theoretically possible for the maximum coupon to be greater than this value if the probability of the reference entity defaulting and the issuer's credit spread were negatively correlated. In this somewhat unlikely scenario, any loss on the CDS would have to be offset by a gain on the deposit's mark-to-market value.

For argument's sake, let us assume that the CLN is issued at a spread of 325 basis points. A potential investor may consider this a more attractive proposition than an asset swap position, which returns a yield 25 basis points lower than the CLN. Indeed, the return is also greater than a short protection position in the reference entity's CDS. The simple example shows that the return on the CLN would be attractive when three conditions prevail:

1. The reference entity trades with a high CDS spread.
2. The issuer funds at a spread to LIBOR.
3. There is low default correlation between the reference entity and the CLN issuer.

7.3.2   Expressing a view on a single reference entity – an example

Consider the following example. You are managing a portfolio and are considering taking credit exposure to Big Bank plc, a UK-headquartered financial services company with a single A credit rating. The following instruments are currently being traded in the market:

- 5-year senior GBP secured term loan (LIBOR + 125bp).
- 5-year asset swap GBP 7% senior bond (LIBOR + 155bp).
- 5-year CDS (quoted in EUR) (155bp).
- 6-year EUR-denominated FRN (EURIBOR + 175bp).
- 5-year GBP credit-linked note (LIBOR + 165bp).
- 3-month ATM long receiver option into 5-year CDS (86bp).

Suppose that you only wish to invest in one of the above, which would you choose?

As with many examples like this, there is very rarely an absolute right or wrong answer. The following points would need to be considered:

- Although the term loan would be secured on the company's assets, it may be illiquid from a secondary market perspective.
- The analyst would have to make some judgement as to the appropriate credit spread between the secured loan and the bond, given that the loan is illiquid, but is likely to have a higher recovery rate in the event of default.
- CDS is an unfunded exposure – i.e., selling protection does not require any upfront payment of premium. So when considering the return on different instruments, the credit portfolio manager needs to consider his own cost of borrowing. If his borrowing cost is LIBOR plus a spread, the return from buying instruments such as the bonds and loans will be reduced relative to the premium received from selling the CDS.
- A position in the FRN may require hedging the FX exposure.

However, the analysis may require the analyst to seek the answers to the following general questions:

- What is the outlook for the company's ratings?
- Is the issuer on positive or negative credit watch?
- Do any of the debt instruments have coupon/spread ratchets?
- Which credit events are included in the CDS?
- What are the relative values of the margins in each currency, given the interest rate differential between EUR and GBP?
- What is the issue size of each debt instrument? (This may give an indication of the issue's liquidity.)

- How liquid are each of the instruments? The trader would want to know the bid/offer spread and the size of transaction that can normally be dealt.
- How long is the investor's time horizon?
- If you invest in the EUR-denominated CDS, but manage your investments in GBP, you will have some element of currency risk.
- In considering the FRN, what is the shape of the credit curve for Big Bank plc between the 5 and 6-year maturities?
- Is the investor seeking to isolate interest rate risk or credit risk?
- If they are seeking to isolate credit risk, are they more interested in capturing spread risk or default risk?

7.4   EXPRESSING A VIEW ON A BASKET OF REFERENCE ENTITIES

In this section we will consider some of the ways in which an investor could take exposure to a basket of reference entities. We approach this in a relatively conservative manner, as this particular area of finance can be complex. In order to maintain our intuitive approach to the subject matter, we will consider the following structures:

- Total return swaps.
- Credit indices (the detail of which is covered in Section 7.1.1).
- Basket default swaps.
- Index tranche investing.

7.4.1   Total return swaps

Total return swaps are designed to replicate the return of a particular index. Whereas index credit default swaps reference CDS contracts, total return swaps will typically reference an index of cash bonds. Some of the key features of total return swaps are:

- The investor can choose the specific index they wish to track.
- A total return swap should replicate exactly the index to which it is referenced, resulting in no tracking error.
- The tenor of the total return swap is also negotiated between the two entities.
- Similar to CLNs, investors entering into total return swaps will be subject to the risk of their counterparty defaulting.
- The "price" of the total return swap is expressed as a spread in basis points to the LIBOR leg.
- The transaction can be executed in either swap format, where no upfront payment is required ("unfunded") or in note format, where the investor will need to invest the par value of the instrument ("funded").

The basic structure of the total return swap would look as shown in Figure 7.9. Here, the investor agrees the underlying index to which the transaction will be referenced with their counterparty bank. The bank then agrees to pay the investor the total return (i.e., price change plus coupons) from the index constituents over an agreed period. In return, the investor pays to the bank LIBOR plus or minus a spread. From the investor's perspective, the structure replicates a purchase of the constituent bonds – they receive the bonds' total return while paying a LIBOR cash flow which replicates their normal borrowing costs.

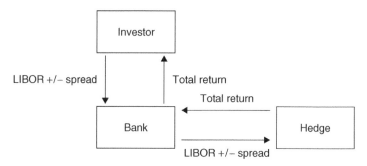

Figure 7.9   Total return swap.

However, the total return swap is operationally easier to execute than an outright bond purchase and easier to manage, particularly if the index is large.

From the bank's perspective, in order to finance the payments to the client they will either buy the physical assets or enter into an offsetting total return swap agreement. Since the transaction's payout to the investor will be referenced to an independently observed index value, any shortfall in the hedge will be a cost to the bank. The profit to the bank arises from the difference between the spreads paid and received on the LIBOR legs. If the hedge consists of an exact physical position in the underlying index, then the bank will be required to finance this purchase. For any profit to be made, the cost of financing the hedge will have to be lower than the spread to LIBOR received from the client. So, a bank with a low cost of funding will be able to offer total return structures at an attractive spread to LIBOR.

7.4.2   Basket default swaps

Basket default swaps come in two flavours – either first- or nth-to-default structures. Although the instruments are relatively illiquid, they are a convenient way to explain the intuition underlying the concept of default correlation.

A first-to-default structure is a CDS that is linked to a variety of underlying reference assets. The seller provides protection against the first reference entity in the basket suffering a credit event. To illustrate the concept consider the example in Table 7.4, in which a bank sells €10m notional protection on a five-name basket.

If there is no credit event on any of the names in the basket, the seller receives the CDS spread every quarter for the full 5 years. If any name suffers a credit event during the life of the trade, the client will pay a cash settlement amount to the buyer as determined by the standard auction process. However, the trade will then terminate and no further rights or liabilities will accrue to either side. This is different from an index CDS, which would continue until either its maturity or the default of all the constituent names.

The motivation for the seller is that he earns an enhanced yield compared to the average spread of 45 basis points per name. This would be the average amount they would have earned if they had sold protection on equal amounts of each credit. In addition, the seller earns an enhanced yield relative to the weakest credit in the basket. From the buyer's perspective it offers a lower-cost method of hedging multiple credits. An equivalent index CDS premium would simply be the total of the constituent premia. However, it is an imperfect hedge for the buyer as he is only compensated for the first default and retains the risk that one of the remaining names may subsequently default.

Table 7.4 Five-name first-to-default basket option (values are illustrative)

Credit	5-year single-name spread (basis points per annum)
Chemical company	43
Retailer	92
Utility	34
Conglomerate	25
Telecom company	31
Sum of spreads	225
Average spread	45
First-to-default price	188

The following list highlights a number of generic features of a CDS basket transaction:

- The basket usually contains three to 12 reference entities, with five being the most common number.
- Maturities range from 1 to 5 years.
- Typical notional trade sizes vary from €10m to €50m.
- They can be traded in either swap or note format.

Default correlation

The concept of default correlation differentiates basket structures and tranches from total return swaps and index CDSs. Default correlation deals with the distribution of defaults throughout a portfolio and considers the likelihood of a single default causing a succession of defaults. This should not be confused with spread correlation, which describes the tendency with which credit spreads move together. There are three ways in which the default correlation between assets can be characterized:

- Low default correlation describes a situation where there is a high probability that an investor will experience a few losses within their portfolio, but a low probability of experiencing either no losses or very significant losses.
- Medium default correlation means that there is a higher probability of experiencing zero losses as well as very large losses.
- High default correlation means the portfolio effectively behaves like a single credit. The assets will either all survive or they will all default.

The first to default basket option has two price boundaries:

1. The premium on the basket option will be greater than the premium on the weakest credit within the basket. This will compensate the seller for the probability that one of the other assets may default prior to the weakest credit. If the basket premium were equal to that of the weakest credit the investor may as well sell protection in this name alone as they are not getting compensation for the possibility that the other names will default.
2. The premium should be just less than the sum of the premiums available for single-name default swaps for each credit in the basket. This is because the buyer is not buying protection on all of the names, just the first to default. Suppose that the default correlation is exactly equal to zero; the basket premium would in this case be equal to the sum of all the single-name default premiums. If this were the case the buyer may as well buy protection on all three names individually. They would then end up with cover for all three names defaulting rather than just one in the first-to-default

structure; this would be achieved at the same cost as the basket option. However, this is an extreme case as it is extremely unlikely that there would be an instance where the correlation is exactly zero.

There are a number of additional factors that could influence the price of the basket option:

- *The number of reference entities* – Assuming that the default correlation remains constant, increasing the number of reference entities within the basket will raise the premium. As more credits are added to the basket, the risk of a credit event increases and so the seller will require a greater level of compensation.
- *Change in default premiums* – As the component CDS spreads increase by equal amounts, the risk of a default within the basket increases. As a result, the premium will increase.

The nth-to-default structures compensate the buyer of protection after an agreed number of defaults have occurred. Say a buyer of protection executes a third-to-default structure on a basket of five names. They will only be compensated upon the default of the third credit, at which point the deal would terminate. If the default correlation of the constituent assets tends towards zero, the possibility of all the assets defaulting becomes remote. Since there is virtually no probability of a large number of assets defaulting, the probability of default moves towards the most likely to default in the basket and away from the other constituents. As the contract only pays out in the instance of the latter names defaulting, and this is now less likely to happen, the premium will tend towards zero. However, this is an extreme case and a correlation of zero would never be used to price these structures.

As the correlation between the entities increases, the likelihood of the structure experiencing significant defaults increases, increasing the spread on the nth-to-default structure. In addition, the spread will tend towards that of the highest individual spread. However, 100% correlation is unlikely as this would imply that all of the reference entities are actually the same underlying credit. Therefore, they would have the same spreads and the same default probabilities. If this condition did not hold then it would represent an arbitrage situation in the underlying CDS market; the trader could buy the CDS with the lowest spread and sell the CDS with the highest spread. If a credit event were to incur, the participant would be neutral in terms of default but will have made a profit from the different spreads.

7.4.3 Index tranche investing

The index tranche market shares common concepts with a number of related credit derivative markets:

- Credit indices.
- First- and nth-to-default structures.
- Collateralized debt obligations (outside the scope of the text).

Participants in the tranche market are generally motivated by a desire to express views on default correlation. Generally speaking, the market splits into two main types of participant:

- *Correlation investors* – Longer-term fundamental credit investors who are seeking to enhance the yield on their portfolios. This is because tranche investments have a higher yield than equivalent CDS or cash instruments.

- *Correlation traders* – Short-term participants who are willing to take risks relating to correlation, volatility and convexity (outside the scope of the text).

Index tranche investments are bilateral investments which are referenced to a common index such as the iTraxx Main. The key word in the previous sentence is "referenced" – neither counterparty is required to either buy or sell protection on the reference index or its constituent CDS contracts, unless they choose to do so for hedging purposes. Tranche products are designed to allow participants to express views on the correlation that exists between the constituent members of the index. Similar to CDS contracts, it is convention to talk about buying and selling protection; buyers will pay a spread to the sellers, who will make a contingent payment to the buyer if a credit event is declared on any of the CDS contracts within the referenced portfolio. However, the distinguishing feature of these contracts is the point from which the seller will incur losses. In an index CDS contract the seller will start to incur losses from the point the first credit event is declared. Although unlikely to happen, they are theoretically exposed to the default of the entire index constituents. The seller of protection in an index tranche transaction may not start to incur losses until a certain number of names have defaulted, but cannot lose more than the notional amount of the transaction. A hypothetical tranche investment is illustrated in Figure 7.10.

In Figure 7.10, the left-hand column represents a hypothetical reference portfolio of 100 CDS contracts each with a notional amount of €10m and therefore a total notional value of €1 billion. The spread of 100 basis points simply represents the average of the constituent CDS spreads. As a result, a seller of protection on such a portfolio would receive a fixed spread of €10m per annum (€1 billion × 100 basis points). It is from this reference portfolio that the tranche investment will derive its value.

With an index tranche investment the seller of protection can select the point from which they will incur losses. The entire index tranche transaction is shown as the middle column

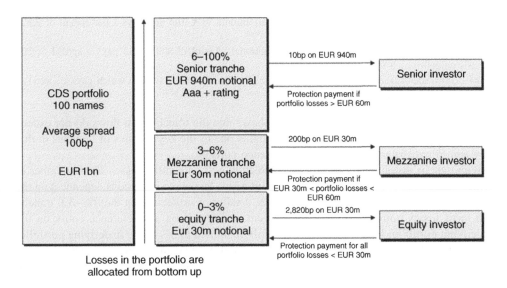

Figure 7.10   An index tranche investment referenced to a portfolio of 100 CDS reference entities.

of Figure 7.10 and in order to simplify the example, the transaction has been split into three slices. A market participant can buy or sell protection on any one (or all) of these tranches.

A tranche is described by its degree of subordination (also known as the "attachment point"), its detachment point and hence its width. In Figure 7.10 the attachment point for the mezzanine tranche is 3%, while the detachment point is 6%. These values are expressed as a percentage of the total underlying reference portfolio but this may be a function of the desired notional on the tranche investment. So, if a mezzanine investor agrees to a 3%–6% tranche with a notional of €30m then this implies a referencing portfolio with a notional value of €1bn. The agreed notional amount on a tranche investment also represents their total possible loss and is sometimes referred to as the "exhaustion amount".

In the tranche market dealers will make markets in a series of standardized tranches to ensure market liquidity. Typically, these may comprise an equity tranche (0%–3%), a mezzanine tranche (3%–6%), senior tranches (6%–9% and 9%–12%) and super senior tranches (12%–22%). The equity and mezzanine tranches will trade in the interdealer market with a typical trade size in the region of €10m for the equity tranche rising to between €20m and €50m in the mezzanine tranches.

One of the many sources of confusion in the index tranche market is the use of the terms "long" and "short" to describe a participant's particular position. By convention, a tranche position describes a participant's exposure to the underlying credit risk. So a short tranche position means the participant has bought default protection and is therefore short the credit risk; a long tranche position means the participant has sold protection and is therefore long the credit risk.

Similar to a regular index investment, they will receive a quarterly spread but the par spread is no longer a straight average; it is a function of how the underlying assets are correlated from a default perspective. One of the key points to understand is that the total spread payable on all the tranches cannot exceed that of the underlying reference index. Consider the spreads on the three tranches in Figure 7.10:

- 0%–3% equity tranche. Tranche has a notional amount of €30m and pays a par spread of 2,820 basis points (a cash flow of €8,460,000).
- 3%–6% mezzanine tranche. Tranche has a notional amount of €30m and pays a spread of 200 basis points (a cash flow of €600,000).
- 6%–100% senior tranche. Tranche has a notional amount of €940 million which pays a spread of 10 basis points (a cash flow of €940,000).

Summing the premiums of each tranche shows that the tranche cash flows do not exceed those of the referencing portfolio. This highlights one of the key features of tranches in that they aim to redistribute the credit of a reference portfolio.

With tranche investments the seller of protection will only suffer losses after a number of defaults have been experienced. The point from which losses are incurred is dependent on the attachment point of their selected tranche. So, a seller of protection on the 0%–3% tranche will incur losses immediately if a credit event is declared on any reference entity on the underlying portfolio. However, their losses will be limited to 3% of the underlying portfolio. To illustrate this consider the mezzanine investor illustrated in Figure 7.10. The width of their transaction is 3%, the notional amount is €30m and the attachment and detachment points are 3% and 6%, respectively. Both entities will be able to observe the performance of the individual CDS names in the referencing portfolio and the tranche investment will pay out solely on declared credit events. Since the attachment point is agreed at 3%, the seller of credit protection will not suffer losses until €30m of losses have been incurred in the referencing portfolio.

Let us suppose that a credit event is declared on one reference entity, which by our definition represents 1% or €10m of the reference portfolio. Assuming that, as a result of the CDS auction process, the recovery rate is fixed at 40%, the hypothetical loss on this €10m position would be €6m. The seller of mezzanine protection on the tranche trade does not suffer any losses, but the cushion of protection afforded by his 3% attachment point now reduces from €30m to €24m. If entities in the referenced CDS portfolio continue to default and the recovery rate is always 40%, then after the fifth default the €30m cushion will have disappeared. As a result, the seller of mezzanine protection will start to lose money on the default of the sixth entity. As these losses become realized, the notional amount on the mezzanine tranche will reduce by the size of the loss on the referencing portfolio. If the underlying reference entities continue to default and the recovery rate remains at 40%, the seller of mezzanine protection will have lost all of their investment after a total of 10 defaults.

In our previous examples we had assumed that the recovery rate in the event of default was always 40%. However, this recovery rate will be set by the normal CDS auction process and its actual value will be unknown until after the process is complete. There is always a possibility that the event of default may occur very close to a scheduled spread payment. In this case the market convention is to assume a 0% recovery value and to adjust the notional amount on the tranche accordingly before calculating the spread payment. When the actual recovery rate is determined, the spread payment would be recalculated and an adjustment payment would be made.

Pricing of tranches can be extremely complex and is on the periphery of the scope of the text. However, we attempt to explain the logic of pricing without getting into the detail of Gaussian copula formulas, compound and base correlation.

The pricing of tranches will depend on a number of key inputs:

- *The expected losses on the reference portfolio* – This will be a function of the constituent CDS spreads and their recovery rates. The higher the constituent CDS spreads the more likely it is for defaults to happen and therefore the higher the tranche spread.
- *The default correlation between the underlying assets* – Since losses will impact different participants in different ways, default correlation between the constituent CDS names in the reference portfolio will need to be taken into consideration. This is different to an index CDS contract where correlation is not a pricing input.
- *The trade specification* – This will encompass such things as the maturity, attachment points and width of each tranche. For example, the lower the attachment point the greater the risk to the protection seller and so the higher the spread. The narrower the tranche the higher the spread as default losses can quickly eat through a narrow tranche.

Table 7.5 shows a hypothetical tranche structure under different assumptions of default correlation. The premiums in the example have been generated by a tranche pricing model while the expected losses (EL) for each tranche are calculated as the product of the premium, the credit DV01 and the width of the particular tranche.

Note that the total expected losses shown on the last line (EL[0%−100%]) are the same irrespective of the default correlation. These expected losses would be equal to those of an equivalent index CDS portfolio that is not tranched. The key point of the table is to illustrate how the risk is redistributed under different assumptions of correlation.

Table 7.5 Example of tranche prices under different assumptions of correlation

	Low correlation (10%)		High correlation (30%)	
	Expected loss	Premium (bp)	Expected loss	Premium (bp)
EL[22%–100%]	0.00%	0	0.02%	1
EL[12%–22%]	0.01%	1	0.13%	29
EL[9%–12%]	0.02%	14	0.12%	90
EL[6%–9%]	0.09%	69	0.24%	178
EL[3%–6%]	0.44%	337	0.50%	386
EL[0-3%]	1.77%	1969	1.32%	1296
EL[0%–100%]	2.33%	50	2.33%	50

Table 7.6 Summary of exposures for trading of tranches

	Equity tranche	Senior tranche
Long correlation	Sell credit protection/long credit exposure	Buy credit protection/short credit exposure
Short correlation	Buy credit protection/short credit exposure	Sell credit protection/long credit exposure

The table shows that a lower correlation assumption increases the expected losses in the junior tranches, while a higher correlation increases the losses in the higher tranches.

The spread on the senior tranches will increase as correlation increases, as the probability of experiencing losses increases. This is because the constituent assets in the reference portfolio tend to act more as a single asset. They will either default or not, and so there is a greater probability that a seller of protection on a higher tranche will experience some form of loss. From this we can say that the premium on the senior tranches is directly related to correlation. As a result, an investor who sells protection in these tranches will lose money if correlation increases; they are short correlation. For the junior tranches the spread will decrease as correlation rises. This is because zero losses are now more likely than a low correlation scenario. In this instance the premium in the equity tranche is inversely related to the correlation. An investor who sells protection on the junior tranches will make money if correlation increases; they are long correlation. For the mezzanine contracts their impact lies somewhere between the equity and the senior tranches and is more difficult to generalize. Table 7.6 summarizes the different exposures using different terminology.

8
Relative Value in Inflation

The fundamental principles of inflation were introduced in Chapter 1 and so it will be assumed that readers are already familiar with these concepts; readers requiring a review of inflation pricing concepts are referred to Chapter 2.

Throughout this chapter we will use the terms "linker" and inflation-linked bond interchangeably.

The inflation market is not as well developed as, say, fixed income and so the relative value triangle framework cannot be fully applied within this asset class. For example, the market in forward inflation is, at the time of writing, still in the very early stages of development and there is currently no inflation bond future. In addition, the market for inflation options is very much linked to the use of structured products and the market for trading volatility is relatively illiquid. However, there is one interesting way in which we can present the triangle and this is by considering the possible linkages within a nominal and real framework (Figure 8.1).

The figure illustrates three possible relationships that we will consider in this chapter:

- Bond breakevens.
- Forward breakevens.
- Swap breakevens.

Despite the limitations of the RV triangle within an inflation context, it is possible to apply the second aspect of our relative value approach: *"What is the most optimal way to express a view on an underlying asset?"* As a result, we will analyse the inflation markets using themes considered in previous chapters – for example, cheap/rich analysis and curve trades. However, at this point it is worth recalling that in the inflation market we actually

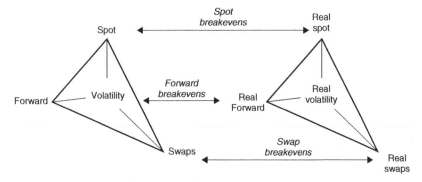

Figure 8.1 The relative value triangle from a nominal and real perspective.

have three underlying "assets" if we use the Fisher equation (presented in Chapter 1) as a point of reference:

- Real yields.
- Inflation expectations ("breakevens").
- Risk premium.

So, curve trades could be constructed to express views on the term structure of either real yields or breakevens.

8.1   PAYERS AND RECEIVERS OF INFLATION

A commonly discussed issue in the inflation market is the balance of demand and supply between those participants who wish to receive inflation and those who wish to pay. Receivers of inflation are typically:

- Pension funds and insurance companies with index-linked liabilities.
- Industries with raw material contracts whose value is index linked.
- Organizations with index-linked wage bills.
- Investors seeking protection against an adverse change in inflation.

Payers of inflation include:

- Companies whose revenues are linked to inflation (e.g., utilities).
- Property companies with inflation-linked rents.
- Retailers selling a broad basket of goods.
- Project finance entities whose revenues are referenced to changes in inflation.

There are, of course, entities that are willing to take either side of the transaction and these mainly comprise investment banks and hedge funds.

One interesting recent development in the inflation market is the increased interest in inflation-linked asset swaps. This product was covered in Section 5.4.5, and so here we merely point out that this structure is seen as a source of inflation supply. That is, an investor buys an inflation-linked bond and then pays fixed in an inflation-linked swap in return for LIBOR +/- spread. It is the paying of fixed under the inflation swap that is regarded as a source of inflation supply.

8.2   TERM STRUCTURE OF BREAKEVEN INFLATION
AND REAL YIELDS

In Figure 8.2 we illustrate the term structure of yields in the UK government bond market. The diagram illustrates the term structures for nominal, breakeven inflation and real yields.

8.2.1   Trading the slope of inflation curves

Figure 8.2 suggests that market participants may choose to express a view on how the shape of both the breakeven and real rate curves may evolve. The basic principles of fixed income curve trades are analysed in Chapter 6. Trade construction within an inflation context is considered in greater detail in Sections 8.6 and 8.8.

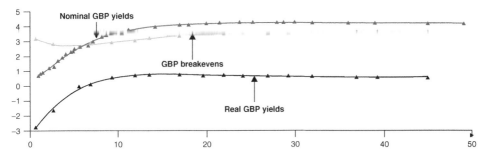

Figure 8.2   Nominal, breakeven and real yields across different maturities. Rates as of 27 December 2010.
Source: Barclays Capital Live. Reproduced with permission.

8.2.2   The importance of liquidity

The relationship illustrated in this figure at the shorter end of the curve is worth pausing to analyse in greater detail. Some market participants would simply interpret the difference between nominal yields and real yields as the market's expectation of future inflation. This stems from the market practice of interpreting the Fisher equation as:

$$\text{Nominal yields} = \text{Real yields} + \text{breakeven inflation} \tag{8.1}$$

In Figure 8.2, 1-year nominal yields were trading at 0.64% while real yields were negative at -2.58%, implying a breakeven inflation rate of 3.22%. However, at the time, 1-year zero-coupon inflation swaps were trading at a level of 4.40%, which we will later show is taken by the market to be the "true" level of breakevens. How can the differences between these two breakeven values be explained?

The Fisher equation actually stated:

$$\text{Nominal yields} = \text{Real yields} + \text{inflationary expectations} + \text{risk premium} \tag{8.2}$$

The risk premium itself can be decomposed into two factors: the premium demanded by nominal investors for unexpected inflation and a liquidity discount. The liquidity discount is defined as the premium that an investor will demand for holding the less liquid inflation-linked bond. However, the use of the word "premium" to define a discount term can be confusing. We will attempt to clarify the importance of inflation-linked bond liquidity with some examples.

Let us first substitute some market values into equation (8.2), but we will use the swap market as our estimate of inflationary expectations:

$$\text{Nominal yields} = \text{Real yields} + \text{inflationary expectations} + \text{risk premium}$$

$$0.64\% = -2.58\% + 4.40\% + \text{risk premium}$$

$$\text{Risk premium} = -1.18\%$$

Although not 100% perfect, it may be possible to estimate a value for the premium demanded for unexpected inflation from forward-starting inflation rates. We explain this in detail in Section 8.8, and Figure 8.10 shows a time series of values for this parameter. The average of the time series in Figure 8.11 is about 3 basis points, suggesting that the liquidity component is about −1.21%. At first glance this does not seem correct − investors appear to be demanding a lower yield to hold a less liquid inflation-linked bond. The analysis is also not helped by the existence of negative real yields. However, this is merely due to the way in which the Fisher equation is expressed. To understand the issue, let us reframe the concept by looking at the yields on both bonds.

The yield on nominal bonds is made up of three components:

$$\text{Real yield} + \text{inflationary expectations} + \text{risk premium for unexpected inflation} \qquad (8.3)$$

The yield on an inflation-linked bond is made up of:

$$\text{Real yield} + \text{risk premium for liquidity} \qquad (8.4)$$

Let us use the following values to illustrate the concept more clearly, and for ease of illustration assume that the premium for unexpected inflation is zero:

- Nominal yields = 4%
- Observed real yields = 3.40%
- Inflation expectations from swap breakevens = 2.5%

At first glance the market shorthand technique of estimating breakevens would appear to return a value of 0.60% (4% − 3.4%). However, if we accept swap breakevens as the most accurate measure of inflation expectations, we could derive an "adjusted" real yield of 1.5% (4.0% − 2.5%) and so this would mean that the quoted real yield of 3.40% comprises a liquidity premium of 1.90% (3.4% − 1.5%). The existence of this liquidity premium will tend to push the shorthand observed breakeven rates below those seen in the swap market. So in some ways this begs the question, what is the "correct" real rate? The issue is made more difficult by noting that there is no assurance that the real rate implied from bonds is equal to that implied by real rate swaps (see Figure 8.12).

8.3 SEASONALITY

Seasonality reflects the fact that the prices of certain goods within the inflation basket have a tendency to increase or decrease at certain times of the year. Each Consumer Price Index (CPI) will display a different seasonal pattern, which is influenced by the timing of changing prices such as energy, rents and food. For example, there is the well-known "driving season" in the USA which extends from May to September, during which time people will be more likely to travel internally. As a consequence, the cost of gasoline and accommodation tends to rise. Another common event is the tendency of shops to discount clothing during the November to January period. As a result of events such as these, inflation indices may deviate from their underlying trend value at certain times of the year.

Seasonality is important for the inflation-linked markets as bonds and swaps that are refer-enced to inflation indices are almost always linked to the non-seasonally adjusted levels. For example, Barclays Capital (2010) show that US non-seasonally adjusted (NSA) core infla-tion tends to rise significantly in February and March, fall off in May to July, rise in October and fall off sharply in November and December. They then relate that to the monthly returns from trading US breakevens and show that these have traditionally risen in the first half of the year and fallen in the second half. As a result, analysts may attempt to strip out the effect of seasonality using different mathematical techniques. However, the different techniques used to calculate the adjustment are beyond the scope of the text and instead we refer interested readers to alternative sources such as the US Bureau of Labor Statistics website.

8.4   IDENTIFYING VALUE IN INFLATION-LINKED BONDS

We showed in Chapters 5 and 6 that there are a number of ways to identify value in bonds:

- Cheap/rich analysis relative to fitted curves.
- Forward rates.
- Butterfly trades.

8.4.1   Fitted curves - cheap/rich analysis

This is a relatively simple way of identifying value, as visually it is easy to identify potentially mispriced bonds (see, for example, Figures 5.13 and 8.2). Within a nominal framework, bonds that sit below the curve are considered "rich" while those that sit above the curve are considered "cheap". However, for inflation-linked securities the issue of seasonality can make this analysis more complex. An example of a typical inflation-linked cheap/rich report

Issue	Price	Expected @ 3M Carry	Yield	Yield @ Chg on Mth	Breakeven Spread @ Current	Breakeven Spread @ Chg on Mth	Breakeven Spread @ 3M Average	Breakeven Spread @ 3M Z Score	Proceeds ASW @ Current	Z Spread ASW @ Current	Z Spread ASW @ Chg on Mth	Z Spread ASW 3M @ Average	Z Spread ASW 3M @ Z Score	ZSpread @ Difference	DV01
UKTI 2.500% Aug 11	309.59	133.90	-2.776	0.2	3.182	-6.04	3.084	0.55	-17.97	-18.14	60.59	-55.92	1.81	42.00	2.00
UKTI 2.500% Aug 13	278.22	48.17	-1.651	5.5	2.834	11.01	2.664	1.41	-14.87	-15.16	6.09	-8.35	-0.80	32.10	7.07
UKTI 2.500% Jul 16	311.89	30.05	-0.039	9.1	2.637	12.88	2.480	1.66	6.88	6.95	-11.85	22.79	-1.77	36.40	16.12
UKTI 1.250% Nov 17	108.03	22.11	0.082	4.2	2.890	10.51	2.743	1.40	-4.51	-4.35	-11.95	15.45	-1.62	17.99	8.23
UKTI 2.500% Apr 20	316.72	20.23	0.539	4.7	2.938	8.35	2.782	1.36	6.95	6.79	-7.75	23.12	-1.55	10.03	26.17
UKTI 1.875% Nov 22	113.42	14.84	0.697	-2.3	3.066	12.39	2.881	1.50	12.99	11.99	-6.46	26.14	-1.22	9.10	13.20
UKTI 2.500% Jul 24	280.31	14.72	0.736	-6.9	3.217	9.27	3.042	1.37	7.22	6.79	-10.03	24.92	-1.58	1.61	32.36
UKTI 1.250% Nov 27	108.09	10.42	0.739	-7.5	3.355	6.27	3.188	1.26	10.72	8.92	-4.92	24.93	-1.46	-0.59	18.95
UKTI 4.125% Jul 30	269.45	11.37	0.671	-5.6	3.543	2.97	3.408	1.08	6.40	6.06	-2.95	21.68	-1.45	-13.21	39.67
UKTI 1.250% Nov 32	111.01	8.19	0.706	-7.9	3.508	5.42	3.358	1.21	19.68	15.13	0.05	25.22	-1.24	-4.14	21.97
UKTI 2.000% Jan 35	166.83	8.55	0.655	-6.7	3.604	4.88	3.457	1.17	15.73	12.52	1.80	22.48	-1.17	-12.00	32.52
UKTI 1.125% Nov 37	111.37	6.69	0.662	-6.4	3.576	3.53	3.451	1.10	31.10	21.84	6.98	24.92	-0.57	-2.96	28.70
UKTI 0.625% Mar 40	98.91	5.88	0.665	-7.0	3.579	3.61	3.456	1.08	42.41	27.07	9.15	26.37	0.15	1.52	27.08
UKTI 0.625% Nov 42	99.83	5.39	0.630	-6.2	3.611	2.55	3.497	0.98	49.84	30.36	11.10	26.77	0.75	2.23	30.17
UKTI 0.750% Nov 47	106.00	4.76	0.569	-5.5	3.650	0.48	3.546	0.83	52.62	30.36	10.75	25.63	0.98	1.92	36.73
UKTI 0.500% Mar 50	98.15	4.32	0.552	-4.5	3.648	-1.21	3.556	0.74	57.01	30.67	11.41	24.83	1.17	2.58	36.34
UKTI 1.250% Nov 55	129.42	4.26	0.515	-2.3	3.648	-4.35	3.580	0.54	53.86	30.03	12.85	23.61	1.25	3.73	53.72
UKRAIL															
UKRAIL 1.750% Nov 27	112.46	11.22	0.949	-8.5	3.145	7.26	2.970	1.29	36.94	31.29	-6.01	48.42	-1.51	21.91	18.01
UKRAIL 1.375% Nov 37	112.14	7.15	0.867	-6.9	3.371	4.02	3.242	1.12	60.38	42.53	6.29	46.45	-0.70	17.83	27.90
UKRAIL 1.125% Nov 47	111.57	5.22	0.764	-6.0	3.398	-0.63	3.320	0.71	83.31	49.21	9.95	45.74	0.75	22.99	36.76

Figure 8.3   Conventional cheap/rich report for GBP inflation-linked bonds.
Source: Barclays Capital Live. Reproduced with permission.

Figure 8.4 A matrix of UK RPI forward breakeven and real rates. Effective dates are read vertically, tenors are read horizontally. Data as of 8 July 2011.

Source: Barclays Capital Live. Reproduced with permission.

Bottom-left matrix:

	0m	1y	2y	3y	4y	5y	7y	10y	15y	20y	25y	30y
1y	4.20	3.29	3.11	3.05	3.02	3.27	3.46	3.86	4.15	3.96	4.01	3.86
2y	3.75	3.20	3.09	3.02	3.14	3.33	3.49	3.93	4.19	3.92	4.04	3.82
3y	3.53	3.15	3.05	3.11	3.22	3.37	3.54	3.96	4.18	3.90	4.05	3.78
4y	3.41	3.11	3.11	3.18	3.28	3.41	3.62	3.98	4.17	3.89	4.06	3.75
5y	3.33	3.15	3.16	3.23	3.33	3.48	3.69	4.01	4.15	3.90	4.04	3.73
6y	3.32	3.19	3.21	3.28	3.38	3.52	3.75	4.03	4.12	3.92	4.01	3.71
7y	3.33	3.23	3.26	3.33	3.45	3.59	3.79	4.05	4.08	3.94	3.98	3.71
8y	3.35	3.26	3.30	3.40	3.52	3.65	3.83	4.07	4.05	3.96	3.94	3.71
9y	3.37	3.30	3.37	3.46	3.57	3.69	3.87	4.08	4.03	3.97	3.91	3.71
10y	3.39	3.36	3.43	3.52	3.62	3.73	3.90	4.08	4.02	3.97	3.88	3.71
15y	3.60	3.59	3.65	3.73	3.80	3.87	3.95	4.02	4.02	3.89	3.82	3.75
20y	3.73	3.72	3.75	3.79	3.83	3.88	3.95	3.96	3.95	3.84	3.82	3.76
25y	3.77	3.76	3.79	3.83	3.87	3.91	3.95	3.96			3.83	3.83
30y	3.81	3.80	3.82	3.84	3.86	3.88	3.90	3.92			3.89	3.83

Bottom-right matrix:

	0m	1y	2y	3y	4y	5y	7y	10y	15y	20y	25y	30y
1y	-2.90	-1.58	-0.62	0.19	0.82	1.00	1.43	1.33	0.70	0.47	0.13	-0.05
2y	-2.24	-1.10	-0.22	0.51	0.92	1.14	1.49	1.26	0.62	0.49	0.05	-0.01
3y	-1.70	-0.67	0.13	0.67	1.03	1.24	1.50	1.23	0.56	0.48	-0.00	0.02
4y	-1.23	-0.30	0.35	0.82	1.13	1.31	1.46	1.18	0.52	0.47	-0.03	0.05
5y	-0.83	-0.04	0.53	0.94	1.22	1.36	1.40	1.12	0.49	0.43	-0.05	0.07
6y	-0.52	0.18	0.68	1.04	1.27	1.35	1.36	1.05	0.49	0.38	-0.04	0.07
7y	-0.27	0.35	0.80	1.11	1.28	1.33	1.32	0.96	0.49	0.32	-0.02	0.07
8y	-0.06	0.50	0.89	1.14	1.28	1.31	1.26	0.91	0.49	0.27	-0.01	0.06
9y	0.12	0.62	0.94	1.15	1.25	1.28	1.20	0.85	0.48	0.23	-0.01	0.06
10y	0.26	0.69	0.97	1.15	1.23	1.24	1.14	0.81	0.46	0.19	0.01	0.06
15y	0.55	0.79	0.93	1.01	1.02	0.99	0.90	0.68	0.29	0.15	0.02	0.01
20y	0.51	0.70	0.81	0.87	0.88	0.85	0.74	0.50	0.23	0.12	-0.01	-0.00
25y	0.51	0.64	0.70	0.72	0.71	0.67	0.58	0.41	0.13	0.08	-0.01	
30y	0.42	0.52	0.57	0.59	0.59	0.57	0.50	0.35	0.15	0.06		

Top-left matrix:

	0m	1y	2y	3y	4y	5y	7y	10y	15y	20y	25y	30y
1y	-2.88	-1.59	-0.62	0.19	0.82	1.01	1.43	1.33	0.70	0.47	0.13	-0.05
2y	-2.23	-1.10	-0.22	0.50	0.91	1.14	1.49	1.26	0.62	0.49	0.05	-0.01
3y	-1.69	-0.67	0.13	0.67	1.03	1.23	1.50	1.23	0.56	0.48	-0.00	0.02
4y	-1.22	-0.30	0.35	0.82	1.13	1.31	1.46	1.18	0.52	0.47	-0.03	0.05
5y	-0.81	-0.04	0.53	0.94	1.21	1.35	1.41	1.13	0.50	0.43	-0.05	0.07
6y	-0.51	0.17	0.67	1.03	1.26	1.33	1.37	1.06	0.49	0.38	-0.05	0.07
7y	-0.26	0.35	0.79	1.10	1.27	1.31	1.32	0.98	0.49	0.32	-0.04	0.07
8y	-0.06	0.49	0.88	1.13	1.26	1.28	1.27	0.92	0.49	0.27	-0.02	0.07
9y	0.12	0.60	0.93	1.14	1.25	1.24	1.21	0.86	0.48	0.23	-0.01	0.06
10y	0.25	0.67	0.95	1.14	1.23	1.24	1.15	0.82	0.46	0.19	0.01	0.06
15y	0.53	0.77	0.93	1.01	1.03	1.00	0.92	0.69	0.29	0.15	0.02	0.01
20y	0.52	0.70	0.81	0.88	0.89	0.87	0.76	0.51	0.24	0.12	-0.01	-0.00
25y	0.50	0.64	0.71	0.74	0.73	0.69	0.60	0.42		0.08	-0.01	
30y	0.42	0.52	0.59	0.62	0.62	0.59	0.52	0.36	0.15	0.06		

Top-right matrix:

	0m	1y	2y	3y	4y	5y	7y	10y	15y	20y	25y	30y
1y	-2.90	-1.60	-0.62	0.19	0.82	1.01	1.43	1.33	0.70	0.47	0.13	-0.05
2y	-2.25	-1.11	-0.22	0.51	0.91	1.14	1.49	1.26	0.62	0.49	0.05	-0.01
3y	-1.70	-0.67	0.13	0.67	1.03	1.23	1.50	1.22	0.56	0.48	-0.00	0.02
4y	-1.22	-0.30	0.35	0.82	1.13	1.31	1.46	1.18	0.52	0.47	-0.03	0.05
5y	-0.81	-0.04	0.53	0.94	1.21	1.35	1.41	1.12	0.50	0.43	-0.05	0.07
6y	-0.51	0.17	0.67	1.03	1.26	1.33	1.36	1.05	0.49	0.38	-0.05	0.07
7y	-0.26	0.35	0.79	1.10	1.27	1.31	1.32	0.98	0.49	0.32	-0.04	0.07
8y	-0.06	0.49	0.88	1.13	1.26	1.30	1.27	0.92	0.49	0.27	-0.02	0.07
9y	0.12	0.60	0.93	1.14	1.25	1.24	1.21	0.86	0.48	0.23	-0.01	0.06
10y	0.25	0.67	0.95	1.14	1.23	1.24	1.14	0.82	0.47	0.19	0.01	0.06
15y	0.53	0.77	0.93	1.01	1.03	1.00	0.92	0.69	0.29	0.15	0.02	0.01
20y	0.52	0.70	0.81	0.88	0.89	0.87	0.76	0.51	0.24	0.13	-0.01	-0.00
25y	0.50	0.64	0.71	0.74	0.73	0.69	0.60	0.42		0.08	-0.01	
30y	0.42	0.52	0.59	0.62	0.62	0.59	0.52	0.36	0.15	0.06		

is shown in Figure 8.3. The report considers the richness or cheapness of a population of bonds from a number of perspectives:

- Breakevens.
- The difference between the yield and the fitted curve.
- The bond's asset swap level.
- Z-spreads.

8.4.2   Forward rate analysis

This technique is useful in identifying points along the curve that may be mispriced, but once again the seasonality has to be taken into account. However, it would be reasonable to assume that the forward curve should be relatively smooth as it is impossible to identify a significant event in advance that may lead to any observed dislocation. Forward rate analysis is most commonly done using swaps and Figure 8.4 shows:

−zero coupon breakeven swap rates (top left)
−zero coupon real rate swap rates (bottom left)
−Real rate swap rates (annual rates top right, semi-annual rates bottom right).

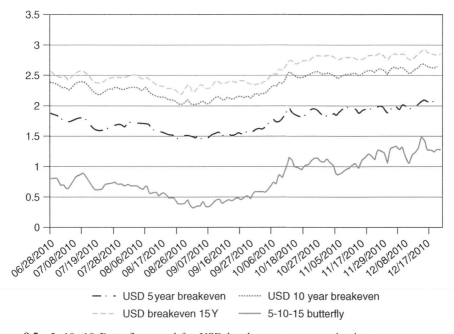

Figure 8.5   5–10–10 Butterfly spread for USD breakevens constructed using zero-coupon swaps. Data covers June–December 2010.
Source: Barclays Capital Live. Reproduced with permission.

8.4.3 Butterfly trades

A third measure of value is a butterfly trade constructed using either bonds or swaps in either the spot or forward markets (Figure 8.5). Butterfly trades were analysed in detail in Section 6.4.1.

Another way of identifying value is to use inflation asset swaps; this was considered in some detail in Section 5.4.5.

8.5   AN OVERVIEW OF INFLATION-LINKED TRADING STRATEGIES

8.5.1 Inflation market risk

Duration within an inflation context

One of the most popular measures of fixed income market risk is duration (either Macaulay or modified). The principles of duration can be applied to inflation-linked bonds to determine how sensitive the price of the bond is to a change in real yields. "Real" duration can be calculated in the same manner as nominal bonds (see Sections 3.3.1 and 3.3.2). When comparing bonds with similar maturities, the duration of a linker is likely to be greater than that of a standard nominal bond as the yield and the coupon are likely to be lower. However, it would be misleading to compare the real duration of a linker with that of the nominal duration of a non-linker instrument, as the nominal measure will capture other effects such as changes in inflationary expectations, the liquidity discount and the risk premium.

Risk-weighted trades: the yield beta

Within a trading environment, risk-weighted trades based on nominal and linker bonds may be constructed using a variety of techniques. One technique sometimes used is the concept of the "yield beta". Within the context of inflation, this is defined as the expected change in the real yield for a given change in the nominal yield. It can be thought of as an estimate of the multiple that could be applied to the real duration to derive the equivalent nominal duration.

There is no single method used to calculate the beta value, and its value can be unstable. For example, the measure is sensitive to:

- The length of the measuring period.
- The frequency of the sampling period (i.e., daily or monthly).
- The selected bonds used in the sample.
- Whether yield levels or yield returns are measured.

The value of beta normally falls between 0 and 1, but on occasions it has been negative or greater than one.

As a crude rule of thumb, market practitioners have used a value of 0.5 for the US, French and UK inflation markets. This can be interpreted to imply that real yields tend to be less volatile than nominal yields.

Although much is made of the use of a yield beta, its adoption in the inflation market is still somewhat sporadic. Anecdotally, it would seem that traders prefer a DV01-weighted approach for trades with a shorter time horizon and a "cash-for-cash" approach for longer horizon trades; that is, at inception the amount of cash required for the long position is equal to the cash received for the short position.

8.5.2   Forward prices and carry

The carry on inflation-linked bonds is calculated in a similar manner to that of a nominal position, except that inflation needs to be included. In some respects it may be helpful to think of the inflation component as being another form of yield. Within the Canadian model of inflation pricing, carry on a long position can be approximated as:

$$\frac{\text{Real yield} + \text{inflation accrual} - \text{financing cost}}{\dfrac{\text{Modified duration}}{100}} \tag{8.5}$$

A more accurate calculation would require cash flow analysis similar to that used for calculating a nominal forward price.

We can illustrate the concept by calculating the 1-month carry on the following position. Let us say that the real yield on a particular linker is 3%, the inflation accrual over the month is 1.2% and the 1-month repo rate is 1.5%. The denominator of the previous equation should be the real forward modified duration of the bond, i.e. the modified duration of a bond for settlement at the end of the investment horizon. If we assume this to be 4%, then the carry expressed in basis points is:

$$3\%/12 + 1.2\% - 1.5\%/12 = 1.325/0.04 = 33.125 \text{ basis points of positive carry}$$

That is, the yield on the bond can rise by 33.125 basis points before a long position loses money. It also implies that the approximate forward real yield on this position would be 3.33125 (3% + 0.33125%). Note that for a given change in inflation the carry on a shorter-dated bond will be greater than that of a longer-dated bond due to the lower value of the forward-modified duration. So, in our above example, if the bond had a modified duration of 3% the carry would have been 44 basis points.

For nominal bonds, carry can move to extreme levels only when the difference between the repo rate and the bond yield is pronounced – i.e., when the yield curve is very steep or inverted. Carry on inflation bonds can be relatively volatile between months as the inflation accrual is a function of published inflation numbers. Equation 8.5 illustrates that if a trader believes inflation for a particular month is expected to be higher than anticipated, the carry on a long position will be very attractive. As a result, this may encourage traders to enter breakeven trades where they take a long position in a linker against a short position in a comparator bond. This carry-related market activity will have an impact on prices, which in turn will have an impact on the level of yields and inflation breakevens.

A trader wishing to calculate the carry on a linker position cannot accurately calculate the inflation accrual for longer-dated investment horizons due to the lack of available inflation data. Recall from Section 2.3.6 that the inflation accrual on the first day of the month is based on the value that occurred 3 months earlier. After this date the accrual is calculated as an interpolated value of the published inflation data from the second and third prior months.

Suppose that inflation figures are published in the middle of each month with a 3-month lag. Today is 10th October and so the most recent inflation figure is for August. A trader wishing to calculate the carry on a new trading position will be able to accurately estimate this value only for positions no further than 1st November – a period of about 3 weeks. Calculating carry beyond this date will require the trader to generate a forecast for inflation. However, a few days later – when the September inflation number is published – he will be able to accurately calculate the carry out to 1st December. This example shows that where the inflation lag is 3 months, carry on a trading position can be accurately estimated for a period of between about 2 and 6 weeks forward.

8.5.3 Summary of popular inflation trades

Inflation-linked trades can be used to express views on a number of different expected market movements:

- *Directional real-yield trades* – Here the trader attempts to express a view on a movement in real yields. This can be constructed by simply going long or short a linker if real yields are expected to fall or rise accordingly.
- *Breakeven trades* – In the cash markets these trades could be constructed by offsetting positions in nominal bonds and linkers. A detailed example is shown in Section 8.6.1. To express a view that breakevens were expected to decline, the trader would buy a nominal bond and sell a linker. A long breakeven position is constructed by shorting a nominal bond and buying a linker. There are a number of different ways in which this trade could be constructed:
  - A DV01-weighted trade is an attempt to benefit from changes in the breakeven but to be insensitive to changes in the real yield which will impact index-linked and nominal bonds alike.
  - A "beta-adjusted trade" is where the DV01 of the real leg is adjusted by the derived value of the yield beta.
  - A "cash-for-cash" trade consists of a position that is cash neutral. However, this may be directional given our discussion on the concept of yield betas. That is, the trade will show a profit or loss if the breakeven does not change but the curves move in a parallel fashion.
- *Real-yield curve trades* – Here the trader expresses a view about relative movements in real yields at different maturities along the curve. This strategy attempts to profit from expected movements in the term structure of real yields. For example, a real-yield steepener trade would be executed as the sale of a long-dated linker and the purchase of a shorter-dated linker.
- *Breakeven curve trades* – Suppose that a trader expects a sharp rise in energy prices. He believes that this will cause an increase in short-term inflation expectations but will cause longer-term breakeven rates to decline as the economy starts to slow down. The trader would buy short-dated breakevens and sell long-dated breakevens on expectations of a flatter breakeven curve.
- *Forward-curve trades referencing real yields and breakeven* – In this example, views on real yield or breakevens are executed on a forward basis rather than in spot space.
- *Intra-market trades* – Here the trades focus on movements of real-yield and breakeven trades between inflation bonds or swaps in different currencies (e.g., GBP vs. EUR trades).

8.6   EXPRESSING VIEWS ON BREAKEVEN INFLATION

8.6.1 Cash strategies

Suppose a trader expects breakevens to increase and decides to implement a trade to exploit this. He decides to select two bonds with market prices as shown in Table 8.1.

Table 8.1 Trade data for an inflation breakeven transaction

Name	Redemption date	Clean price	Dirty price	Yield	Modified duration
$1\frac{1}{4}$% index-linked bond 2027	22-Nov-2027	108.89	109.19	0.753267	17.17%
$4\frac{1}{4}$% Treasury stock 2027	07-Dec-2027	94.04	94.876066	4.723540	12.73%

Note: The dirty price of the index-linked bond is 121.548006 based on an index ratio of 1.113179.

The existing breakeven inflation rate is the difference between the nominal yield on the comparator bond and the real yield on the linker – 3.970273%. In order to go long breakevens, the trader would need to execute two transactions – buy the linker and sell the comparator bond.

If breakevens do increase as per the trader's expectation, but the real yield stays the same, it will not impact the price of the linker as this is only influenced by a change in real yields. An increase in breakevens will push the nominal yield on the comparator higher, reducing its price and thus returning a profit to the short position. A change in real yields should have no overall effect on this position as both bonds have a real-yield component, which effectively cancels out.

The DV01 (per 100 nominal) of both trades can be calculated using the following formula:

$$\text{(Modified duration/100)} \times \text{(dirty price/100)}$$

For the comparator bond the DV01 is $12.73/100 \times 94.876066/100 = 0.12077$ or 12.0777. The DV01 of the linker is $17.17/100 \times 109.19/100 = 0.187479$ or 18.7479. In this example we have chosen to weight trades by their yield beta, which means the DV01 of the linker should be multiplied by 0.5 (we use the "rule-of-thumb" measure for the value of beta).

The trader decides that the appropriate notional position for the linker is GBP 10m. Multiplying the linker's DV01 by 0.5 returns a value of 0.09374. The ratio of the two DV01s is therefore $0.09374/0.12077 = 0.776183$. So, if the nominal value of the linker is chosen to be GBP 10m, the nominal value of the comparator bond will be £7,760,000 (we round this down to £7,700,000 in the example). The instrument with the more volatile yield will have the lower notional exposure.

To calculate the net carry on the trade, we will assume:

- A 31-day month.
- A 182-day coupon period.
- A repo rate of 5% p.a.
- An inflation uplift for holding period = 1.11234 (RPI for holding period/base RPI).

The first step is to calculate the carry on the short comparator position, which comprises repo income and coupon expense. The repo income is calculated as:

$$\text{Nominal} \times \text{dirty price} \times \text{repo rate} \times \text{day fraction}$$

$$= £7,700,000 \times 94.876066/100 \times 5\% \times 31/365 = £31,023.17$$

The coupon expense for the holding period is:

$$\text{Nominal} \times \text{coupon}/2 \times \text{day fraction}$$

$$= £7,700,000 \times 4.25\%/2 \times 31/182 = £27,870.19$$

The carry on the comparator position is therefore:

$$\text{Repo income} - \text{interest accrual}$$

$$= £3,152.98$$

The second step is to calculate the carry on the long linker position. This comprises a repo cost and coupon income. The repo cost is:

$$\text{Nominal} \times \text{dirty price} \times \text{repo rate} \times \text{day fraction}$$

$$= £10,000,000 \times 121.548006/100 \times 5\% \times 31/365 = £51,616.28$$

The real coupon accrual income uplifted by inflation is:

$$\text{Nominal} \times \text{real yield}/2 \times \text{day fraction} \times \text{inflation uplift}$$

$$= £10,000,000 \times 1.25\%/2 \times 31/182 \times 1.11234$$

$$= £11,841.53$$

The carry on the linker position is therefore:

$$\text{Interest accrual} - \text{repo cost}$$

$$= (£39,774.75)$$

The total net carry on both positions is therefore:

$$£3,152.98 - £39,774.75 = (£36,621,77)$$

Let us suppose that 1 month later, the yields shown in Table 8.2 were observed.

Table 8.2 shows that breakevens have fallen to 3.93% (4.644166% − 0.718516%, rounded), which represents a change of about 4 basis points. Nominal yields changed with respect to real yields by a ratio of 1:0.4378, which is reasonably close to our yield beta estimate of 0.5.

Table 8.2 Evolution of market prices for breakeven position

Name	Original yield (%)	New yield (%)	Change (%)
$1\frac{1}{4}$% index-linked bond 2027	0.753267	0.718516	−0.034751
$4\frac{1}{4}$% Treasury stock 2027	4.723540	4.644166	−0.079374
Breakevens (rounded)	3.97%	3.93%	

The overall profit and loss on the trade comprises two elements:

(a) The profit or loss from the change in prices over the holding period (calculated as nominal position × number of basis points change × DV01/100).
(b) The cost of carrying the position. The profit/loss due to a change in price is as follows.

Nominal position

$$£7,700,000 \times 7.9374 \times 0.12077/100 = £73,812.18 \text{ loss}$$

Linker position

$$£10,000,000 \times 3.4751 \times 0.187479/100 = £65,150.83 \text{ profit}$$

The profit on the linker is uplifted by the index ratio of 1.11234 to give a value of £72,469.87, but overall the position loses £1,342.31 from the fall in breakevens and since the position carried negatively by £36,621.77 the total loss on the position is £37,964.08. Essentially the trader's view on the evolution of breakeven rates was wrong. He expected breakevens to rise but in fact they fell. Interestingly, if the trader had opted for a DV01-weighted trade the ratio of the two values would have implied a trade size of about £15.5m for the comparator and £10m for the linker. Based on these trade sizes the losses on the comparator bond alone due to the change in rates would have been much greater than the beta-adjusted trade.

8.6.2 Derivative strategies

Zero-coupon inflation swaps

The majority of inflation swaps are zero coupon in style, meaning there is no exchange of cash flows until the maturity of the swap. One counterparty agrees to pay the cumulative percentage increase in the inflation index over the tenor of the swap, while the other party pays a compounded fixed rate (see Figure 8.6).

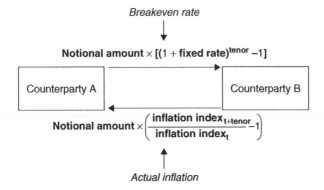

Figure 8.6 Zero-coupon inflation swap.

It is worth noting that the quoting conventions for inflation swaps are different from those used in the nominal market. A "receiver" inflation swap position means the market participant is receiving accrued inflation and paying the fixed rate; this may also be described as a "long" inflation position. A "payer" inflation swap position means the market participant is paying the accrued inflation leg and receiving fixed; this is a "short" inflation position.

Although the fixed rate on the swap is the average inflation rate needed over the period in order for the swap to have zero value at maturity, the market interprets this figure as the "pure" breakeven inflation rate. For example, on a 5-year deal, if the fixed rate equals 2.25% then it can be said that the market discounts inflation from the base reference index period to the final reference index level to be equal to 2.25% on an annualized basis. The net cash flow at maturity will only be zero if the average inflation rate over the period is equal to this initial fixed rate.

The inflation index used on the swap is subject to a lag and for most markets this is similar to that used in the associated inflation-linked bond market. However, the index value may or may not be interpolated using the techniques outlined in Section 2.3.6. Some of the more important market conventions for swaps in four major inflation markets are summarized in Table 8.3.

The implications of the different interpolation methods are worth mentioning. For those instruments with no interpolation, a swap traded on any given day of a particular month will have the same starting index reference value. For example, a UK Retail Price Index (RPI) swap executed on any day in November will accrue inflation based on the published September value. Recall that in the bond markets this would only hold true for the first day of the month. The swap market convention does have an advantage in that a trader who wishes to implement and unwind a position within the same month will not be faced with a residual risk with respect to the inflation accrual. For an interpolated trade the base inflation index value will change every single day using the same methodology as the underlying bond market.

To illustrate the settlement cash flows on the swap, consider the following example. On 15th September you enter into a €50m 2-year zero-coupon inflation swap based on HICPx where you have agreed to pay a fixed rate of 2.21% and where the base date inflation index is 114.842. Suppose that the inflation index applicable 2 years later turns out to be 121.000. The associated cash flows are as follows.

Fixed payment:

$$\text{Notional} \times \left((1 + \text{fixed})^{\text{tenor}} - 1\right)$$

$$= \text{EUR } 50\text{m} \times \left((1.0221)^2 - 1\right) = \text{EUR } 2{,}234{,}420$$

Table 8.3 Zero-coupon swap market conventions

	Euro	France	USA	UK
Inflation index	Euro HICP ex-tobacco (HICPx)	CPI ex-tobacco (CPIx)	US CPI (non-seasonally adjusted)	RPI
Indexation	3-month lag, not interpolated	3-month lag, interpolated	3-month lag, interpolated	2-month lag, not interpolated
Effective date	Trade date + 2 days	Trade date + 2 days	Trade date + 2 days	Trade date

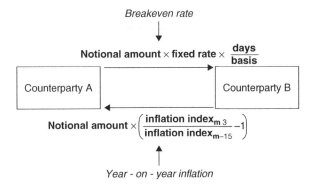

Figure 8.7   Deal structure for year-on-year inflation swap.

Floating payment:

$$\text{Notional} \times \left(\frac{\text{PI}_{\text{base+tenor}}}{\text{PI}_{\text{base}}} - 1 \right)$$

$$= \text{EUR 50m} \times \left(\frac{121.000}{114.842} - 1 \right) = \text{EUR } 2,681,075$$

The receiver of the floating rate (i.e., actual inflation) will receive a net payment of EUR 446,655. This implies that actual inflation was greater than the initial breakeven. In this case, inflation averaged 2.68% per annum over the period.

Year-on-year inflation swaps

Year-on-year (yoy; also sometimes referred to as year-over-year or period-on-period) inflation swaps involve one counterparty agreeing to receive an annual coupon determined by the yoy rate of inflation while paying a fixed rate in return (see Figure 8.7). Once again, the fixed rate could be thought of as the breakeven rate but since there is annual settlement of cash flows the impact of compounding means it is not a "pure" measure in the same sense as the zero-coupon structure.

Sometimes the fixed-rate leg is replaced with a floating leg where the cash flow is typically LIBOR +/− spread. In this case the spread to LIBOR represents the price of the transaction.

This type of transaction was popular in the early days of the swap market as it was often linked to corporate inflation bond issuance.

8.6.3   Expressing views on swap breakevens

In Figure 8.1 we presented a framework that illustrated the relationships that could exist between nominal and real interest rates. One of the relationships highlighted the linkage between nominal swaps and real rate swaps (which are explained in Section 8.7.2). In Figure 8.8 we show pricing matrices for nominal and real rate swaps, respectively, for both spot and forward-starting maturities. If we took the 10-year spot-starting values from these figures, nominal rates are 3.22% (Figure 8.8(a)) and real rates are −0.01% (Figure 8.8(b)),

	0m	3m	6m	12m	2y	3y	4y	5y	7y	10y	15y	20y	25y	30y
3m	1.07	1.15	1.18	1.31	1.83	2.56	3.17	3.69	4.44	4.88	4.68	4.41	4.12	3.73
6m	1.12	1.17	1.21	1.37	1.93	2.65	3.25	3.76	4.50	4.91	4.70	4.43	4.13	3.73
1y	1.16	1.22	1.29	1.49	2.11	2.81	3.39	3.87	4.56	4.91	4.68	4.42	4.11	3.72
2y	1.32	1.42	1.53	1.80	2.46	3.09	3.62	4.06	4.65	4.91	4.65	4.40	4.07	3.69
3y	1.58	1.71	1.84	2.13	2.76	3.34	3.83	4.22	4.72	4.90	4.62	4.38	4.03	3.67
4y	1.88	2.01	2.15	2.43	3.03	3.56	4.00	4.34	4.77	4.88	4.59	4.35	3.99	3.65
5y	2.17	2.30	2.43	2.71	3.26	3.75	4.14	4.44	4.79	4.86	4.57	4.32	3.96	3.65
6y	2.43	2.56	2.69	2.94	3.45	3.90	4.25	4.51	4.80	4.83	4.54	4.29	3.92	3.65
7y	2.67	2.79	2.91	3.15	3.62	4.02	4.33	4.56	4.80	4.80	4.52	4.26	3.89	3.65
8y	2.88	2.99	3.11	3.33	3.75	4.12	4.39	4.59	4.80	4.78	4.50	4.22	3.86	3.65
9y	3.06	3.17	3.27	3.48	3.86	4.19	4.43	4.61	4.79	4.75	4.48	4.19	3.83	3.65
10y	3.22	3.31	3.41	3.59	3.95	4.24	4.47	4.62	4.77	4.73	4.46	4.16	3.81	3.65
15y	3.66	3.72	3.79	3.92	4.16	4.36	4.51	4.61	4.69	4.62	4.32	4.02	3.77	3.65
20y	3.82	3.87	3.92	4.02	4.21	4.37	4.48	4.56	4.61	4.50	4.20	3.95	3.75	3.66
25y	3.88	3.92	3.97	4.05	4.21	4.34	4.43	4.48	4.50	4.39	4.13	3.91	3.75	3.69
30y	3.89	3.92	3.96	4.03	4.17	4.28	4.36	4.41	4.42	4.32	4.08	3.89	3.76	3.71

(a)

	0m	1y	2y	3y	4y	5y	7y	10y	15y	20y	25y	30y
1y	-2.86	-1.52	-1.02	-0.28	0.22	0.66	1.16	1.20	0.73	0.66	0.24	-0.00
2y	-2.19	-1.27	-0.65	-0.03	0.44	0.82	1.22	1.16	0.70	0.66	0.17	0.02
3y	-1.79	-0.93	-0.36	0.20	0.62	0.93	1.24	1.11	0.68	0.64	0.11	0.04
4y	-1.41	-0.64	-0.10	0.40	0.75	1.02	1.23	1.06	0.66	0.62	0.08	0.05
5y	-1.08	-0.38	0.12	0.55	0.86	1.07	1.21	1.01	0.65	0.57	0.06	0.06
6y	-0.79	-0.16	0.28	0.67	0.93	1.09	1.18	0.96	0.66	0.52	0.04	0.06
7y	-0.54	0.03	0.42	0.75	0.96	1.09	1.14	0.92	0.66	0.46	0.04	0.07
8y	-0.33	0.18	0.53	0.81	0.98	1.09	1.10	0.89	0.65	0.40	0.05	0.07
9y	-0.15	0.30	0.60	0.84	0.98	1.06	1.06	0.86	0.64	0.35	0.05	0.08
10y	-0.01	0.39	0.65	0.85	0.98	1.04	1.02	0.84	0.61	0.32	0.06	0.08
15y	0.31	0.55	0.70	0.82	0.89	0.92	0.90	0.75	0.43	0.23	0.07	0.04
20y	0.39	0.57	0.69	0.78	0.82	0.84	0.77	0.58	0.34	0.20	0.04	0.03
25y	0.43	0.56	0.63	0.68	0.69	0.69	0.63	0.48		0.15	0.04	
30y	0.37	0.47	0.53	0.57	0.59	0.59	0.54	0.42	0.24	0.13		

(b)

Figure 8.8   Values for (a) GBP nominal swaps and (b) GBP real rate swaps for spot and forward maturities. Effective dates are read vertically, tenors are read horizontally. Rates as of 29 July 2011. *Source:* Barclays Capital Live. Reproduced with permission.

implying a swap breakeven value of 3.23%. If the trader expected the value of breakevens to increase, they would pay fixed on the nominal swap and receive fixed on the real rate swap. Although we have considered this trade within a spot framework, Figure 8.8 indicates that the transactions could also be executed within forward space.

8.7   EXPRESSING VIEWS ON REAL YIELDS

One of the simplest ways to express a view on real yields is to simply trade index-linked bonds. In Chapter 2 we considered the pricing of inflation-linked bonds and concluded that their price was impacted only by a change in real yields; they are immune to direct changes in inflation. However, if inflation is anticipated to become a problem, this could lead to an increase in demand for inflation protection which would cause the price of linkers to rise and real yields to fall.

In this section we consider two alternative ways to express a view on real rates:

- Total return swaps.
- Real rate swaps.

8.7.1   Total return inflation swaps

Total return swaps exist within a number of different asset classes and within the context of inflation are designed to mimic the returns of either a single inflation-linked bond or a designated portfolio of instruments. A typical structure is illustrated in Figure 8.9.

The key features of a total return swap are:

- The swap allows an investor to take either a long or short exposure to inflation bonds without actually owning the asset. This would allow a fund manager to track a particular index with no tracking error.
- The cash flows consist of the total return (i.e., price change and coupon) of the underlying assets against a floating rate which is referenced to LIBOR +/− spread.
- If the price of the bond during the period falls by more than the coupon payment, the total return will be negative and so an entity that is "long inflation" (counterparty B in Figure 8.6) will have to pay both the total return and the floating LIBOR component.
- The bank paying the total return normally finances this payment by holding a physical position in the underlying asset(s). They will finance this physical holding at their normal cost of funding. As a result, the difference between this cost and the spread to LIBOR earned from the client represents their overall compensation.
- If the bank holding the bonds as a hedge can fund itself at an attractive level, the spread to LIBOR demanded under the swap will be lower than that of a weaker credit-rated entity.
- Certain customers are not allowed to enter into swap transactions and so banks may create the same return by creating a bond-like structure (a so-called "funded note"). The transaction would have a deal size of, say, €10m and this amount would be invested by the client at the start of the transaction.

8.7.2   Real rate swap

A real rate swap can be thought of as an inflation bond in swap format. In this type of deal one party receives a cash flow that accretes in line with realized levels of inflation (i.e., a real yield uplifted by an inflation accrual) and in return pays a LIBOR-based return. In order to mimic the cash market there will be an adjustment at maturity that will reflect the impact of inflation on the notional value of the transaction. The major difference between the bond and the swap is that the latter does not require any initial upfront financing.

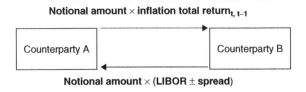

Figure 8.9   Total return inflation swap.

To illustrate how this might look, consider the following simple termsheet:

Amount	€50,000,000
Start date	Spot
Maturity	5 years
Bank pays	6m EURIBOR flat, semi-annual, act/360 (trade could also be done using a fixed rate, annual 30/360)
Bank receives	Real coupon of X%
	X% × [HICP(P − 3months)/HICP(S − 3months)]
	×day fraction × notional amount, annual, 30/360
	Additional receipt at maturity:
	Notional × Max{0%, [HICP(M − 3)/HICP(S − 3) − 1]}

where:

P = payment date

S = start date

M = maturity date

In this example the transaction has been structured with an inflation floor of 0% at maturity. Again this structure shares some similar advantages with the total return swap, such as the ability to take a long or short position on inflation, and requires no upfront funding.

8.8   FORWARD BREAKEVENS

8.8.1   Background

One of the key concepts introduced earlier in the text is that all fixed income strategies revolve around the idea of "beating the forward". That is, a trader's decision to buy or sell a particular bond would be driven by their expectation of how the price (or yield) of the bond would evolve relative to the initial implied forward price (or yield). Within the inflation market, forward trading is not as liquid as nominal fixed income markets; however, it is becoming increasingly important. The matrices of prices shown in Figures 8.4 and 8.8 show that it is possible to create a forward curve for both nominal and real rates.

One popular reason why forward analysis is important is that Central Banks such as the Federal Reserve use measures such as the 5-year breakeven rate, 5 years forward as a market-based indicator of long-term inflation expectations. This longer-dated measure is preferred as it is constructed from 5 and 10-year spot breakevens which are considered to be liquid points on the inflation curve. As a result of this Central Bank focus, traders could exploit movements in the 5-year, 5-year forward rate by going long or short breakevens if they believe that it is trading at an extreme of a particular range. If the market felt that the breakeven rate was too high and they expected the Central Bank to take action, then they may decide to take a short breakeven position.

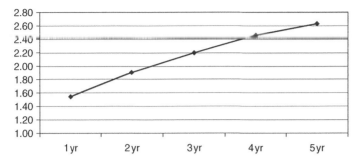

Figure 8.10   1-year rates at different forward effective dates. Rates are derived from Figure 8.4.
Source: Barclays Capital Live. Reproduced with permission.

One of the features of forward analysis is that analysis of forward rates often highlights dislocations along the spot curve as a result of the bootstrapping process. A forward curve which is not smooth in nature would lend itself to trades such as butterflies on forward rates. However, care has to be taken when analysing forward rates as their value may be exaggerated by the influence of seasonal factors. So, one popular technique may be to construct a series of 1-year rates with differing forward-starting dates – 1 year, 1 year forward; 1 year, 2 years forward; 1 year, 3 years forward and so on. An example of 1-year rates, effective at different future time periods, is shown in Figure 8.10.

One would expect such a forward curve to be relatively smooth, similar to that illustrated in Figure 8.10 unless there was a specific reason that could explain the deviation. For example, a linker of a particular maturity may be attractive as it may suit a particular hedging need and so its real yield will force breakevens for that maturity to increase, all other things being equal.

8.8.2   Assessing the risk premium

In the original Fisher equation (see Sections 1.2.3 or 8.2), one component of a bond's nominal yield was the inflation risk premium. This was defined as the compensation an investor earns for accepting undesirable inflation risk. If one believes that forward inflation expectations should be fairly constant, differences between long-dated forward breakevens may be useful in assessing the inflation risk premium. So it may be possible to assess this parameter by measuring, say, the difference between 5-year, 5-year forward breakeven and 10-year, 10-year forward breakeven (see Figure 8.11). However, the Fisher equation included a liquidity premium and so analysing the risk premium is perhaps more of an art than a science.

8.8.3   Trading forward breakevens using bonds

Trading forwards using bonds may be somewhat difficult given there are limited tenors available in the cash market and, since a single forward position would have four components, crossing the bid/offer spread on this many occasions may render the economics of the trade unattractive.

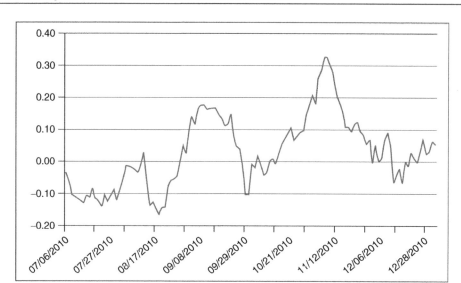

Figure 8.11   Using forward rates to assess the inflation risk premium. Chart shows the 10-year rate, 10 years forward minus the 5-year rate, 5 years forward.
Source: Barclays Capital Live. Reproduced with permission.

Forward breakeven rates can be calculated using techniques similar to those seen in the nominal markets. One shortcut method (Barclays Capital, 2010) for approximating forward breakeven rates is:

$$\text{Forward breakeven} = (W_2 \times BE_2) - (W_1 \times BE_1)$$

$$W_1 = \frac{MD_1}{MD_2 - MD_1}, \ W_2 = \frac{MD_2}{MD_2 - MD_1}$$

where:

BE_1 = breakeven rate for shorter-dated position

BE_2 = breakeven rate for longer-dated position

MD_1 = modified duration of shorter-dated inflation-linked instrument

MD_2 = modified duration of longer-dated inflation-linked instrument

To illustrate how a forward trade could be constructed, consider the data shown in Table 8.4 for settlement on 25 November 2010.

The 12-year breakeven value is calculated as 2.95% (3.64% − 0.69%) while the 17-year breakeven value is calculated as 3.29% (4.10% − 0.81%). Inputting these values into the formula presented earlier to calculate an approximation for the forward breakeven (i.e., the 5-year breakeven in 12 years' time), we derive a value of 4.11%.

Although there are a number of possible ways to approach the construction of this trade, we have broken the process down into a number of steps. On this occasion we have not applied the principle of the yield beta.

Table 8.4   Market data for forward breakeven position for settlement on 25 November 2010

Bond type	Short-dated breakeven position		Long-dated breakeven position	
	Linker	Comparator	Linker	Comparator
Position	Buy	Sell	Short	Long
Issue	1⅞% November 2022	4% March 2022	1¼% November 2027	4¼% December 2027
Dirty price	136.19	104.17	143.97	103.83
Yield (%)	0.69	3.64	0.81	4.10
Index ratio	1.09460		1.15998	
DV01	0.134998	0.093651	0.190757	0.123137
Modified duration	10.85	8.99	15.37	11.86
BE DV01	11.88		17.83	
Nominal trade size	100.00	144.15	94.36	146.18
Proceeds	136.19	150.16	135.85	151.77

Note: The dirty prices of the linkers are their actual settlement amount – i.e., their dirty values multiplied by their index ratios.
Source: UK DMO.

- *Step I*. For the shorter-dated breakeven position we create a DV01-neutral trade assuming a nominal linker position of £100m. This is based on the ratio of the DV01s, which is 1.44 (0.134998/0.093651) and so returns a nominal value of £144.15m for the comparator position.
- *Step II*. Here we need to determine a nominal value for the long-dated linker position. The aim is to make sure that until the forward-starting date, the overall position is not impacted by any inflation accrual. To achieve this we solve the following identity:

$$2022 \text{ linker nominal} \times \text{index ratio} - 2027 \text{ linker nominal} \times \text{index ratio} = 0$$

$$100 \times 1.09460 - 2027 \text{ linker nominal} \times 1.15998 = 0$$

$$2027 \text{ nominal} = 94.36$$

- *Step III*. Based on the result of step II, we create a DV01-weighted longer-dated breakeven position. Step II derived a nominal value for the longer-dated linker position of £94.36m and so using the ratio of the two longer-dated DV01s of 1.549144 (0.190757/0.123137), the appropriate nominal trade size for the longer-dated comparator position is £146.18m.

The associated settlement cash flows for the position are given in the last line of the table. The shorter-dated breakeven position has an initial net cash inflow of 13.97, while the longer-dated breakeven position has a net cash outflow of 15.92. As a result, there is an overall net cash outflow of −1.95.

One additional concept is introduced, and that is the "breakeven DV01" (sometimes referred to as the "inflation 01"). This is defined as the change in the profit or loss as a result of a one basis point change in breakevens. This can be calculated by multiplying the modified duration of the inflation-linked security multiplied by the index ratio.

Having constructed the trade it would be useful to consider how it would perform under different market movements. The essence of this trade is that it will show some profit or loss as the market's expectation of the forward breakeven rate changes. Since both legs of the transaction are constructed to be DV01 neutral, parallel movements in real and breakeven

Table 8.5 Profit and loss from long forward breakeven position under different movements in the forward breakeven rate

	100m long Nov 2022 position (BE DV01 11.87)	Profit and loss	94.3636 short Nov 2027 position (BE DV01 17.83)	Profit and loss	Forward breakeven rate	Net profit and loss
At entry	2.95%		3.29%		4.11%	
Scenario #1	3.05%	−1,187,000	3.39%	+1,682,502	4.21%	+495,502
Scenario #2	2.85%	+1,187,000	3.29%	0	4.35%	+1,187,000
Scenario #3	2.85%	+1,187,000	3.19%	−1,682,502	4.01%	−495,502
Scenario #4	2.95%	0	3.24%	−841,251	3.94%	−841,252

yields will not have an impact on the position. However, we will consider the following movements, all other things assumed equal:

- Ten basis point increase in both 12 and 27-year breakeven rates (scenario #1). Forward breakevens increase by 10 basis points.
- A 10 basis point fall in 12-year breakevens but no change in longer-dated rates (scenario #2). Forward breakevens increase by 24 basis points.
- Ten basis point decrease in both 12 and 27-year breakeven rates (scenario #3). Forward breakevens decrease by 10 basis points.
- A 5 basis point fall in 27-year breakevens but no change in shorter-dated rates (scenario #4). Forward breakevens decrease by 17 basis points.

The different profit and loss scenarios are shown in Table 8.5.

8.8.4   Trading forward breakevens using swaps

Arguably a more efficient way to express a view on forward breakevens is to use zero-coupon swaps rather than bonds. The reader may wonder why the forward breakeven trade illustrated earlier involved relatively odd dates (i.e., 12 and 17 years). This was due to the fact that there are a limited number of maturity points in the UK cash linker market. Figure 8.12 illustrates the population of UK government-issued inflation-linked bonds against zero-coupon and real rate swaps. The chart shows swaps being quoted most frequently for shorter-dated maturities, but traders would theoretically be willing to quote any maturity to about 30 years.

There are a number of reasons why investors may prefer swaps to bonds:

- A forward position can be created by just two transactions rather than four, reducing transaction costs.
- Bonds could go "on special" in the repo market.
- There is a wider range of available maturities offering greater trading opportunities.
- When setting up the trade, swaps will not have accreted principal values as in the bond market.
- One of the advantages of using the swaps market for forward analysis is that an analyst can derive a series of shorter-term forward rates (i.e., 1-year forwards), which is not possible in the cash markets. This type of shorter-term analysis would allow traders to identify those areas of the curve that are trading cheap or rich to the curve.

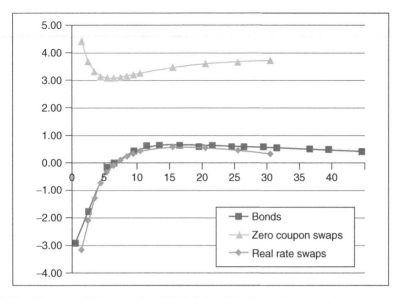

Figure 8.12 Chart of yield curve for UK inflation-linked bonds, UK real rate swaps and UK zero-coupon inflation swaps. Data as of 31 December 2010.
Source: Barclays Capital Live. Used with permission.

8.8.5   Calculating forward swap rates

To calculate a forward-starting swap rate S with a tenor of B at a forward date A, the following formula, using zero-coupon rates, can be used. This formula is similar to that used to calculate forward rates within a non-inflation environment:

$$S = \left[\frac{(1 + S_{A+B})^{A+B}}{(1 + S_A)^A} \right]^{(1/B)} - 1$$

To illustrate the concept we use the 10 and 15-year spot-starting USD zero-coupon breakeven rates shown in Figure 8.4 to calculate a theoretical value for the 5-year rate, 10 years forward:

$$S = \left[\frac{(1 + S_{15})^{15}}{(1 + S_{10})^{10}} \right]^{(1/5)} - 1$$

$$S = \left[\frac{(1.0284)^{15}}{(1.0265)^{10}} \right]^{(1/5)} - 1$$

$$S = 3.22\%$$

Figure 8.4 returns a quoted market value of 3.23%.

If a market participant wished to pay inflation on a forward-starting basis, this trade could be constructed by paying inflation on a longer-dated transaction and while receiving inflation on the shorter-dated transaction. To receive forward-starting inflation the trader would receive inflation on the longer-dated position and pay inflation on the shorter-dated position.

One of the challenges faced by a trader looking to construct a forward-starting swap transaction is deciding on the spot-starting deal sizes that will result in the desired notional exposure for the forward-starting period. Suppose that a trader wished to express a 5-year, 5-year forward view on inflation with a notional equal to $100m. The common practice amongst traders is to discount this forward-starting notional amount using the current 5-year breakeven rate. So if the current 5-year inflation breakeven is trading at 2.5%, then the initial notional amount on both the 5 and 10-year swap trades would be $88.39m ($100m/1.025^5). This would ensure that there is no net exposure to inflation over the period preceding the forward-starting date. However, to maintain a constant forward-starting notional, the spot-starting positions would have to be rebalanced if actual inflation does not move in line with breakevens. If breakeven rates increase, the size of the forward-starting notional will also increase and so the trader would need to reduce the size of the spot-starting notionals as a result. Equally, the notionals would have to be reduced and – if actual inflation does not rise as fast – the initial breakeven levels.

8.8.6 Forward real-yield trades

Although we have focused on forward breakevens it would also be possible to construct forward real-yield trades using similar principles to those just outlined. These could be created using bonds and possibly swaps where they are traded.

8.9   USING OPTIONS TO EXPRESS VIEWS ON BREAKEVEN AND REAL YIELDS

At the time of writing, the inflation options market is not as mature as, say, the nominal swaptions market. As a result, rather than have a market that trades volatility as a distinct asset class, the use of options has been most commonly seen within structured products. Arguably, the most popular type of inflation-linked option is the inflation cap or floor, which, similar to nominal structures, comprises a series of caplets/floorlets on inflation. There is, however, one difference between the nominal and inflation-linked market, and that relates to the number of options within the structure. A 5-year cap referencing to year-on-year inflation will consist of five caplets. However, the nominal equivalent with the same payment frequency would be made up of just four options. This is because, in the inflation-linked market, realized inflation is not known in advance. The buyer of this inflation cap will receive compensation if realized inflation is above the strike rate. The actual inflation rate to which the cap/floor is referenced is based on the swap market convention of the particular currency.

One of the reasons that interest in inflation options has increased came about as a result of a number of structured products which contained embedded 0% inflation floors. The banks who had sold these inflation floors suffered considerable mark-to-market losses as expectations of deflation grew after the default of Lehman Brothers.

It is also possible to trade "real" volatility via options on TIPS or real swaptions, however, activity in this market at the time of writing is relatively illiquid and so we have chosen not to cover this topic in any depth.

9

Trading Axioms: An A to Z

A

People will pay more money to be able to get out of the theatre first than they will to get the best seat. Markets are not rational – fear and greed are important.

Are markets really efficient? The market frequently overshoots: prices look silly, only to get sillier. When markets are volatile, having smaller stop losses should lead to higher expected profits. The aim is to stop losses accumulating.

B

If you are right and the market is wrong, **you** lose.

C

Don't try to be too clever. Positions that are too intelligent are likely to lose money. The market is too basic to understand them.

D

Keynes claimed, *"Markets can remain irrational longer than you can remain solvent"*. Markets are amoral, changeable and the extraordinary does happen. Always abide by your principles and be disciplined. But that doesn't mean you should be too dogmatic. Be prepared to change your mind. Lemmings believe that the sea is filled with carrots and jump into it.

E

Prices can move significantly even if there are no trades taking place. The supply and demand curves for various assets tell you how much of those assets people want to buy or sell at a particular price, other things being equal. Those other things include tastes, expectations and new technologies. These are not stable and can change. They can change unpredictably, especially expectations. So supply and demand curves can shift to establish a new equilibrium price regardless of whether or not there has been any significant trade flow.

F

It is impossible to explain all market moves since investors may need to buy and/or sell for reasons that are not obvious. Do not even bother to try!

G

Understand that high risk does not mean bad risk, and that low risk does not mean good risk. What is also important is that the trades pay off. A high-risk trade with an exceptionally high expected payoff may be a good trade relative to a low-risk trade with a low expected payoff.

Consider the risk/reward ratio. As a rule of thumb, some traders adopt a 3-to-1 reward-to-risk ratio. That is, the profit potential must be at least three times the possible loss. Make sure to use protective stops to limit losses.

H

What is the difference between knowledge and wisdom? Knowing that a tomato is a fruit is knowledge. Wisdom is knowing not to put it in a fruit salad.

I

It always pays to do sound fundamental economic and political analysis:
   Good sources
      Personal research
      Leading financial institutions
      Opinions of informed market participants
      Taxi drivers
   Bad sources
      Politicians
      Political party millionaires

J

Make sure that when expressing a view, it is backed up with fundamental analysis.

Hypothetical example: "Due to the high propensity to consume in the USA, there will continue to be a substantial trade deficit. This will result in net dollar sales so in the medium term the dollar will continue to be weak."

K

Be suspicious of unrealistic market rumours. Presidents only die once, and little green men from Mars do not buy Bolivian stocks.

L

Economies are not linear. We do not understand enough about their complexities. So, always expect to see crises forming – we *CANNOT* avoid them. Unconvinced? Have a look at "chaos mathematics".

M

Don't dismiss the principles of technical analysis even if you think it is the modern-day equivalent of reading tea leaves. The fact of the matter is that there are sufficient people in the market who do believe in the principles! Be aware of key market technicals, such as open interest, support and resistance points. Understanding these principles is particularly useful at times of major market swings or, conversely, at times of consolidation when the market is short of ideas and trades technically.

N

Be creative in making use of cross-market correlations in both risk-taking and risk-reduction. Take advantage of differences in market volatilities.
   Examples:
      Buy pork bellies; sell cattle.
      Short €/USD; buy out-of-the-money puts on Spanish Treasury bonds.

Most traders specialize in one or two markets and are not aware of cross-market opportunities.

O

Everybody knows how to make money going long. Fewer investors use short positions. Short positions can be extremely profitable if the longs panic.

P

Always remember that in any investment there is a long and a short position. If you buy gold, you are long gold and short cash. If you short US Treasuries, you are short US Treasuries and long cash. There is no reason why you should not buy gold with US Treasuries if you think that the exchange rate is favourable, i.e. sell US Treasuries, buy cash, sell cash, buy gold.

Q

All fixed income trading strategies revolve around *"beating the forward"*! But the forward price and the expected future price of any risky investment are not the same.

R

Consider the use of short-term limited-risk option strategies to "scrape" value. An example of this trade would be to sell a short-dated volatility (e.g., a strangle) if no critical market data is expected. This type of strategy allows a trader to take advantage of a probable decrease in volatility and enjoy rapid time decay.

S

Take losses or consider the use of options to "repair" positions. For example, in certain market conditions it may be worth selling out of the money call options on long positions.

T

Consider the following two examples.

Scenario #1

In addition to whatever you own, you have been given $1,000. You are then asked to choose between:
   A sure gain of $500.
   A 50% chance of gaining $1,000 and a 50% chance of gaining nothing.

Which do you choose?

Scenario #2

In addition to whatever you own, you have been given $2,000. You are then asked to choose between:
   A sure loss of $500.
   A 50% chance of losing $1,000 and a 50% chance of losing nothing.

Which do you choose?

In the original experiment,[1] 84% chose A in scenario #1. In scenario #2, 69% chose B. However, the two problems are identical in terms of net cash (i.e., you end up with $1,500 – the expected value). However, the way in which the question is framed leads the problem to be interpreted differently. These scenarios give a simple insight into risk-aversion. People tend to be **risk-averse** when gains are at stake and **risk-seeking** when losses are involved.

Run profits, do not be modest when you get it right, but cut losses early!

U

Take advantage of when the market panics or when prices look really silly. Always trade with a plan, do not gamble and trade impulsively. Be careful though; remember that the herd can trample you!

V

Only add to winning positions and never chase losing positions. If you are going to add to a position, each addition should be smaller than before. Adjust your protective stops to the breakeven point.

W

If everyone is bullish, they have already bought and the price is still there; they need the next guy to buy them out. If they have not bought, they are probably either liars or broke and should not be trusted!

X

Remember volatility and what it measures. If you have, say, 20% implied volatility on an asset, it means that asset prices can move up and down by 10% a year and that will capture about 68% of market moves. However, that's hardly significant. It also means that prices can be expected to move by about 1.26% per day ($20\%/\sqrt{250}$) without it being considered a significant move.

Opportunities have a bell-shaped distribution but are not emotional. Do not be afraid to have missed the boat if catching it means you may be drowned. There will be another boat tomorrow. However, 50% probability is not enough! The potential rewards should outweigh the potential losses.

Y

Never reach........

Z

There is always one more principle you still need to learn.

Notes

Chapter 1

1. Standard & Poor's "Ratings: FAQ". Sourced from www.standardandpoors.com.
2. Standard & Poor's "Introduction – Corporate Ratings Criteria". Available from www.standardand-poors.com.

Chapter 2

1. Antti Ilmanen, *Understanding the Yield Curve*, Salomon Brothers, New York, 1995.
2. A repo or repurchase agreement is the most popular way of financing a bond transaction. An institution would buy a fixed income instrument and then enter into a repo transaction to finance the deal. Under the terms of the repo, the institution would sell the bond at the current market value with an agreement to repurchase it at the same price at an agreed time in the future. When the bond is returned under the terms of the second leg of the transaction, the bank will repay the cash element with interest. This interest is termed the repo rate. Although the actions of buying a bond and then selling it under repo immediately to pay for it may seem self-defeating, under the conventions of the repo market the original purchaser will retain all of the economic benefits associated with owning the bond. So even though the bond will be in the possession of another institution, they will retain all the price and credit risk as well as being eligible to receive any interest payment. The repo is legally a sale and repurchase of a bond, but economically it is a collateralized loan. Hence the interest paid on the cash element is lower (by about 1/8th of 1%) than the equivalent unsecured rate.
3. These concepts are analysed in greater detail in Section 7.1.2.
4. Galitz, L., *Financial Engineering*, FT Prentice Hall, 1996.
5. Most FRNs would pay a fixed margin, expressed in basis points per annum, in addition to the LIBOR rate.
6. In reality, swaps will be traded with a slightly positive value to the market maker that they would then hedge.
7. Quote taken from "The evolution of swap pricing", *Risk Magazine*, March 2011.
8. See Gregory (2010) for more details on the calculation of CVA.
9. See www.bba.org.uk.

Chapter 3

1. Kopprasch, R. (2004). "A look at a variety of duration measures", Citigroup.
2. The interested reader is referred to Tompkins (1994) for an easy-to-understand explanation of this concept.

3. See Natenberg (1994) for an extended discussion.
4. *Source:* Barclays 2008 annual report.

Chapter 4

1. See Gregory (2010) for a complete discussion on pricing counterparty risk.
2. See Chapter 5 Tompkins (1994) for an example.
3. See JP Morgan (2007).

Chapter 5

1. The call is typically exercised if the issuer's credit standing improves. If this did happen they would call the bond and finance its repayment by borrowing at a lower rate.
2. Readers interested in the detail of fixed income mathematics are referred to Fabozzi (1997).
3. See, for example, "Britain worse credit risk than McDonalds", *The Independent*, Wednesday 10 December 2008.
4. A zero-coupon inflation swap is an exchange of cash flows where there is only one settlement which occurs at the maturity of the transaction. The fixed cash flow is based on breakeven inflation rates of the same maturity as the swap, while the floating cash flow is based on actual inflation over the period.

Chapter 6

1. For readers requiring a greater insight into the technique, we can suggest either Tuckman (2002) or Watsham and Parramore (1997).
2. Z-scores were introduced in Chapter 5.

Chapter 9

1. Taken from Daniel Kahnemann and Amos Tversky, "Prospect theory – an analysis of decision making under risk", *Econometrica*, 1979.

Bibliography

Bank of England (2006) The framework for the Bank of England's operations in the sterling money markets.

Barclays Capital (2010) Global inflation-linked products. Internal Research Document.

Blake, D. (1990) *Financial Market Analysis*. McGraw-Hill, New York.

Burghardt, G. (2003) *The Eurodollar Futures and Options Handbook*. Irwin, New York.

Burghardt, G., Belton, T., Lane, M. and Papa, J. (2005) *The Treasury Bond Basis*, 3rd edn. McGraw-Hill, New York.

Chapelton, S., Kurpiel, A. and Sasura, M. (2007) *Introduction to CMS Products*. Société Générale, Paris.

Chisholm, A. (2009) *An Introduction to Capital Markets*, 2nd edn. John Wiley & Sons Ltd, Chichester.

Choudhry, M. (2005) *Fixed Income Securities and Derivatives Handbook*. Bloomberg Press, New York.

Choudhry, M. (2005) Understanding the z-spread. Available from www.yieldcurve.com.

De Weert, F. (2008) *Exotic Options Trading*. John Wiley & Sons Ltd, Chichester.

Dubil, R. (2004) *An Arbitrage Guide to Financial Markets*. John Wiley & Sons Ltd, Chichester.

Eckl, S., Robinson, J.N. and Thomas, D.C. (1990) *Financial Engineering*. Blackwell, Oxford.

Fabozzi, F. (1997) *Fixed Income Mathematics*,, 3rd edn. Irwin, New York.

Gale, G. (2006) Using and trading asset swaps. Morgan Stanley Fixed Income Research.

Galitz, L. (1996) *Financial Engineering*. FT/Prentice Hall, London.

Goyal, P. and Mirani, C. (2008) Interest rate derivatives: a relative value framework. Barclays Capital Research.

Greer, R.J. (1997) What is an asset class anyway? *The Journal of Portfolio Management*, Winter.

Gregory, J. (2010) *Counterparty Credit Risk*. John Wiley & Sons Ltd, Chichester.

Grieves, R. (1999) Butterfly trades. *Journal of Portfolio Management*, Fall.

Haug, E.G. (2007) *The Complete Guide to Option Pricing Formulas*, 2nd edn. McGraw-Hill, New York.

Henderson, T.M. (2003) *Fixed Income Strategy*. John Wiley & Sons Ltd, Chichester.

Hull, J. (2008) *Options, Futures and Other Derivatives*, 7th edn. Prentice Hall, New Jersey.

Ilmanen, A. (1995) *Understanding the Yield Curve*. Salomon Brothers, New York.

Jorion, P. (2009) *Financial Risk Manager Handbook*, 5th edn. John Wiley & Sons Ltd, Chichester.

JP Morgan (2007) Fixed income correlation trading using swaptions. Research Note, 4 April.

Kay, J. (2009) *The Long and the Short of it*. Erasmus Press.

Kerkhof, J. (2005) Inflation derivatives explained. Lehman Brothers Internal Research Document.

Kopprasch, R. (1985) *Understanding Duration and Volatility*. Salomon Brothers Inc.

Kopprasch, R. (2004) A look at a variety of duration measures. Citigroup.

Kritzman, M. (1995) *The Portable Financial Analyst*. Probus, Chicago.

Labuszewski, J.W. and Sturm, F. (2008) Understanding US Treasury Futures. CME Group.

Leeming, M. and Hagemans, R. (2009) CDS butterflies. Barclays Capital.

Leeming, M., Willemann, S., Ghosh, A. and Hagemans, R. (2010) *Standard Corporate CDS Handbook*. Barclays Capital.

Manson, B. (1992) *The Practitioner's Guide to Interest Rate Risk Management*. Graham and Trotman, London.

Nashikkar, A. (2011) Understanding OIS discounting. Barclays Capital.

Natenberg, S. (1994) *Option Volatility and Pricing*. McGraw-Hill, New York.

O'Kane, D. and McAdie, R. (2004) Trading the default swap basis. Risk and Return.

O'Kane, D. and Sen, S. (2004) Credit spreads explained. Lehman Brothers Research, March.

Plona, C. (1997) *The European Bond Basis*. Irwin, New York.

Pradhan, A. (2010) Waiting for a newer low market strategy Americas. Barclays Capital, 5 March.

Ray, C.I. (1993) *The Bond Market*. McGraw-Hill, New York.

Rennison, G., Erlandsson, U. and Ghosh, A. (2008) Systematic CDS Index Trading. Barclays Capital.

Risk (2009) The asset swap lifeline, November.

Risk (2009) Scaling the peaks, December.

Risk (2011) The evolution of swap pricing, March.

Sadr, A. (2009) *Interest Rate Swaps and their Derivatives*. John Wiley & Sons Ltd, Chichester.

Sasura, M. (2008) Buy vol via swaption triangles. Barclays Capital Research.

Sasura, M. (2008) Euro wedges at attractive levels. Barclays Capital Research.

Schofield, N.C. (2008) *Commodity Derivatives*. John Wiley & Sons Ltd, Chichester.

Taksler, G. (2004) Guide to credit default swaptions. Bank of America.

Taksler, G. (2006) *Credit Default Swap Primer*, 2nd edn. Bank of America.

Tompkins, R. (1994) *Options Explained*, 2nd edn. Palgrave, London.

Tonge, D. (2001) Using asset swap spreads to identify government bond relative value. Citibank.

Tuckman, B. (2002) *Fixed Income Securities*, 2nd edn. John Wiley & Sons Ltd, Chichester.

Veronesi, P. (2010) *Fixed Income Securities*. John Wiley & Sons Ltd, Chichester.

Vine, S. (2005) *Options: Trading Strategy and Risk Management*. John Wiley & Sons Ltd, Chichester.

Watsham, T.J. and Parramore, K. (1997) *Quantitative Methods in Finance*. Thomson, Andover.

Willemann, S. and Bicer, B. (2010) CDS option trading. Barclays Capital Research, 14 May.

Willermann, S., Leeming, M., Duggar, M. and Bicer, B. (2009) Single name credit-linked notes. Barclays Capital Research, 6 August.

Index

Printed and bound by CPI Group (UK) Ltd, Croydon, CR0 4YY

16/04/2025

14658507-0002